FIRST COURSE
in
FUNCTIONAL ANALYSIS

PRENTICE-HALL SERIES IN MODERN ANALYSIS

R. CREIGHTON BUCK, *editor*

PRENTICE-HALL INTERNATIONAL, INC., *London*
PRENTICE-HALL OF AUSTRALIA PTY., LTD., *Sydney*
PRENTICE-HALL OF CANADA, LTD., *Toronto*
PRENTICE-HALL OF INDIA (PRIVATE) LTD., *New Delhi*
PRENTICE-HALL OF JAPAN, INC., *Tokyo*

FIRST COURSE *in* FUNCTIONAL ANALYSIS

CASPER GOFFMAN   GEORGE PEDRICK

Department of Mathematics
Purdue University

PRENTICE-HALL, INC.

Englewood Cliffs, N.J.

Library of Congress Catalog Card Number: 64-21171

Second printing. . . . . June, 1965

PRINTED IN THE UNITED STATES OF AMERICA

31838-C

To Gertrude and Dorothy

PREFACE

Portions of this book have been used by the authors in beginning graduate courses at Purdue University during the past several years.

Our view is that analysis itself is basic and that the abstract theories to which it leads are primarily of interest as tools which may be used in treating problems in analysis. This includes the theories of metric spaces, compactness and lower semicontinuity, normed vector spaces, Hilbert spaces, ordered vector spaces, Banach algebras, etc. Thus, we consider the abstract theories themselves only in part and then indicate their roles in analysis by giving various applications. In this regard, many important applications have not been considered because they are too complicated to be treated in an introductory study.

We assume that the reader is familiar with the symbols of set theory. For the most part, then, the book is self-contained.

There are many exercises at the end of each chapter. Each exercise is numbered so as to indicate the section to which it refers. Thus the exercise numbered 8.12 is concerned with the material of section 8 of the chapter. Some of the exercises are simple applications of the material in the text, whereas others should challenge the reader's ingenuity.

We take this occasion to express our thanks to Judy Wolf for her excellent typing of the manuscript.

We are grateful to R. C. Buck and J. J. Price for reading the text. Several improvements in form and content were made at their suggestion.

Casper Goffman George Pedrick

CONTENTS

Chapter 1—Metric Space 1

1.1 Definitions and Examples . . . 1
1.2 Inequalities of Hölder and Minkowski . . . 2
1.3 Examples Continued; l_p Spaces . . . 4
1.4 Examples Continued; Function Spaces . . . 6
1.5 Convergence and Related Notions . . . 8
1.6 Separable Space, Examples . . . 9
1.7 Complete Space, Examples . . . 11
1.8 Contractions, Applications to Differential and Integral Equations . . . 16
1.9 Completion . . . 20
1.10 Category, Nowhere Differentiable Continuous Functions . . 21
1.11 Compactness, Continuity . . . 24
1.12 Equicontinuity, Application to Differential Equations . . . 28
1.13 Stone-Weierstrass Theorems . . . 32
1.14 Normal Families . . . 35
1.15 Semi-continuity, Application to Arc Length . . . 38
1.16 Space of Compact, Convex Sets . . . 41
Exercises . . . 43

Chapter 2—Banach Spaces 50

2.1 Vector Space . . . 50
2.2 Subspace . . . 52
2.3 Quotient Space . . . 54
2.4 Dimension, Hamel Basis . . . 55
2.5 Algebraic Dual, Second Dual . . . 57
2.6 Convex Sets . . . 58
2.7 Ordered Groups . . . 59
2.8 Hahn-Banach Theorem, Separation Form . . . 60
2.9 Hahn-Banach Theorem, Extension Form . . . 62
2.10 Applications, Banach Limits, Invariant Measure . . . 64
2.11 Banach Space, Dual Space . . . 71
2.12 Hahn-Banach Theorem in Normed Space . . . 73
2.13 Uniform Boundedness Principle, Applications . . . 76

2.14 Lemma of F. Riesz, Applications 81
2.15 Application to Compact Transformations 83
2.16 Applications, Weak Convergence, Summability Methods, Approximate Integration 86
2.17 Second Dual Space 91
2.18 Dual of l_p 93
2.19 Dual of $C[a, b]$, Riesz Representation Theorem 94
2.20 Open Mapping and Closed Graph Theorems 97
2.21 Application, Projections 100
2.22 Application, Schauder Expansion 101
2.23 A Theorem on Operators in $C[0, 1]$ 102
Exercises 103

Chapter 3—Measure and Integration, L_p Spaces 109

3.1 Lebesgue Measure for Bounded Sets in E_n 109
3.2 Lebesgue Measure for Unbounded Sets 113
3.3 Totally σ Finite Measures 114
3.4 Measurable Functions, Egoroff Theorem 115
3.5 Convergence in Measure 118
3.6 Summable Functions 120
3.7 Fatou and Lebesgue Dominated Convergence Theorems . . 125
3.8 Integral as a Set Function 128
3.9 Signed Measure, Decomposition into Measures 129
3.10 Absolute Continuity and Singularity of Measures 132
3.11 The L_p Spaces, Completeness 135
3.12 Approximation and Smoothing Operations 138
3.13 The Dual of L_p, $p > 1$ 142
3.14 The Dual of L_1 146
3.15 The Individual Ergodic Theorem 148
3.16 L_p Convergence of Fourier Series 150
3.17 Functions Whose Fourier Series Diverge Almost Everywhere 153
3.18 Continuous Functions Which Differ from All Those Having a Given Modulus 155
Exercises 159

Chapter 4—Hilbert Space 165

4.1 Inner Product, Hilbert Space 165
4.2 Basic Lemma, Projection Theorem, Dual 168
4.3 Application, Mean Ergodic Theorem 171
4.4 Orthonormal Sets, Fourier Expansion 173
4.5 Application, Isoperimetric Theorem 178
4.6 Müntz Theorem 179
4.7 Dimension, Riesz-Fischer Theorem 182
4.8 Reproducing Kernel 184
4.9 Application, Bergman Kernel 187

4.10 Examples of Complete Orthonormal Sets 191
4.11 Systems of Haar, Rademacher, Walsh; Applications 194
Exercises 201

Chapter 5—Topological Vector Spaces 206

5.1 Topology 206
5.2 Tychonoff Theorem, Application in Banach Space 207
5.3 Topological Vector Space 210
5.4 Normable Space 211
5.5 Space of Measurable Functions 212
5.6 Locally Convex Space 217
5.7 Metrizable Space, Space of Entire Functions 219
5.8 FK Spaces 224
5.9 Application to Summability Methods 228
5.10 Ordered Vector Spaces 232
5.11 Banach Lattice 235
5.12 Köthe Spaces 238
Exercises 242

Chapter 6—Banach Algebras 248

6.1 Definition and Examples 248
6.2 Adjunction of Identity 250
6.3 Haar Measure 250
6.4 Commutative Banach Algebras, Maximal Ideals 254
6.5 The Set $C(\mathscr{M})$ 258
6.6 Gelfand Representation for Algebras with Identity 260
6.7 Analytic Functions 261
6.8 Isomorphism Theorem for Algebras with Identity 263
6.9 Algebras without Identity 266
6.10 Application to $L_1(G)$ 269
Exercises 272

References 276

Index 279

FIRST COURSE
in
FUNCTIONAL ANALYSIS

CHAPTER 1

METRIC SPACE

1.1 Definitions and Examples

A **metric space** consists of a set X, together with a notion of distance between pairs of elements of X, satisfying certain conditions. Thus, if X is a set, a **metric** in X is defined by a mapping

$$\rho: X \times X \to R,$$

of the space $X \times X$ into the real numbers, such that

(a) $\rho(x, x) = 0$ for every $x \in X$, and
$\rho(x, y) > 0$ for every $x, y \in X$, $x \neq y$,
(b) $\rho(x, y) = \rho(y, x)$ for every $x, y \in X$, and, **the triangle inequality**,
(c) $\rho(x, z) \leq \rho(x, y) + \rho(y, z)$ for every $x, y, z \in X$.

We give several examples of metric spaces, some of which are already familiar to the reader.

(i) Let X be any set of real numbers, and **let** ρ be defined by

$$\rho(x, y) = |x - y|.$$

(ii) Let X be any subset of the plane $R \times R$, and let ρ be defined by

$$\rho(x, y) = [(x_1 - y_1)^2 + (x_2 - y_2)^2]^{1/2},$$

where $x = (x_1, x_2)$ and $y = (y_1, y_2)$.

(iii) Let X be any set, and let ρ be defined by

$$\rho(x, y) = \begin{cases} 0 \text{ if } x = y \\ 1 \text{ if } x \neq y. \end{cases}$$

This is called the **discrete** metric in the set X.

We shall sometimes designate a space X with metric ρ as the **metric space** (X, ρ).

(iv) If (X, ρ) is a metric space and $Y \subset X$, then the restriction of ρ to

$Y \times Y$ determines a metric in Y which we shall also designate by ρ. The metric space (Y, ρ) is said to be a **subspace** of (X, ρ).

(v) Let X be real n-space (complex n-space) for a positive integer n. Then X consists of all n-tuples of real numbers (respectively, complex numbers),

$$x = (x_1, x_2, \ldots, x_n).$$

We shall consider a variety of metrics in this set. The most important metric is the euclidean metric given by

$$\rho_2(x, y) = \left[\sum_{i=1}^{n} |x_i - y_i|^2\right]^{1/2}$$

where $x = (x_1, x_2, \ldots, x_n)$ and $y = (y_1, y_2, \ldots, y_n)$.

In analogous fashion, for every $p \geq 1$, a metric is given by

$$\rho_p(x, y) = \left[\sum_{i=1}^{n} |x_i - y_i|^p\right]^{1/p}.$$

That these functions ρ_p satisfy the triangle inequality is the content of the Minkowski inequality, whose proof follows from another inequality—the Hölder inequality. In the next section, we present proofs of these inequalities.

1.2 Inequalities of Hölder and Minkowski

THEOREM 1 (Hölder's inequality). If $p > 1$ and q is defined by $1/p + 1/q = 1$,

$$\sum_{i=1}^{n} |x_i y_i| \leq \left[\sum_{i=1}^{n} |x_i|^p\right]^{1/p} \left[\sum_{i=1}^{n} |y_i|^q\right]^{1/q}$$

for any complex numbers $x_1, x_2, \ldots, x_n; y_1, y_2, \ldots, y_n$.

Proof. We first prove the inequality

$$a^{1/p} b^{1/q} \leq \frac{a}{p} + \frac{b}{q}, \quad a \geq 0, b \geq 0.$$

In order to prove this, we consider the function

$$f(t) = t^\alpha - \alpha t + \alpha - 1$$

defined for $0 < \alpha < 1$, $t \geq 0$.

Then

$$f'(t) = \alpha(t^{\alpha - 1} - 1),$$

so that

$$f(1) = f'(1) = 0,$$

$$f'(t) > 0 \quad \text{for } 0 < t < 1,$$

and

$$f'(t) < 0 \quad \text{for } t > 1.$$

It follows that

$$f(t) \leq 0 \quad \text{for } t \geq 0.$$

The inequality is obvious for $b = 0$. Suppose $b > 0$, and let $t = a/b$ and $\alpha = 1/p$. Then

$$f\left(\frac{a}{b}\right) = \left(\frac{a}{b}\right)^{1/p} - \frac{1}{p}\frac{a}{b} + \frac{1}{p} - 1 \leq 0.$$

Multiplying by b, we obtain

$$a^{1/p}b^{1-1/p} \leq \frac{a}{p} + b\left(1 - \frac{1}{p}\right),$$

which is our inequality.

Applying this to the numbers

$$a_j = \frac{|x_j|^p}{\sum_{i=1}^{n}|x_i|^p},$$

$$b_j = \frac{|y_j|^q}{\sum_{i=1}^{n}|y_i|^q},$$

for each $j = 1, 2, \ldots, n$, we get

$$\frac{|x_j y_j|}{\left[\sum_{i=1}^{n}|x_i|^p\right]^{1/p}\left[\sum_{i=1}^{n}|y_i|^q\right]^{1/q}} \leq \frac{a_j}{p} + \frac{b_j}{q}, \quad j = 1, 2, \ldots, n.$$

By adding these n inequalities, we obtain the Hölder inequality, since

$$\sum_{j=1}^{n}\left(\frac{a_j}{p} + \frac{b_j}{q}\right) = \frac{\sum_{j=1}^{n} a_j}{p} + \frac{\sum_{j=1}^{n} b_j}{q} = \frac{1}{p} + \frac{1}{q} = 1.$$

We prove now the

THEOREM 2 (Minkowski's inequality). If $p \geq 1$, then

$$\left[\sum_{i=1}^{n}|x_i + y_i|^p\right]^{1/p} \leq \left[\sum_{i=1}^{n}|x_i|^p\right]^{1/p} + \left[\sum_{i=1}^{n}|y_i|^p\right]^{1/p}$$

for any complex numbers $x_1, x_2, \ldots, x_n; y_1, y_2, \ldots, y_n$.

Proof. The case $p = 1$ is obvious. Suppose $p > 1$. It is obvious that

$$\left[\sum_{i=1}^{n}|x_i + y_i|^p\right]^{1/p} \leq \left[\sum_{i=1}^{n}(|x_i| + |y_i|)^p\right]^{1/p}.$$

Now

$$(|x_i| + |y_i|)^p = (|x_i| + |y_i|)^{p-1}\,|x_i| + (|x_i| + |y_i|)^{p-1}\,|y_i|.$$

Summing these identities for $i = 1, 2, \ldots, n$,

$$\sum_{i=1}^{n}(|x_i| + |y_i|)^p = \sum_{i=1}^{n}(|x_i| + |y_i|)^{p-1}|x_i| + \sum_{i=1}^{n}(|x_i| + |y_i|)^{p-1}|y_i|.$$

The first sum on the right may be estimated by Hölder's inequality as follows (similarly for the second sum).

$$\sum_{i=1}^{n}(|x_i| + |y_i|)^{p-1}|x_i| \le \left[\sum_{i=1}^{n}|x_i|^p\right]^{1/p}\left[\sum_{i=1}^{n}((|x_i| + |y_i|)^{p-1})^q\right]^{1/q}$$
$$= \left[\sum_{i=1}^{n}|x_i|^p\right]^{1/p}\left[\sum_{i=1}^{n}(|x_i| + |y_i|)^p\right]^{1/q}.$$

Thus,

$$\sum_{i=1}^{n}(|x_i| + |y_i|)^p \le \left\{\left[\sum_{i=1}^{n}|x_i|^p\right]^{1/p} + \left[\sum_{i=1}^{n}|y_i|^p\right]^{1/p}\right\}\left[\sum_{i=1}^{n}(|x_i| + |y_i|)^p\right]^{1/q}.$$

Dividing $\left(\text{we may suppose } \sum_{i=1}^{n}(|x_i| + |y_i|)^p \neq 0\right)$, we obtain

$$\left[\sum_{i=1}^{n}(|x_i| + |y_i|)^p\right]^{1/p} \le \left[\sum_{i=1}^{n}|x_i|^p\right]^{1/p} + \left[\sum_{i=1}^{n}|y_i|^p\right]^{1/p},$$

from which Minkowski's inequality follows, since

$$\left[\sum_{i=1}^{n}|x_i + y_i|^p\right]^{1/p} \le \left[\sum_{i=1}^{n}(|x_i| + |y_i|)^p\right]^{1/p}.$$

The triangle inequality for the metric ρ_p is obtained by putting $x_i - z_i$ in place of x_i and $z_i - y_i$ in place of y_i in the statement of Minkowski's inequality.

The special case of Hölder's inequality with $p = q = 2$ is known as the **Cauchy-Schwarz** inequality:

$$\left[\sum_{i=1}^{n}|x_i y_i|\right]^2 \le \left[\sum_{i=1}^{n}|x_i|^2\right]\left[\sum_{i=1}^{n}|y_i|^2\right].$$

1.3 Examples Continued; l_p Spaces

Continuing the examples of Sec. 1.1, we mention an additional metric for n-space, namely,

$$\rho_\infty(x, y) = \max_{1 \le i \le n} |x_i - y_i|.$$

The notation is motivated by the fact that for any x and y,

$$\lim_{p \to \infty} \rho_p(x, y) = \max_{1 \le i \le n} |x_i - y_i|.$$

Spaces of sequences of real (complex) numbers provide natural extensions of the foregoing examples. These are obtained by considering the expression

$$\left[\sum_{i=1}^{\infty}|x_i - y_i|^p\right]^{1/p}, \quad p \geq 1,$$

for two sequences $x = (x_1, x_2, \ldots)$ and $y = (y_1, y_2, \ldots)$.

(vi) The space l_p, for $1 \leq p < \infty$, is the set of all sequences $x = (x_1, x_2, \ldots)$ satisfying

$$\sum_{i=1}^{\infty}|x_i|^p < \infty,$$

with the metric

$$d_p(x, y) = \left[\sum_{i=1}^{\infty}|x_i - y_i|^p\right]^{1/p}, \quad y = (y_1, y_2, \ldots).$$

To see that the series for d_p converges under the assumptions on x and y, and that the triangle inequality holds, we extend Minkowski's inequality as follows.

THEOREM 1 (Minkowski's inequality). If $1 \leq p < \infty$ and if $x, y \in l_p$, then

$$\left[\sum_{i=1}^{\infty}|x_i + y_i|^p\right]^{1/p} \leq \left[\sum_{i=1}^{\infty}|x_i|^p\right]^{1/p} + \left[\sum_{i=1}^{\infty}|y_i|^p\right]^{1/p}.$$

Proof. For any n we have

$$\left[\sum_{i=1}^{n}|x_i + y_i|^p\right]^{1/p} \leq \left[\sum_{i=1}^{n}|x_i|^p\right]^{1/p} + \left[\sum_{i=1}^{n}|y_i|^p\right]^{1/p}$$
$$\leq \left[\sum_{i=1}^{\infty}|x_i|^p\right]^{1/p} + \left[\sum_{i=1}^{\infty}|y_i|^p\right]^{1/p}.$$

The convergence of the series $\sum_{i=1}^{\infty}|x_i + y_i|^p$ and the inequality follow at once.

It is now an easy matter to verify that l_p, $1 \leq p < \infty$, is in fact a metric space.

(vii) The space l_∞ is defined to be the space of all bounded sequences, i.e., all $x = (x_1, x_2, \ldots)$ for which $\sup_{1\leq i<\infty} |x_i| < \infty$, with the metric

$$d_\infty(x, y) = \sup_{1\leq i<\infty} |x_i - y_i|.$$

The Hölder inequality has an extension to sequence spaces, which we state in terms of the following notations.

If $1 \leq p \leq \infty$, then we call q the **conjugate index** of p if

$$\frac{1}{p} + \frac{1}{q} = 1 \quad \text{for } 1 < p < \infty$$
$$q = \infty \quad \text{for } p = 1$$
$$q = 1 \quad \text{for } p = \infty.$$

The distance $d_p(x, 0)$ of x from the sequence $0 = (0, 0, 0, \ldots)$ is called the **norm** of the sequence x and denoted $\|x\|_p$.

THEOREM 2 (Hölder's inequality). If $1 \leq p \leq \infty$, q is conjugate to p, $x \in l_p$ and $y \in l_q$, then

$$(x_1 \cdot y_1, x_2 \cdot y_2, \ldots) \in l_1,$$

and

$$\sum_{i=1}^{\infty} |x_i y_i| \leq \|x\|_p \, \|y\|_q.$$

The proof is easy and is left to the reader.

The space l_2 is of special importance; it is called **sequential Hilbert space.** The above statement with $p = q = 2$ gives the Cauchy-Schwarz inequality:

$$\left[\sum_{i=1}^{\infty} |x_i y_i|\right]^2 \leq \left(\sum_{i=1}^{\infty} |x_i|^2\right)\left(\sum_{i=1}^{\infty} |y_i|^2\right).$$

1.4 Examples Continued; Function Spaces

Many important examples of metric spaces whose elements are functions (or equivalence classes of functions) occur naturally in the various branches of analysis. We shall mention only three examples of such function spaces here, restricting ourselves to real-valued functions defined on a closed interval $[a, b]$ of the real line. Further examples may be supplied by the reader.

(viii) $C[a, b]$ is the space of all continuous functions on $[a, b]$ with the metric

$$\rho(x, y) = \sup_{a \leq t \leq b} |x(t) - y(t)|.$$

(ix) $M[a, b]$ is the space of all bounded functions on $[a, b]$ with the above metric.

Of course, $C[a, b]$ is a subspace of $M[a, b]$.

(x) Let $BV[a, b]$ denote the class of all functions of bounded variation on $[a, b]$, i.e., all f for which the total variation

$$V(f) = \sup \sum_{i=1}^{n} |f(x_i) - f(x_{i-1})|$$

is finite, where the supremum is taken over all partitions $a = x_0 < x_1 < \ldots < x_n = b$. It is easily seen that

$$\rho(f, g) = V(f - g)$$

has all the properties of a metric except that $V(f - g)$ may be zero for distinct functions f and g. Indeed, $V(f - g) = 0$ if and only if f and g differ by a constant.

If BV is decomposed into equivalence classes according to the equivalence relation defined by

$$f \simeq g \quad \text{if} \quad f(t) - g(t) \quad \text{is constant on} \quad [a, b],$$

then this $\rho(f, g)$ determines a metric $\tilde{\rho}$ on the space $\widetilde{BV}$ of such equivalence classes in an obvious way.

Alternatively, we may modify the definition of ρ so as to obtain a metric on the original class BV. For example,

$$\rho(f, g) = |f(a) - g(a)| + V(f - g)$$

is a metric on BV. The subspace of this metric space, consisting of all $f \in BV$ for which $f(a) = 0$, can be identified in a natural way with the space $\widetilde{BV}$.

(xi) An example of a metric space which is of a somewhat different nature than those discussed so far is the space of non-empty, closed, bounded, convex subsets of the plane.

A set is **convex** if for each pair of its points it contains the line segment joining them. This segment, for points P and Q, has the parametric representation

$$tP + (1 - t)Q, \quad 0 \leq t \leq 1,$$

where tP denotes the point with coordinates (tx, ty) if P has the coordinates (x, y) relative to a cartesian coordinate system in the plane.

Let Γ denote the collection of all non-empty, closed, bounded, convex sets. For $A \in \Gamma$ and $\delta > 0$, denote by A_δ the union of all closed disks of radius δ centered at points of A.

Let $d(A, B)$ be defined by

$$d(A, B) = \inf \{\delta > 0 \colon A_\delta \supset B \text{ and } B_\delta \supset A\}.$$

We show that d is a metric on Γ. Clearly $d(A, A) = 0$, $d(A, B) \geq 0$ and $d(A, B) = d(B, A)$. If $d(A, B) = 0$, then for every $\delta > 0$, $A \subset B_\delta$. It follows that A is a subset of the closure of B. Since B is closed, $A \subset B$. By symmetry, $B \subset A$, so that $B = A$.

For the triangle inequality we first observe that

$$A \in \Gamma \text{ implies } A_\delta \in \Gamma \text{ for any } \delta > 0 \text{ and } (A_\delta)_\epsilon = A_{\delta+\epsilon}, \text{ for any } \epsilon > 0.$$

Now let

$$R = \{\rho > 0 : A_\rho \supset B \text{ and } B_\rho \supset A\}$$
$$S = \{\sigma > 0 : A_\sigma \supset C \text{ and } C_\sigma \supset A\}$$
$$T = \{\tau > 0 : C_\tau \supset B \text{ and } B_\tau \supset C\}.$$

We must show

$$\inf R \leq \inf S + \inf T.$$

The right-hand side equals

$$\inf \{\sigma + \tau : \sigma \in S \text{ and } \tau \in T\}.$$

The result will follow if we show that $\sigma + \tau \in R$ for all $\sigma \in S$ and $\tau \in T$. But this is the case since

$$A_{\sigma+\tau} = (A_\sigma)_\tau \supset (C)_\tau \supset B$$

and

$$B_{\sigma+\tau} = (B_\tau)_\sigma \supset (C)_\sigma \supset A.$$

1.5 Convergence and Related Notions

The metric space provides an abstract setting for a discussion of the convergence of sequences and related notions. By a sequence $\{x_n\}$ of elements of X is meant a mapping $n \to x_n$ of the positive integers into X.

A sequence $\{x_n\}$ **converges** to an element $x \in X$ if $\lim_n \rho(x_n, x) = 0$. We shall write $x = \lim_n x_n$ when $\{x_n\}$ converges to x.

It is immediately seen that a sequence can have at most one limit:

$$\lim_n x_n = x \text{ and } \lim_n x_n = y \text{ imply } x = y.$$

Application of this definition in a particular case may yield a familiar notion of convergence, as in the space $C[a, b]$, for example, where we have the

PROPOSITION 1. In $C[a, b]$, $\lim_n x_n = x$ if and only if $\{x_n(t)\}$ converges to $x(t)$ uniformly on $[a, b]$.

In view of this fact, the metric in $C[a, b]$

$$\rho(x, y) = \sup_{a \le t \le b} |x(t) - y(t)|$$

is called the **uniform** metric.

In other particular metric spaces, the above definition yields a new notion of convergence. Thus, in l_p, $p \geq 1$, there appears a notion of the convergence "in mean of order p" of a sequence of sequences of numbers.

Finally, it should be noted that some fundamental notions of convergence are not derivable from a metric space convergence. Indeed, the ordinary notion of point-wise convergence of a sequence of functions on $[a, b]$,

$$\lim_n f_n = f \quad \text{if} \quad \lim_n f_n(t) = f(t) \quad \text{for each } t \in [a, b]$$

cannot be described by any metric on a non-trivial class of functions (see Sec. 5.1).

In a metric space (X, ρ) the set

$$S(x_0, r) = \{x \in X : \rho(x_0, x) < r\}, \quad r > 0, x_0 \in X,$$

is called the **open sphere** of radius r and center x_0. We speak of the **closed sphere** if the inequality is replaced by $\rho(x_0, x) \leq r$ and denote the set by $\bar{S}(x_0, r)$.

A subset $G \subset X$ is called **open** if it contains a sphere about each of its points. A set F is **closed** if its complement $X \sim F$ is open. An open sphere is an open set and a closed sphere is a closed set.

The collection $\mathcal{G}$ of all open sets has the following properties.

(1) $0 \in \mathcal{G}$ and $X \in \mathcal{G}$, where 0 is the empty set.
(2) Any union of members of $\mathcal{G}$ is a member of $\mathcal{G}$.
(3) The intersection of finitely many members of $\mathcal{G}$ is a member of $\mathcal{G}$.

These facts are easily proved, as are the dual facts about closed sets, namely,

(1′) 0 and X are closed.
(2′) Any intersection of closed sets is closed.
(3′) A finite union of closed sets is closed.

A **neighborhood** of a point $x_0 \in X$ is any set which contains an open set to which x_0 belongs. We say that x_0 is an **interior** point of a set A if A is a neighborhood of x_0. The **interior** of a set A consists of all interior points of A and can easily be seen to coincide with the largest open set contained in A.

If $A \subset X$ and $x_0 \in X$, then x_0 is called a **limit point** of A if every neighborhood of x_0 contains points of A distinct from x_0 (x_0 may or may not be in A). One easily sees that x_0 is a limit point of A if, and only if, A contains an infinite sequence of distinct points which converges to x_0.

For each $A \subset X$, the set $\bar{A}$ consisting of all points which are either points of A or limit points of A is called the **closure** of the set A. The closure of A is a closed set and is in fact the smallest closed set containing A.

1.6 Separable Space, Examples

If A and B are subsets of X, then we say that **A is dense in B** if $\bar{A} \supset B$; every element of B is a point or a limit point of A. In particular, A is said to be **everywhere dense** if $\bar{A} = X$. This means that for every $x \in X$ and $\epsilon > 0$ there is a $y \in A$ such that $\rho(x, y) < \epsilon$.

If the metric space X has a countable subset which is everywhere dense, it is called a **separable** metric space.

Since the rational numbers form a countable set which is everywhere dense in the real line, the latter is a separable space.

In n-space with any of the metrics we have introduced, the countable set consisting of all $x = (x_1, x_2, \ldots, x_n)$ for which each coordinate x_i is rational, is easily seen to be everywhere dense (a complex number is called rational in case its real and imaginary parts are both rational).

The spaces l_p for $1 \leq p < \infty$ are separable, but l_∞ is not separable. If e_k denotes the sequence consisting of 1 in the kth place and zeros elsewhere, then the set of all finite sums of rational multiples of the e_k's (i.e., all sequences with only finitely many non-zero coordinates, each of which is rational) is dense in l_p, $1 \leq p < \infty$. For, if $x = (x_1, x_2, \ldots) \in l_p$, and $r_1, r_2, \ldots, r_k$ are rational, then

$$d_p^p\left(x, \sum_{i=1}^{k} r_i e_i\right) = \sum_{i=1}^{k} |x_i - r_i|^p + \sum_{i=k+1}^{\infty} |x_i|^p$$

and, for any $\epsilon > 0$, k may be chosen so that

$$\sum_{i=k+1}^{\infty} |x_i|^p < \frac{\epsilon^p}{2}.$$

Then $r_1, r_2, \ldots, r_k$ may be chosen to give

$$|x_i - r_i|^p < \frac{\epsilon^p}{2k}, \qquad i = 1, 2, \ldots, k,$$

with the result,

$$d_p\left(x, \sum_{i=1}^{k} r_i e_i\right) < \epsilon$$

from which the separability follows in case $1 \leq p < \infty$.

In the case $p = \infty$, we observe that the set of all sequences of zeros and ones is an uncountable set (may be put in one-one correspondence with the interval [0, 1] by means of binary representation) and that any two members of this set have distance 1 apart in l_∞. The impossibility of a countable dense set is then apparent.

That the space $C[a, b]$ is separable can be seen by means of the Weierstrass approximation theorem (see Sec. 1.13), which says that any element of $C[a, b]$ can be approximated uniformly on $[a, b]$ by a polynomial. But any polynomial can be uniformly approximated by a polynomial with rational coefficients. Since there are countably many polynomials with rational coefficients, the result follows.

The property of separability has the following reformulation.

PROPOSITION 1. X is separable if, and only if, there is a countable collection B of open sets such that an arbitrary open set can be expressed as a union of members of B.

The proof is left as an exercise.

If $\mathcal{C}$ is a collection of open sets in a metric space X with the property that every $x \in X$ is a member of at least one set $G \in \mathcal{C}$, then $\mathcal{C}$ is called an **open covering** of X. A **subcovering** of the open covering $\mathcal{C}$ is any subcollection $\mathcal{C}' \subset \mathcal{C}$ which is also an open covering of X. It is often of use, for technical reasons, to know when a space X has the property that every open covering contains a countable subcovering. We have the

PROPOSITION 2 (Lindelöf). If X is separable and $\mathcal{C}$ is an open covering of X, then there is a countable subcovering $\mathcal{C}' \subset \mathcal{C}$.

The proof, based on the preceding proposition, is left as an exercise.

1.7 Complete Space, Examples

In a metric space, certain sequences, called Cauchy sequences, or fundamental sequences, are of primary importance. A sequence $\{x_n\}$ in a metric space $X = (X, \rho)$ is said to be a **Cauchy sequence** if, for every $\epsilon > 0$, there is an N such that

$$m > N \text{ and } n > N \text{ implies } \rho(x_m, x_n) < \epsilon.$$

More briefly, $\{x_n\}$ is a Cauchy sequence if

$$\lim_{m,n\to\infty} \rho(x_m, x_n) = 0.$$

An equivalent statement is that $\rho(x_{n+k}, x_n)$ converges to 0 uniformly in k as n tends to infinity.

Every convergent sequence is a Cauchy sequence. For, suppose $\{x_n\}$ converges to x. Let $\epsilon > 0$. Then there is an N such that $n > N$ implies $\rho(x, x_n) < \epsilon/2$. But this implies

$$\rho(x_n, x_m) \le \rho(x_n, x) + \rho(x, x_m) < \epsilon,$$

for every $m > N$, $n > N$, so that $\{x_n\}$ is a Cauchy sequence.

The converse is not always true. In some metric spaces there are Cauchy sequences which do not converge. A classical example is the space of rational numbers with

$$\rho(x, y) = |x - y|.$$

The sequence .1, .101, .101001, .1010010001, . . . is easily seen to be a Cauchy sequence which does not converge.

A metric space (X, ρ) is said to be **complete** if every Cauchy sequence in the space converges. The space of rational numbers is, accordingly, not complete. It turns out that every metric space may be imbedded in a complete metric space in which it is dense. For the space of rational numbers, the corresponding complete metric space is the space of real numbers. However, the reals play a special role and their completeness must already be known before the general imbedding theorem can be established.

In many basic developments in analysis, the completeness of the reals is used in the form of the so-called nested intervals theorem. It has the following counterpart in general metric spaces.

PROPOSITION 1. A metric space (X, ρ) is complete if and only if for every sequence $\{\bar{S}_n\}$ of closed spheres, with

$$\bar{S}_{n+1} \subset \bar{S}_n, \quad n = 1, 2, \ldots$$

and

$$\lim_{n \to \infty} r_n = 0,$$

where r_n is the radius of $\bar{S}_n$, the intersection

$$\bigcap_{n=1}^{\infty} \bar{S}_n$$

consists of exactly one point.

The proof is left to the reader.

We consider some examples.

(i) The space $C[a, b]$ is complete.

Let $\{x_n\}$ be a Cauchy sequence. Then for every $\epsilon > 0$ there is an N such that $m, n > N$ implies $\rho(x_n, x_m) < \epsilon$. But this means that

$$\max \{|x_n(t) - x_m(t)| : t \in [a, b]\} < \epsilon.$$

In particular, for every $t \in [a, b]$, $\{x_n(t)\}$ is a Cauchy sequence of real numbers. By the completeness of the real numbers, $\{x_n(t)\}$ converges to a number $x(t)$, so that we have determined a function x on $[a, b]$. Now, for every $n > N$

$$\max \{|x(t) - x_n(t)| : x \in [a, b]\} \leq \epsilon.$$

This implies that $\{x_n\}$ converges uniformly to x, that x is continuous, and that $\lim_{n \to \infty} \rho(x, x_n) = 0$. Thus $C[a, b]$ is complete.

(ii) Again, let S be the set of continuous functions on a closed interval $[a, b]$. But now let

$$\rho(x, y) = \int_a^b |x(t) - y(t)|\, dt.$$

Then (S, ρ) is a metric space. We observe that it is not complete.

Let $a < c < b$, and for every n so large that $a < c - 1/n$, define x_n as:

$$x_n(t) = \begin{cases} 0 & \text{if } a \leq t \leq c - \dfrac{1}{n} \\ nt - nc + 1 & \text{if } c - \dfrac{1}{n} \leq t \leq c \\ 1 & \text{if } c \leq t \leq b. \end{cases}$$

Then $\rho(x_n, x_m) \leq \dfrac{1}{n} + \dfrac{1}{m}$, from which it is obvious that $\{x_n\}$ is a Cauchy sequence.

Now, let $x \in S$. Then

$$\rho(x_n, x) = \int_a^{c-(1/n)} |x(t)|\, dt + \int_{c-(1/n)}^{c} |x_n(t) - x(t)|\, dt + \int_c^b |1 - x(t)|\, dt$$

and $\lim_{n\to\infty} \rho(x_n, x) = 0$ implies

$$x(t) = 0,\ t \in [a, c) \quad\text{and}\quad x(t) = 1,\ t \in (c, b].$$

Since it is impossible for a continuous function to have this property, $\{x_n\}$ does not have a limit.

This example suggests the consideration of $\int_a^b |x(t) - y(t)|\, dt$ as a metric for a wider class of functions; in particular, on the class of all absolutely integrable functions. The sense in which the term integrable is to be understood depends on the definition of the integral being used. We wish to accept the integral in the Riemann sense and make some observations about the associated metric space. For simplicity, we take the interval $[a, b]$ to be $[0, 1]$, which is typical of the general case.

It is possible for $\int_0^1 |x(t) - y(t)|\, dt = 0$ with $x \neq y$. For example, let

$$x(t) = 0 \quad \text{if } x \in [0, 1]$$

$$y(t) = \begin{cases} 0 & \text{if } x \in [0, 1) \\ 1 & \text{if } x = 1. \end{cases}$$

We shall call x and y equivalent if $\rho(x, y) = 0$ and consider ρ on the equivalence classes of functions so determined, i.e., the distance of two equivalence classes is $\rho(x, y)$ where x and y are, respectively, any representatives of these classes. In this way, a metric is determined on the set of equivalence classes of absolutely integrable functions.

(iii) The resulting metric space is not complete. A simple example shows this. Let

$$x_n(t) = \begin{cases} \sqrt{n} & \text{if } 0 \le t \le \dfrac{1}{n} \\ \dfrac{1}{\sqrt{t}} & \text{if } \dfrac{1}{n} \le t \le 1 . \end{cases}$$

Then $\{x_n\}$ is easily seen to be a Cauchy sequence which does not converge in our space. However, if we were to extend the interpretation of integrability to include unbounded functions for which an improper integral exists and extend the definition of $\rho(x, y)$ as an improper integral, then this sequence would have the limit

$$x(t) = \begin{cases} t^{-1/2} & \text{if } 0 < t \le 1 \\ 0 & \text{if } x = 0. \end{cases}$$

Our next example shows that the completeness property breaks down in a more serious way.

(iv) Define a sequence $\{S_n\}$ of sets as follows:

$$S_0 = [0, 1]$$

$S_1 = S_0$ with the middle open interval of length $1/4$ removed,

$S_2 = S_1$ with the middle open intervals of the component intervals of S_1 removed, each of length $1/4^2$.

Then, by induction, having already defined S_n so as to consist of 2^n disjoint closed intervals, of equal length, let

$S_{n+1} = S_n$ with the middle open intervals of the component intervals of S_n removed, each of length $1/4^{n+1}$.

For each $n = 1, 2, \ldots$, the sum of the lengths of the component open intervals of S_n is given by

$$m(S_n) = 1 - \sum_{i=0}^{n-1} \frac{1}{4^{i+1}} \cdot 2^i = \frac{1}{2} + \frac{1}{2^{n+1}}.$$

For every $n = 1, 2, \ldots$, let x_n be defined by

$$x_n(t) = \begin{cases} 1 & \text{if } t \in S_n \\ 0 & \text{if } t \notin S_n. \end{cases}$$

We note that $\{x_n\}$ is a Cauchy sequence. For, let $m > n$. Then

$$\begin{aligned} \rho(x_n, x_m) &= \int_0^1 |x_n(t) - x_m(t)|\, dt \\ &= m(S_n) - m(S_m) \\ &= \frac{1}{2^{n+1}} - \frac{1}{2^{m+1}}. \end{aligned}$$

We shall show that $\{x_n\}$ does not converge to any Riemann integrable function. Let x be a Riemann integrable function and suppose

$$(*) \quad \lim_{n\to\infty} \int_0^1 |x(t) - x_n(t)|\, dt = 0.$$

Let I_1 be the open interval removed in forming S_1; I_1, I_2, I_3 the open intervals removed in forming S_2, etc.

For each $k = 1, 2, \ldots$ there is an N so that $n > N$ implies $x_n(t) = 0$, $t \in I_k$. It follows that x is equivalent to a function which is identically zero on

$$T = \bigcup_{k=1}^{\infty} I_k.$$

But the lower Riemann integral of such a function is zero. Since x is integrable,

$$\int_0^1 x(t)\,dt = 0.$$

But

$$\int_0^1 x_n(t)\,dt > \tfrac{1}{2}, \quad n = 1, 2, \ldots.$$

This contradicts (*).

The failure of the space of absolutely integrable functions to be complete is to be regarded as a defect in the definition of the integral. The definition of Lebesgue, which will be discussed later, corrects this and other defects of the Riemann integral.

(v) The spaces l_p, $1 \le p < \infty$, are complete. Let $\{x^{(n)}\}$ be a Cauchy sequence in l_p, where

$$x^{(n)} = \{x_1^{(n)}, x_2^{(n)}, \ldots\}, \quad n = 1, 2, \ldots.$$

For each $\epsilon > 0$, there is an N such that $m, n > N$ implies

$$\sum_{i=1}^{\infty} |x_i^{(n)} - x_i^{(m)}|^p < \epsilon^p.$$

It follows that, for each i, the sequence of numbers $\{x_i^{(n)}\}$ is a Cauchy sequence, since $m, n > N$ implies

$$|x_i^{(n)} - x_i^{(m)}| < \epsilon.$$

Let

$$x_i = \lim_{n\to\infty} x_i^{(n)}, \quad i = 1, 2, 3, \ldots,$$

and let

$$x = \{x_1, x_2, \ldots\}.$$

We show that $x \in l_p$ and that $\{x^{(n)}\}$ converges to x in l_p. Let $n > N$ and fix k. Then

$$\sum_{i=1}^{k} |x_i|^p \le \left\{\left[\sum_{i=1}^{k} |x_i^{(n)} - x_i|^p\right]^{1/p} + \left[\sum_{i=1}^{k} |x_i^{(n)}|^p\right]^{1/p}\right\}^p$$
$$\le \{\epsilon + \|x^{(n)}\|\}^p.$$

It follows that $\sum_{i=1}^{\infty} |x_i|^p$ converges, so that $x \in l_p$.

Moreover, the observation that for every $n > N$ and every k,

$$\left[\sum_{i=1}^{k} |x_i^{(n)} - x_i|^p\right]^{1/p} \le \epsilon$$

implies that

$$\|x^{(n)} - x\| \le \epsilon, \quad n > N,$$

so that $\{x^{(n)}\}$ converges to x in the l_p norm.

(vi) The space l_∞, of bounded sequences with sup norm, is complete.

Let $\{x^{(n)}\}$ be a Cauchy sequence in l_∞. Then for each $\epsilon > 0$, there is an N such that $m, n > N$ implies

$$\sup_i |x_i^{(n)} - x_i^{(m)}| < \epsilon.$$

It follows that, for each i, $\{x_i^{(n)}\}$ is a Cauchy sequence. Let

$$x_i = \lim_{i \to \infty} x_i^{(n)}$$

and let

$$x = \{x_1, x_2, \ldots\}.$$

Now, for each i and $n > N$, it follows that

$$|x_i - x_i^{(n)}| \leq \epsilon,$$

from which both facts, that $x \in l_\infty$ and that $\{x^{(n)}\}$ converges to x in the l_∞ norm, follow.

The n-space is complete under the various metrics we have introduced.

Proposition 2. A subspace of a complete metric space is complete if and only if it is closed.

The proof is left for the reader.

(vii) The Baire-classes of bounded functions form a family of closed subspaces of the space of bounded functions with the uniform metric.

For real-valued functions on [0, 1], let M be the metric space of bounded functions with

$$d(f, g) = \sup [|f(x) - g(x)| : x \in [0, 1]].$$

The Baire subspaces of M are defined as follows.

$$B_0 = C[0, 1].$$

B_1 is the set of bounded functions which are point-wise limits of sequences of functions in B_0. B_2 is the set of all bounded functions which are point-wise limits of sequences of functions in B_1.

In general, if α is any ordinal number, of countable cardinal, then B_α is the set of all bounded functions which are point-wise limits of sequences of functions in $\bigcup [B_\beta : \beta < \alpha]$.

Each B_α is a closed subspace of M and so is complete (for the proof see Goffman [1]).

For every ordinal α, of countable cardinal, $\bigcup [B_\beta : \beta < \alpha]$ is a proper subspace of B_α (for the proof see Hausdorff [1]).

1.8 Contractions, Applications to Differential and Integral Equations

In this section, we show how various existence theorems in analysis follow from a very simple fact about mappings in a metric space.

Let $X = (X, \rho)$ be a metric space. A mapping $T : X \to X$ is called a **contraction in** X if there is a number K, with $0 < K < 1$, such that $x, y \in X$, $x \neq y$, implies

$$\rho(Tx, Ty) \leq K\rho(x, y).$$

THEOREM 1. If X is a complete metric space, and T is a contraction in X, then T has a fixed point and it is unique. That is to say, there is a unique $x_0 \in X$ such that $Tx_0 = x_0$.

Proof. We first prove uniqueness. Suppose $Tx = x$ and $Ty = y$. Then, if $x \neq y$, $\rho(x, y) = \rho(Tx, Ty) < \rho(x, y)$, which is impossible. Hence $x = y$.

For the existence of a fixed point, we may start with any $x \in X$ and consider the sequence of images of x under repeated application of T,

$$x, Tx, T^2x = T(Tx), \ldots, T^n x = T(T^{n-1}x), \ldots.$$

We show that $\{T^n x\}$ is a Cauchy sequence. For every $n > 1$ and $p > 0$,

$$\begin{aligned}\rho(T^{n+p}x, T^n x) &\leq K\rho(T^{n+p-1}x, T^{n-1}x) \leq \ldots \leq K^n\rho(T^p x, x)\\ &\leq K^n[\rho(T^p x, T^{p-1}x) + \ldots + \rho(Tx, x)]\\ &\leq K^n\rho(Tx, x)(K^{p-1} + K^{p-2} + \ldots + K + 1)\\ &< \frac{K^n}{1 - K}\rho(Tx, x).\end{aligned}$$

Since $K < 1$ and $\rho(Tx, x)$ are fixed, it follows that $\{T^n x\}$ is Cauchy.

Let $x_0 = \lim_{n \to \infty} T^n x$. Since T is a contraction, the interchange of operations in

$$Tx_0 = T \lim T^n x = \lim T^{n+1} x = x_0$$

is easily justified so that x_0 is a fixed point.

As a first example of the application of this theorem, we prove a standard existence and uniqueness theorem for ordinary differential equations.

Let D be a connected open set in the plane, and let f be a real function defined on D. We shall say that f satisfies a **Lipschitz condition** in y on D, with Lipschitz constant M, if for every (x, y_1) and (x, y_2) in D, we have

$$|f(x, y_2) - f(x, y_1)| \leq M|y_2 - y_1|.$$

We shall show that if f satisfies a Lipschitz condition, then there exists a unique solution, through each point in D, to the differential equation

$$\frac{dy}{dx} = f(x, y),$$

and this solution extends across the domain.

We shall make the above statement precise and shall give the proof in steps. Let $(x_0, y_0) \in D$. By a local solution passing through (x_0, y_0) we mean a function φ defined on an open interval I such that $x_0 \in I$, $\varphi(x_0) = y_0$, $(x, \varphi(x)) \in D$ for every $x \in I$, and $\varphi'(x) = f(x, \varphi(x))$ for every $x \in I$.

THEOREM 2. If f is continuous on an open connected set D and satisfies a Lipschitz condition in y on D, then for every $(x_0, y_0) \in D$, the differential equation $dy/dx = f(x, y)$ has a unique local solution passing through (x_0, y_0).

Proof. We leave it for the reader to verify that a function φ defined on an open interval I is such that $\varphi(x_0) = y_0$ and $\varphi'(x) = f(x, \varphi(x))$ for every $x \in I$ if and only if

$$\varphi(x) = y_0 + \int_{x_0}^{x} f(t, \varphi(t))\, dt$$

for every $x \in I$.

Now, let $D' \subset D$ be open, connected, containing (x_0, y_0), and such that f is bounded on D', and let $|f(x, y)| < A$ for all $(x, y) \in D'$.

Let $d > 0$ be such that

(a) the rectangle $R \subset D'$, where

$$R = [x_0 - d, x_0 + d] \times [y_0 - dA, y_0 + dA],$$

(b) $Md < 1$, where M is the Lipschitz constant for f in D.

Let $J = [x_0 - d, x_0 + d]$. The set B of continuous functions ψ on J such that $\psi(x_0) = y_0$ and $|\psi(x) - y_0| \leq dA$ for every $x \in J$ is a complete metric space under the uniform metric ρ. Consider the mapping T defined by

$$(T\psi)(x) = y_0 + \int_{x_0}^{x} f(t, \psi(t))\, dt \quad \text{for } \psi \in B \text{ and } x \in J.$$

Now, $(T\psi)(x_0) = y_0$, $T\psi$ is continuous, and for every $x \in J$,

$$|(T\psi)(x) - y_0| = \left| \int_{x_0}^{x} f(t, \psi(t))\, dt \right| \leq \int_{x_0}^{x} |f(t, \psi(t))|\, dt \leq dA.$$

Hence $T\psi \in B$. Thus T maps B into B.

We show that T is a contraction. Let $\psi_1, \psi_2 \in B$. Then, for every $x \in J$,

$$\begin{aligned} |(T\psi_1)(x) - (T\psi_2)(x)| &= \left| \int_{x_0}^{x} \{f(t, \psi_1(t)) - f(t, \psi_2(t))\}\, dt \right| \\ &\leq \int_{x_0}^{x} |f(t, \psi_1(t)) - f(t, \psi_2(t))|\, dt \\ &\leq Md \max\,[|\psi_1(t) - \psi_2(t)| : t \in J], \end{aligned}$$

so that $\rho(T\psi_1, T\psi_2) \leq Md\rho(\psi_1, \psi_2)$. Hence T is a contraction. By theorem 1, we obtain theorem 2.

We next show that the local solution can be extended across D'. Let $J = J_1$, $d = d_1$ and $x_0 + d = x_1$, $\varphi(x_1) = y_1$. By theorem 2, applied to (x_1, y_1), we obtain J_2, d_2 and (x_2, y_2), and the solution functions $\varphi_1 = \varphi$ on J_1 and φ_2 on J_2 agree on an interval and so yield a solution on $J_1 \cup J_2$. In this way, we obtain a sequence $\{(x_n, y_n)\}$ with $x_{n+1} > x_n$, $n = 1, 2, \ldots$. We assume D' bounded and show that the distance of (x_n, y_n) from the boundary of D' converges to zero. If this distance is δ_n, the above $d_1, d_2, \ldots, d_n, \ldots$ may be chosen so that

$$d_n = \min\left[\frac{\delta_n}{A^2 + 1}, \frac{1}{2M}\right].$$

Since $\sum_{n=1}^{\infty} d_n < \infty$ it follows that $\sum_{n=1}^{\infty} \delta_n < \infty$ and $\lim \delta_n = 0$. We thus have (using the fact that D is the union of an increasing sequence of sets each having the above properties of D'):

THEOREM 3. If f is continuous on an open connected set D and satisfies a Lipschitz condition in y on D, then for every $(x_0, y_0) \in D$ the differential equation $dy/dx = f(x, y)$ has a unique solution $y = \varphi(x)$ such that $y_0 = \varphi(x_0)$ and such that the curve given by the solution passes across D from boundary to boundary.

Thus the solutions to the equation form a simple covering of D.

The condition that f satisfies a Lipschitz condition may be localized, but we shall not discuss these details.

We next consider an integral operator. Let K be defined and continuous on the closed square $[a, b] \times [a, b]$, let g be continuous on $[a, b]$, and let λ be a real number. We seek a function f satisfying

$$f(x) = \lambda \int_a^b K(x, y) f(y)\, dy + g(x), \quad x \in [a, b].$$

In other words, we seek a fixed point, in the space $C[a, b]$, of the mapping T, where

$$(T\psi)(x) = \lambda \int_a^b K(x, y)\psi(y)\, dy + g(x), \quad x \in [a, b].$$

Clearly, T maps $C[a, b]$ into itself and a sufficient condition for the existence and uniqueness of a solution is that T be a contraction in $C[a, b]$. If M is an upper bound for $|K(x, y)|$ on the square, then

$$\begin{aligned}\rho(T\psi_1, T\psi_2) &= \sup\left\{\left|\lambda \int_a^b K(x, y)\{\psi_1(y) - \psi_2(y)\}\, dy\right| : x \in [a, b]\right\} \\ &\leq |\lambda|\, M(b - a) \sup\{|\psi_1(y) - \psi_2(y)| : y \in [a, b]\} \\ &= |\lambda|\, M(b - a)\rho(\psi_1, \psi_2).\end{aligned}$$

The condition thus takes the form

$$|\lambda| < \frac{1}{M(b - a)}.$$

1.9 Completion

By following a procedure similar to that which yields the real number system from the rationals in terms of equivalence classes of Cauchy sequences, it can be shown that any metric space (X, ρ) can be imbedded in a complete metric space, as a dense subspace, in essentially a unique way. The enlarged space is called the **completion** of the space (X, ρ).

This section is devoted to a precise formulation of this statement and an outline of the proof.

A transformation of a metric space (X, ρ) into a metric space (Y, σ) is called an **isometry** if, for every $x, y \in X$,

$$\sigma(Tx, Ty) = \rho(x, y).$$

Such an isometry is said to **imbed** (X, ρ) in (Y, σ). (X, ρ) and (Y, σ) are **isomorphic** as metric spaces if there is an isometry of (X, ρ) onto (Y, σ).

THEOREM 1. If (X, ρ) is any metric space, it can be imbedded, as a dense subspace, in a complete metric space $(\tilde{X}, \tilde{\rho})$. Two complete spaces in which (X, ρ) can be so imbedded are isomorphic.

Outline of Proof. We assume that the real numbers are a complete metric space. Let $\mathfrak{X}$ be the set of all Cauchy sequences in X. Define an equivalence relation in $\mathfrak{X}$ by letting $\{x_n\} \simeq \{y_n\}$ if $\{\rho(x_n, y_n)\}$ converges to 0. The set of equivalence classes so formed is denoted by $\tilde{X}$ and a metric $\tilde{\rho}$ is defined in $\tilde{X}$ as follows:

If $\{x_n\}, \{y_n\} \in \mathfrak{X}$, then $\{\rho(x_n, y_n)\}$ is a Cauchy sequence of real numbers. Let $\tilde{\rho}$ be defined as $\lim_{n \to \infty} \rho(x_n, y_n)$. This limit is unchanged if $\{x_n\}$ and $\{y_n\}$ are replaced by equivalent sequences. Then

$$\tilde{\rho}(\tilde{x}, \tilde{y}) = \lim_{n \to \infty} \rho(x_n, y_n)$$

when $\{x_n\} \in \tilde{x} \in \tilde{X}$ and $\{y_n\} \in \tilde{y} \in \tilde{X}$.

We omit the proof that $(\tilde{X}, \tilde{\rho})$ is a complete metric space.

The imbedding is accomplished by associating with each $x \in X$ the equivalence class Tx in $\tilde{X}$ to which the Cauchy sequence $\{x, x, x, \ldots\}$ belongs. Then T is easily shown to be an isometry.

To see that $T(X)$ is dense in $\tilde{X}$, let $\{x_n\} \in \tilde{x} \in \tilde{X}$, and observe that the sequence $\{Tx_n\}$ converges to $\tilde{x}$ in $\tilde{X}$. This shows that a completion of (X, ρ) exists.

For the uniqueness, we must realize that a completion of (X, ρ) consists of both a metric space $(\tilde{X}, \tilde{\rho})$ and an imbedding map T. Thus, we must show that if $(\tilde{X}, \tilde{\rho}, T)$ and $(\tilde{Y}, \tilde{\sigma}, S)$ are completions of (X, ρ), then an isomorphism exists between $(\tilde{X}, \tilde{\rho})$ and $(\tilde{Y}, \tilde{\sigma})$.

Now T^{-1} is an isomorphism of $T(X)$ onto X, and S is an isomorphism of

X onto $S(X)$. The composite mapping ST^{-1} is then an isomorphism of $T(X)$ onto $S(X)$. We obtain a mapping φ by extending this mapping to all of $\tilde{X}$ from the dense subset $T(X)$. Choose $\tilde{x} \in \tilde{X}$ and $\{Tx_n\}$, a sequence in $T(X)$ converging to $\tilde{x}$. Then $\{ST^{-1}Tx_n\} = \{Sx_n\}$ is a Cauchy sequence in Y whose limit is defined to be $\varphi\tilde{x}$. The mapping φ defined in this way can be shown to be an isomorphism of $\tilde{X}$ onto $\tilde{Y}$.

1.10 Category, Nowhere Differentiable Continuous Functions

An important fact about complete metric spaces, which has many interesting applications to analysis, is that they are of the second category.

If (X, ρ) is a metric space, a set $A \subset X$ is said to be **nowhere dense** if its closure $\bar{A}$ contains no sphere, or equivalently if $\bar{A}$ has no interior points.

The union of any finite set of nowhere dense sets is nowhere dense. However, the union of countably many nowhere dense sets need not be nowhere dense.

A set $A \subset X$ is said to be of the **first category** in X if it is the union of countably many nowhere dense sets in X. Otherwise, A is said to be of the **second category** in X.

PROPOSITION 1. (X, ρ) is of the second category in itself, if and only if, in any representation of X as the union

$$X = \bigcup_{i=1}^{\infty} F_i$$

of countably many closed sets F_i, at least one of the F_i contains a sphere.

The proof is easy and will be omitted.

THEOREM 1. Every complete metric space (X, ρ) is of the second category in itself.

Proof. Suppose, on the contrary, that

$$X = \bigcup_{i=1}^{\infty} F_i,$$

where each F_i is closed and contains no sphere. Then $X \sim F_1$ is a non-empty open set. Choose x_1 and $\epsilon_1 < 1$ so that $x_1 \in X \sim F_1$ and

$$S(x_1, \epsilon_1) \cap F_1 = 0.$$

The sphere $S(x_1, \epsilon_1/2)$ is not contained in F_2. Hence there is an $x_2 \in S(x_1, \epsilon_1/2)$ and an $\epsilon_2 < \frac{1}{2}$ such that

$$S(x_2, \epsilon_2) \cap F_2 = 0 \quad \text{and} \quad S(x_2, \epsilon_2) \subset S\left(x_1, \frac{\epsilon_1}{2}\right).$$

Proceeding inductively, we can choose a sequence $\{x_n\}$ of points and a sequence $\{\epsilon_n\}$ of radii for which

(a) $S(x_{n+1}, \epsilon_{n+1}) \subset S\left(x_n, \dfrac{\epsilon_n}{2}\right)$,

(b) $\epsilon_{n+1} < \dfrac{1}{2^n}$,

and

(c) $S(x_{n+1}, \epsilon_{n+1}) \cap F_{n+1} = 0$.

The sequence $\{x_n\}$ is Cauchy, for

$$\begin{aligned}\rho(x_{n+k}, x_n) &\leq \rho(x_n, x_{n+1}) + \rho(x_{n+1}, x_{n+2}) + \dots + \rho(x_{n+k-1}, x_{n+k})\\ &< \frac{\epsilon_n}{2} + \frac{\epsilon_{n+1}}{2} + \dots + \frac{\epsilon_{n+k-1}}{2}\\ &< \frac{1}{2^n} + \frac{1}{2^{n+1}} + \dots + \frac{1}{2^{n+k-1}}\\ &< \frac{1}{2^{n-1}}.\end{aligned}$$

Since X is complete, there is an x such that

$$x = \lim_{n\to\infty} x_n.$$

Now, fix n. Then $x \in S(x_n, \epsilon_n)$, since $x_{n+k} \in S(x_n, \epsilon_n/2)$ for every $k = 1, 2, \dots$. Hence, by (c), $x \notin F_n$. Thus $x \notin \bigcup_{n=1}^{\infty} F_n = X$, an obvious contradiction.

As an application of theorem 1, we prove the existence of continuous functions on [0, 1] which are nowhere differentiable. For this purpose, we consider the metric space $C_0[0, 1]$ of continuous functions f for which $f(0) = f(1)$, with

$$d(f, g) = \max\,[|f(x) - g(x)| : x \in [0, 1]].$$

Then $C_0[0, 1]$ is a complete metric space. We show that those functions in $C_0[0, 1]$ which are somewhere differentiable form a subset of the first category. Since the space $C_0[0, 1]$ is of the second category, this proves the existence of nowhere differentiable functions.

It will be convenient to extend the functions of $C_0[0, 1]$ to the entire axis by periodicity and to treat the space Γ of such extensions with the metric d defined above.

Let $K \subset \Gamma$ be the set of functions f such that, for some ξ, the set of numbers

$$\left[\frac{f(\xi + h) - f(\xi)}{h} : h > 0\right]$$

is bounded. K contains the set of functions which are somewhere differentiable. We shall show that K is of the first category in Γ. Let

$$K_n = \left[f \in \Gamma : \text{for some } \xi, \left| \frac{f(\xi + h) - f(\xi)}{h} \right| \leq n, \text{ for all } h > 0 \right].$$

Then

$$K = \bigcup_{n=1}^{\infty} K_n.$$

We shall show that for every $n = 1, 2, \ldots$,

(a) K_n is closed,
(b) $\Gamma \sim K_n$ is dense.

Then (a) and (b) imply that each K_n is nowhere dense, so that K is of the first category.

For (a), let f be a limit point of K_n and let $\{f_k\}$ be a sequence in K_n converging to f.

For each $k = 1, 2, \ldots$ let ξ_k be in $[0, 1]$ and such that

$$\left| \frac{f_k(\xi_k + h) - f_k(\xi_k)}{h} \right| \leq n \text{ for all } h > 0.$$

Let ξ be a limit point of $\{\xi_k\}$ and let $\{\xi_{k_i}\}$ converge to ξ.

We may suppose, by considering the proper sequence $\{f_k\}$, that $\{\xi_k\}$ converges to ξ.

For $h > 0$ and $\epsilon > 0$,

$$\begin{aligned} \left| \frac{f(\xi + h) - f(\xi)}{h} \right| & \\ &\leq \left| \frac{f_k(\xi_k + h) - f_k(\xi_k)}{h} \right| \\ &\quad + \frac{1}{h} \{ |f(\xi + h) - f(\xi_k + h)| + |f(\xi_k + h) - f_k(\xi_k + h)| \\ &\quad + |f_k(\xi_k) - f(\xi_k)| + |f(\xi_k) - f(\xi)| \}. \end{aligned}$$

There is an $N = N(\epsilon, h)$ such that $k > N$ implies

$$\sup |f_k(t) - f(t)| < \frac{\epsilon h}{4}.$$

By continuity of f, there is an $M > N$ such that $k > M$ implies

$$|f(\xi + h) - f(\xi_k + h)| < \frac{\epsilon h}{4} \quad \text{and} \quad |f(\xi_k) - f(\xi)| < \frac{\epsilon h}{4},$$

since $\lim_{k \to \infty} \xi_k = \xi$. Hence, if $k > M$, we have

$$\left| \frac{f(\xi + h) - f(\xi)}{h} \right| < \left| \frac{f_k(\xi_k + h) - f_k(\xi_k)}{h} \right| + \epsilon \leq n + \epsilon.$$

It follows that

$$\left|\frac{f(\xi + h) - f(\xi)}{h}\right| \leq n$$

for all $h > 0$. Thus, $f \in K_n$ and K_n is closed.

For (b), suppose $g \in \Gamma$. Let $\epsilon > 0$. We may partition [0, 1] into k equal intervals so that if x, x' are in the same interval of the partitioning then

$$|g(x) - g(x')| < \frac{\epsilon}{2}.$$

Thus, in the ith subinterval $\frac{i-1}{k} \leq x \leq \frac{i}{k}$, if we consider the rectangle formed with

$$g\left(\frac{i-1}{k}\right) - \frac{\epsilon}{2} \leq y \leq g\left(\frac{i-1}{k}\right) + \frac{\epsilon}{2},$$

then the point $\left(\frac{i}{k}, g\left(\frac{i}{k}\right)\right)$ lies on the right-hand side and the point

$$\left(\frac{i-1}{k}, g\left(\frac{i-1}{k}\right)\right)$$

lies on the left-hand side of the rectangle. By joining the two points by a

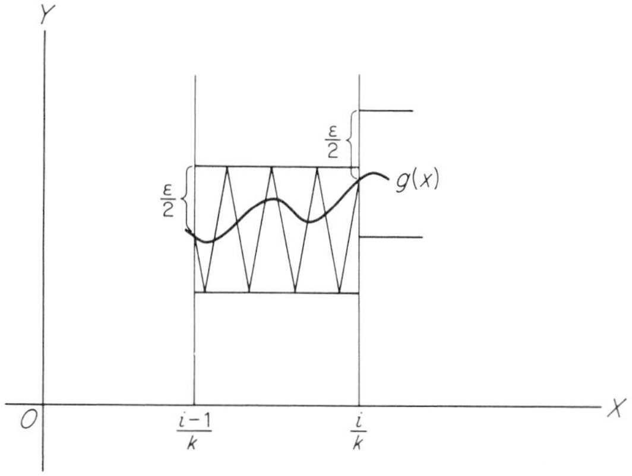

Figure 1

polygonal graph which remains within the rectangle and whose line segments have slopes exceeding n in absolute value, we obtain a continuous function which is within ϵ of g and is in $\Gamma \sim K_n$. This proves (b).

1.11 Compactness, Continuity

A metric space (X, ρ) is said to be **compact** if every infinite subset of X has at least one limit point.

A set $K \subset X$ is then compact if the space (K, ρ) is compact.

PROPOSITION 1. K is compact if and only if every sequence with values in K has a subsequence which converges to a point in K.

The proof is easy after a distinction is made between sequences which assume infinitely many values and those assuming only finitely many values.

Another fact, easy to prove and whose proof we omit, is given by

PROPOSITION 2. Every compact set in a metric space X is a closed, bounded subset of X. If X itself is compact then every closed subset of X is compact.

If X is a metric space and K is a subset, such that its closure $\bar{K}$ is compact, then K is said to be **relatively compact.**

The property of being closed and bounded is characteristic of the compact sets in euclidean n-space. This is the familiar Bolzano-Weierstrass theorem. In a general metric space, however, there may exist closed and bounded sets which are not compact. An example is the subset of l_2 consisting of the elements $e_1 = (1, 0, 0, \ldots)$, $e_2 = (0, 1, 0, 0, \ldots)$, $e_3 = (0, 0, 1, 0, 0, \ldots)$, ... This set is obviously bounded and it is closed since it has no limit points. For the same reason, it is not compact.

PROPOSITION 3. Every compact metric space is complete.

The proof is obvious.

Among the complete metric spaces, the compact ones are distinguished by a property called **total boundedness.**

A metric space X is said to be totally bounded if, for every $\epsilon > 0$, X contains a finite set, called an **ϵ-net**, such that the finite set of open spheres of radius ϵ and centers in the ϵ-net covers X.

THEOREM 1. A metric space X is compact if and only if it is complete and totally bounded.

We shall first show that the theorem follows from a lemma.

LEMMA 1. X is totally bounded if and only if every sequence in X has a Cauchy subsequence.

Proof of theorem 1. Suppose X is complete and totally bounded. By lemma 1, every sequence in X has a Cauchy subsequence, which converges since X is complete. Hence X is compact.

Suppose X is compact. Then X is complete. Moreover, every sequence in X has a convergent, hence a Cauchy, subsequence.

Proof of lemma 1. (Sufficiency) Let $\epsilon > 0$, and let $x_1 \in X$. If $X \sim S(x_1, \epsilon)$ is empty, we have found an ϵ-net. Otherwise, choose $x_2 \in X \sim S(x_1, \epsilon)$. If $X \sim [S(x_1, \epsilon) \cup S(x_2, \epsilon)]$ is empty, we have an ϵ-net. Otherwise, choose $x_3 \in X \sim [S(x_1, \epsilon) \cup S(x_2, \epsilon)]$. Clearly, it is only necessary to show that this process terminates. If it did not terminate, then $x_1, x_2, x_3, \ldots$ would be an infinite sequence each pair of which would have distance at least ϵ apart, and so no subsequence could be Cauchy, contrary to hypothesis.

(Necessity) Let $\{x_n\}$ be a sequence in X whose value set may be assumed infinite. Choose a $\frac{1}{2}$-net in X. Then one of the spheres of radius $\frac{1}{2}$, with center in the net, contains the values of an infinitely many-valued subsequence of the sequence. Proceeding in this way, we obtain a sequence of sequences, each a subsequence of the preceding, call them

$$\{x_n\}, \{x_n^{(1)}\}, \ldots, \{x_n^{(k)}\}, \ldots,$$

so that for every $k = 1, 2, \ldots, \{x_n^{(k)}\}$ is infinite-valued and all the values lie in a sphere of radius $\frac{1}{2^k}$.

Now, $\{x_n^{(n)}\}$ is a subsequence of $\{x_n\}$. Let $\epsilon > 0$. Choose N so that

$$\frac{1}{2^{n-1}} < \epsilon.$$

Then

$$n > N,\ p > 0 \text{ implies } \rho(x_{n+p}^{(n+p)}, x_n^{(n)}) < \frac{1}{2^{n-1}} < \epsilon,$$

so that $\{x_n^{(n)}\}$ is a Cauchy sequence.

PROPOSITION 4. Every totally bounded metric space is separable.

Proof. The union of $1/n$-nets for $n = 1, 2, \ldots$ is a countable dense set.

COROLLARY 1. Every compact metric space is separable.

Compactness is characterized in metric spaces by the property of the familiar Borel covering theorem; namely, we have the

PROPOSITION 5. A metric space X is compact if and only if for every collection $\mathcal{G}$ of open sets which covers X there is a finite subset $G_1, \ldots, G_n$ of $\mathcal{G}$ which covers X.

Proof. Suppose X is compact, and $\mathcal{G}$ is a collection of open sets which covers X. By corollary 1 and the Lindelöf theorem, there is a countable subset $G_1, G_2, \ldots$ of $\mathcal{G}$ which covers X. Suppose

$$X \sim \bigcup_{i=1}^{N} G_i$$

is non-empty for every N and let x_N be a point of this set. By compactness, a subsequence $\{x_{N_k}\}$ converges to some $x \in X$. Now, $x \in G_j$ for some j, and since G_j is open it contains all x_{N_k} with sufficiently large index. But this contradicts the way these points were chosen.

Conversely, suppose X is not compact. Let A be an infinite set in X which has no limit point. Then the distance d_x of x from $A \sim \{x\}$ is positive for every $x \in X$. The spheres $S(x, d_x)$ cover X. If a finite number of them were to cover X, then at least one of them would contain an infinite number of points of A. But these spheres were chosen to contain at most one point of A. Hence, there is an open covering of X which has no finite subcovering.

For mappings between metric spaces, the notions of continuity and uniform continuity have meaning. Let T map (X, ρ) into (Y, σ). T is said to be **continuous at** $x \in X$ if for every sequence $\{x_n\}$ converging to x, $\{Tx_n\}$ converges to Tx in Y. T is said to be **continuous** if it is continuous at every $x \in X$.

A useful reformulation of the latter property is given by the

PROPOSITION 6. T is continuous if and only if for every open $G \subset Y$ the inverse image

$$T^{-1}(G) = [x : x \in X, Tx \in G]$$

is open in X.

We leave the proof for the reader.

T is said to be **uniformly continuous** on X if for every $\epsilon > 0$ there is a $\delta > 0$ such that

$$\rho(x, x') < \delta \text{ implies } \sigma(Tx, Tx') < \epsilon$$

for all $x, x' \in X$.

The proofs of the next two propositions are not difficult and are left as exercises for the reader.

PROPOSITION 7. If X is compact, then every T which is continuous on X is uniformly continuous.

PROPOSITION 8. If T is continuous, then the image of a compact set is compact.

In particular, if (Y, σ) is the real line, then the image of a compact set $A \subset X$ is closed and bounded, hence contains its supremum and infimum. This yields

COROLLARY 1. If f is a real-valued continuous function defined on a metric space (X, ρ), then for every compact $A \subset X$ the values

$$\sup [f(x) : x \in A], \quad \inf [f(x) : x \in A]$$

are finite and are attained by f at some points of A.

Another important property of continuous functions of a real variable, the intermediate-value property, also has a generalization to arbitrary metric spaces.

A set A in a metric space (X, ρ) is said to be **connected** if it cannot be represented as the union of two sets, each of which is disjoint from the closure of the other.

PROPOSITION 9. If T is continuous, then the image of a connected set is connected.

1.12 Equicontinuity, Application to Differential Equations

There are many applications of compactness in analysis, some of which we shall give below. For this reason, it is important to characterize the compact sets in the spaces which appear most often in analysis. We do this for C here and for other spaces later.

Let X be a compact metric space. The metric space of continuous real-valued functions on X with the metric

$$\rho(f, g) = \max\,[|f(x) - g(x)| : x \in X]$$

is a complete metric space, which we denote by $C(X)$. We have already discussed the special case $C[a, b]$.

A collection $\mathfrak{F}$ of functions on a set X is said to be **uniformly bounded** if there is an $M > 0$ such that

$$|f(x)| \leq M \text{ for all } x \in X \text{ and all } f \in \mathfrak{F}.$$

For subsets of $C(X)$, uniform boundedness agrees with boundedness in the metric space, i.e., a set $\mathfrak{F}$ is uniformly bounded if and only if it is contained in a sphere.

A collection $\mathfrak{F}$ of functions defined on a metric space X is called **equicontinuous** if for each $\epsilon > 0$ there is a $\delta > 0$ such that $\rho(x, x') < \delta$ implies $|f(x) - f(x')| < \epsilon$ for all $x, x' \in X$ and all $f \in \mathfrak{F}$.

According to this definition, the functions belonging to the equicontinuous collection are uniformly continuous.

The following theorem is of great historical importance in the development of general topology and of functional analysis, as well as being of great use.

THEOREM 1 (Arzelà-Ascoli). If X is a compact metric space, a subset $K \subset C(X)$ is relatively compact if and only if it is uniformly bounded and equicontinuous.

Proof. Suppose K is relatively compact. It then follows that K is totally bounded. Let $\epsilon > 0$ and let $f_1, f_2, \ldots, f_n$ be an $\epsilon/3$-net in K. Now, let $f \in K$ and $x, x' \in X$. For each $i = 1, 2, \ldots, n$,

$$|f(x) - f(x')| \leq |f(x) - f_i(x)| + |f_i(x) - f_i(x')| + |f_i(x') - f(x')|.$$

Choose j so that

$$\sup\,[|f(x) - f_j(x)| : x \in X] < \frac{\epsilon}{3}.$$

Then

$$|f(x) - f(x')| < |f_j(x) - f_j(x')| + \frac{2\epsilon}{3}.$$

Since X is compact, the functions f_i, $i = 1, \ldots, n$, are uniformly continuous. There is then a $\delta > 0$ so that $\rho(x, x') < \delta$ implies

$$|f_i(x) - f_i(x')| < \frac{\epsilon}{3}, \quad i = 1, \ldots, n.$$

It follows that $\rho(x, x') < \delta$ implies

$$|f(x) - f(x')| < \epsilon \text{ for every } f \in K.$$

Hence, K is equicontinuous.

Suppose, conversely, that K is uniformly bounded and equicontinuous. Suppose M is an integer such that

$$|f(x)| \leq M \text{ for all } x \in X \text{ and } f \in K.$$

Let $\epsilon > 0$. Choose δ so that $\rho(x, x') < \delta$ implies $|f(x) - f(x')| < \epsilon/4$ for all $f \in K$. Since X is compact, it has a δ-net $x_1, \ldots, x_n$. Choose a positive integer m such that $1/m < \epsilon/4$ and divide $[-M, M]$ into $2Mm$ equal parts by the points

$$y_0 = -M < y_1 < y_2 < \ldots < y_k = M,$$

where $k = 2Mm$.

Consider those n-tuples $(y_{i_1}, y_{i_2}, \ldots, y_{i_n})$ of the numbers y_i, $i = 0, 1, \ldots, k$, such that some $f \in K$ has the property

$$|f(x_j) - y_{i_j}| < \frac{\epsilon}{4}, \quad j = 1, 2, \ldots, n$$

and choose one such $f \in K$ for each such n-tuple.

We shall show that the resulting finite subset E of K is an ϵ-net for K. If $f \in K$ then we may choose $y_{i_1}, y_{i_2}, \ldots y_{i_n}$ so that

$$|f(x_j) - y_{i_j}| < \frac{\epsilon}{4}, \quad j = 1, 2, \ldots, n,$$

and so there is a corresponding $e \in E$.

Let $x \in X$ and choose j so that $\rho(x, x_j) < \delta$. Then

$$|f(x) - e(x)| \leq |f(x) - f(x_j)| + |f(x_j) - y_{i_j}| + |y_{i_j} - e(x_j)| + |e(x_j) - e(x)| < \epsilon.$$

Hence

$$\sup_{x \in X} |f(x) - e(x)| < \epsilon.$$

An application of the Arzelà-Ascoli theorem yields the existence of solutions to the differential equation $y' = f(x, y)$ in case f is only assumed to be continuous. To be precise we have the

THEOREM 2. If f is continuous on an open set D, then for every $(x_0, y_0) \in D$ the differential equation $dy/dx = f(x, y)$ has a local solution passing through (x_0, y_0).

Proof. Let R be a closed, non-degenerate rectangle contained in D having center (x_0, y_0) and sides parallel to the axes. Let $M > 0$ be such that

$$|f(x, y)| < M \text{ for all } (x, y) \in R.$$

The two lines through (x_0, y_0) with slopes $\pm M$ may intersect the horizontal sides of R. If so, take I to be the projection on the x-axis of the interval between the points of intersection. Otherwise, I is the projection of the entire horizontal side. In either case, I has the form $[x_0 - a, x_0 + a]$ for some

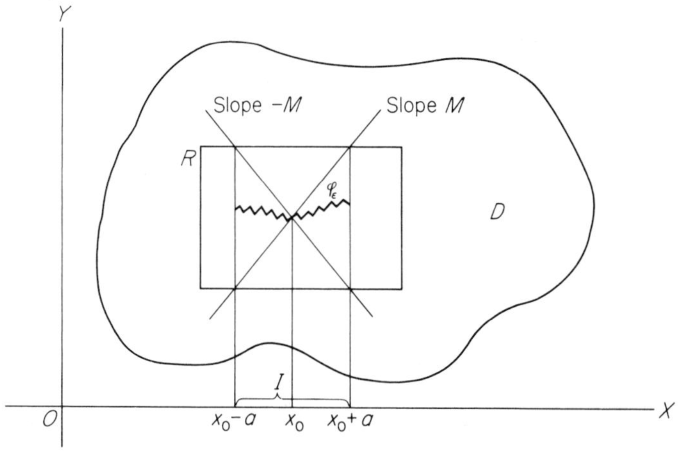

Figure 2

$a > 0$. Our solution φ will be defined on I. It will be obtained by applying the Arzelà-Ascoli theorem in $C(I)$ to a set of "approximate" solutions.

For $\epsilon > 0$ we shall call a function φ_ϵ defined on I an ϵ-approximate solution if its graph is a polygonal arc through (x_0, y_0), lying between the two lines of slope $\pm M$ and the lines $x = x_0 \pm a$ and satisfying

$$|\varphi_\epsilon'(x) - f(x, \varphi_\epsilon(x))| < \epsilon$$

at each $x \in I$ where φ_ϵ' exists (i.e., except at the finite number of points where the vertices occur).

Since f is uniformly continuous on R, there is a $\delta > 0$ such that, for (x, y) and $(\bar{x}, \bar{y})$ in R,

$$|x - \bar{x}| < \delta \text{ and } |y - \bar{y}| < \delta \text{ imply } |f(x, y) - f(\bar{x}, \bar{y})| < \epsilon.$$

It is enough to describe φ_ϵ on the interval $[x_0, x_0 + a]$. Divide this interval by the points

$$x_0 < x_1 < x_2 < \ldots < x_n = x_0 + a$$

so that

$$|x_i - x_{i-1}| < \min\left(\delta, \frac{\delta}{M}\right), \quad i = 1, \ldots, n.$$

Let $\varphi_\epsilon(x_0) = y_0$ and, in $[x_0, x_1]$ let φ_ϵ be linear with slope $f(x_0, y_0)$. Then $\varphi_\epsilon(x_1)$ is defined. In $[x_1, x_2]$, take φ_ϵ to be linear with slope $f(x_1, \varphi_\epsilon(x_1))$. Continuing in a way which should now be clear, φ_ϵ is defined on $[x_0, x_0 + a]$.

Since the slope of φ_ϵ nowhere exceeds M in absolute value, we obtain

$$|\varphi_\epsilon(x) - \varphi_\epsilon(\bar{x})| \le M\,|x - \bar{x}| \text{ for all } x, \bar{x} \in I.$$

In other words, the functions φ_ϵ, where we consider one such function for each $0 < \epsilon < a$, are an equicontinuous collection.

Fix ϵ. If $x \in I$ and $x \ne x_i$, $i = 0, 1, \ldots, n$, then $x_{j-1} < x < x_j$ for some j and

$$|\varphi_\epsilon(x) - \varphi_\epsilon(x_{j-1})| \le M\,|x - x_{j-1}| < M \cdot \frac{\delta}{M} = \delta.$$

But this implies

$$|f(x_{j-1}, \varphi_\epsilon(x_{j-1})) - f(x, \varphi_\epsilon(x))| < \epsilon.$$

But $\varphi_\epsilon'(x)$ exists and equals $f(x_{j-1}, \varphi_\epsilon(x_{j-1}))$. It follows that φ_ϵ is an ϵ-approximate solution,

$$|\varphi_\epsilon'(x) - f(x, \varphi_\epsilon(x))| < \epsilon, \quad x \in I \text{ and } x \ne x_i, \quad i = 1, \ldots, n.$$

We now write

$$(*) \qquad \varphi_\epsilon(x) = y_0 + \int_{x_0}^{x} \{f(u, \varphi_\epsilon(u)) + [\varphi_\epsilon'(u) - f(u, \varphi_\epsilon(u))]\}\,du,$$

where φ_ϵ' can have any values at the vertices. Choose them so that the term in brackets vanishes there.

The collection φ_ϵ, $a > \epsilon > 0$, is uniformly bounded on I (since the graphs all lie in R) and is equicontinuous. Hence if $\{\epsilon_n\}$ is a null sequence, it has a subsequence, which we again call $\{\epsilon_n\}$, such that $\{\varphi_{\epsilon_n}\}$ converges uniformly to a function φ on I.

Since f is uniformly continuous, $\{f(u, \varphi_{\epsilon_n}(u))\}$ converges uniformly to $f(u, \varphi(u))$ on I. Moreover, $\{\varphi'_{\epsilon_n}(u) - f(u, \varphi(u))\}$ converges uniformly to zero on I. It then follows by (*) that

$$\varphi(x) = y_0 + \int_{x_0}^{x} f(u, \varphi(u))\, du.$$

But this implies that φ is differentiable on I and is the required solution.

1.13 Stone-Weierstrass Theorems

Our next topic is the Weierstrass approximation theorem and its generalization by Stone. The Weierstrass theorem asserts that if $[a, b]$ is a closed interval on the real line, then the polynomials are dense in $C[a, b]$. In other words, every continuous function on $[a, b]$ is the limit of a uniformly convergent sequence of polynomials. In order to prove this we need only show that for every continuous f and $\epsilon > 0$ there is a polynomial p such that

$$\max \{|f(x) - p(x)| : x \in [a, b]\} < \epsilon.$$

It follows from the fact that f is uniformly continuous on $[a, b]$ that there is a g, whose graph is a polygonal arc, such that

$$\max \{|f(x) - g(x)| : x \in [a, b]\} < \frac{\epsilon}{3}.$$

It is easy to prove that the Fourier series of g converges uniformly to g on $[a, b]$. We assume that $f(b) = f(a)$ and $g(b) = g(a)$, leaving it to the reader to note that this entails no loss in generality. There accordingly exists a trigonometric polynomial

$$t(x) = a_0 + \sum_{k=1}^{n} (a_k \cos k\alpha x + b_k \sin k\alpha x),$$

where α is the proper positive number, such that

$$\max \{|g(x) - t(x)| : x \in [a, b]\} < \frac{\epsilon}{3}.$$

But the Taylor series of the functions $\cos k\alpha x$, $\sin k\alpha x$, $k = 1, \ldots, n$ converge uniformly to them, so there is a polynomial p such that

$$\max \{|t(x) - p(x)| : x \in [a, b]\} < \frac{\epsilon}{3}.$$

It follows that

$$\max \{|f(x) - p(x)| : x \in [a, b]\} < \epsilon$$

and the theorem is proved.

This remarkable theorem has a large number of proofs. There are two famous proofs where the polynomials are given directly in terms of the function f. These proofs are relegated to the exercises. Another proof shows that the theorem follows almost immediately after it is proved for the function $|x|$. This fact is used also in the generalization given by Stone, which we now discuss.

Let (X, ρ) be a compact metric space, and let $C(X)$ be the space of continuous real functions on X, with the usual metric

$$\rho(f, g) = \max\,[|f(x) - g(x)| : x \in X].$$

We define algebraic operations in $C(X)$ as follows: If $f, g \in C(X)$ and a is real, then, for every $x \in X$,

$$\begin{aligned}(f + g)(x) &= f(x) + g(x),\\ (fg)(x) &= f(x)g(x),\\ (af)(x) &= a\,f(x).\end{aligned}$$

A set $A \subset C(X)$ is called an **algebra** if $f, g \in A$ and a real imply $f + g \in A$, $fg \in A$ and $af \in A$.

For example, the polynomials and the trigonometric polynomials are algebras in $C[a, b]$.

If $E \subset C(X)$, the intersection of all algebras in $C(X)$ containing E, which is itself an algebra containing E, is denoted by $A(E)$ and is called the **algebra generated by *E*.**

For example, the polynomials on $[a, b]$ are generated by the pair $1, x$.

We shall need the fact, easy to prove, that if $A \subset C(X)$ is an algebra then its closure $\bar{A}$ is also an algebra.

We also make use of the Weierstrass theorem for $[a, b] = [-1, 1]$. We shall not need the full force of the theorem, only the fact that the function $|x|$ is the limit of a uniformly convergent sequence of polynomials. In order to prove this directly, we note that for every $\eta > 0$ the Taylor series of

$$(t + \eta^2)^{1/2}$$

converges uniformly to the function on $[0, 1]$. Hence for $\epsilon > 0$ there is a polynomial $p(x)$ such that

$$|(t + \eta^2)^{1/2} - p(t)| < \frac{\epsilon}{2} \text{ for all } t \in [0, 1].$$

For $x \in [-1, 1]$, let $|x|^2 = t$. Then

$$\left|(|x|^2 + \eta^2)^{1/2} - p(|x|^2)\right| < \frac{\epsilon}{2} \text{ for all } x \in [-1, 1].$$

Thus if $\eta = \epsilon/2$,

$$\begin{aligned}\big||x| - p(x^2)\big| &\le \big||x| - (|x|^2 + \eta^2)^{1/2}\big|\\ &\quad + \big|(|x|^2 + \eta^2)^{1/2} - p(x^2)\big| < \epsilon.\end{aligned}$$

The idea of basing the proof of the Weierstrass theorem on this special case is due to Lebesgue.

We now state Stone's theorem.

THEOREM 1. Let A be a closed algebra in $C(X)$, X a compact metric space, such that $1 \in A$ and if $x, y \in X$, $x \neq y$, there is an $f \in A$ for which $f(x) \neq f(y)$. Then $A = C(X)$.

Proof. We first show that $f \in A$ implies $|f| \in A$. Suppose at first that $\max [|f(x)| : x \in X] \leq 1$. Let $\epsilon > 0$ and let $p(t) = a_0 + a_1 t + \ldots + a_n t^n$ be a polynomial such that

$$\big||t| - p(t)\big| < \epsilon \text{ for every } t \in [-1, 1].$$

Then if $p(f) = a_0 + a_1 f + \ldots + a_n f^n$, $p \in A$ and

$$\big||f(x)| - p(f(x))\big| < \epsilon \text{ for every } x \in X.$$

Thus $|f| \in A$, since A is closed in $C(X)$. For any $f \in A$ there is an $a \neq 0$ with $|af(x)| \leq 1$ for every $x \in X$ and since $|af|$ is in A, so is $|f|$.

We next note that if $f, g \in A$ then $\min(f, g)$ and $\max(f, g)$ are in A, where, for example,

$$[\min(f, g)](x) = \min(f(x), g(x)).$$

This follows since

$$\min(f, g) = \tfrac{1}{2}(f + g) - \tfrac{1}{2}|f - g|,$$

and $|f - g| \in A$ if $f, g \in A$.

Let $x, y \in X$ with $x \neq y$. Let $f \in C(X)$. The constant function g with the value $f(x)$ is in A. Let $h \in A$ be such that $h(x) \neq h(y)$. There is no loss in generality in assuming $h(x) = 0$. There is a constant a such that the function f_{xy} given by

$$f_{xy} = g + ah$$

satisfies $f_{xy}(x) = f(x)$ and $f_{xy}(y) = f(y)$ and belongs to A. Let $\epsilon > 0$. For every $y \in X$ there is an open sphere S_y such that $y \in S_y$ and $f_{xy}(z) < f(z) + \epsilon$ for every $z \in S_y$. Since the space X is compact, a finite number of these spheres covers X; call them $S_{y_1}, \ldots, S_{y_n}$. Let

$$f_x = \min(f_{xy_1}, \ldots, f_{xy_n}).$$

Then $f_x \in A$, $f_x(x) = f(x)$ and, for every $z \in X$, $f_x(z) < f(z) + \epsilon$. Now for every $x \in X$, x is in an open sphere T_x such that, for every $z \in T_x$,

$$f_x(z) > f(z) - \epsilon.$$

Since X is compact, a finite number of these spheres $T_{x_1}, \ldots, T_{x_m}$ covers X. Let

$$F = \max(f_{x_1}, \ldots, f_{x_m}).$$

Then $F \in A$ and, for every $z \in X$,

$$|f(z) - F(z)| < \epsilon.$$

This proves the theorem.

1.14 Normal Families

Let G be a connected open set in the plane, considered as the complex $z = x + iy$ plane. For functions defined in G, a natural and fruitful notion of convergence is that of convergence in G, uniformly on each compact subset of G. For example, according to a theorem of Weierstrass, if a sequence of functions holomorphic in G converges in this sense, then the limit function is holomorphic in G.

We assume the functions involved are bounded on compact sets. The above convergence may then be obtained from a metric $d(f, g)$ as follows. Let K_n, $n = 1, 2, \ldots$, be a sequence of compact subsets of G such that

$$K_n \subset K_{n+1}, \quad n = 1, 2, \ldots,$$

and

$$G = \bigcup_{n=1}^{\infty} K_n.$$

Let d_n be the uniform metric on K_n, $d_n(f, g) = \sup [|f(z) - g(z)| : z \in K_n]$, and put

$$d(f, g) = \sum_{n=1}^{\infty} \frac{1}{2^n} \frac{d_n(f, g)}{1 + d_n(f, g)}.$$

It can be shown that d is a metric. It is not hard to prove the

PROPOSITION 1. $\{f_n\}$ converges to f in the metric d if and only if $\{f_n\}$ converges to f uniformly on each compact subset of G.

The theorem of Weierstrass mentioned above gives at once the completeness of the space of all functions holomorphic in G, under the metric d. The space of all functions continuous on G is also complete under d. These facts are easily seen and are left to the reader.

We consider the question of compactness in these spaces. The term **normal family** is used for a collection of functions which is relatively compact for the above notion of convergence. Such families have important and surprising applications in complex variable theory.

The Arzelà-Ascoli theorem yields the

PROPOSITION 2. F is a normal family of continuous functions on G if and only if F is uniformly bounded and equicontinuous on each compact $K \subset G$.

Proof. We only discuss the sufficiency. Let K_n, $n = 1, 2, \ldots$, be compact subsets of G as above. Let $\{f_n\}$ be any sequence in F. A subsequence $\{f_n^{(1)}\}$ of $\{f_n\}$ converges uniformly on K_1. A subsequence $\{f_n^{(2)}\}$ of $\{f_n^{(1)}\}$ converges uniformly on K_2. Continuing in this way and then choosing the diagonal sequence $\{f_k^{(k)}\}$, we obtain a subsequence of $\{f_n\}$ which converges uniformly on each compact $K \subset G$.

It is a noteworthy fact that if F consists of holomorphic functions on G, then the equicontinuity assumption need not be made explicitly.

THEOREM 1 (Montel). A family F of functions holomorphic in a domain G is normal if and only if F is uniformly bounded on each compact subset of G.

Proof. Let $K \subset G$ be compact. We shall show that F is equicontinuous on K.

Let $r > 0$ be so small that the set $K^{(r)}$ of points whose distance from K does not exceed r is a subset of G. $K^{(r)}$ is compact, so that F is uniformly bounded there. Let M be a uniform bound, i.e.,

$$|f(z)| \leq M, \quad f \in F, \quad z \in K^{(r)}.$$

Let $0 < \epsilon < M$, and set

$$\delta = \frac{\epsilon r}{2M}.$$

Then $\delta < r/2$.

Now, if $z, z' \in K$ and $|z - z'| < \delta$, then the circle C, with center z and radius r, is in $K^{(r)}$. Hence, for every $f \in F$,

$$|f(z) - f(z')| = \left| \frac{1}{2\pi i} \int_C f(t) \left[\frac{1}{t - z} - \frac{1}{t - z'} \right] dt \right|$$

$$\leq \frac{1}{2\pi} \int_C \frac{|f(t)|\,|z - z'|}{|t - z|\,|t - z'|} |dt|$$

$$< \frac{M\delta \cdot 2\pi r}{2\pi \cdot r \cdot r/2} = \epsilon.$$

We consider next a variant of proposition 2 in which equicontinuity is replaced by a condition on the convergence of the integral means of the functions. An analogous treatment will be given other spaces in Chapter 3.

Let K be a compact set in G and let $d > 0$ be less than half the distance from K to the boundary of G. Let K' be the set of all points whose distance from K does not exceed d. K' is compact.

If f is defined in G and $z \in K'$, then for $0 < r \leq d$, let

$$M_r(f; z) = \frac{1}{\pi r^2} \int_0^{2\pi} \int_0^r f(z + \rho e^{i\theta}) \rho \, d\rho \, d\theta.$$

Of course, the function f is assumed to be integrable. The function M_r is called the **integral mean** of f.

The function M_r is continuous; if f is continuous, then M_r has partial derivatives, which are continuous, on the interior of K', and are given by the formulas:

$$\frac{\partial M_r(f; z)}{\partial x} = \frac{1}{\pi r} \int_0^{2\pi} f(z + re^{i\theta}) \cos \theta \, d\theta$$

$$\frac{\partial M_r(f; z)}{\partial y} = \frac{1}{\pi r} \int_0^{2\pi} f(z + re^{i\theta}) \sin \theta \, d\theta.$$

We leave the details of the proofs to the reader.

Let f be continuous on G. The identity

$$M_r(f; z) - f(z) = \frac{1}{\pi r^2} \int_0^{2\pi} \int_0^r [f(z + \rho e^{i\theta}) - f(z)]\rho \, d\rho \, d\theta$$

shows that $M_r(f)$ converges to f, as r goes to zero, uniformly on compact subsets of G. Moreover, if F is a normal family, then it is equicontinuous and it follows, by the same identity, that the convergence is uniform for $f \in F$, i.e.,

$$\sup [|M_r(f; z) - f(z)| : z \in K, \quad f \in F]$$

converges to zero as r converges to zero. This proves the necessity in the

THEOREM 2. The family F of continuous functions in G is normal if and only if, for each compact $K \subset G$, F is uniformly bounded on K and the convergence of $M_r(f)$ to f, uniform on K as r goes to zero, is uniform with respect to $f \in F$.

Proof. We need only show the equicontinuity of F on K under the above conditions.

The functions f will be supposed real-valued. The complex case then follows.

Let M denote a uniform bound for $|f(z)|$ for $f \in F$ and $z \in K'$, where K' is defined as above. Let $\epsilon > 0$.

For any $f \in F$ and $z, z' \in K$,

$$\begin{aligned} |f(z) - f(z')| &\leq |f(z) - M_r(f; z)| + |M_r(f; z) - M_r(f; z')| \\ &\quad + |M_r(f; z') - f(z')| < |M_r(f; z) - M_r(f; z')| + \frac{\epsilon}{2}, \end{aligned}$$

for r sufficiently small, independent of f, z and z'.

Choose $\delta > 0$ so that $\dfrac{2M}{r}\delta < \dfrac{\epsilon}{2}$ and if $z, z' \in K$ with $|z - z'| < \delta$, then the segment joining z to z' and the circles of radius r with centers on this segment are contained in K'. By the mean value theorem, there is a $\tilde{z}$ on the segment for which

$$\begin{aligned} M_r(f; z) - M_r(f; z') &= (z - z') \left\{ \frac{\partial M_r(f; \tilde{z})}{\partial x} + i \frac{\partial M_r(f; \tilde{z})}{\partial y} \right\} \\ &= \frac{z - z'}{\pi r} \int_0^{2\pi} f(\tilde{z} + re^{i\theta})(\cos \theta + i \sin \theta) \, d\theta. \end{aligned}$$

Thus, for $|z - z'| < \delta$, $z, z' \in K$ and $f \in F$,

$$|f(z) - f(z')| < \frac{2\delta M}{r} + \frac{\epsilon}{2} < \epsilon.$$

It should be remarked that the uniform boundedness is essential to the above proof of equicontinuity. Simple examples can be given of families for which the convergence of the integral means has the above uniformity but which are not equicontinuous.

1.15 Semi-continuity, Application to Arc Length

It is known that if f is a continuous real function on a closed interval $[a, b]$, then f has an absolute minimum on $[a, b]$, i.e., there is an $x \in [a, b]$ such that $f(y) \geq f(x)$ for every $y \in [a, b]$.

This theorem remains true for continuous functions on compact metric spaces. However, in most applications the function which arises is not continuous. Fortunately, the more general result, given in proposition 1 below, which is of great importance, is valid. We first must define semi-continuity.

If X is a metric space and f is a real function on X then f is said to be **lower semi-continuous** at $x \in X$ if, for every $\epsilon > 0$, there is a $\delta > 0$ such that $\rho(x, y) < \delta$ implies

$$f(y) > f(x) - \epsilon.$$

Upper semi-continuity is defined in a similar fashion, and it is then easy to show that f is continuous at x if and only if it is both upper semi-continuous at x and lower semi-continuous at x.

f is said to be **lower semi-continuous on** X if it is lower semi-continuous at every $x \in X$. We now state the

Proposition 1. If X is a compact metric space and f is a lower semi-continuous real function on X, then f has an absolute minimum on X.

Proof. We first note that the set of values of f on X has a lower bound. Otherwise, there would be an $x_n \in X$, for every $n = 1, 2, \ldots,$ such that $f(x_n) < -n$. Since X is compact, $\{x_n\}$ has a convergent subsequence. Let $\{y_n\}$ be this subsequence and let $y = \lim_n y_n$. Then $\lim_n f(y_n) = -\infty$ and, since $f(y)$ is real, this is easily seen to contradict the lower semi-continuity of f.

Now, let

$$L = \inf [f(x) : x \in X].$$

There is a $\xi_n \in X$, for every $n = 1, 2, \ldots$ such that $f(\xi_n) < L + \dfrac{1}{n}$. Since X is compact, $\{\xi_n\}$ has a convergent subsequence. Let $\{\eta_n\}$ be this subsequence, and let $x = \lim \eta_n$. Then $\lim_n f(\eta_n) = L$. But it follows from the definition of lower semi-continuity that $f(x) \leq \lim_n f(\eta_n) = L$. However, by the definition of L, $f(x) \geq L$. This proves the proposition.

We shall give one simple application. For this purpose it is necessary to define the length of a curve. We shall consider continuous mappings $T = (x, y, z)$ on the unit interval $I = [0, 1]$ into euclidean 3-space E_3, i.e., the functions x, y, z are continuous real functions. Let ρ be the euclidean metric. For each $t \in I$, $T(t) = (x(t), y(t), z(t))$ is a point in E_3. For mappings T_1 and T_2 let

$$d(T_1, T_2) = \max\,[\rho(T_1(t), T_2(t)) : t \in I\,].$$

It is easy to show that if $\mathcal{T}$ is the set of all T then $(\mathcal{T}, d)$ is a complete metric space. Curves will be defined as certain equivalence classes in $\mathcal{T}$. In the first place T_1 will be equivalent to T_2 if there is a homeomorphism h of I onto itself such that T_2 is the composite

$$T_2 = T_1 \circ h.$$

It is not satisfactory to take these equivalence classes as curves since they will not form a metric space (with the natural metric defined from d). However, the closures of these equivalence classes also form equivalence classes, and these will be called curves.

Precisely, if T_1 and T_2 are in $\mathcal{T}$ we shall say that T_1 is **equivalent to** T_2 if, for every $\epsilon > 0$, there is a homeomorphism h of I onto itself such that

$$d(T_2, T_1 \circ h) < \epsilon.$$

It is fairly routine to show that this is an equivalence relation in T. We shall designate the equivalence classes as $C, C_1, C_2, \ldots$, and let $\mathcal{C}$ be the set of all equivalence classes, or **curves**. A member T of an equivalence class C will be called a **representation** of the curve C.

We define a metric δ in $\mathcal{C}$ as

$$\delta(C_1, C_2) = \inf\,[d(T_1, T_2) : T_1 \in C_1, T_2 \in C_2].$$

We leave it to the reader to verify that $(\mathcal{C}, \delta)$ is a metric space.

Having defined curves, we now define the length of a curve. Let C be a curve and let $T \in C$. For every partition

$$\pi = [0 = t_0 < t_1 < \ldots < t_n = 1]$$

of $[0, 1]$, let

$$l(T, \pi) = \sum_{i=1}^{n} \rho(T(t_i), T(t_{i-1}))$$

and let

$$L(T) = \sup l(T, \pi),$$

where the supremum is taken for all partitions π, and may assume the value $+\infty$.

It is not hard to show that if T_1 is equivalent to T_2 then $L(T_1) = L(T_2)$. We may thus define the **length $L(C)$ of the curve C** to be the common value of $L(T)$ for all $T \in C$.

We prove

PROPOSITION 2. $L(C)$ is a lower semi-continuous non-negative (extended) real-valued function on the metric space $\mathcal{C}$.

Proof. Let $C \in \mathcal{C}$ and suppose $L(C) < \infty$. Let $T \in C$. Fix $\epsilon > 0$. There is a partition

$$\pi = [0 = t_0 < t_1 < \ldots < t_n = 1]$$

of $[0, 1]$ such that

$$l(T, \pi) > L(C) - \frac{\epsilon}{2}.$$

But, there is a $\delta > 0$ such that $d(T', T) < \delta$ implies

$$l(T', \pi) > l(T, \pi) - \frac{\epsilon}{2}$$

so that

$$L(C') = L(T') \geq l(T', \pi) > L(C) - \epsilon.$$

Now, let C' be such that $\delta(C', C) < \delta$. There is then a $T' \in C'$ such that $d(T', T) < \delta$. We have thus shown that $\delta(C', C) < \delta$ implies

$$L(C') > L(C) - \epsilon.$$

For the case $L(C) = +\infty$, lower semi-continuity at C means that for every $M > 0$ there is a $\delta > 0$ such that $\delta(C, C') < \delta$ implies $L(C') > M$. The proof for this case is similar to the finite case and is left to the reader.

Now let A be the closed cube of points (x, y, z) where $|x| \leq a$, $|y| \leq a$, $|z| \leq a$, $a > 0$. We let $\mathcal{C}_A$ be the set of curves in A, i.e., for every $C \in \mathcal{C}_A$ and $T \in C$, $T(t) \in A$ for every $t \in I$.

Next, let $M > 0$ and let $\mathcal{C}_{AM}$ be the space of curves in $\mathcal{C}_A$ of length not greater than M. We now prove

PROPOSITION 3. The metric space $\mathcal{C}_{AM}$ is compact.

Proof. In order to prove this result, it is convenient to consider a particular representation $R \in C$ for every $C \in \mathcal{C}_{AM}$. Let $T \in C$. For every $t \in I$ we consider the mapping T restricted to the interval $[0, t]$. Call this mapping T_t. Consider $L(T_t)$. This is a monotonically non-decreasing function on $[0, 1]$ and is easily seen to be continuous. For every $t \in [0, 1]$, there is a unique $u \in [0, 1]$ such that $L(T_t) = uL(T)$. Define R so that

$$R(u) = T(t).$$

Then R is defined everywhere on [0, 1], and $L(R_u) = uL(T)$. The case where T is constant must be treated separately; here, $R = T$.

It is not hard to show that $R \in C$ and we leave the proof to the reader. We shall call R the **arc length representation** of C. Now for every $C \in \mathcal{C}_{AM}$, with $R \in C$

$$\rho(R(t_1), R(t_2)) \leq M\,|t_1 - t_2|.$$

Thus the collection of arc length representations of curves in $\mathcal{C}_{AM}$ is equicontinuous. Since it is uniformly bounded, every sequence has a Cauchy subsequence. Since

$$\delta(C, C') \leq d(R, R'),$$

the same holds for $\mathcal{C}_{AM}$.

It remains only to show that $\mathcal{C}_{AM}$ is complete. But this is an obvious consequence of the lower semi-continuity of L.

Since L is a lower semi-continuous functional on the compact space C_{AM}, it has a minimum. Since L is 0 for the curves consisting of one point, this result is trivial. However, we may consider closed subspaces of $\mathcal{C}_{AM}$. For example, consider two points (x_1, y_1, z_1) and (x_2, y_2, z_2) and consider those curves for which these are the end points. This is a closed subspace of $\mathcal{C}_{AM}$ and so it is compact. Moreover, L is still lower semi-continuous. This yields the result that among the curves in A joining two points, there is one of shortest length. This result is still not very exciting. However, let S be an arbitrary closed subset of A, and let (x_1, y_1, z_1) and (x_2, y_2, z_2) be any points in S. Suppose there is a curve of length not greater than M, with these points as end points, which lies in S. It is easy to see that the set of all curves lying in S, with these points as end points, and of length not greater than M, is a non-empty closed subspace of $\mathcal{C}_{AM}$. It then follows that we have

THEOREM 1. Let S be a closed bounded set in euclidean 3-space, let (x_1, y_1, z_1) and (x_2, y_2, z_2) be in S, and suppose there is a curve in S, with these end points, which has finite length. Then there is a curve in S, among those with these end points, for which the length is a minimum.

For example, if S is a torus, every pair of points in S is joined by an arc in S of minimum length.

1.16 Space of Compact, Convex Sets

To conclude this chapter, we return to some considerations in the space (Γ, d) of all non-empty, compact, convex subsets of the plane introduced in example (xi), Sec. 1.3.

We shall need the following lemma, whose proof is left to the reader.

LEMMA 1. If $\{A_n\}$ is a decreasing sequence of sets in Γ, then $A = \bigcap_{n=1}^{\infty} A_n$ is in Γ and $\{A_n\}$ converges to A in the metric of (Γ, d).

We now prove the

PROPOSITION 1. (Γ, d) is complete.

Proof. Let $\{A_n\}$ be a Cauchy sequence in Γ. For $\epsilon > 0$, there is an N such that

$$d(A_n, A_{n+p}) < \epsilon,\ n \geq N, \quad p = 1, 2, 3, \ldots .$$

For each $n = 1, 2, 3, \ldots$, let H_n be the smallest closed convex set containing the set

$$A_n \cup A_{n+1} \cup A_{n+2} \cup \ldots ,$$

i.e., the intersection of all closed convex sets containing this set. Then, for every n, $H_n \supset H_{n+1}$, and it follows that

$$H = \bigcap_{n=1}^{\infty} H_n$$

is a non-empty, closed, convex set.

Now, for $\epsilon > 0$, choose N as above. We obtain, for $n \geq N$,

$$(A_n)_\epsilon \supset A_{n+p}, \quad p = 1, 2, 3, \ldots$$

so that

$$(A_n)_\epsilon \supset A_{n+1} \cup A_{n+2} \cup \ldots ,$$

and

$$(A_n)_\epsilon \supset H_{n+1} \supset H.$$

In particular, this shows that $H \in \Gamma$, since it is bounded.

By lemma 1, there is an M such that $n \geq M$ implies $H_n \subset H_\epsilon$, so that, since $A_n \subset H_n$, we have $A_n \subset H_\epsilon$. It follows that, for $n \geq \max(N, M)$,

$$H_\epsilon \subset A_n \quad \text{and} \quad (A_n)_\epsilon \subset H,$$

so that

$$d(A_n, H) < \epsilon$$

and the proof is complete.

The space (Γ, d) is introduced as a tool in the general theory of convex sets (all of our considerations are valid for sets in n-space). The main fact is the following compactness criterion.

THEOREM 1. Let Q be a closed square. The subset Γ_Q of Γ, of those sets belonging to Γ which are contained in Q, is a compact metric space.

Proof. In view of proposition 1, we need only show that Γ_Q is totally bounded, i.e., if $A_n \in \Gamma_Q$, $n = 1, 2, \ldots$, then $\{A_n\}$ has a Cauchy subsequence.

Let s denote the length of the sides of Q, and for each $i = 1, 2, 3, \ldots$, consider the subdivision of Q into 4^i equal squares of side length $s/2^i$. For each n and i, we associate with A_n the set of those squares of the ith subdivision which meet A_n. There will be a subsequence $\{A_{1n}\}$ of $\{A_n\}$ for each of whose terms the associated set of squares in the first subdivision is always the same set σ_1. There will then be a subsequence $\{A_{2n}\}$ of $\{A_{1n}\}$ for each of whose terms the associated set of squares in the second subdivision is always the same set σ_2. We then obtain

$$\{A_{1n}\}, \{A_{2n}\}, \ldots, \{A_{in}\}, \ldots,$$

each sequence being a subsequence of the preceding and such that for each term of $\{A_{in}), i = 1, 2, \ldots$, the associated set of squares in the ith subdivision is always the same set σ_i.

The diagonal sequence $\{A_{nn}\}$ is a subsequence of $\{A_n\}$. We show that it is a Cauchy sequence. We first note that if S_i is the set consisting of the union of squares in σ_i, then

$$d(S_i, A_{in}) \leq \frac{s}{2^i}\sqrt{2}, \quad n = 1, 2, 3, \ldots.$$

But the sets of the diagonal sequence with index not less than i are all among the A_{in}. Hence,

$$d(S_i, A_{kk}) \leq \frac{s}{2^i}\sqrt{2}, \quad k \geq i.$$

It follows that $m, n \geq i$ implies

$$d(A_{nn}, A_{mm}) \leq d(S_i, A_{nn}) + d(S_i, A_{mm}) \leq \frac{s}{2^{i-1}}\sqrt{2},$$

and $\{A_{nn}\}$ is a Cauchy sequence.

We consider the area $a(A)$ and the perimeter $c(A)$ of $A \in \Gamma$. It is easily seen that the first of these functionals is continuous on Γ, and the second is continuous at any $A \in \Gamma$ for which $a(A) > 0$.

Let $\Gamma_{QL\alpha}$ be the subset of sets A in Γ_Q for which $c(A) = L$ and $a(A) \geq \alpha > 0$. (We suppose L, α chosen so that this set is non-empty.) Then $\Gamma_{QL\alpha}$ is closed, and so it is compact.

It follows that among all convex sets of a given perimeter, there is one which encloses the largest area. By means of another consideration, which we do not discuss here, it can be shown that this convex set must be enclosed by a circle.

EXERCISES

1.1 Show that examples (i) and (ii) satisfy the conditions of a metric space.

1.2 Let X be the set of continuous functions on (0, 1) and for every $x, y \in X$, let

$$E(x, y) = [t \in (0, 1) : x(t) \neq y(t)].$$

$E(x, y)$ is the union of disjoint open intervals. Define $\rho(x, y)$ to be the sum of the lengths of these intervals. Show that (X, ρ) is a metric space.

1.3 The real line with

$$\rho(x, y) = \frac{|x - y|}{1 + |x - y|}$$

is a metric space.

1.4 For what values of p is $|x - y|^p$ a metric on the real line?

2.1 Give necessary and sufficient conditions for equality to hold in Hölder's inequality.

2.2 Is n-space a metric space if ρ is taken to be

$$\rho(x, y) = \left[\sum_{i=1}^{n} |x_i - y_i|^p\right]^{1/p}$$

with $0 < p < 1$?

3.1 Prove that

$$\lim_{p\to\infty} \rho_p(x, y) = \max\,[|x_i - y_i| : 1 \leq i \leq n].$$

3.2 Prove that if $x \in l_p$ and $y \in l_p$, then the series for $d_p(x, y)$ converges, without using Minkowki's inequality.

3.3 Let X consist of all sequences of complex numbers. Show that

$$\rho(x, y) = \sum_{i=1}^{\infty} \frac{1}{2^i} \frac{|x_i - y_i|}{1 + |x_i - y_i|}$$

is a metric in X.

3.4 Show that if $p > p' \geq 1$, then $l_p \supset l_{p'}$ and the inclusion is proper.

3.5 Show that for $p > 1$, the union of all the $l_{p'}$ spaces, $p > p' > 1$, is a proper subspace of l_p.

3.6 Give an example of a sequence which converges to 0 but is not in any l_p space, $1 \leq p < \infty$.

3.7 Prove theorem 2.

4.1 Show that $C[a, b]$ and $M[a, b]$ are metric spaces.

4.2 Define the metric $\tilde{\rho}$ on $\widetilde{BV}$ and show that it is indeed a metric.

4.3 Let X be the set of all continuous functions on $(-\infty, \infty)$ which vanish outside of some interval (the interval depending on the particular function). Show that X is a metric space under

$$\rho(x, y) = \max\,[|x(t) - y(t)| : -\infty < t < \infty].$$

4.4 Extending the definition of S_δ to arbitrary sets S in the plane, show that $\bigcap\,[S_\delta : \delta > 0] = \bar{S}$, where $\bar{S}$ is the closure of S. Defining $d(S, T)$ for arbitrary sets S and T as in the text, show that $d(S, T) = 0$ if and only if $\bar{S} = \bar{T}$.

4.5 For the class of all bounded sets in the plane, an equivalence relation is given by S equivalent to T if $\bar{S} = \bar{T}$. Show that $d(S, T)$ is a metric on these equivalence classes of sets.

5.1 Prove proposition 1.

5.2 Prove that the collection $\mathscr{G}$ of open sets satisfies the properties 1, 2 and 3.

5.3 Prove that the closure of a set A is the intersection of all closed sets containing A.

5.4 Is the space of exercise 1.2 separable?

5.5 In the space l_2, let

$$A = \left[x = (x_1, x_2, \ldots) : |x_n| \leq \frac{1}{n}, \quad n = 1, 2, \ldots\right].$$

Prove that A is closed.

6.1 Show that $C[0, 1]$ is separable by exhibiting a countable set of functions, which is dense in $C[0, 1]$, each of whose graphs consists of a finite number of line segments.

6.2 Is the space of all bounded continuous functions on $(-\infty, \infty)$ with $\rho(x, y) = \sup\,[|x(t) - y(t)| : -\infty < t < \infty]$ separable?

6.3 Prove proposition 1.

6.4 Prove proposition 2.

7.1 Show that $\{x_n\}$ is a Cauchy sequence if and only if $\rho(x_{n+k}, x_n)$ converges to zero uniformly in k.

7.2 Prove that the sequence

$$.1, .101, .101001, .1010010001, \ldots$$

is a Cauchy sequence of rationals which does not converge in the space of rationals.

7.3 Exhibit a non-convergent Cauchy sequence in the space of polynomials on $[0, 1]$ with the uniform metric.

7.4 Exhibit a non-convergent Cauchy sequence in the space of exercise 1.2.

7.5 Prove proposition 1.

7.6 In example (ii), give the details of the proof that the limit function x must be $x(t) = 0$, $t \in [a, c)$ and $x(t) = 1$, $t \in (c, b]$.

7.7 Show that a necessary and sufficient condition that

$$\int_0^1 |x(t)|\, dt = 0$$

is that x be bounded and that, for every $\epsilon > 0$, the set

$$[t \in [0, 1] : |x(t)| < \epsilon]$$

contains a finite set of intervals the sum of whose lengths exceeds $1 - \epsilon$.

7.8 Show that the sequence $\{x_n\}$ in example (iii) is a Cauchy sequence but is not convergent.

7.9 For the set $S = \bigcap_{n=1}^{\infty} S_n$ of example (iv), show that for every partition of

[0, 1], the sum of the lengths of the intervals of the partition, which contain points of S, exceeds $\frac{1}{2}$.

7.10 Show that the bounded functions on an arbitrary set, with the uniform metric, form a complete metric space.

7.11 Show that the set of continuous functions on $(-\infty, \infty)$ with the metric

$$\rho(x, y) = \sum_{n=1}^{\infty} \frac{1}{2^n} \frac{\max [|x(t) - y(t)| : |t| \leq n]}{1 + \max [|x(t) - y(t)| : |t| \leq n]}$$

is a complete metric space.

8.1 Show that theorem 1 fails to hold if T has only the property

$$\rho(Tx, Ty) < \rho(x, y).$$

8.2 Prove that if T is a contraction in a complete metric space X and $x \in X$, then

$$T \lim_n T^n x = \lim_n T^{n+1} x.$$

8.3 Show that a function φ, defined on an interval I containing x_0, is such that $\varphi(x_0) = y_0$ and $\varphi'(x) = f(x, \varphi(x))$, for all $x \in I$, where φ is differentiable on I and f is continuous, if and only if

$$\varphi(x) = y_0 + \int_{x_0}^{x} f(t, \varphi(t))\, dt$$

for every $x \in I$.

8.4 Show that if D is an open connected set, and a differential equation

$$\frac{dy}{dx} = f(x, y)$$

is such that its solutions form a simple covering of D, then f is the limit of a sequence of continuous functions.

8.5 Show that the system

$$\begin{aligned} x &= \tfrac{1}{3}x - \tfrac{1}{4}y + \tfrac{1}{4}z - 1 \\ y &= -\tfrac{1}{2}x + \tfrac{1}{5}y + \tfrac{1}{4}z + 2 \\ z &= \tfrac{1}{5}x - \tfrac{1}{3}y + \tfrac{1}{4}z - 2 \end{aligned}$$

has a unique solution by using the contraction mapping theorem.

9.1 Give the details of the proof that the space $(\tilde{X}, \tilde{\rho})$, associated with (X, ρ), is a complete metric space.

9.2 Show that the extension φ of ST^{-1} is indeed an isomorphism of the two completions $(\tilde{X}, \tilde{\rho})$ and $(\tilde{Y}, \tilde{\sigma})$.

10.1 Prove proposition 1.

10.2 Let X be a separable metric space and let $S \subset X$. Call $x \in X$ a point of the first category relative to S if some nieghborhood of x meets S in a set of the first category in X. Show that the set composed of those points of S, which are points of the first category relative to S, is a set of the first category.

10.3 A point is of the strong second category relative to S if it has a neighborhood none of whose points are of the first category relative to S. Show that the subset of S, of points that are not of the strong second category relative to S, is a set of the first category.

10.4 Prove the assertions in exercises 10.2 and 10.3 without the separability assumption.

10.5 Let X be the space of functions on $[0, 1]$ which are differentiable and have a continuous first derivative (one-sided at the end points) with the metric

$$\rho(x, y) = \max [|x(t) - y(t)| : t \in [0, 1]] + \max [|x'(t) - y'(t)| : t \in [0, 1]].$$

Show that the set of all polynomials is of the first category in X.

10.6 In the space $BV[0, 1]$ with

$$\rho(x, y) = |x(0) - y(0)| + V(x - y)$$

show that the continuous functions of bounded variation form a set of the first category.

11.1 Let us say that metric spaces (X, ρ) and (Y, σ) are equivalent if there is a one-one mapping between them which preserves open sets. Show that a space equivalent to a complete space need not be complete. Show that a space equivalent to a compact space is necessarily compact.

11.2 Prove proposition 1.

11.3 Prove proposition 2.

11.4 Show that the subset of l_2 of points $\{x_n\}$ such that

$$|x_n| \leq \frac{1}{n}, \quad n = 1, 2, \ldots$$

is compact.

11.5 Show that the unit sphere in $C[0, 1]$ of points

$$[x : \max |x(t)| \leq 1, t \in [0, 1]]$$

is not compact.

11.6 Show that X is compact if and only if for any collection $\mathfrak{F}$ of closed sets with the property that $\bigcap_{i=1}^{n} F_i \neq 0$ for any finite collection in $\mathfrak{F}$, it follows that $\bigcap [F : F \in \mathfrak{F}] \neq 0$.

11.7 Prove proposition 6.

11.8 Prove proposition 7.

11.9 Prove proposition 9.

11.10 Give necessary and sufficient conditions for a subset of l_p, $p > 1$, to be compact.

11.11 If X is a compact metric space, show that $C(X)$ is separable.

12.1 Show that a uniformly bounded sequence of functions has a subsequence which converges point-wise on a prescribed countable set.

12.2 By using the result of exercise 12.1, give an alternate proof of the sufficiency part of theorem 1.

12.3 Give an example of a continuous function f on an open set D and an $(x_0, y_0) \in D$ such that the differential equation

$$\frac{dy}{dx} = f(x, y)$$

has several distinct local solutions through (x_0, y_0).

12.4 Prove theorem 2 by considering auxiliary differential equations

$$\frac{dy}{dx} = p_n(x, y), \quad n = 1, 2, \ldots,$$

where the p_n are polynomials which converge uniformly to f on an appropriate rectangle.

13.1 If P_n, $n = 1, 2, \ldots$, is the polynomial $P_n(x) = c_n(1 - x^2)^n$, where c_n is chosen so that

$$\int_{-1}^{1} P_n(x)\, dx = 1,$$

show that for any continuous f such that $f(x) = 0$ for $x \leq 0$ and for $x \geq 1$, the polynomials

$$L_n(x) = \int_{-1}^{1} P_n(x + t) f(t)\, dt$$

converge uniformly to f on $[0, 1]$.

13.2 Prove an analogous result in the two dimensional case.

13.3 The polynomials

$$B_n(f, x) = \sum_{k=0}^{n} \binom{n}{k} f\left(\frac{n}{k}\right) x^k (1 - x)^{n-k},$$

where $\binom{n}{k} = \dfrac{n!}{k!(n-k)!}$, are called the Bernstein polynomials of f. If $0 \leq x \leq 1$, these polynomials have a probabilistic interpretation. Discuss.

13.4 Show that if f is continuous on $[0, 1]$ then $B_n(f, x)$ converges uniformly to f on $[0, 1]$.

13.5 Prove that the closure $\bar{A}$ of an algebra $A \subset C(X)$ is an algebra.

13.6 Show that the Weierstrass theorem holds for $|x|$ on $[-1, 1]$ by showing that the Fourier series of $|x|$ converges uniformly to $|x|$ on $[-1, 1]$.

13.7 Show that the Stone theorem is false when $C(X)$ is the space of complex-valued continuous functions on X. (Let X be the set $[z : |z| \leq 1]$ in the complex plane and let A be the set of polynomials in z.)

13.8 Show that the additional hypothesis $f \in A$ implies $\bar{f} \in A$ corrects the above deficiency.

13.9 Show that the closed algebra generated by the pair $1, x^2$ is $C[0, 1]$ but is not $C[-1, 1]$.

13.10 For each natural number k, for which closed real intervals I is the closed algebra generated by 1, x^k the space $C(I)$?

13.11 Show that $\int_a^b f(x) \cdot x^n \, dx = 0$, $n = 1, 2, \ldots$, implies $f = 0$.

14.1 Prove proposition 1.

14.2 Prove that the space of all functions continuous on G is complete under the metric d.

15.1 Show that f is lower semi-continuous at x if and only if $\lim_n x_n = x$ implies $\underline{\lim}\, f(x_n) \geq f(x)$.

15.2 Show that if we define T_1 to be equivalent to T_2 if, for every $\epsilon > 0$, there is a homeomorphism h of I onto itself such that

$$d(T_2, T_1 \circ h) < \epsilon,$$

then this is an equivalence relation.

15.3 Verify that $(\mathcal{C}, \delta)$ is a metric space.

15.4 Prove the lower semi-continuity of L at C when $L(C) = \infty$.

15.5 For any C, with $L(C) < \infty$, show that the arc length representation R belongs to C.

16.1 Prove lemma 1.

16.2 Extend theorem 1 to n-space.

16.3 Show that area is a continuous function on Γ.

16.4 Show that perimeter is continuous at those $A \in \Gamma$ for which $a(A) > 0$.

CHAPTER 2

BANACH SPACES

2.1 Vector Space

Many of the metric spaces which arise in analysis are endowed with a vector space structure, and the metrics are derived from norms related to this structure.

The first few sections of this chapter are concerned with vector spaces. A **vector space X over a field F** consists of the set X, a mapping $(x, y) \to x + y$ of X^2 into X, and a mapping $(a, x) \to ax$ of $F \times X$ into X, such that

(a) X is an abelian group with group operation $(x, y) \to x + y$,
(b) the associative law $a(bx) = (ab)x$ holds,
(c) the distributive laws $(a + b)x = ax + bx$, $a(x + y) = ax + ay$ hold,
(d) $1x = x$.

It is easy to show that $0 \cdot x = 0$, where 0 is the scalar zero on the left, and is the group identity on the right. It is also easy to show that $(-1)x = -x$, where $-x$ is the group inverse of x.

The most important cases, by far, are those for which the field F is either R, the real number field, or C, the complex number field. We shall consider these cases only. Most of our general discussion will involve R, although the complex case is often more important, and so will be considered at the appropriate times.

We list some examples of vector spaces over R.

(i) R itself is a vector space over R. In this case, $X = R$ is the real additive group and $F = R$ is the real field. The operation ax is multiplication for the real field.

(ii) The set R^n of n-tuples of real numbers $x = (x_1, x_2, \ldots, x_n)$, with the standard operations $(x_1, x_2, \ldots, x_n) + (y_1, y_2, \ldots, y_n) = (x_1 + y_1, x_2 + y_2, \ldots, x_n + y_n)$ and $a(x_1, x_2, \ldots, x_n) = (ax_1, ax_2, \ldots, ax_n)$, is a vector space.

(iii) More generally, for any set A, the set R^A of all $[x_\alpha]$, $\alpha \in A$, where $[x_\alpha] + [y_\alpha] = [x_\alpha + y_\alpha]$ and $a[x_\alpha] = [ax_\alpha]$, is a vector space. This is the vector space of real functions on A. The notation $x(\alpha)$ may be used instead of $[x_\alpha]$. This is also an example of the direct product of vector spaces, which we now define.

Let X_α, $\alpha \in A$, be a set of vector spaces. The **direct product**

$$X = \Pi[X_\alpha : \alpha \in A]$$

has as elements the functions $[x_\alpha]$, where $x_\alpha \in X_\alpha$ for each $\alpha \in A$, and addition and scalar multiplication are given by $[x_\alpha] + [y_\alpha] = [x_\alpha + y_\alpha]$ and $a[x_\alpha] = [ax_\alpha]$. It is easy to verify that X is a vector space. Example (ii) above is the special case where A is a finite set and $X_\alpha = R$ for every $\alpha \in A$, and example (iii) is the case where A is an arbitrary set and $X_\alpha = R$ for every $\alpha \in A$.

Now, let X_α, $\alpha \in A$, again be a set of vector spaces whose identity elements are all designated as 0. Let

$$\tilde{X} = \Sigma[X_\alpha : \alpha \in A]$$

consist of those $[x_\alpha] \in \Pi[X_\alpha : \alpha \in A]$ for which $x_\alpha = 0$ for all but a finite number of the $\alpha \in A$. It is easily verified that $\Sigma[X_\alpha : \alpha \in A]$ is a vector subspace of $\Pi[X_\alpha : \alpha \in A]$, and that the two spaces are identical if and only if A is finite. $\tilde{X}$ is called the **direct sum** of the vector spaces X_α, $\alpha \in A$.

In each of the above examples, the values of the coordinates may be complex. In that case the scalars may be taken to be real as well as complex. In general, for any complex vector space, we obtain the **associated real space** by restricting the scalars to the real subfield of the complex field.

It is not always immediately obvious that a certain system is a vector space. For example, let X consist of all real sequences $(x_1, x_2, \ldots, x_n, \ldots)$ for which the corresponding series $\sum_{n=1}^{\infty} x_n^2$ converges. In order to know that X is a vector space, with the usual operations, we must show that $\sum_{n=1}^{\infty} x_n^2 < \infty$ and $\sum_{n=1}^{\infty} y_n^2 < \infty$ implies $\sum_{n=1}^{\infty} (x_n + y_n)^2 < \infty$. We have seen in Chapter 1 that this is true but not immediately obvious.

Indeed, if we allow functions as integrable if an improper integral exists, then the functions on [0, 1] for which

$$\int_0^1 (e^{|f(x)|} - 1)\, dx < \infty$$

may be shown to not form a vector space.

Examples of important vector spaces of functions are

(α) the continuous functions on a metric space,
(β) the differentiable functions of a real variable,
(γ) the analytic functions,
(δ) the functions which are integrable in some sense.

For any two vector spaces X and Y, the set of linear transformations of

X into Y is also a vector space, which is designated by $L(X, Y)$. A **linear transformation** f is a mapping

$$f : X \rightarrow Y$$

on X into Y such that $f(ax_1 + bx_2) = af(x_1) + bf(x_2)$ for all $x_1, x_2 \in X$ and $a, b \in R$. It is evident that $L(X, Y)$ is a vector space if the operations are defined point-wise. Of special interest is the case where $Y = R$, i.e., Y is the vector space of real numbers. Then the elements of $L(X, R)$ are called **linear functionals** (also linear forms) on X. We call $L(X, R)$ the **algebraic dual** of X, and designate it by X^*. The qualifying adjective "algebraic" is introduced in order to distinguish this space from the various dual spaces of continuous linear functionals on X associated with the possible topologies in X.

2.2 Subspace

Let X be a vector space. A subset $Y \subset X$ is called a vector subspace, or simply a **subspace** of X if it is itself a vector space with the same operations as for X. A necessary and sufficient condition that a subset $Y \subset X$ should be a vector subspace of X is that for every $x_1, x_2 \in X$ and $a, b \in R$ the element $ax_1 + bx_2 \in Y$. The condition is evidently necessary. For the sufficiency, we need only observe that if Y is closed under the above operations, then, since $0x = 0$ and $(-1)x = -x$, it follows that $0 \in Y$ and the group inverse of every element in Y is also in Y. Two special subspaces of a vector space X are X itself and the null subspace $\{0\}$ of X whose only member is 0. These are called **improper** subspaces of X. All other subspaces of X are called **proper.**

We now consider operations on subspaces of a vector space X which yield other subspaces of X.

If Y_α, $\alpha \in A$, is a set of subspaces of X, then the set $Y = \bigcap[Y_\alpha : \alpha \in A]$ is also a subspace of X. It is called the **intersection** of the subspaces Y_α, $\alpha \in A$, and is evidently the largest vector space contained in all of them.

The union of a set of subspaces of X need not be a subspace of X. Indeed, if Y and Z are subspaces of X, then the set $Y \cup Z$ is a subspace of X if and only if $Y \subset Z$ or $Z \subset Y$. For suppose $y \in Y$, $y \notin Z$ and $z \in Z$, $z \notin Y$. Then $y + z \notin Y \cup Z$. For, if $u = y + z \in Y$, then $z = u - y \in Y$, contradicting the assumption that $z \notin Y$. Similarly, $u \in Z$ implies $y \in Z$. It follows that $Y \cup Z$ is not a vector space.

There is, however, an operation on vector spaces which does yield a vector space and is, in a sense, the dual of the intersection operation. Let Y_α, $\alpha \in A$, be a set of subspaces of X. Let Y be the intersection of all the subspaces of X which contain all the Y_α, $\alpha \in A$. X itself is a subspace of X which contains all the Y_α, so that Y, as the intersection of a non-empty set of subspaces of X, is also a subspace of X. It is the smallest subspace of X which contains all the Y_α, $\alpha \in A$.

We shall use the notation $\vee[Y_\alpha : \alpha \in A]$ for this space. It is the least upper bound, or supremum, of the spaces Y_α, $\alpha \in A$, in the partial ordering of all subspaces of X, ordered by means of set inclusion. We sometimes use the notation $\wedge[Y_\alpha : \alpha \in A]$ instead of $\bigcap[Y_\alpha : \alpha \in A]$ for the intersection operation, in order to emphasize the fact that it is the greatest lower bound, or infimum, of the spaces Y_α, $\alpha \in A$. It follows that, with these operations, the subspaces of a vector space X form a complete lattice, i.e., every set of subspaces of X has a supremum and an infimum.

Let S be any subset of X. By the subspace $(S) \subset X$ **generated by** S we mean the smallest subspace of X which contains S. Then (S) is the intersection of all subspaces of X which contain S. We note that (S) is the set L of all linear combinations $\sum_{i=1}^{n} a_i x_i$, of finite sets in S. It is obvious that L is a vector space containing S. Moreover, every subspace containing S contains all elements of L.

Two subspaces Y and Z of X are called **disjoint** if $Y \cap Z = \{0\}$, the subspace of X which consists of the one element 0. Two disjoint subspaces Y and Z of X are called **complementary** if $Y \vee Z = X$. We shall show that every subspace of X has complementary subspaces which, however, are not unique. In this, we need Zorn's lemma, which we now state without proof.

A **partially ordered set** is a set S together with a relation $x \leq y$, between pairs of elements of S, satisfying: $x \leq x$, $x \leq y$ and $y \leq x$ implies $x = y$, and $x \leq z$ whenever $x \leq y$ and $y \leq z$. If every pair of elements of a subset C of S are comparable, i.e., $x \in C$ and $y \in C$ implies either $x \leq y$ or $y \leq x$, then C is called a **chain** or a **totally ordered** subset of S. An **upper bound** of a set $A \subset S$ is any $y \in S$ such that $x \leq y$ for all $x \in A$. A **maximal element** of S is any $y \in S$ such that $y \leq x$ implies $y = x$.

ZORN'S LEMMA. If S is a partially ordered set in which every totally ordered subset has an upper bound, then S has a maximal element.

Zorn's lemma was first proved by Hausdorff, but its importance as a tool was first recognized by Zorn. For further discussion see Kelley [1].

Now, let X be a vector space and Y a subspace of X. We consider the partially ordered set $\chi(Y)$ of all subspaces of X which are disjoint with Y, ordered by inclusion. Let Z_α, $\alpha \in A$, be a totally ordered subset of $\chi(Y)$. Then $Z = \bigcup [Z_\alpha : \alpha \in A]$ is also a subspace of X. Moreover $Y \wedge Z = Y \cap Z = \bigcup [Y \cap Z_\alpha : \alpha \in A] = \{0\}$, so that $Z \in \chi(Y)$. Hence, $\chi(Y)$ satisfies the condition of Zorn's lemma so that it has a maximal element M. We show that M is a complement of Y. For, let $W = Y \vee M$. Suppose there is an $x \in X$, $x \notin W$. Let M' be the subspace of X generated by M and x. Then M' is also disjoint with Y, contradicting the fact that M is maximal in $\chi(Y)$. Accordingly, $X = Y \vee M$, so that M is a complement of Y.

PROPOSITION 1. If X is a vector space, and Y and Z are complementary subspaces of X, then for every $x \in X$ there are $y \in Y$, $z \in Z$ such that $x = y + z$ and this representation is unique.

Proof. That every $x \in X$ has a representation $x = y + z$, $y \in Y$, $z \in Z$ follows from the fact that $X = Y \vee Z$. Suppose now that $x = u + v$, $u \in Y, v \in Z$. Then $y + z = u + v$, so that $w = y - u = z - v$ is in $Y \cap Z$. However, since $Y \cap Z = \{0\}$, we have $y = u$ and $z = v$.

2.3 Quotient Space

Let X be a vector space and Y a subspace of X. Then Y is a subgroup of the abelian group X, so that we may consider the quotient group X/Y. The elements of X/Y are the cosets modulo Y in X. These are the translations $x + Y$ of Y as x varies over X, where $x + Y = [z : z = x + y, y \in Y]$. It is well known, and easily shown, that the cosets of Y are disjoint sets whose union is X. It is also easy to show that if A and B are cosets modulo Y and $a \in R$ then $A + B$ and aA are also cosets modulo Y where $S + T = [x + y : x \in S, y \in T]$, and $aS = [ax : x \in S]$. This allows us to define vector space operations in X/Y, and it may be readily verified that X/Y is then a vector space. We leave all these easy details to the reader.

The notion of a homomorphism between vector spaces is of importance in connection with subspaces and quotient spaces. Let X and Z be vector spaces. By a **homomorphism** h of X **into** Z we mean a function defined on X with values in Z such that $h(x + y) = h(x) + h(y)$ and $h(ax) = ah(x)$. Thus a homomorphism is merely a linear mapping on X into Z. The homomorphism h is said to be **onto** Z if, for every $z \in Z$, there is an $x \in X$ such that $h(x) = z$. The set $K \subset X$ of all x for which $h(x) = 0$ is called the **kernel** of the homomorphism. The kernel K of a homomorphism is evidently a subspace of X. If a homomorphism is onto and its kernel contains only 0, then it is called an **isomorphism.**

Let X be a vector space and Y a subspace of X. Let φ be the mapping of X onto X/Y which takes every element of X into the element of X/Y which contains it when considered as a subset of X. The mapping φ is a homomorphism and is known as the **canonical homomorphism** of X onto X/Y.

We state one further fact. Let h be a homomorphism of X onto Z whose kernel is Y. Then the inverse images in X of the elements of Z are cosets modulo Y, so that h induces an isomorphism ψ of X/Y onto Z. It follows that the homomorphism h is the product of the canonical homomorphism φ of X onto X/Y followed by the induced isomorphism ψ of X/Y onto Z.

We now obtain a connection between the quotient space X/Y and any subspace Z of X complementary to Y.

PROPOSITION 1. If X is a vector space, Y and Z are subspaces of X, and Y is complementary to Z, then every element of X/Y contains exactly one element of Z.

Proof. By proposition 1, Sec. 2.2, every $x \in X$ has a unique representation $x = y + z$, where $y \in Y$ and $z \in Z$. Thus the cosets $z + Y$, $z \in Z$, are the totality of cosets of Y. That each of them contains exactly one element of Z follows since $z + y \in Z$, $z \in Z$, $y \in Y$ implies $y = 0$.

We also have the

COROLLARY. If X is a vector space, Y is a subspace of X, and Z a complement of Y in X, then X/Y is isomorphic to Z under the mapping which takes each element of X/Y into the element of Z which it contains.

2.4 Dimension, Hamel Basis

Let X be a vector space, and S a subset of X. S generates a subspace (S) of X. We say that the elements of S are **linearly independent** if the subspace (T) generated by any proper subset $T \subset S$ is a proper subspace of (S).

We prove the

PROPOSITION 1. Every vector space X contains a set of linearly independent elements which generates X.

Proof. Let $\mathcal{S}$ be the totality of linearly independent subsets of X, partially ordered by inclusion. We show that for every totally ordered subset S_α, $\alpha \in A$, of $\mathcal{S}$, the set $S = \bigcup [S_\alpha : \alpha \in A]$ is also in $\mathcal{S}$. For, if not, (S) would be generated by a proper subset $T \subset S$. Then for every $\alpha \in A$, (S_α) is generated by $T_\alpha = T \cap S_\alpha$. But the independence of S_α implies $T_\alpha = S_\alpha$. Thus

$$T = \bigcup [T \cap S_\alpha : \alpha \in A] = \bigcup [T_\alpha : \alpha \in A] = \bigcup [S_\alpha : \alpha \in A] = S,$$

contradicting the assumption that T is a proper subset S. The condition of Zorn's lemma being satisfied, there is a maximal $M \in \mathcal{S}$. Suppose (M) a proper subspace of X. Let $y \in X$, $y \notin (M)$. The subspace Y of X generated by M and y then contains (M) as a proper subspace. If for any proper subset $T \subset M$, T and y also generate Y, it follows that T also generates (M), thus contradicting the fact that M is linearly independent. There is thus no $y \in X$, $y \notin (M)$. Hence M generates X.

A set S of linearly independent elements which generates a vector space X is called a **Hamel basis** in X. Proposition 1 says that every vector space has a Hamel basis.

Although a given vector space has many Hamel bases, we note that they all have the same number (cardinal) of elements. Indeed, let S and T be Hamel bases of X.

Suppose S is finite and has n elements $x_1, x_2, \ldots, x_n$. If there were $n + 1$ elements $y_1, y_2, \ldots, y_n, y_{n+1}$ in T, then

$$y_i = \sum_{j=1}^{n} a_{ij} x_j, \quad i = 1, \ldots, n$$

and since $y_1, y_2, \ldots, y_n$ are linearly independent, the matrix (a_{ij}) has rank n. But

$$y_{n+1} = \sum_{j=1}^{n} a_{n+1,j} x_j$$

and the vector $(a_{n+1,1}, \ldots, a_{n+1,n})$ is a linear combination of the row vectors of the matrix (a_{ij}). But this implies $y_1, y_2, \ldots, y_n, y_{n+1}$ not linearly independent. Hence T has $m \leq n$ elements. By the same argument $n \leq m$.

Suppose S is infinite and has cardinal number a. Let b be the cardinal number of T. Every $y \in T$ is a linear combination, with non-zero coefficients, of a finite number $x_1, x_2, \ldots, x_n$ of elements of S, and only a finite number n of elements of T are associated in this way with the same set $x_1, x_2, \ldots, x_n$ or some subset of it. Since the cardinal number of the set of finite subsets of S is the same as that of S itself, it follows that $b \leq \aleph_0 \cdot a = a$. Similarily, $a \leq b$, so that $a = b$. This completes the proof of

Proposition 2. If X is a vector space, all Hamel bases of X have the same cardinal number.

This cardinal number is called the **dimension** of X.

Proposition 3. If S is a Hamel basis of X, then every $x \in X$ has a unique representation as a linear combination of a finite number of elements of S.

The proof is left to the reader.

Proposition 4. If the dimension of X is at least as great as the cardinal number of the reals, then the dimension of X and the cardinal number of X are equal.

The proof is left to the reader.

We recall that vector spaces X and Y are called **isomorphic** if there is a mapping φ which is one-one and onto such that

$$\varphi(ax_1 + by_1) = a\varphi(x_1) + b\varphi(x_2) \text{ for all } x_1, x_2 \in X \text{ and } a, b \in R.$$

We prove

Proposition 5. Two vector spaces X and Y are isomorphic if and only if they have the same dimension.

Proof. Suppose X and Y have the same dimension and S and T are Hamel bases of X and Y, respectively. Let φ be a one-one correspondence between S and T. We extend φ to X by letting

$$\varphi(x) = a_1\varphi(x_1) + \ldots + a_n\varphi(x_n)$$

for $x = a_1x_1 + \ldots + a_nx_n$, $x \in X$, $x_1, \ldots, x_n \in S$. It readily follows that this is an isomorphism between X and Y. The converse is obvious.

There are thus many different one-one correspondences between X and Y, called isomorphisms, which establish the fact that X and Y are isomorphic. We notice that a vector space can be isomorphic to a proper subspace.

By the **deficiency** of a subspace Y of a vector space X we mean the dimension of X/Y. The deficiency of Y is then the dimension of any subspace Z of X which is complementary to Y.

In particular, a subspace of X of deficiency 1 is called a **hyperplane** in X; its cosets are also called hyperplanes. We note that if S is a Hamel basis of X and $x \in S$, then $S \sim \{x\}$ is a Hamel basis of a hyperplane in X.

In the same way as we showed that every vector space X has a Hamel basis, we may show that if Y is a subspace of X then X has a Hamel basis S, which has a subset T which is a Hamel basis of Y. We omit the proof. It follows that every proper subspace of a vector space X is contained in a hyperplane.

2.5 Algebraic Dual, Second Dual

Let X be a vector space and let X^* be the algebraic dual of X. Then X^* is a vector space with operations $f + g$ and af defined by

$$(f + g)(x) = f(x) + g(x), \quad x \in X,$$

$$(af)(x) = af(x), \qquad x \in X.$$

For any $f \in X^*$, the set

$$Z(f) = [x : x \in X, f(x) = 0]$$

is a vector subspace of X and is called the **null space** of f.

Proposition 1. If $f \in X^*$, then $Z(f)$ has deficiency 0 or 1 in X. Conversely, if Z is a subspace of X of deficiency 0 or 1, there is an $f \in X^*$ such that $Z = Z(f)$.

Proof. Suppose $x \in X$ and $f(x) \neq 0$. Then, for every $y \in X$ there is a real number a such that $f(y) = af(x) = f(ax)$, or $f(y - ax) = 0$. Thus $y - ax \in Z(f)$. In other words, X is generated by $Z(f)$ and x, so that the deficiency of $Z(f)$ is 1. If $f(x) \equiv 0$ on X, then $Z(f) = X$ and its deficiency is 0.

For the converse, if $Z = X$, i.e., Z has deficiency 0, then $Z(f) = Z$ for $f(x) \equiv 0$. Suppose, Z has deficiency 1. Let $x_0 \notin Z$. Then every $y \in X$ has a unique representation $y = x + ax_0$, where $x \in Z$. Let $f(y) = a$. A simple calculation shows that f is linear and $Z(f) = Z$.

Now, let $S^* \subset X^*$ be a set of linear functionals on X. By the **null space** $Z(S^*)$ of S^* we shall mean the set of all $x \in X$ for which $f(x) = 0$ for all $f \in S^*$. That $Z(S^*)$ is a subspace of X follows since it is the intersection of the subspaces $Z(f), f \in S^*$.

A subspace $Y^* \subset X^*$ is called **total** if $Z(Y^*) = \{0\}$. Thus Y^* is total if and only if for every $x \neq 0$ in X there is an $f \in Y^*$ such that $f(x) \neq 0$. Most important subspaces are total.

PROPOSITION 2. For every vector space X, with algebraic dual X^*, $\dim X^* \geq \dim X$.

The proof is left to the reader.

For any vector space X, the dual X^* is also a vector space and so it has its own algebraic dual X^{**}. There is a natural isomorphism between a certain subspace of X^{**} and X itself, which we now discuss.

Fix $x_0 \in X$. For every $f \in X^*$, let $x_0(f) = f(x_0)$. Then $x_0(f)$ is a linear functional on X^*. For,

$$x_0(f + g) = (f + g)(x_0) = f(x_0) + g(x_0) = x_0(f) + x_0(g)$$

and

$$x_0(af) = (af)(x_0) = af(x_0) = ax_0(f).$$

Hence, for every $x_0 \in X$, $x_0(f) \in X^{**}$. Consider the mapping

$$\varphi : X \to X^{**}$$

defined by $\varphi(x_0) = x_0(f), f \in X^*$. We show that this is an isomorphism between X and a subspace of X^{**}. For,

$$(x_0 + y_0)(f) = f(x_0 + y_0) = x_0(f) + y_0(f)$$

and

$$(ax_0)(f) = f(ax_0) = af(x_0) = ax_0(f).$$

Moreover, the mate of 0 is the functional on X^* which is identically zero, and for any $x_0 \neq 0$, there is an $f \in X^*$ such that $f(x_0) \neq 0$, whence $x_0(f) \neq 0$.

Now, let $Y^* \subset X^*$ be any total subspace of X^*. Then for every $x_0 \in X$, $x_0(f)$ is a linear functional on Y^* so that it belongs to Y^{**}. The mapping defined by $\varphi(x_0) = x_0(f)$, $f \in Y^*$ is an isomorphism between X and Y^{**}, by the same discussion as above. Indeed, all of the interesting applications are concerned with this isomorphism for special subspaces Y^* of X^*.

If X is finite dimensional, the natural isomorphism $\varphi(x_0) = x_0(f), f \in X^*$ is between X and all of X^{**}. This is never true if X is infinite dimensional.

2.6 Convex Sets

Let X be a vector space. A set $S \subset X$ is called **convex** if for every $x, y \in S$ and every $a \in R$, with $0 \leq a \leq 1$, the element $ax + (1 - a)y \in S$. In other words, the line segment joining x and y is contained in S.

We first state some elementary properties of convex sets.

Every subspace Y of X is convex. For if $x, y \in Y$ then $ax + by \in Y$ for every $a, b \in R$.

The intersection, $S = \bigcap [S_\alpha : \alpha \in A]$ of any collection S_α, $\alpha \in A$, of convex sets is a convex set. For, let $x, y \in S$. Then $x, y \in S_\alpha$ for every $\alpha \in A$. Then for every $a \in R$, $0 \leq a \leq 1$, $ax + (1 - a)y \in S_\alpha$, for every $\alpha \in A$, so that $ax + (1 - a)y \in S$.

For every set $S \subset X$, there is a smallest convex set $C(S)$ such that $S \subset C(S)$. $C(S)$ is called the **convex hull** of S. In order to prove this, we observe that there are convex sets which contain S. For example, X itself is such a set. The intersection of all the convex sets containing S is convex. This is the convex hull of S.

The translations $x + S$ of convex sets and the products aS of convex sets by real numbers are convex sets. We leave the proofs to the reader.

If S is a convex set, and $x_0 \in S$, we shall say that x_0 is an **interior** point of S if every line through x_0 meets S in a line segment which has x_0 as interior point. Precisely, this means that for every $x \in X$, $x \neq 0$, there is a $k > 0$ such that $|a| < k$ implies $x_0 + ax \in S$.

Let H be a hyperplane in X such that $0 \in H$. Then H is a subspace of deficiency 1. There is a linear functional f whose null space is H. The sets for which $f(x) \geq 0$ and $f(x) \leq 0$ are called the two **sides** of H.

A **ray** with vertex x_0, determined by $x \neq 0$, is the set of all $x_0 + ax$, $a \geq 0$. A **cone** with vertex x_0 is the union of a set of rays with vertex x_0. For every $x_0 \in X$ and $S \subset X$, the cone $c(x_0, S)$ with vertex x_0 determined by S, is the union of the set of all rays with vertex x_0 determined by points of S.

PROPOSITION 1. If $x_0 \in X$ and S is convex, then $c(x_0, S)$ is convex.

Proof. Let $x, y \in c(x_0, S)$ and $0 \leq a \leq 1$. We note that $x = x_0 + a_1x_1$ $y = x_0 + a_2x_2$ where $a_1 \geq 0$, $a_2 \geq 0$ and $x_1, x_2 \in S$. Then,

$$\begin{aligned} ax + (1 - a)y &= a(x_0 + a_1x_1) + (1 - a)(x_0 + a_2x_2) \\ &= x_0 + aa_1x_1 + (1 - a)a_2x_2 \\ &= x_0 + [aa_1 + (1 - a)a_2] \\ &\quad \times \left[\frac{aa_1}{aa_1 + (1 - a)a_2} x_1 + \frac{(1 - a)a_2}{aa_1 + (1 - a)a_2} x_2\right] \end{aligned}$$

so that $ax + (1 - a)y \in c(x_0, S)$.

2.7 Ordered Groups

We shall give a proof of the so-called Hahn-Banach theorem. Our proof depends on some elementary facts concerning ordered groups which we present in this section.

Let G be an abelian group with identity 0. A set $P \subset G$ is called a **positive cone** for G if $0 \in P$ and $x, y \in P$ implies $x + y \in P$. A positive cone P induces an "order relation" in G for which $x \geq y$ if $x - y \in P$. An abelian group G together with an order relation given by a positive cone in G is called a **preordered group.** It is called an **ordered group** if $P \cap (-P) = \{0\}$.

If $P \cap (-P) = \{0\}$ and $P \cup (-P) = G$, it is called a **totally ordered group.** G is evidently totally ordered if and only if, for every $x, y \in G$, either $x \leq y$ or $y \leq x$ and both $x \leq y$ and $y \leq x$ implies $x = y$. Instead of $x \geq y$ we may write $y \leq x$, as we have done above.

If G is a preordered group, the set $H = P \cap (-P)$ is a subgroup. Let G/H be the quotient group, and φ the canonical mapping $\varphi(x) = \xi$, where ξ is the coset modulo H to which x belongs. Let $\mathfrak{T}$ be the image in G/H of P under the mapping φ. It is easy to see that G/H is an ordered group with positive cone $\mathfrak{T}$ which is totally ordered if $P \cup (-P) = G$.

A totally ordered group is **archimedean** if for every $x, y \in P \sim \{0\}$ there are positive integers n, m such that $nx - y \in P$ and $my - x \in P$. Two totally ordered groups G and H, with positive cones P and Q, respectively, are said to be isomorphic if there is a group isomorphism between them which maps P onto Q. We then have

PROPOSITION 1. If G is an archimedean totally ordered group, then G is isomorphic to a subgroup of the totally ordered group of real numbers.

Proof. Let 0 be the identity in G, and P the positive cone of G. We let $\varphi(0) = 0$, and $\varphi(x_0) = 1$ where $x_0 \in P \sim \{0\}$. We now associate a positive real number with every $x \in P$ as follows: The rational number n/m belongs to the upper segment of the Dedekind cut defining $\varphi(x)$ if and only if $nx \leq mx_0$. That $x \in P$ actually defines a Dedekind cut in this way follows since G is archimedean, for this implies that the upper segment is non-empty. It is an exercise to show that $x \neq y$ implies $\varphi(x) \neq \varphi(y)$. We let $\varphi(-x) = -\varphi(x)$, so that we now have a one-one correspondence between G and a subset of the reals. It is a routine calculation, which we leave for the reader, to show that this mapping is an isomorphism.

2.8 Hahn-Banach Theorem, Separation Form

A variety of results, which are closely related to each other, and deal either with the separation of sets by hyperplanes, or the extension of linear functionals, are known as the Hahn-Banach theorem. The form which we first give is due to J. Dieudonné.

THEOREM 1. If S is a convex set which contains an interior point and $0 \notin S$, there is a hyperplane H, passing through 0, such that all of S is on the same side of H.

Proof. The cone $c(0, S)$ with vertex 0, determined by S, is convex. Let x_0 be an interior point of S. Then $-x_0 \notin c(0, S)$. Otherwise, there would be an $x \in S$ and $a > 0$ such that $-x_0 = ax$, but then $x_0 + ax = 0$, so that

$$\frac{1}{1+a} x_0 + \frac{a}{1+a} x = 0$$

and, since $\dfrac{1}{1+a} + \dfrac{a}{1+a} = 1$, we have $0 \in S$. The condition for Zorn's lemma is evidently satisfied by the collection of convex cones, ordered by inclusion, which contain $c(0, S)$ but do not contain $-x_0$. Let C be a maximal cone in this collection.

We first show that $X = C \cup (-C)$. Suppose then that $x \notin C$. Then the convex cone generated by C and x contains $-x_0$ since C is maximal among the convex cones not containing $-x_0$. Hence $-x_0 = ax + by$, where $a > 0$, $b \geq 0$ and $y \in C$. Thus $-x = \dfrac{1}{a} x_0 + \dfrac{b}{a} y \in C$, so that $x \in -C$.

Now $x, y \in C$ implies $x + y \in C$. For since C is convex, $\frac{1}{2}(x + y) \in C$, and since C is a cone, $x + y = 2(\frac{1}{2}(x + y)) \in C$. Thus the abelian group X is preordered with C as positive cone. Let $H = C \cap (-C)$. H is easily seen to be a subgroup, indeed a subspace, of X and the quotient group X/H is totally ordered.

We finally prove that X/H is archimedean, so that H has deficiency 1 and our theorem is proved. For this, we show that for every $x \in C \sim H$ there are $a, b > 0$ such that $x - ax_0 \in -C$ and $x - bx_0 \in C$. Since x_0 is an interior point of C, there is an $\alpha > 0$ such that $y = x_0 - \alpha(x - x_0) \in C$. Then $x - \dfrac{2+\alpha}{\alpha} x_0 \in -C$. For, if it were in C, then

$$x_0 - \alpha(x - x_0) + \alpha\left(x - \frac{2+\alpha}{\alpha} x_0\right) \in C,$$

but this last term is just $-x_0$. We need only let $a = \dfrac{2+\alpha}{\alpha} > 0$. Moreover, $-x \notin C$, so that the smallest convex cone containing C and $-x$ contains $-x_0$, since C is maximal among the convex cones not containing $-x_0$. Hence there are $\gamma > 0$, $\delta \geq 0$, with $-x_0 = \gamma(-x) + \delta y$, $y \in C$. Thus $x - \dfrac{1}{\gamma} x_0 \in C$. We need only let $b = 1/\gamma > 0$.

The condition that the convex set S should contain an interior point cannot be dropped entirely. Thus, let X have dimension $\aleph_0$ with basis

$$x_1, x_2, \ldots, x_n, \ldots.$$

Every $x \in X$, $x \neq 0$, has a unique representation $x = a_1x_1 + \ldots + a_mx_m$, where $m > 0$ and $a_m \neq 0$. Let S be the set of those $x \in X$ whose last coefficient in this representation is positive. Then $0 \notin S$. The set S is convex. For, if $x = a_1x_1 + \ldots + a_mx_m$, $a_m > 0$ and $y = b_1x_1 + \ldots + b_nx_n$, $b_n > 0$, if $0 \leq a \leq 1$, and $z = ax + (1 - a)y$, then clearly $z = c_1x_1 + \ldots + c_kx_k$ with $c_k > 0$. Let f be a linear functional on X which is non-negative on S. For every n and $a \in R$, we have $ax_n + x_{n+1} \in S$, so that $af(x_n) + f(x_{n+1}) \geq 0$.

This implies $f(x_n) = 0$ for every n, so that $f(x) \equiv 0$ on X. This means that there is no hyperplane H such that all of S is on one side of H. Of course, the above set S contains no interior points.

As a corollary to theorem 1 we have

THEOREM 2. If X is a vector space and S is a convex set in X which contains an interior point, and if Y is a subspace of X which has no points in common with S, then there is a hyperplane H such that $Y \subset H$ and all points of S are on the same side of H.

Proof. Let x_0 be an interior point of S. Then $-x_0$ is not in the cone of vertex 0 generated by $S \cup Y$. For, if it were, there would be a $y \in Y$, $x \in S$, $a > 0$, $b > 0$, with $-x_0 = ax + by$. Hence, $-y = \frac{1}{a} x_0 + \frac{b}{a} x$ and so $-\frac{a}{b+1} y \in S$. This means that $S \cap Y$ is non-empty, contradicting our original assumption. We may now complete the proof as for theorem 1.

The above theorem has the

COROLLARY. If X and S are as in the theorem, and Y is a translation of a subspace of X which has no points in common with S, then there is a hyperplane H (not necessarily a subspace) containing Y, such that all points in S are on the same side of H.

This means there is a linear functional f and $k \geq 0$ such that $f(x) \geq k$ for every $x \in S$.

Theorem 2 and its corollary are the separation form of the Hahn-Banach theorem. The following extension form follows from it.

THEOREM 3. Let X be a vector space, Y a subspace of X, and p a real function on X such that $p(x) \geq 0$, $p(x + y) \leq p(x) + p(y)$, and $p(ax) = |a|\, p(x)$. If f is a linear functional on Y such that $|f(x)| \leq p(x)$ for every $x \in Y$, there is a linear F on X such that $F(x) = f(x)$ on Y and $|F(x)| \leq p(x)$ on X.

The proof is left to the reader. In the next section we prove an important extension theorem of which theorem 3 is also an immediate consequence.

2.9 Hahn-Banach Theorem, Extension Form

We now prove

THEOREM 1. Let X be a (real) vector space, p a real-valued function on X such that $p(x + y) \leq p(x) + p(y)$ and $p(ax) = ap(x)$ for $a \geq 0$, and Y a subspace of X. If f is linear on Y and $f(x) \leq p(x)$ for every $x \in Y$, there is a linear F on X such that $F(x) = f(x)$ on Y and $F(x) \leq p(x)$ on X.

Proof. The main problem is to extend f to a φ defined on $(Y \cup \{x_0\})$ for any $x_0 \notin Y$ so that

$$\varphi(x) \leq p(x) \text{ for all } x \in (Y \cup \{x_0\}).$$

Assuming this can be done, the existence of F is obtained using Zorn's lemma as follows:

Let E be the class of all linear extensions of f which are dominated by p on their domains. Partially order E by

$$F_1 \leq F_2 \text{ if } F_2 \text{ is an extension of } F_1,$$

i.e., the domain of F_2 contains that of F_1 and $F_2(x) = F_1(x)$ for every x in the domain of F_1. Let $\mathfrak{C}$ be a chain in E and define a linear functional U by

(a) the domain of U is the union of the domains of the F for all $F \in \mathfrak{C}$,

(b) if x is in the domain of U, define $U(x) = F(x)$, where $F \in \mathfrak{C}$ and x is in the domain of F. This is consistent, since $\mathfrak{C}$ is a chain.

It is clear that U is a linear extension of f and $U(x) \leq p(x)$ on its domain, so that $U \in E$ and it is an upper bound of $\mathfrak{C}$. By Zorn's lemma, E has a maximal element F. F must be an extension to X since if its domain were a proper subspace M and $x_0 \in X \sim M$, then an extension to $(M \cup \{x_0\})$ would be possible.

We now suppose f defined on Y and extend it to φ on $(Y \cup \{x_0\}) = Z$. Since $x \in Z$ has a unique representation $x = y + cx_0$, $y \in Y$, c real, it follows that $\varphi(x) = f(y) + ca_0$ is such that $\varphi(x) = f(x)$ for every $x \in Y$ no matter how we choose a_0. The problem is to show that a_0 may be chosen so that $\varphi(x) \leq p(x)$ for all $x \in Z$, i.e., so that $f(y) + ca_0 \leq p(y + cx_0)$. In other words, $ca_0 \leq p(y + cx_0) - f(y)$.

For $c = 0$, this always holds. For $c > 0$, the relation $ca_0 \leq p(y + cx_0) - f(y)$ is equivalent to

$$a_0 \leq \frac{1}{c} p(y + cx_0) - \frac{1}{c} f(y) = p\left(\frac{y}{c} + x_0\right) - f\left(\frac{y}{c}\right).$$

For $c < 0$, it is equivalent to

$$a_0 \geq -p\left(-\frac{y}{c} - x_0\right) - f\left(\frac{y}{c}\right).$$

Hence, we must show the existence of an a_0 such that, for every $y \in Y$,

$$-p(-y - x_0) - f(y) \leq a_0 \leq p(y + x_0) - f(y).$$

But this follows from the fact that, for every $y, z \in Y$,

$$-p(-y - x_0) - f(y) \leq p(z + x_0) - f(z),$$

since

$$f(z) - f(y) = f(z - y) \leq p[(z + x_0) + (-y - x_0)]$$
$$\leq p(z + x_0) + p(-y - x_0).$$

A corollary to this theorem is theorem 3, section 2.8.

2.10 Applications, Banach Limits, Invariant Measure

The Hahn-Banach theorem will be seen to have many applications in the development of the general theory of normed linear spaces and, more generally, locally convex topological vector spaces.

We give two direct applications of the theorem. The first is to the generalized notion of the limit of a sequence.

Let m denote the vector space of all bounded sequences of real numbers, c the subspace of all convergent sequences. If $x \in c$, then $l(x) = \lim_n x_n$ is defined, and l is a linear functional on c.

A **Banach limit** is any linear functional L defined on m such that

(a) $L(x) \geq 0$ if $x_n \geq 0$ for all n,
(b) $L(x) = L(\sigma x)$ where σ denotes the shift

$$\sigma x = \sigma(x_1, x_2, x_3, \ldots) = (x_2, x_3, \ldots),$$

(c) $L(x) = 1$ if $x = (1, 1, 1, \ldots)$.

These are properties which a generalized limit may be expected to have.

Proposition 1. *If L is a Banach limit, then*

$$\underline{\lim}\, x_n \leq L(x) \leq \overline{\lim}\, x_n \text{ for all } x \in m.$$

Proof. Since $\underline{\lim}\, x_n = \lim_k \inf_{n \geq k} x_n$ and $\overline{\lim}\, x_n = \lim_k \sup_{n \geq k} x_n$, it follows by (b) that we need only show that

$$\inf x_n \leq L(x) \leq \sup x_n.$$

For $\epsilon > 0$, choose n_0 so that

$$\inf x_n \leq x_{n_0} < \inf x_n + \epsilon,$$

whence

$$x_n + \epsilon - x_{n_0} > 0 \text{ for all } n.$$

By (a) and (c), we get

$$L(x) + \epsilon \geq x_{n_0} \geq \inf x_n,$$

so that $L(x) \geq \inf x_n$. Similarly $L(x) \leq \sup x_n$.

In particular, for $x \in c$, the Banach limit equals the ordinary limit.

Define, on m,

$$q(x) = \overline{\lim_{n \to \infty}} \frac{x_1 + x_2 + \ldots + x_n}{n}.$$

Then

$$-q(-x) = \underline{\lim}_{n\to\infty} \frac{x_1 + x_2 + \ldots + x_n}{n}.$$

If $\{x_n\}$ is convergent, it is easy to show that

$$\lim_{n\to\infty} x_n = \lim_{n\to\infty} \frac{x_1 + x_2 + \ldots + x_n}{n}.$$

We leave this for the reader to prove.

Thus, for $x \in c$,

$$q(x) = l(x).$$

Moreover, $q(x + y) \leq q(x) + q(y)$ and $q(ax) = aq(x)$, $a \geq 0$.

Let L be an extension of l from c to m given by the Hahn-Banach theorem (theorem 1, Sec. 2.9). Then

$$-q(-x) \leq L(x) \leq q(x)$$

for all $x \in m$.

In order to show that L is a Banach limit, it is only necessary to show that (b) holds. For this,

$$q(x - \sigma x) = \overline{\lim}_{n\to\infty} \left(\frac{x_{n+1} - x_1}{n}\right) = 0.$$

We thus have

THEOREM 1. Banach limits exist.

In order to characterize the sequences for which all Banach limits agree, it is convenient to give another proof of theorem 1.

Define, on m,

$$p(x) = \inf \overline{\lim}_{j\to\infty} \frac{1}{k} \sum_{i=1}^{k} x_{n_i+j}$$

where the infimum is taken over all finite sets of integers $n_1, n_2, \ldots, n_k$. Also define

$$p'(x) = -p(-x), \qquad x \in m.$$

Observe that

$$p'(x) = \sup \underline{\lim}_{j\to\infty} \frac{1}{k} \sum_{i=1}^{k} x_{n_i+j}.$$

PROPOSITION 2. For any $x \in m$,

$$\underline{\lim}\, x_n \leq p'(x) \leq p(x) \leq \overline{\lim}\, x_n.$$

In particular, $p(x) = l(x)$ for $x \in c$.

PROPOSITION 3. For any Banach limit L and $x \in m$,

$$p'(x) \leq L(x) \leq p(x).$$

Proof. Apply proposition 1 to the sequence $\left\{\frac{1}{k}\sum_{i=1}^{k} x_{n_i+j}\right\}$ for fixed k, $n_1, \ldots, n_k$ to get

$$\underline{\lim}_{j\to\infty} \frac{1}{k}\sum_{i=1}^{k} x_{n_i+j} \le L\left(\left\{\frac{1}{k}\sum_{i=1}^{k} x_{n_i+j}\right\}\right) = L(x) \le \overline{\lim}_{j\to\infty} \frac{1}{k}\sum_{i=1}^{k} x_{n_i+j}.$$

Proposition 4. $p(x)$ is such that $p(x + y) \le p(x) + p(y)$, and $p(ax) = ap(x)$ if $a \ge 0$.

Proof. We need only prove $p(x + y) \le p(x) + p(y)$. Let x, $y \in m$ and $\epsilon > 0$. There are $k, n_1, \ldots, n_k$ such that

$$\overline{\lim}_{j\to\infty} \frac{1}{k}\sum_{i=1}^{k} x_{n_i+j} < p(x) + \frac{\epsilon}{2}$$

and $l, m_1, \ldots, m_l$ such that

$$\overline{\lim}_{j\to\infty} \frac{1}{l}\sum_{i=1}^{l} x_{m_i+j} < p(y) + \frac{\epsilon}{2}.$$

Consider the kl integers $n_r + m_s$, $r = 1, \ldots, k$, $s = 1, \ldots, l$. Using the subadditive property of $\overline{\lim}$ we get

$$p(x + y) \le \overline{\lim}_{j\to\infty} \frac{1}{kl}\sum_{r=1}^{k}\sum_{s=1}^{l}(x_{n_r+m_s+j} + y_{n_r+m_s+j})$$

$$\le \overline{\lim}_{j\to\infty} \frac{1}{kl}\sum_{r=1}^{k}\sum_{s=1}^{l} x_{n_r+m_s+j} + \overline{\lim}_{j\to\infty} \frac{1}{kl}\sum_{r=1}^{k}\sum_{s=1}^{l} y_{n_r+m_s+j}.$$

Continuing with the first term only, it is no larger than

$$\frac{1}{l}\sum_{s=1}^{l} \overline{\lim}_{j\to\infty} \frac{1}{k}\sum_{r=1}^{k} x_{n_r+m_s+j}.$$

But each

$$\overline{\lim}_{j\to\infty} \frac{1}{k}\sum_{r=1}^{k} x_{n_r+m_s+j} < p(x) + \frac{\epsilon}{2},$$

so that the average also has this property. Similarly, the second term is less than $p(y) + \frac{\epsilon}{2}$ and

$$p(x + y) < p(x) + p(y) + \epsilon,$$

for every $\epsilon > 0$.

We now apply the Hahn-Banach theorem to $l(x)$ on c to obtain linear functionals $L(x)$ on m satisfying $L(x) \le p(x)$, $x \in m$. Putting $-x$ for x we obtain the other part of

$$p'(x) \le L(x) \le p(x), \qquad x \in m.$$

It remains to show that L satisfies (b). For any $x \in m$,

$$L(\sigma x) - L(x) = L(\sigma x - x) \le p(\sigma x - x)$$

and

$$p(\sigma x - x) \leq \overline{\lim_{j\to\infty}} \frac{1}{k} \sum_{i=1}^{k} (x_{n_i+1+j} - x_{n_i+j}).$$

So, if we take $n_i = i$, $i = 1, \ldots, k$, we have

$$p(\sigma x - x) \leq \overline{\lim_{j\to\infty}} \frac{1}{k} \sum_{i=1}^{k} (x_{i+1+j} - x_{i+j})$$

$$= \frac{1}{k} \overline{\lim_{j\to\infty}} (x_{k+1+j} - x_{1+j}).$$

If M is an upper bound for $|x_n|$, for all n, then for arbitrary k we have

$$p(\sigma x - x) \leq \frac{2M}{k},$$

so that $p(\sigma x - x) \leq 0$, and

$$L(\sigma x) \leq L(x).$$

Similarly,

$$L(x) - L(\sigma x) \leq p(x - \sigma x) \leq 0.$$

Hence

$$L(\sigma x) = L(x).$$

This completes the second proof of the existence of Banach limits.

All Banach limits are the same for the convergent sequences. However, there are other sequences which have this property; in particular, $\{1, 0, 1, 0, \ldots\}$. $x \in m$ is called **almost convergent** and the number s is called the ***F*-limit** of x if $L(x) = s$ for all Banach limits L. This notion was introduced and studied by G. Lorentz.

PROPOSITION 5. x is almost convergent if and only if $p'(x) = p(x)$.

Proof. The sufficiency follows by proposition 3. If $p'(x) < p(x)$ then $x \notin c$. There are distinct extensions of $l(x)$ from c to $(c \cup \{x\})$, since in the proof of the Hahn-Banach theorem the extensions can have any value at x on the interval

$$\left(\sup_{x \in c} [-p(-y - x) - l(y)], \qquad \inf_{x \in c} [p(y + x) - l(y)]\right)$$

and these end points reduce to $p'(x)$ and $p(x)$, respectively.

PROPOSITION 6. x is almost convergent and the F-limit of x is s if and only if

$$\lim_{p\to\infty} \frac{1}{p} (x_n + x_{n+1} + \ldots + x_{n+p-1}) = s$$

holds uniformly in n.

Proof. Under the condition of the theorem, for $\epsilon > 0$, we have

$$s - \epsilon < \frac{1}{p}(x_n + x_{n+1} + \dots + x_{n+p-1}) < s + \epsilon$$

for all n and all sufficiently large p. It then readily follows that

$$s - \epsilon \leq p'(x) \leq p(x) \leq s + \epsilon,$$

so that F-lim $x_n = s$.

Conversely, suppose F-lim $x_n = s$. Let $\epsilon > 0$. Since $s = p(x)$, there are $k, n_1, \dots, n_k$ such that

$$\overline{\lim_{j \to \infty}} \frac{1}{k} \sum_{i=1}^{k} x_{n_i+j} < s + \epsilon.$$

Thus, if j is sufficiently large, say $j \geq N$,

$$\frac{1}{k} \sum_{i=1}^{k} x_{n_i+j} < s + \epsilon.$$

Replacing j by $j - N$ and n_i by $m_i = n_i + N$, for $i = 1, 2, \dots, k$, we obtain

$$\frac{1}{k} \sum_{i=1}^{k} x_{m_i+j} < s + \epsilon, \quad j = 0, 1, 2, \dots.$$

Now, for any $n = 1, 2, 3, \dots$ and $p = 1, 2, 3, \dots$,

$$\frac{1}{p} \sum_{j=1}^{p} \frac{1}{k} \sum_{i=1}^{k} x_{m_i+j+n} < s + \epsilon.$$

This sum can be evaluated as

$$\frac{1}{pk} \sum_{i=1}^{k} \sum_{j=m_i+1}^{m_i+p} x_{j+n} = \frac{1}{pk} \sum_{i=1}^{k} \sum_{j=1}^{p-1} [x_{j+n} + (x_{m_i+1+j+n} - x_{j+n})]$$

$$= \frac{1}{p} \sum_{j=0}^{p-1} x_{j+n} + \frac{1}{p} \left\{ \frac{1}{k} \sum_{i=0}^{k} \sum_{j=0}^{p-1} (x_{m_i+1+j+n} - x_{j+n}) \right\}.$$

The quantity in brackets is bounded for large p, uniformly in n. In fact, if kp exceeds m_i for all $i = 1, 2, \dots, k$, then cancellations occur in the inner sum, leaving only $2m_i$ terms. Thus, if M is a bound for $|x_n|$ for all $n = 1, 2, 3, \dots$, the quantity in brackets does not exceed in absolute value the quantity

$$\frac{2M}{k} \sum_{i=1}^{k} m_i.$$

It follows that p can be chosen so large that

$$\frac{1}{p} \sum_{j=0}^{p-1} x_{j+n} < s + 2\epsilon$$

uniformly in n.

The reverse inequality is obtained by a similar argument using $s = p'(x)$.

As a second application, we show the existence of a finitely additive invariant measure for the set of all subsets of a circle σ. By this we mean a non-negative function $m(S)$ defined for all subsets of σ such that

(α) $m(\sigma) = 1$,
(β) if $S \cap T$ is empty, then $m(S \cup T) = m(S) + m(T)$,
(γ) for every rotation f of σ and every S, $m(fS) = m(S)$.

It is equivalent to prove the existence of a generalized integral for the space X of bounded real functions $x(t)$ on σ; in other words, the existence of a $\varphi(x)$ on X such that

(α') $\varphi(1) = 1$, where $1(t) = 1$, $t \in \sigma$,
(β') $\varphi(ax + by) = a\varphi(x) + b\varphi(y)$ for all $x, y \in X$ and $a, b \in R$,
(γ') $\varphi(x) \geq 0$ if $x(t) \geq 0$,
(δ') $\varphi(x_\tau) = \varphi(x)$, where $x_\tau(t) = x(t + \tau)$.

We now define a special function p on X with the following properties:

(α'') $p(1) = 1$, $p(-1) = -1$,
(β'') $p(x + y) \leq p(x) + p(y)$ for all $x, y \in X$,
(γ'') $p(ax) = ap(x)$ for all $a \geq 0$ and $x \in X$,
(δ'') $p(x_\tau - x) \leq 0$ for all $x \in X$ and τ.

That the upper Riemann integral cannot serve as the p is clear if we consider the function $x(t) = 1$, t rational, $x(t) = 0$, t irrational, and let $\tau = \sqrt{2}$. Then $x_\tau - x$ is equal to 1 on a dense set so that its upper Riemann integral is equal to 1. However, Banach found a p which has the desired properties. For every $x \in X$ and $t_1, t_2, \ldots, t_n$ consider the set of mean values

$$\frac{1}{n}\sum_{j=1}^{n} x(t + t_j)$$

obtained as t varies over σ. Let

$$U(x; t_1, \ldots, t_n) = \sup_t \frac{1}{n}\sum_{j=1}^{n} x(t + t_j),$$

and let $p(x) = \inf U(x\,; t_1, \ldots, t_n)$ for all n and $t_1, \ldots, t_n$.

(α'') That $p(1) = 1$ and $p(-1) = -1$ are obvious since $1(t + t_j) = 1$ for all choices of t_j and t.

(β'') Let $x, y \in X$. For every $\epsilon > 0$, there are $t_1, \ldots, t_n$; $s_1, \ldots, s_m$ for which

$$p(x) \geq U(x; t_1, \ldots, t_n) - \frac{\epsilon}{2}$$

and

$$p(y) \geq U(y; s_1, \ldots, s_m) - \frac{\epsilon}{2}.$$

Now, for every t,

$$\begin{aligned}\frac{1}{nm}\sum_{i=1}^{n}\sum_{j=1}^{m}[x(t+t_i+s_j)+y(t+t_i+s_j)]\\ &= \frac{1}{m}\left\{\frac{1}{n}\sum_{i=1}^{n}x((t+s_1)+t_i)+\dots+\frac{1}{n}\sum_{i=1}^{n}x((t+s_m)+t_i)\right\}\\ &\quad+\frac{1}{n}\left\{\frac{1}{m}\sum_{j=1}^{m}y((t+t_1)+s_j)+\dots+\frac{1}{m}\sum_{j=1}^{m}y((t+t_n)+s_j)\right\}\\ &\le U(x;t_1,\dots,t_n)+U(y;s_1,\dots,s_m),\end{aligned}$$

so that

$$\begin{aligned}U(x+y;t_1+s_1,\dots,t_n+s_m)&\le U(x;t_1,\dots,t_n)\\ &\quad+U(y;s_1,\dots,s_m)\le p(x)+p(y)+\epsilon.\end{aligned}$$

Since $\epsilon > 0$ is arbitrary, it follows that $p(x+y) \le p(x)+p(y)$.

(γ'') Since, for every $a \ge 0$ and $x \in X$ we have, for every n, t and $t_1, \dots, t_n$,

$$\frac{1}{n}\sum_{i=1}^{n} ax(t+t_i) = a\left\{\frac{1}{n}\sum_{i=1}^{n} x(t+t_i)\right\},$$

it follows that $p(ax) = ap(x)$.

(δ'') Consider $x \in X$ and fix τ. For a given n, let $t_1 = \tau$, $t_2 = 2\tau, \dots$, $t_n = n\tau$. Then

$$\frac{1}{n}\sum_{j=1}^{n}[x(t+\tau+j\tau)-x(t+j\tau)] = \frac{1}{n}[x(t+(n+1)\tau)-x(t+\tau)] \le \frac{2M}{n},$$

where $M = \sup_t |x(t)|$. It follows that $p(x_\tau - x) \le \inf_n \dfrac{2M}{n} = 0$.

We now apply theorem 1, Sec. 2.9, to the above space X and functional p, where Y is the null space $\{0\}$. There is a linear functional $\varphi(x)$ on X such that $\varphi(x) \le p(x)$. We show that this is the required functional. By theorem 1, Sec. 2.9, φ satisfies (β'). Now, $\varphi(1) \le p(1) = 1$ and $\varphi(-1) \le p(-1) = -1$, so that $1 \ge \varphi(1) = -\varphi(-1) \ge 1$. Hence $\varphi(1) = 1$, so that (α') holds. Suppose $x = x(t) \ge 0$. Then $p(-x) \le 0$. Hence

$$\varphi(x) = -\varphi(-x) \ge -p(-x) \ge 0$$

so that (γ') holds. Consider any $x \in X$ and any τ. Now $\varphi(x_\tau - x) \le p(x_\tau - x) \le 0$. Moreover, $\varphi(x_\tau - x) = -\varphi(x - x_\tau) \ge -p(x - x_\tau) \ge 0$. Hence $\varphi(x_\tau) - \varphi(x) = \varphi(x_\tau - x) = 0$, so that ($\delta'$) holds.

We observe that in proving that p satisfies (β''), the t_i and s_j were interchanged. In other words, we used the fact that the group of rotations of the circle is abelian. The above argument cannot be applied to the group of rotations of a 2-sphere since it is not an abelian group. Indeed, Hausdorff showed that there is no non-trivial finitely additive invariant measure for all the subsets of the 2-sphere.

2.11 Banach Space, Dual Space

We now turn to a discussion of normed vector spaces. A **norm** is a non-negative real function on a vector space X, written $\|x\|$, such that

(a) $x \neq 0$ implies $\|x\| > 0$,
(b) $\|ax\| = |a| \, \|x\|$,
(c) $\|x + y\| \leq \|x\| + \|y\|$.

Thus the function p of theorem 3, Sec. 2.8, would be a norm if $x \neq 0$ implied $p(x) > 0$. Such a function on X is called a **seminorm.**

We present some simple properties of normed spaces.

First of all a normed space may be given a natural metric by means of

$$d(x, y) = \|x - y\|.$$

It is easy to verify that d is a metric. Moreover, it is an invariant metric, i.e., $d(x, y) = d(x + z, y + z)$.

The norm is then a continuous function on this metric space.

We leave these proofs to the reader.

Since a normed vector space X is a metric space, it has a completion $\tilde{X}$ as a metric space. It is easy to define vector space operations and a norm in $\tilde{X}$ so that it is a normed vector space in which X is a subspace.

A complete (with the associated metric) normed vector space is called a **Banach space.**

We give some examples of normed vector spaces, some of which are Banach spaces.

(a) The vector space $C[0, 1]$ with the norm

$$\|x\| = \max \, [|x(t)| : t \in [0, 1]]$$

is a Banach space.

(b) The vector space $P[0, 1]$ of polynomials on $[0, 1]$ with the norm

$$\|x\| = \max \, [|x(t)| : t \in [0, 1]]$$

is a normed vector space which is not complete.

(c) The vector space m of bounded sequences with the norm

$$\|x\| = \sup \, [|x_n| : n = 1, 2, \ldots]$$

is a Banach space.

(d) The vector space c of convergent sequences with the norm

$$\|x\| = \sup \, [|x_n| : n = 1, 2, \ldots]$$

is a Banach space.

(e) The vector space l_p, $p \geq 1$, of sequences for which $\sum_{n=1}^{\infty} |x_n|^p < \infty$ with the norm

$$\|x\| = \left[\sum_{n=1}^{\infty} |x_n|^p \right]^{1/p}$$

is a Banach space.

Let X and Y be normed vector spaces. Linear transformations T of X into Y have been defined in Sec. 2.1. Since X and Y are metric spaces, we may discuss the continuity of such transformations. We prove

PROPOSITION 1. If T is continuous at $x = 0$, then it is continuous everywhere and the continuity is uniform.

Proof. Since T is continuous at $x = 0$, for every $\epsilon > 0$ there is a $\delta > 0$ such that $\|x\| < \delta$ implies $\|Tx\| < \epsilon$. But for every $x \in X$, $\|x - y\| < \delta$ then implies $\|Tx - Ty\| = \|T(x - y)\| < \epsilon$.

The point $x = 0$ could be replaced by any other point of X. Thus a linear transformation is either uniformly continuous or everywhere discontinuous. We shall accordingly refer to the property simply as continuity.

We shall refer to a linear transformation T as **bounded** if there is an M such that $\|Tx\| \le M\,\|x\|$ for all $x \in X$.

PROPOSITION 2. T is bounded if and only if T is continuous.

Proof. Suppose T is bounded and M is a bound. Let $\epsilon > 0$ and $\delta = \epsilon/M$. Then $\|x\| < \delta$ implies $\|Tx\| < \epsilon$, so that T is continuous. Suppose T is continuous. Then there is a $\delta > 0$ such that $\|x\| = \delta$ implies $\|Tx\| < 1$. Let $x \in X$, then

$$\|Tx\| = \left\| T\left(\frac{\delta x}{\|x\|}\right) \right\| \cdot \frac{\|x\|}{\delta} < \frac{1}{\delta}\,\|x\|$$

so that T is bounded.

Now let T be a bounded linear transformation and let

$$\|T\| = \inf\,[M : \|Tx\| \le M\,\|x\|, \quad x \in X].$$

Then $\|T\|$ is called the **norm** or **bound** of T. Evidently, $\|Tx\| \le \|T\|\,\|x\|$ for every $x \in X$.

Let $B(X, Y)$ be the set of bounded linear transformations on X into Y. We shall show that $B(X, Y)$ is a normed vector space which is a Banach space if Y is a Banach space.

Let $T_1, T_2 \in B(X, Y)$. Define $T_1 + T_2$ by

$$(T_1 + T_2)(x) = T_1(x) + T_2(x)$$

and aT by

$$(aT)(x) = aT(x),$$

for every $x \in X$. Then

$$\|T_1 + T_2\| \le \|T_1\| + \|T_2\|$$

and

$$\|aT\| = |a|\,\|T\|.$$

These imply that $B(X, Y)$ is a vector space. Moreover, since $\|T\| = 0$ implies $T = 0$, it is a normed vector space.

Suppose now that Y is complete. Let $\{T_n\}$ be a Cauchy sequence in $B(X, Y)$. Then, for any $x \in X$,

$$\|T_m x - T_n x\| \leq \|T_m - T_n\| \, \|x\|,$$

so that $\{T_n x\}$ is a Cauchy sequence in Y. Since Y is complete we may define

$$Tx = \lim_n T_n x \quad \text{for } x \in X.$$

It is obvious that T is linear. Since $\{T_n\}$ is Cauchy, $\{\|T_n\|\}$ is bounded, i.e., there is an M such that $\|T_n\| \leq M$, $n = 1, 2, \ldots$. For every x, $\|T_n x\| \leq M\|x\|$. So, $\|Tx\| \leq M\|x\|$. Hence $T \in B(X, Y)$.

Let $\epsilon > 0$. Choose n_0 so that $\|T_m - T_n\| < \epsilon$ if $m, n > n_0$. Then

$$\|T_m x - T_n x\| < \epsilon \|x\| \text{ for } m, n > n_0, \quad x \in X.$$

Letting n converge to infinity, we get

$$\|T_m x - Tx\| \leq \epsilon \|x\| \text{ for } m > n_0, \quad x \in X.$$

This implies $\|T_m - T\| \leq \epsilon$ for $m > n_0$, so that $\{T_n\}$ converges to T in $B(X, Y)$.

In particular, if Y is one-dimensional, we write X' instead of $B(X, Y)$. If X is a normed vector space, the space X' of continuous linear functionals on X, with norm

$$\begin{aligned} \|x'\| &= \sup\,[|x'(x)| : \|x\| = 1] \\ &= \inf\,[M : |x'(x)| \leq M\|x\|, \quad x \in X] \end{aligned}$$

is called the **dual** of X. We then have the

COROLLARY. The dual of a normed vector space is a Banach space.

2.12 Hahn-Banach Theorem in Normed Space

In a normed vector space, the Hahn-Banach theorem (theorem 3, Sec. 2.8) assumes the following form.

PROPOSITION 1. If X is a normed vector space, Y a subspace of X, and f a bounded linear functional on Y with bound $\|f\|$, relative to Y, then f has a continuous linear extension to an $x' \in X'$ with $\|x'\| = \|f\|$.

Proof. By theorem 3, Sec. 2.8 with $p(x) = \|f\| \, \|x\|$.

The following proposition assures that X' is a total subspace of X^*.

PROPOSITION 2. For any $x \neq 0$ in X there is an $x' \in X'$ such that $x'(x) = \|x\|$ and $\|x'\| = 1$.

Proof. Let Y be the one-dimensional space generated by x, let $x'(ax) = a\,\|x\|$ and apply proposition 1.

So far, we have only given the Hahn-Banach theorem for real vector spaces. The theorem also holds for complex vector spaces. In proving the analog of proposition 1 for complex vector spaces, we first recall that every complex vector space is also a real vector space. Let f be a complex linear functional on the complex vector space X. Then

$$f(x) = f_1(x) + if_2(x),$$

where f_1 and f_2 are real linear functionals on the real vector space X.

Now, let X be a complex normed vector space, Y a subspace of X, and $f = f_1 + if_2$ a linear functional on Y. Then $f(ix) = f_1(ix) + if_2(ix)$ and $f(ix) = if(x) = -f_2(x) + if_1(x)$, so that $f_2(x) = -f_1(ix)$. Hence, $f(x) = f_1(x) - if_1(ix)$. We suppose that f is bounded on Y and let $\|f\|$ be its norm on Y. If $p(x) = \|f\| \cdot \|x\|$ on X, then $|f(x)| \leq p(x)$ on Y so that $|f_1(x)| \leq p(x)$ on Y. By proposition 1, f_1 may be extended to an F_1 such that $|F_1(x)| \leq p(x)$ on X. We consider the extension $F(x) = F_1(x) - iF_1(ix)$ of f to X. For every real φ,

$$|\mathrm{Re}\,(e^{i\varphi}F(x))| = |\mathrm{Re}\,F(e^{i\varphi}x)| = |F_1(e^{i\varphi}x)| \leq p(e^{i\varphi}x) = p(x).$$

But there is a real φ for which $\mathrm{Re}\,(e^{i\varphi}F(x)) = |F(x)|$. Hence $|F(x)| \leq p(x)$ on X, so that $\|F\| = \|f\|$. This proves the

PROPOSITION 3. If X is a complex normed vector space, and f is a continuous linear functional on Y, a subspace of X, then f may be extended to a continuous linear functional F on X such that $\|F\| = \|f\|$.

Proposition 2 readily yields a representation theorem for normed vector spaces.

PROPOSITION 4. For every normed vector space X there is a set A such that X is isomorphic with a subspace of the Banach space of bounded functions f on A with norm $\|f\| = \sup\,[|f(t)| : t \in A]$.

Proof. Let x_α, $\alpha \in A$, be a dense set in X. For every $\alpha \in A$, let $f(x, \alpha)$ be a linear functional on X such that

$$\|f(x, \alpha)\| = 1 \text{ and } f(x_\alpha, \alpha) = \|x_\alpha\|.$$

Now, for every $x \in X$, $x \neq 0$, and $\alpha \in A$, we have

$$1 = \|f(x, \alpha)\| \geq \frac{|f(x, \alpha)|}{\|x\|}$$

so that $\|x\| \geq |f(x, \alpha)|$. The function $[f(x, \alpha)]$, x fixed, $\alpha \in A$, is thus bounded. Let φ be defined on X by

$$\varphi(x) = [f(x, \alpha)].$$

Then evidently $\varphi(x + y) = \varphi(x) + \varphi(y)$ and $\varphi(ax) = a\varphi(x)$. We need only show that

$$\|x\| = \sup [|f(x, \alpha)| : \alpha \in A]$$

in order to complete the proof that φ is a norm preserving isomorphism. We already know that $\|x\| \geq \sup [|f(x, \alpha)| : \alpha \in A]$. Now,

$$\big|\, |f(x_\alpha, \alpha)| - \|x\| \,\big| = \big|\, \|x_\alpha\| - \|x\| \,\big| \leq \|x_\alpha - x\|$$

and

$$\big|\, |f(x, \alpha)| - |f(x_\alpha, \alpha)| \,\big| \leq |f(x, \alpha) - f(x_\alpha, \alpha)| \leq \|x_\alpha - x\|,$$

so that

$$\big|\, |f(x, \alpha)| - \|x\| \,\big| \leq 2\, \|x_\alpha - x\|.$$

Since, for every $\epsilon > 0$ there is an $\alpha \in A$ such that $\|x_\alpha - x\| < \epsilon$, it follows that $\|x\| \leq \sup [|f(x, \alpha)| : \alpha \in A]$. This completes the proof.

This theorem also follows from the imbedding of X in X'', with the unit sphere of X' as A (see Sec. 2.17), but this proof does not yield the interesting

COROLLARY. If X is a separable normed vector space, X is isomorphic to a subspace of the Banach space m of bounded sequences with the norm $\|x\| = \sup [|x_n| : n = 1, 2, \ldots]$.

As another application of the Hahn-Banach theorem we have

PROPOSITION 5. If X is an infinite dimensional Banach space, then $\dim X \geq c$.

Proof. Let x_1' be a non-zero continuous linear functional on X and let Z_1 be its null space. The existence of such a functional is assured by proposition 2. Let $x_1 \in X \sim Z_1$ with $\|x_1\| = 1$. The subspace Z_1 has deficiency 1 and so is also infinite dimensional. Let x_2' be a non-zero continuous linear functional on Z_1 and let Z_2 be its null space. Let $x_2 \in Z_1 \sim Z_2$ be such that $\|x_2\| = \frac{1}{2}$. By induction, we obtain a sequence $\{x_n\}$ such that, for every n, $\|x_n\| = 1/2^{n-1}$, and a decreasing sequence of closed subspaces

$$X \supset Z_1 \supset Z_2 \supset \ldots \supset Z_n \supset \ldots$$

such that, for every n, $x_1, \ldots, x_n \notin Z_n$.

We now establish a vector space isomorphism between the vector space m of bounded sequences and a subspace of X. Let $\{a_n\} \in m$. The series $\sum_{n=1}^{\infty} a_n x_n$ has as its sequence of partial sums a Cauchy sequence and so, since X is complete, it converges. The mapping

$$\varphi : \{a_n\} \to \sum_{n=1}^{\infty} a_n x_n$$

is clearly a vector space homomorphism of m into X. In order to show that it is an isomorphism, we must show that $\sum_{n=1}^{\infty} a_n x_n = 0$ implies all the $a_n = 0$. Now, $\sum_{n=1}^{\infty} a_n x_n = 0$ implies $a_1 x_1 = \sum_{n=2}^{\infty} -a_n x_n$, $\sum_{n=2}^{\infty} -a_n x_n \in Z_1$ but $x_1 \notin Z_1$. Hence $\sum_{n=2}^{\infty} -a_n x_n = 0$ and $a_1 = 0$. In similar fashion $a_2 = a_3 = \ldots = 0$. This proves that the dimension of X is at least as great as that of m.

It remains to be shown that m has dimension c. For every $\xi \in (0, 1)$ the sequence $(\xi, \xi^2, \ldots, \xi^n, \ldots)$ is in m. It is easy to show that these sequences are linearly independent. Hence $\dim m \geq c$. But the cardinality of m is c.

2.13 Uniform Boundedness Principle, Applications

We turn now to one of the most important properties of Banach spaces, the so-called principle of **uniform boundedness.** Although this principle was discovered by Lebesgue in 1908 in investigations on Fourier series, it was isolated as a general principle by Banach and Steinhaus. It states that if $\{f_n\}$ is a sequence of continuous linear functionals and, for every $x \in X$, the sequence $\{|f_n(x)|\}$ is bounded, then the sequence $\{\|f_n\|\}$ of norms is bounded.

We first observe that this is not true for every normed vector space X. For this, let X be the space of polynomials $x = x(t) = \sum_{n=0}^{\infty} a_n t^n$ where $a_n = 0$ for all $n > N(x)$, with $\|x\| = \max [|a_n|, n = 1, 2, \ldots]$. Let $f_n(x) = \sum_{k=0}^{n-1} a_k$. The functions f_n are continuous linear functionals on X. Moreover, for every $x = a_0 + a_1 t + \ldots + a_m t^m$, it is clear that for every n, $|f_n(x)| \leq (m + 1) \|x\|$, so that $\{|f_n(x)|\}$ is bounded. On the other hand, $\|f_n\| \geq n$, since for $x = 1 + t + \ldots + t^{n-1}$, $\|x\| = 1$ and $|f_n(x)| = n$. Hence $\{\|f_n\|\}$ is unbounded. We now state

THEOREM 1. If X is a Banach space, and $\{f_n(x)\}$ a sequence of continuous linear functionals on X such that $\{|f_n(x)|\}$ is bounded for every $x \in X$, then the sequence $\{\|f_n\|\}$ is bounded.

Proof. For every m, let $X_m \subset X$ be the set of all x such that $|f_n(x)| \leq m$ for all n. Then X_m, as the intersection of closed sets, is closed. Moreover, $X = \bigcup_{m=1}^{\infty} X_m$, so that, since X, as a complete metric space, is of the second category, some X_m contains a sphere. There is thus an $x_0 \in X$ and a $k > 0$ such that $\|x - x_0\| \leq k$ implies $|f_n(x)| \leq m$ for every n. Since $\{|f_n(x_0)|\}$ is bounded, there is a p such that $\|x\| \leq k$ implies $|f_n(x)| \leq m + p$ for every n, so that $\|f_n\| \leq \dfrac{m+p}{k}$ for every n.

Theorem 1 also holds for linear transformations from a Banach space X to a normed vector space Y. The proof is almost identical and will be omitted.

THEOREM 1′. If X is a Banach space, Y a normed vector space, and $\{T_n\}$ a sequence of continuous linear transformations on X into Y such that for every $x \in X$ the sequence $\{\|T_n(x)\|\}$ is bounded, then the sequence $\{\|T_n\|\}$ of norms is bounded.

An interesting application of the principle of uniform boundedness is to a proof that there are continuous functions of period 2π whose Fourier series diverge at a given point. For this purpose, let X be the Banach space of such functions with $\|x\| = \max |x(t)|$. The nth partial sum of the Fourier series of $x = x(t)$ at $t = 0$ may be written in the form

$$f_n(x) = \frac{1}{2\pi} \int_0^{2\pi} x(t) D_n(t)\, dt,$$

where

$$D_n(t) = \frac{\sin (n + \frac{1}{2})t}{\sin \frac{1}{2}t}.$$

Now, for each $x \in X$,

$$|f_n(x)| \leq \frac{1}{2\pi} \int_0^{2\pi} |D_n(t)|\, dt \cdot \|x\|.$$

Evidently, f_n is linear and it is bounded with

$$\|f_n\| \leq \frac{1}{2\pi} \int_0^{2\pi} |D_n(t)|\, dt.$$

Let y be the function which is $+1$ for those t for which $D_n(t) \geq 0$ and which is -1 for those t for which $D_n(t) < 0$. For every $\epsilon > 0$, y may be modified to a continuous x of norm 1 so that

$$\left| f_n(x) - \frac{1}{2\pi} \int_0^{2\pi} |D_n(t)|\, dt \right| = \frac{1}{2\pi} \left| \int_0^{2\pi} (x(t) - y(t)) D_n(t)\, dt \right| < \epsilon.$$

It follows that

$$\|f_n\| = \frac{1}{2\pi} \int_0^{2\pi} |D_n(t)|\, dt.$$

We show that the sequence

$$\left\{ \int_0^{2\pi} \left| \frac{\sin (n + \frac{1}{2})t}{\sin \frac{1}{2}t} \right| dt \right\}$$

is unbounded. Since $\sin u \leq u$, $0 \leq u \leq \pi$, this follows if we show that

$$\left\{ \int_0^{\pi} \left| \frac{\sin (2n + 1)u}{u} \right| du \right\}$$

is unbounded. Now,

$$\int_0^{\pi} \left| \frac{\sin (2n+1)u}{u} \right| du = \sum_{k=0}^{2n} \int_{\frac{k\pi}{2n+1}}^{\frac{(k+1)\pi}{2n+1}} \left| \frac{\sin (2n+1)u}{u} \right| du$$

$$\geq \sum_{k=0}^{2n} \frac{2n+1}{(k+1)\pi} \int_{\frac{k\pi}{2n+1}}^{\frac{(k+1)\pi}{2n+1}} |\sin (2n+1)u| \, du$$

$$= \sum_{k=0}^{2n} \frac{1}{(k+1)\pi} \int_{k\pi}^{(k+1)\pi} |\sin x| \, dx = \frac{2}{\pi} \sum_{k=0}^{2n} \frac{1}{k+1}.$$

But the series $\sum_{n=1}^{\infty} \frac{1}{n}$ diverges, so that the assertion is proved.

Thus, the sequence $\{\|f_n\|\}$ is unbounded. By theorem 1, there is thus an $x \in X$ whose Fourier series diverges at $t = 0$.

The uniform boundedness theorem has a similar application to interpolation theory. For any function x defined on the interval [0, 1] and any partition

$$0 \leq t_1 < t_2 < \ldots < t_n \leq 1$$

of [0, 1], there is a polynomial of degree $n - 1$ which interpolates to x at the given points, i.e., takes the values $x(t_i)$ at t_i, $i = 1, \ldots, n$. This is called the Lagrange interpolation polynomial and is given by

$$L_{t_1 \ldots t_n}(x, t) = \sum_{i=1}^{n} x(t_i) \frac{(t - t_1) \ldots (t - t_{i-1})(t - t_{i+1}) \ldots (t - t_n)}{(t_i - t_1) \ldots (t_i - t_{i-1})(t_i - t_{i+1}) \ldots (t_i - t_n)}.$$

Consider any sequence of partitions

$$(*) \qquad \begin{array}{l} t_{1,1} \\ t_{2,1}, t_{2,2} \\ \quad \cdot \quad \cdot \quad \cdot \\ t_{n,1}, t_{n,2}, \ldots, t_{n,n} \\ \quad \cdot \quad \cdot \quad \cdot \end{array}$$

and the corresponding sequence of polynomials

$$(**) \qquad L_{t_{n,1} t_{n,2} \ldots t_{n,n}}(x, t).$$

THEOREM 2. For every choice of (*) there is an $x \in C[0, 1]$ for which (**) does not converge uniformly to x.

Proof. Denote by $l^{(i)}_{t_1 \ldots t_n}(t)$ the fraction appearing in the ith term of $L_{t_1 \ldots t_n}(x, t)$. Let

$$\lambda_{t_1 \ldots t_n}(t) = \sum_{i=1}^{n} |l^{(i)}_{t_1 \ldots t_n}(t)|.$$

The mapping $f \to L_{t_1 \ldots t_n}(f)$ is a linear transformation of $C[0, 1]$ into itself and

$$|L_{t_1 \ldots t_n}(x, t)| \leq \|f\| \cdot \lambda_{t_1 \ldots t_n}(t), \text{ for every } t \in [0, 1].$$

It follows that this transformation is bounded and that its norm does not exceed

$$\Lambda_{t_1 \ldots t_n} = \sup\,[\lambda_{t_1 \ldots t_n}(t) : t \in [0, 1]].$$

We show that its norm is precisely $\Lambda_{t_1 \ldots t_n}$. Since $\lambda_{t_1 \ldots t_n}$ is continuous on $[0, 1]$, there is $\xi \in [0, 1]$ such that

$$\Lambda_{t_1 \ldots t_n} = \lambda_{t_1 \ldots t_n}(\xi).$$

Let

$$x(t_i) = \operatorname{sgn} l^{(i)}_{t_1 \ldots t_n}(\xi), \quad i = 1, \ldots, n,$$

and let x be linear on the intervals $[t_i, t_{i+1}]$ and constant on $[0, t_1]$ and $[t_n, 1]$. Then $x \in C[0, 1]$, $\|x\| = 1$, and

$$L_{t_1 \ldots t_n}(x, \xi) = \sum_{i=1}^{n} \operatorname{sgn} l^{(i)}_{t_1 \ldots t_n}(\xi) \cdot l^{(i)}_{t_1 \ldots t_n}(\xi)$$

$$= \lambda_{t_1 \ldots t_n}(\xi) = \Lambda_{t_1 \ldots t_n}.$$

This proves the norm of the transformation is $\Lambda_{t_1 \ldots t_n}$. Corresponding to (*) we have the sequence of norms $\Lambda_{t_{1,1}}, \Lambda_{t_{2,1}t_{2,2}}, \ldots$.

It is a fact, which in this case is not easy to prove (for a proof see Natanson [1], p. 370) that

$$\Lambda_{t_{k,1} \ldots t_{k,k}} > \frac{\log k}{8\pi}.$$

Thus our sequence of operators is unbounded and the theorem follows by theorem 1′.

Closely related to the principle of uniform boundedness is the so-called principle of the **condensation of singularities.** In its classical form, this says that under certain conditions, if for every point t_0 in a set S, there is a function x, in a given set X of functions, which has a singularity at $t = t_0$, then there is an $x \in X$ which has the singularity at every $t \in S$. The easiest case is that for which S is countable. This principle has been made precise in terms of linear operators on a Banach space for this case.

THEOREM 3. Let X be a Banach space and Y a normed vector space. For every $m = 1, 2, \ldots$, let $\{T_n(x, m)\}$ be a sequence of continuous linear operators on X with values in Y such that for every m there is an $x_m \in X$ for which $\overline{\lim_n} \|T_n(x_m, m)\| = +\infty$. Then there is an $x \in X$ for which $\overline{\lim_n} \|T_n(x, m)\| = +\infty$, $m = 1, 2, \ldots$.

Proof. We show that for every m, n and k, the set X_{mnk} of points $x \in X$ for which $\|T_\nu(x, m)\| > k$, for some $\nu > n$, is a dense open set. It is open since $X_{mnk} = \bigcup [Y_{m\nu k} : \nu > n]$, where $Y_{m\nu k}$ is the set for which $\|T_\nu(x, m)\| > k$, and every $Y_{m\nu k}$ is evidently open. That X_{mnk} is dense in X follows since for every real a and $x \in X$,

$$\|T_\nu(x + ax_m, m)\| \geq |a| \, \|T_\nu(x_m, m)\| - \|T_\nu(x, m)\|$$

so that either $\|T_\nu(x, m)\| > k$ or else $\|T_\nu(x + ax_m, m)\| > k$ for some $\nu > n$. Hence X_{mnk}, as a dense open set, is residual (i.e., its complement is of the first category in X). But the set

$$\bigcap [X_{mnk} : m, n, k = 1, 2, \ldots]$$

consists of those $x \in X$ for which $\overline{\lim}_n \|T_n(x, m)\| = +\infty$ for every m. Since this set is also residual and X is of the second category, the theorem is proved.

We prove a variant of this theorem, but first obtain the

Lemma 1. If X is a Banach space and Y is a subspace of X which is a Borel set, then Y is either of the first category in X or is identical with X.

Proof. Suppose Y is of the second category in X. By a theorem of Banach and Blumberg (see Chapter 1, exercise 10.2), there is an open sphere S in X such that Y meets every subsphere of S in a set of the second category. Since Y is a subspace of X, the sphere S may be taken with center 0 and radius, say, $r > 0$. Moreover, since Y is a Borel set, it has the property of Baire (see Kuratowski [1]), which means here that it is residual in S. Since $0 \in S$, it follows that $x \in S$ implies $x \in x + S$, so that $S \cap (x + S)$ is non-empty. Let T be a sphere, center x, such that $T \subset S \cap (x + S)$. But then both Y and $x + Y$ are residual relative to T, so that $Y \cap (x + Y)$ is non-empty. There is thus a $y \in Y$ such that $y - x \in Y$. Since Y is a vector space, this implies $x \in Y$. Hence $S \subset Y$ and, since Y is a vector space,

$$X = \bigcup_{n=1}^{\infty} nS \subset Y.$$

We now prove

Theorem 3′. Let X be a Banach space and Y a normed vector space. For every $m = 1, 2, \ldots$, let $\{T_n(x, m)\}$ be a sequence of continuous linear operators on X with values in Y such that, for every m, there is an $x_m \in X$ for which $\{T_n(x_m, m)\}$ does not converge. Then there is an $x \in X$ for which $\{T_n(x, m)\}$ does not converge for any $m = 1, 2, \ldots$.

Proof. The set X_m of points $x \in X$ for which $\{T_n(x, m)\}$ converges is easily seen to be a proper subspace and a Borel set, so that, by lemma 1, and the hypothesis, it is of the first category. But then there is an $x \in X$, $x \notin \bigcup_{m=1}^{\infty} X_m$ and the theorem is proved.

The above two principles are usually used together. Thus, by the principle of uniform boundedness, we showed that there are continuous functions whose Fourier series diverge at a single point. By then applying the principle of the condensation of singularities, we can show the existence of continuous functions whose Fourier expansions diverge on a dense (countable) set in $[0, 2\pi]$. The details of this and other similar applications are now easy to supply. It is worth mentioning that it is now not hard to show that there is a continuous function whose Fourier series diverges except at the points of a subset of $[0, 2\pi]$ of the first category.

2.14 Lemma of F. Riesz, Applications

If X is a finite dimensional normed vector space and Y is a proper subspace of X, then there is a point x_1 on the unit sphere of X, i.e., $\|x_1\| = 1$, such that the distance of x_1 from Y is one;

$$\inf\,[\|x - x_1\| : x \in Y] = 1.$$

This observation is intuitively evident and is, indeed, easy to prove. However, if the assumption of finite dimensionality is dropped, the conclusion no longer holds in general, as the following example shows.

Let X be the subspace of $C[0, 1]$ which consists of those functions x for which $x(0) = 0$. Let Y be the subspace of X whose elements satisfy

$$\int_0^1 x(t)\,dt = 0.$$

Clearly, Y is a closed subspace of X. Now, if $x_1 \in X$ and $\|x_1\| = \sup\,[|x_1(t)| : t \in [0, 1]] = 1$, then necessarily

$$\left|\int_0^1 x_1(t)\,dt\right| < 1,$$

because x_1 is continuous and $x_1(0) = 0$. We shall show that this conclusion is contradicted if it is assumed that $\|x - x_1\| \geq 1$ for all $x \in Y$. In fact for any $y \in X$, with $\|y\| = 1$, we would have

$$\left|\int_0^1 y(t)\,dt\right| \leq \left|\int_0^1 x_1(t)\,dt\right|.$$

This is obvious for $y \in Y$, and if $y \notin Y$, then we can form

$$x_1 - \frac{\int_0^1 x_1(t)\,dt}{\int_0^1 y(t)\,dt}\,y,$$

which is in Y, and so

$$1 \leq \left\| x_1 - \left(x_1 - \frac{\int_0^1 x_1(t)\,dt}{\int_0^1 y(t)\,dt}\,y \right) \right\| = \frac{\left|\int_0^1 x_1(t)\,dt\right|}{\left|\int_0^1 y(t)\,dt\right|}.$$

The contradiction follows from the observation that y may be chosen in such a way that $\left|\int_0^1 y(t)\,dt\right|$ is arbitrarily close to 1.

A result which holds in a general normed vector space is the

PROPOSITION 1. If Y is a closed proper subspace of X and $\epsilon > 0$, there is an x_ϵ on the unit sphere such that

$$\inf\,[\|x_0 - x_\epsilon\| : x_0 \in Y] > 1 - \epsilon.$$

Proof. Let $x \in X \sim Y$ and put

$$d = \inf\,[\|x - x_0\| : x_0 \in Y].$$

Since Y is closed, $d > 0$. Choose $y_0 \in Y$ so that

$$d \leq \|y_0 - x\| < d(1 + \epsilon)$$

and put

$$x_\epsilon = -\frac{y_0 - x}{\|y_0 - x\|}.$$

It is clear that $\|x_\epsilon\| = 1$. If $x_0 \in Y$,

$$\|x_0 - x_\epsilon\| = \left\| x_0 + \frac{y_0 - x}{\|y_0 - x\|} \right\|$$

$$= \frac{1}{\|y_0 - x\|}\,\|(y_0 + \|y_0 - x\|\,x_0) - x\|$$

$$\geq \frac{d}{\|y_0 - x\|} > \frac{d}{d(1 + \epsilon)} = 1 - \frac{\epsilon}{1 + \epsilon} > 1 - \epsilon.$$

This proposition has some interesting applications. If X is a normed vector space with the property that closed bounded sets are compact, then X is finite dimensional. For, if $x_1 \in X$ and x_1 does not generate X, there is x_2 with $\|x_2\| = 1$, so that $\|x_2 - x_1\| > \frac{1}{2}$. If x_1 and x_2 do not generate X, there is x_3 with $\|x_3\| = 1$, so that $\|x_3 - x_1\| > \frac{1}{2}$ and $\|x_3 - x_2\| > \frac{1}{2}$. This process must terminate, since otherwise we would obtain a sequence of points on the unit sphere which has no convergent subsequence, contrary to the assumed compactness of this set.

It is not hard to show that, conversely, the closed bounded sets in any finite dimensional normed vector space are compact. We may thus state the

PROPOSITION 2. A normed vector space is finite dimensional if and only if the closed bounded sets are compact.

A second application occurs in connection with the Baire classes of bounded functions, B_α, $\alpha < \omega_1$. We have noted that each B_α is a closed subspace of the space M of bounded functions and, hence, is a Banach space (see Sec. 1.7).

We consider now the class

$$B = \bigcup [B_\alpha : \alpha < \omega_0]$$

of all bounded functions of finite Baire type. Since each B_α, $\alpha < \omega_0$, is a closed proper subspace of B, hence is nowhere dense in B, it follows that B is of the first category in itself and so is not complete. Since the norm in M is the uniform norm, this conclusion may be stated as the

PROPOSITION 3. There is a uniformly convergent sequence of functions of finite Baire type whose limit is not of finite Baire type.

The limit is in $B_{\omega_0} \sim B$. The question arises whether every function in $B_{\omega_0} \sim B$ is the uniform limit of some sequence from B. The negative answer is obtained as follows.

Let $0 = a_0 < a_1 < \ldots < a_n < \ldots < 1$ and $\lim_{n\to\infty} a_n = 1$. Consider the Baire classes on $[a_{n-1}, a_n)$, say $B_\alpha^{(n)}$, $\alpha < \omega_1$. Each $B_\alpha^{(n)}$ is a closed proper subspace of the succeeding class $B_{\alpha+1}^{(n)}$. In particular, therefore, there exists a function f_n on $[a_{n-1}, a_n)$, of norm 1 in $B_n^{(n)}$, whose distance from $B_{n-1}^{(n)}$ exceeds $\frac{1}{2}$.

Let g_m, $m = 1, 2, 3, \ldots$, be defined on $[0, 1]$ by $g_m = f_1$ on $[a_0, a_1)$, $g_m = f_2$ on $[a_1, a_2), \ldots, g_m = f_m$ on $[a_{m-1}, a_m)$, and $g_m = 0$ on $[a_m, 1]$. The sequence $\{g_m\}$ converges on $[0, 1]$ to a function g.

If $f \in B$ then, for some n, $f \in B_n$, so that

$$\|g - f\| \geq \sup [|g(t) - f(t)| : t \in [a_n, a_{n+1})] > \tfrac{1}{2}.$$

Thus g is not the uniform limit of any sequence in B.

That $g \in B_{\omega_0}$ is a consequence of the fact that each g_m is of finite Baire type, a fact which is not hard to verify.

2.15 Application to Compact Transformations

We give some applications of proposition 1 of the last section to the theory of compact (completely continuous) operators.

Let X and Y be Banach spaces. A linear transformation T on X into Y is called **compact** if every bounded set in X is taken by T into a set whose closure is compact.

We give an example of a compact operator. Let $X = C[a, b]$. Let K be a continuous real function on $[a, b] \times [a, b]$. Define T by means of

$$Tf(x) = \int_a^b K(x, y) f(y)\, dy.$$

Then T is a linear operator on X into X.

Let $\epsilon > 0$. There is a $\delta > 0$ such that $|x_1 - x_2| < \delta$, $y \in [a, b]$ implies $|K(x_1, y) - K(x_2, y)| < \dfrac{\epsilon}{b - a}$, so that

$$\int_a^b |K(x_1, y) - K(x_2, y)|\, dy < \epsilon.$$

Thus

$$|Tf(x_1) - Tf(x_2)| \leq \int_a^b |K(x_1, y) - K(x_2, y)|\, |f(y)|\, dy$$
$$\leq \epsilon\, \|f\|$$

whenever $|x_1 - x_2| < \delta$. This means that if B is any bounded set in $C[0, 1]$, the set $TB = [Tf : f \in B]$ is equicontinuous. It then follows that T is a compact operator.

We have already discussed the Banach space $B(X, Y)$ of bounded transformations of a Banach space X into a Banach space Y. It is clear that a compact transformation is bounded. We consider the subset $C(X, Y) \subset B(X, Y)$ of compact transformations. $C(X, Y)$ is easily seen to be a vector space. We show that it is a closed subspace of $B(X, Y)$, whereby we have

PROPOSITION 1. $C(X, Y)$ is a Banach space.

Proof. Let T_n, $n = 1, 2, \ldots$ be a sequence of compact transformations which converges in $B(X, Y)$ to a transformation T, let $\{x_n\}$ be such that $x_n \in X$, $\|x_n\| \leq M$, $n = 1, 2, \ldots$. Then $\{x_n\}$ has a subsequence $\{x_{1,n}\}$ such that $\{T_1 x_{1,n}\}$ is Cauchy; $\{x_{1,n}\}$ has a subsequence $\{x_{2,n}\}$ such that $\{T_2 x_{2,n}\}$ is Cauchy. Continuing in this way and taking the diagonal sequence $y_n = x_{n,n}$, we obtain a subsequence $\{y_n\}$ of $\{x_n\}$ such that $\{T_m y_n\}$, $m = 1, 2, \ldots$ are all Cauchy sequences. Let $\epsilon > 0$. There is an m such that $\|T - T_m\| < \epsilon/4M$. Let N be such that $n, k > N$ implies $\|T_m y_n - T_m y_k\| < \epsilon/2$. Then

$$\|Ty_n - Ty_k\| \leq \|T - T_m\|\, \|y_n\| + \|T - T_m\|\, \|y_k\|$$
$$+ \|T_m y_n - T_m y_k\| < \epsilon,$$

so that $\{Ty_n\}$ is Cauchy.

We next define the adjoint of a transformation of X into Y. Let X' be the dual of X and Y' the dual of Y. Then X' and Y' are Banach spaces. Let $T \in B(X, Y)$. The **adjoint** T^* of T is a transformation $T^* \in B(Y', X')$ defined as follows: T^*y', $y' \in Y'$, is the element of X' which for each $x \in X$ has the value

$$(T^*y')(x) = y'(Tx).$$

It is easy to see that $T^* \in B(Y', X')$ and $\|T^*\| = \|T\|$. Moreover, if $T \in C(X, Y)$, it can be shown that $T^* \in C(Y', X')$ but we do not give the proof.

We now give two applications to compact operators of the proposition 1, Sec. 2.14.

PROPOSITION 2. If $T \in C(X, X)$, X a Banach space, the vector space of solutions of $x - Tx = 0$ is finite dimensional.

Proof. Suppose, on the contrary, that the equation has an infinite set x_n, $n = 1, 2, \ldots$ of linearly independent solutions. For every n, let X_n be the vector space spanned by $x_1, \ldots, x_n$.

For every $n > 1$, there is, by proposition 1, Sec. 14, a $y_n \in X_n$ such that $\|y_n\| = 1$ and $\|y_n - x\| > \frac{1}{2}$ for every $x \in X_{n-1}$. Now, $y_n = Ty_n$, $n = 1, 2, \ldots$, implies that $\{y_n\}$ has a Cauchy subsequence, contradicting the assertion that $\|y_m - y_n\| > \frac{1}{2}$, $m \neq n$.

We next consider the equation

$$x - \lambda Tx = 0.$$

A real number λ_0 is called a **characteristic number** of the equation if $x - \lambda_0 Tx = 0$ has a non-zero solution.

PROPOSITION 3. If $T \in C(X, X)$, the set of characteristic numbers of

$$x - \lambda Tx = 0$$

is an isolated set.

Proof. Let $\{\lambda_n\}$ be a sequence of distinct characteristic numbers and let $x_n \neq 0$, $x_n = \lambda_n Tx_n$, $n = 1, 2, \ldots$.

We show the x_n, $n = 1, 2, \ldots$, are linearly independent. Suppose

$$x_{n+1} = \sum_{i=1}^{n} a_i x_i.$$

Then

$$x_{n+1} = \lambda_{n+1} Tx_{n+1} = \sum_{i=1}^{n} \lambda_{n+1} a_i Tx_i$$

so that

$$x_{n+1} = \sum_{i=1}^{n} a_i \frac{\lambda_{n+1}}{\lambda_i} x_i.$$

It follows that

$$\sum_{i=1}^{n} a_i \left(1 - \frac{\lambda_{n+1}}{\lambda_i}\right) x_i = 0,$$

so that, since each $\lambda_{n+1}/\lambda_i \neq 1$, the $x_1, \ldots, x_n$ are linearly dependent. Consequently, x_1 is linearly dependent, which is a contradiction.

Now, for every $n = 1, 2, \ldots$, let X_n be the vector space spanned by $x_1, \ldots, x_n$. We note that $X_{n+1} \supset X_n$, where the inclusion is proper and X_n is closed. There is $y_{n+1} \in X_{n+1}$, $\|y_{n+1}\| = 1$ and $\|y_{n+1} - x\| > \frac{1}{2}$ for every $x \in X_n$, $n = 1, 2, \ldots$. Suppose $\{\lambda_n\}$ converges. Then since $\{\lambda_n y_n\}$ is bounded, $\{T(\lambda_n y_n)\}$ has a convergent subsequence.

But

$$\|T(\lambda_n y_n) - T(\lambda_m y_m)\| = \|y_n - (y_n - T(\lambda_n y_n) + T(\lambda_m y_m))\|$$

and $y_n \in X_n$ implies

$$y_n - \lambda_n T(y_n) = \sum_{i=1}^{n} a_i x_i - \sum_{i=1}^{n} \lambda_n \frac{a_i}{\lambda_i} x_i$$

$$= \sum_{i=1}^{n-1} a_i \left(1 - \frac{\lambda_n}{\lambda_i}\right) x_i \in X_{n-1},$$

and $T(\lambda_m y_m) \in X_m$. Hence, if $m < n$, $y_n - T(\lambda_n y_n) + T(\lambda_m y_m) \in X_{n-1}$, so that $\|T(\lambda_n y_n) - T(\lambda_m y_m)\| > \frac{1}{2}$. This contradicts the assertion that $\{T(\lambda_n y_n)\}$ has a convergent subsequence.

2.16 Applications, Weak Convergence, Summability Methods, Approximate Integration

The point-wise convergence of functionals is a type of convergence which is important in many applications. Various such notions of "weak" convergence and "weak" topology arise naturally in vector space theory and have extensive application. In this section we shall give a characterization of weak convergence for bounded linear functionals on a Banach space X and indicate some applications.

If X is a normed vector space and $x'_n \in X'$, $n = 1, 2, 3, \ldots$, we say that x'_n **converges weakly** to $x' \in X'$ if for each $x \in X$, $\lim_{n\to\infty} x'_n(x) = x'(x)$.

We shall call a subset of X **total** if its closed linear span is X.

PROPOSITION 1. If X is a Banach space, then $\{x'_n\}$ converges weakly to x' in X' if and only if the sequence $\{\|x'_n\|\}$ of norms is bounded and $\lim_n x'_n(x) = x'(x)$ for every x in some total subset of X.

Proof. (Sufficiency) If $x \in X$ and $\epsilon > 0$, we may choose a finite linear combination x_0 of elements in the total subset so that

$$\|x - x_0\| < \frac{\epsilon}{4M}$$

where M is an upper bound for the numbers $\|x'_n\| + \|x'\|$, $n = 1, 2, 3, \ldots$. For n sufficiently large

$$|x'_n(x_0) - x'(x_0)| < \frac{\epsilon}{2}.$$

For such indices n, we then obtain

$$\begin{aligned}|x'_n(x) - x'(x)| &\leq |x'_n(x) - x'_n(x_0)| + |x'_n(x_0) - x'(x_0)| \\ &\quad + |x'(x_0) - x'(x)| \\ &\leq \|x'_n\|\,\|x - x_0\| + \frac{\epsilon}{2} + \|x'\|\,\|x - x_0\| < \epsilon.\end{aligned}$$

(Necessity) If x'_n converges weakly to x', then in particular $[x'_n(x) : n = 1, 2, \ldots]$ is a bounded set of numbers for each $x \in X$. By the principle of uniform boundedness the sequence $\{\|x'_n\|\}$ is bounded.

We should remark that in the necessity, as we stated it, we have assumed the continuity of the limiting linear functional x'. But this is in fact a consequence of the existence of $\lim_n x'_n(x)$ for each $x \in X$.

Applying the above result we may obtain a basic theorem in the theory of divergent sequences. A matrix method of summability is characterized by a doubly infinite matrix

$$\mathcal{A} = \begin{pmatrix} a_{11} & a_{12} & \ldots & a_{1n} & \ldots \\ a_{21} & a_{22} & \ldots & a_{2n} & \ldots \\ & & \ldots & & \\ a_{m1} & a_{m2} & \ldots & a_{mn} & \ldots \\ & & \ldots & & \end{pmatrix}.$$

A sequence $x = (x_1, x_2, \ldots)$ is said to have $\mathcal{A}$-limit $= A(x)$ if for each $i = 1, 2, 3, \ldots$, the sum

$$A_i(x) = \sum_{k=1}^{\infty} a_{ik} x_k$$

is convergent and $\lim_i A_i(x) = A(x)$.

The method $\mathcal{A}$ is said to be **regular** if for every convergent sequence x, the $\mathcal{A}$-limit exists and equals the ordinary limit of the sequence x. We shall prove a characterization, due to O. Toeplitz, of regular methods.

THEOREM 1. $\mathcal{A}$ is regular if and only if

(i) $\sum_{k=1}^{\infty} |a_{ik}| \leq M$, $i = 1, 2, \ldots$, for some M,

(ii) $\lim_i a_{ik} = 0$, $k = 1, 2, \ldots$

(iii) $\lim_i \sum_{k=1}^{\infty} a_{ik} = 1$.

Proof. The class of all convergent sequences is a Banach space c under $\|x\| = \sup |x_i|$. Suppose $\mathcal{A}$ is regular. Then the series $\sum_{k=1}^{\infty} a_{ik} x_k$ converges for each $x \in c$, $i = 1, 2, \ldots$. The partial sums $\sum_{k=1}^{n} a_{ik}x_k$ are clearly bounded linear functionals on c and the last remark amounts to the weak convergence in c' of the partial sums. Thus the limits A_i are in c' and have uniformly bounded norms, $\|A_i\| \leq M$ for all $i = 1, 2, \ldots$, by proposition 1. Taking $x_k = \operatorname{sgn} a_{ik}$ for $k = 1, \ldots, N$ and $x_k = 0$, $k > N$ gives, for any N,

$$\sum_{k=1}^{N} |a_{ik}| \leq \|A_i\|, \quad i = 1, 2, \ldots.$$

Thus $\sum_{k=1}^{\infty} |a_{ik}| \leq M$, 1, 2, ..., proving the necessity of (i).

The choice $x = e_k = (0, 0, \ldots, 0, 1, 0, \ldots)$, with the 1 in the kth place, yields $A_i(x) = a_{ik}$ and the necessity of (ii) follows. Similarly, by choosing $x = e_0 = (1, 1, \ldots)$ we find $A_i(x) = \sum_{k=1}^{\infty} a_{ik}$ converges to 1, which completes the proof of necessity.

Suppose now that $\mathcal{A}$ has the three properties and, for a fixed i, consider the partial sum functionals

$$B_N(x) = \sum_{k=1}^{N} a_{ik}x_k, \quad N = 1, 2, 3, \ldots.$$

These functionals belong to c' and their norms are bounded by $\sum_{k=1}^{\infty} |a_{ik}|$. Whenever x is one of the points $e_0, e_1, e_2, \ldots$, the functionals converge as N increases. But these points form a total set in c, so that the B_N converge weakly and the limit functional $A_i(x) = \sum_{k=1}^{\infty} a_{ik}x_k$ is in c'.

The norms of the functionals A_i, $i = 1, 2, \ldots$, are bounded by M, by (i), and (ii), and (iii) express the fact that $\lim_i A_i(x)$ exists and equals the limit of the sequence x in case x is one of the points $e_0, e_1, e_2, \ldots$. Then this condition holds for any $x \in c$, which proves that $\mathcal{A}$ is regular.

We make a slight extension of the above result; $\mathcal{A}$ will be called **almost regular** if, for every convergent sequence $x = (x_1, x_2, \ldots)$, there is an N (which depends on x) such that, for every $m > N$, $\sum_{n=1}^{\infty} a_{mn}x_n$ converges and $\lim_{m\to\infty} \sum_{n=1}^{\infty} a_{mn}x_n = \lim_{n\to\infty} x_n$. We show that $\mathcal{A}$ is almost regular if and only if there is a fixed m_0 such that

(i) $\sum_{m=1}^{\infty} |a_{mn}| < M$ for fixed M and every $m > m_0$,

(ii) $\lim_m a_{mn} = 0$ for every n,

(iii) $\lim_m \sum_{n=1}^{\infty} a_{mn} = 1$.

This has the surprising implication that the above N may be taken to be independent of x. The proof depends upon the following lemma, whose proof we omit.

LEMMA 1. If $\{s_n^{(m)}\}$ is a sequence of sequences such that $\sum_{n=1}^{\infty} |s_n^{(m)}| = \infty$, $m = 1, 2, \ldots$, there is a sequence $\{t_n\}$, converging to zero, such that all the series $\sum_{n=1}^{\infty} s_n^{(m)} t_n$, $m = 1, 2, \ldots$, diverge.

The lemma implies there is an N such that $\sum_{n=1}^{\infty} |a_{mn}| < \infty$ for every $m > N$. Otherwise, there would be an $\{x_n\}$ converging to zero with infinitely many of the series $\sum_{n=1}^{\infty} a_{mn}x_n$ diverging, contrary to hypothesis.

For each $m > N$, let $E_m \subset c$ be the set of convergent sequences $x = (x_1, x_2, \ldots)$ for which $\sum_{n=1}^{\infty} a_{mn}x_n$ converges. Since $\sum_{n=1}^{\infty} |a_{mn}| < \infty$, it follows that E_m is a closed subspace of c. Let $S_m = \bigcap_{i=m}^{\infty} E_i$, $m = N + 1, N + 2 \ldots$. The S_m are closed subspaces of c such that

$$S_{N+1} \subset S_{N+2} \subset \ldots \subset S_m \subset \ldots.$$

Now, a closed subspace T of a Banach space X is either nowhere dense in X or else $T = X$. By hypothesis, $c = \bigcup_{m=N+1}^{\infty} S_m$. Since c is of the second category, there is an m_0 such that $c = S_{m_0}$.

It follows that $\mathcal{A}$, with its first $m_0 - 1$ rows removed, is regular and the result follows by theorem 1.

We make one further remark regarding matrix summability. Using theorem 1, it is not hard to show that if $\mathcal{A}$ is regular then there is a bounded sequence $x = \{x_n\}$ whose $\mathcal{A}$-limit does not exist. Let m be the vector space of bounded sequences with $\|x\| = \sup_n |x_n|$. It is easy to show that the subspace of m of sequences which are transformed by $\mathcal{A}$ into convergent sequences is a closed vector space. It is nowhere dense. Hence, there is no countable set of regular $\mathcal{A}_n$, $n = 1, 2, \ldots$ such that every bounded sequence is taken into a convergent one by at least one of the $\mathcal{A}_n$.

We give a second application of proposition 1.

Let $\alpha(t)$, $t \in [0, 1]$, be a non-decreasing function. The problem is to approximate $\int_0^1 x(t)\, d\alpha(t)$ by a sequence of finite sums of the form

$$S_n(x) = \sum_{k=1}^{k_n} a_{nk}x(t_{nk}), \quad n = 1, 2, \ldots,$$

where, for each n, $t_{nk} \in [0, 1]$, $k = 1, \ldots, k_n$, and $x \in C[0, 1]$.

A selection of points t_{nk} and coefficients a_{nk} determines a prospective method of approximate integration. If the choice yields the result

$$\lim_n S_n(x) = \int_0^1 x\, d\alpha$$

for every $x \in C[0, 1]$, then we have in fact a method of approximate integration. In other words, we require weak convergence on $C[0, 1]$ of the functionals S_n to the functional I given by

$$I(x) = \int_0^1 x\, d\alpha.$$

We shall say in this case that the method is convergent.

Various methods which suggest themselves, e.g., by integrating certain interpolating or approximating polynomials, have the property that $S_n(x) = I(x)$ whenever x is a polynomial of degree at most n, $n = 1, 2, 3, \ldots$. Such a condition serves to relate the numbers a_{nk} and the points t_{nk} by the system of equations

$$\int_0^1 t^i\, da = \sum_{k=1}^{k_n} a_{nk} t_{nk}^i, \quad i = 0, 1, \ldots, n.$$

Under the above condition, it makes sense to characterize the convergent methods by conditions on the coefficients a_{nk}. We have the

Proposition 2. The method $\{S_n\}$ satisfying $S_n(x) = I(x)$, whenever x is a polynomial whose degree does not exceed n, is convergent if and only if the sums

$$\sum_{k=1}^{k_n} |a_{nk}|, \quad n = 1, 2, 3, \ldots,$$

are bounded.

Proof. We note that

$$|S_n(x)| \leq \|x\| \sum_{k=1}^{k_n} |a_{nk}|.$$

It follows that S_n is in the dual of $C[0, 1]$, and $\|S_n\|$ is no greater than the above sum. A proper choice of x shows that $\|S_n\|$ equals the sum.

The result follows from proposition 1 since the polynomials are dense in $C[0, 1]$.

Corollary. If each $a_{nk} \geq 0$, the method is convergent.

Proof. Since $S_n(x) = I(x)$ for all n, if x is the function $x(t) = 1$, $t \in [0, 1]$, we have

$$S_n(1) = \sum_{k=1}^{k_n} a_{nk} = I(1), \quad n = 1, 2, 3, \ldots,$$

so that the sums in proposition 2 are bounded.

2.17 Second Dual Space

We discuss the second dual of a normed vector space briefly.

Let X be a normed vector space, and let X' be the dual of X. For every $x_0 \neq 0$ in X, consider the functional $\tilde{x}_0$ on X' defined by

$$\tilde{x}_0(x') = x'(x_0).$$

Then $\tilde{x}_0$ is a linear functional, since

$$\begin{aligned}\tilde{x}_0(ax' + by') &= (ax' + by')(x_0) = ax'(x_0) + by'(x_0)\\ &= a\tilde{x}_0(x') + b\tilde{x}_0(y').\end{aligned}$$

Moreover, $\tilde{x}_0$ is bounded, since $|\tilde{x}_0(x')| = |x'(x_0)| \leq \|x'\| \, \|x_0\|$. The norm of $\tilde{x}_0$ satisfies

$$\|\tilde{x}_0\| \leq \|x_0\|.$$

By proposition 2, Sec. 2.12, there is an $x' \in X'$ such that $x'(x_0) = \|x_0\|$ and $\|x'\| = 1$. Hence

$$|\tilde{x}_0(x')| = |x'(x_0)| = \|x_0\|.$$

It follows that

$$\|\tilde{x}_0\| = \|x_0\|.$$

The mapping

$$x \to \tilde{x}$$

of X into X'' is thus norm preserving.

X is said to be **reflexive** if $X = X''$, where equality is understood in the sense of isomorphism under the canonical mapping. Thus reflexivity occurs if and only if the above mapping carries X onto X''.

We shall see that there exist reflexive spaces—necessarily Banach spaces, since X'' is complete. Any incomplete space is of course non-reflexive, but there are also non-reflexive Banach spaces.

Examples of these possibilities will arise as we discuss cases of the following general question: Given a particular normed vector space, find a concrete representation of its dual (i.e., a specific Banach space which can be mapped isomorphically onto the dual space in question).

Before doing this, let us prove another useful consequence of the Hahn-Banach theorem.

PROPOSITION 1. If Y is a proper subspace of a normed vector space X and x_0 is at positive distance $d > 0$ from Y, i.e.,

$$d = \inf\,[\|x - x_0\| \, : x \in Y] > 0,$$

then there is an $x' \in X'$ such that $\|x'\| = 1$, x' vanishes at all points of Y and $x'(x_0) = d$. The hypotheses are fulfilled, in particular, if Y is closed and $x_0 \notin Y$.

Proof. Define f on $(Y \cup \{x_0\})$ by

$$f(x + ax_0) = ad, x \in Y.$$

Clearly, f is a linear functional on $(Y \cup \{x_0\})$ and the result will follow if we show that f is bounded with $\|f\| = 1$.

First, f is bounded with $\|f\| \leq 1$, i.e., $|f(x + ax_0)| = |a|\, d \leq \|x + ax_0\|$ for all $x \in Y$ and all a. This is obvious for $a = 0$ and, for $a \neq 0$, it follows from

$$\left\|\frac{x}{a} + x_0\right\| = \left\|-\frac{x}{a} - x_0\right\| \geq \inf\,[\|z - x_0\| : z \in Y] = d,$$

since $-x/a \in Y$.

Finally, $\|f\| \geq 1$. For if $\{x_n\}$ is a sequence in Y such that $\lim\limits_{n\to\infty} \|x_n - x_0\| = d$, then

$$\frac{|f(x_n - x_0)|}{\|x_n - x_0\|} = \frac{d}{\|x_n - x_0\|},$$

which converges to 1 as n goes to infinity. Thus

$$\|f\| = \sup\left[\frac{|f(z)|}{\|z\|} : z \in (Y \cup \{x_0\})\right] \geq 1.$$

A consequence of this result is that a Banach space X is either reflexive or its successive second dual spaces X'', X'''', . . . are all distinct. Namely, one can show that $X \neq X''$ implies $X' \neq X'''$ and then use an induction argument.

Another consequence of proposition 1 is the

PROPOSITION 2. If X' is separable, then X is separable.

(*Remark.* We shall see that the dual of l_1 is l_∞ and so, in view of the present proposition, l_1 is not reflexive. This example also shows that the converse of the proposition is false.)

Proof. Let $\{x'_n\}$ be a countable dense subset of the unit sphere in $X' : \|x'_n\| = 1, n = 1, 2, \ldots.$

For each n, choose an $x_n \in X$ with $\|x_n\| = 1$ and $|x'_n(x_n)| \geq \frac{3}{4}$. This is possible since $\|x'_n\| = 1$.

Let Y be the closed subspace of X generated by $x_1, x_2, \ldots.$ We shall show that $Y = X$, so that X is separable, since then the linear combinations, with rational coefficients, of the x_n form a dense set.

Suppose $Y \neq X$. Then with $x_0 \in X \sim Y$, there is an x' on the unit sphere of X' which vanishes on Y but not at x_0. Thus for any $n = 1, 2, \ldots$

$$\begin{aligned}\tfrac{3}{4} \leq |x'_n(x_n)| &= |x'_n(x_n) - x'(x_n)| \\ &= |(x'_n - x')(x_n)| \leq \|x'_n - x'\|,\end{aligned}$$

which is impossible, since $\{x'_n\}$ is dense on the unit sphere in X'.

2.18 Dual of l_p

We now describe the duals of the l_p spaces, $1 \leq p < \infty$.

THEOREM 1. If $1 \leq p < \infty$, and q is conjugate to p, then $(l_p)' = l_q$.

(*Remark*. It follows that if $1 < p < \infty$, then l_p is reflexive, while l_1 and l_∞ are non-reflexive.)

Proof. Let

$$e_n = (0, \ldots, 0,1, 0, \ldots)$$

be the vector with 1 in the nth place and 0 in every other place. Then for all p and n, $e_n \in l_p$ and $\|e_n\|_p = 1$.

If $f \in (l_p)'$, for $1 \leq p < \infty$, we define

$$a_n = f(e_n), \quad n = 1, 2, \ldots,$$

and consider the mapping

$$\tau : f \to \{a_n\}.$$

We shall show that

(a) $f \in (l_p)'$ implies $\tau f = \{a_n\} \in l_q$ and

$$\|\tau f\|_q = \|\{a_n\}\|_q \leq \|f\|,$$

and

(b) τ maps $(l_p)'$ onto l_q and

$$\|\tau f\|_q \geq \|f\|.$$

Since τ is obviously linear, this will establish the isomorphism of the normed vector spaces $(l_p)'$ and l_q.

For (a), observe that

$$|a_n| = |f(e_n)| \leq \|f\| \, \|e_n\| = \|f\|, n = 1, 2, \ldots.$$

Hence $\{a_n\}$ is a bounded sequence and

$$\|\{a_n\}\|_\infty \leq \|f\|,$$

proving (a) in the case $p = 1$.

For the case $1 < p < \infty$, we must estimate the partial sums $\sum_{n=1}^{k} |a_n|^q$, $k = 1, 2, \ldots.$ We do this by finding elements $x_k \in l_p$ such that $f(x_k)$ is the kth partial sum.

Let $x_k = (\xi_1, \xi_2, \ldots, \xi_k, 0, \ldots)$, where

$$\xi_i = |a_i|^{q-1} \operatorname{sgn} a_i, \; i = 1, 2, \ldots, k.$$

(sgn z means $z/|z|$ if $z \neq 0$ and 0 if $z = 0$.)

Clearly, $x_k \in l_p$ for all k, and we find

$$f(x_k) = f\left(\sum_{n=1}^{k} \xi_n e_n\right) = \sum_{n=1}^{k} \xi_n f(e_n) = \sum_{n=1}^{k} \xi_n a_n$$
$$= \sum_{n=1}^{k} |a_n|^{q-1} a_n \operatorname{sgn} a_n = \sum_{n=1}^{k} |a_n|^q.$$

Hence,

$$\sum_{n=1}^{k} |a_n|^q = |f(x_k)| \leq \|f\| \, \|x_k\|_p.$$

But,

$$\|x_k\|_p = \left(\sum_{n=1}^{k} |a_n|^{(q-1)p}\right)^{1/p} = \left(\sum_{n=1}^{k} |a_n|^q\right)^{1/p}.$$

We obtain, by dividing by $\|x_k\|_p$, if this is not 0, and by inspection otherwise, the inequality

$$\left(\sum_{n=1}^{k} |a_n|^q\right)^{1/q} \leq \|f\|, \quad k = 1, 2, \ldots,$$

from which (a) follows.

For (b), choose any $\{a_n\} \in l_q$ and define a linear functional f as follows (to obtain $\tau f = \{a_n\}$). Let

$$f(e_n) = a_n, \; n = 1, 2, \ldots$$

(this is permissible since the e_n's form a linearly independent set) and extend by linearity to all of l_p. Thus, if $x = (x_1, x_2, \ldots) \in l_p$, we put

$$f(x) = \sum_{n=1}^{\infty} a_n x_n.$$

The convergence of this series results from Hölder's inequality

$$|f(x)| \leq \sum_{n=1}^{\infty} |a_n x_n| \leq \|\{a_n\}\|_q \|x\|_p,$$

which also shows that f is a bounded linear functional on l_p and that

$$\|f\| \leq \|\{a_n\}\|_q.$$

This completes the proof.

2.19 Dual of $C[a, b]$, Riesz Representation Theorem

The dual space of the space $C[a, b]$ can be identified with a subspace of the space $BV[a, b]$ of functions of bounded variation on $[a, b]$ (see example (x), Sec. 1.1).

The major step in the identification is the Riesz representation theorem, which asserts that any bounded linear functional F on $C[a, b]$ is a Riemann-Stieltjes integral with respect to a function $g \in BV[a, b]$:

$$F(f) = \int_a^b f \, dg, \qquad f \in C[a, b].$$

We begin by recalling the definition of the Riemann-Stieltjes integral. Let $f \in C[a, b]$ and $g \in BV[a, b]$. For every partition $a = x_0 < x_1 < \dots < x_{n-1} < x_n = b$ of $[a, b]$ and $x_{i-1} \leq t_i \leq x_i$, $i = 1, 2, \dots, n$, consider the sum

$$\sum_{i=1}^{n} f(t_i)[g(x_i) - g(x_{i-1})].$$

There is a real number I such that for every $\epsilon > 0$ there is a $\delta > 0$ such that $\max [|x_i - x_{i-1}| : i = 1, \dots, n] < \delta$ implies

$$\left| I - \sum_{i=1}^{n} f(t_i)[g(x_i) - g(x_{i-1})] \right| < \epsilon.$$

The number I is the Riemann-Stieltjes integral of f with respect to g and is denoted $\int_a^b f\,dg$.

It is easy to show that the integral depends linearly on $f \in C[a, b]$ and on $g \in BV[a, b]$, so that

$$\int_a^b (\alpha f_1 + \beta f_2)\,dg = \alpha \int_a^b f_1\,dg + \beta \int_a^b f_2\,dg,$$

and

$$\int_a^b f\,d(\alpha g_1 + \beta g_2) = \alpha \int_a^b f\,dg_1 + \beta \int_a^b f\,dg_2.$$

Moreover, the inequality

$$\left| \int_a^b f\,dg \right| \leq \max [|f(x)| : x \in [a, b]] \cdot V(g)$$

holds.

In view of the definitions of the norms in C and BV (we use $\|g\| = |g(a)| + V(g)$ as norm in BV), we see that any $g \in BV$ determines a bounded linear functional F on C by the formula,

$$F(f) = \int_a^b f\,dg, \quad f \in C$$

and that

$$\|F\| \leq V(g).$$

Clearly, any two choices of g which differ by an additive constant define the same functional F. Thus, in order to specify a unique g determining F it is necessary to impose a normalizing condition, e.g., $g(a) = 0$. There remains a further ambiguity in g. It is easily seen that F may be the same for distinct functions in BV which vanish at a. A normalizing condition which removes this ambiguity consists of requiring that g be continuous from the right. The justification for this normalization lies in the fact that corresponding to any $g \in BV[a, b]$ there is exactly one $\bar{g} \in BV[a, b]$, continuous from the right, and such that

$$\int_a^b f\,d\bar{g} = \int_a^b f\,dg, \quad f \in C.$$

Moreover, $V(\bar{g}) \leq V(g)$.

The functions satisfying these normalizing conditions form a subspace BVN of $BV[a, b]$, and our observations so far show that the mapping

$$g \to \int_a^b f\,dg$$

is a one-one, linear, norm decreasing transformation of BVN into C'. We now show that the mapping is onto C' and preserves norms.

THEOREM 1. If $F \in C'[a, b]$, there exists a $g \in BVN[a, b]$ such that

$$F(f) = \int_a^b f\,dg, \quad f \in C[a, b]$$

and

$$\|g\| = V(g) = \|F\|.$$

Proof. We consider $C[a, b]$ as a subspace of the space $M[a, b]$ of bounded functions on $[a, b]$ and apply the Hahn-Banach theorem to extend F to all of $M[a, b]$, preserving the norm $\|F\|$. We may now apply F to the functions

$$\varphi_x(t) = \begin{cases} 1, a \le t < x \\ 0, x \le t \le b \end{cases}, a < x \le b,$$

$$\varphi_a(t) = 0, a \le t \le b,$$

and define

$$g(x) = F(\varphi_x), a \le x \le b.$$

To compute $V(g)$, we choose

$$a = x_0 < x_1 < \ldots < x_{n-1} < x_n = b,$$

and evaluate

$$\begin{aligned} \sum_{i=1}^n |g(x_i) - g(x_{i-1})| &= \sum_{i=1}^n \{g(x_i) - g(x_{i-1})\} \operatorname{sgn}(g(x_i) - g(x_{i-1})) \\ &= F\left(\sum_{i=1}^n \{\varphi_{x_i} - \varphi_{x_{i-1}}\} \operatorname{sgn}(g(x_i) - g(x_{i-1}))\right) \\ &\le \|F\| \cdot \left\| \sum_{i=1}^n \{\varphi_{x_i} - \varphi_{x_{i-1}}\} \operatorname{sgn}(g(x_i) - g(x_{i-1})) \right\| \\ &= \|F\|. \end{aligned}$$

We see that $g \in BV$ and $V(g) \le \|F\|$. Since $g(a) = F(\varphi_a) = F(0) = 0$, this means $\|g\| \le \|F\|$. The reverse inequality has been shown earlier. Hence $\|g\| = \|F\|$.

Now, if $f \in C$, we define a sequence of functions $f_n \in M$ such that $\{f_n\}$ converges to f in the space M and the values $F(f_n)$ are approximating sums for the integral $\int_a^b f\,dg$. Namely, writing s for $b - a$,

$$f_n(t) = \sum_{k=1}^n f\left(\frac{ks}{n}\right)[\varphi_{ks/n}(t) - \varphi_{(k-1)s/n}(t)].$$

Notice that f_n is a step function having the value $f(ks/n)$ in the interval $(k-1)s/n < t \leq ks/n$, $k = 1, 2, \ldots, n$.

It is evident that f_n converges uniformly to f.

Now

$$F(f_n) = \sum_{k=1}^{n} f\left(\frac{ks}{n}\right)[F(\varphi_{ks/n}) - F(\varphi_{(k-1)s/n})]$$

$$= \sum_{k=1}^{n} f\left(\frac{ks}{n}\right)\left[g\left(\frac{ks}{n}\right) - g\left(\frac{(k-1)s}{n}\right)\right],$$

so that $\{F(f_n)\}$ converges to $\int_a^b f\,dg$.

On the other hand, $F(f_n)$ converges to $F(f)$ by the continuity of F. Hence

$$F(f) = \int_a^b f\,dg.$$

By a remark above, g may be modified so as to belong to BVN and the proof is complete.

2.20 Open Mapping and Closed Graph Theorems

Differential operators provide important examples of linear transformations. Let us consider the simplest differential operator d/dt as an illustration of some general facts.

If X and Y are both taken to be the space $C[0, 1]$, then the subspace of X consisting of all continuously differentiable functions constitutes a natural domain on which d/dt defines a linear transformation from X into Y. Call this subspace C_1 and put

$$Tx = \frac{dx}{dt} \quad \text{for } x \in C_1.$$

The linear transformation T is not bounded since, for example, the functions

$$x_n(t) = t^n, \; n = 1, 2, \ldots$$

all have norm 1 in X while their images

$$(Tx_n)(t) = nt^{n-1}$$

have norms arbitrarily large.

In general, linear transformations defined by differential operators are not bounded. They do, however, enjoy a related property.

A linear transformation T from a Banach space X into a Banach space Y, with domain $D(T) \subset X$, is said to be **closed** if $x_n \in D(T)$, $\lim_n x_n = x$ and $\lim_n Tx_n = y$ imply $x \in D(T)$ and $y = Tx$.

Proposition 1. If $D(T)$ is closed in X and T is bounded, then T is closed.

We verify that the first order differential operator discussed above yields a closed transformation.

Let $x_n \in C_1$, $\lim_n x_n = x$ and $\lim_n \dfrac{dx_n}{dt} = y$, where the convergence is uniform. Then

$$\int_0^t y(s)\, ds = \int_0^t \lim_n \frac{dx_n}{dt}\, ds = \lim_n \int_0^t \frac{dx_n}{dt}\, ds$$

$$= \lim_n [x_n(t) - x_n(0)] = x(t) - x(0).$$

Thus

$$x(t) = x(0) + \int_0^t y(s)\, ds,$$

and it follows that $x \in C_1$ and $dx/dt = y$.

The property of being closed has a simple geometric interpretation in terms of the concept of the graph of the transformation.

The product $X \times Y$ of normed vector spaces X and Y is a normed vector space under the norm

$$\|(x, y)\| = \|x\| + \|y\|,$$

and $X \times Y$ is a Banach space if X and Y are such.

The **graph** of a mapping $T : X \to Y$ is the set of points $(x, Tx) \in X \times Y$, with $x \in D(T)$. It is designated as $G(T)$.

If T is linear, $G(T)$ is a vector subspace of $X \times Y$. The following proposition is immediate.

PROPOSITION 2. T is a closed linear transformation if and only if $G(T)$ is a closed vector subspace of $X \times Y$.

THEOREM 1 (Closed Graph Theorem). If X and Y are Banach spaces and T is a linear transformation from X into Y, then $D(T)$ closed and $G(T)$ closed imply T is bounded.

The proof is accomplished by an application of the

THEOREM 2 (Open Mapping Theorem). If X and Y are Banach spaces and T is a bounded linear transformation which maps X onto all of Y, then T is an open mapping (i.e., the image under T of an open set in X is open in Y).

Thus, if the mapping is also one-one, then T^{-1} is continuous.

Proof of Closed Graph Theorem. Since $D(T)$ is closed, it is itself a Banach space. Again $G(T)$, as a closed subspace of the Banach space $X \times Y$, is a Banach space. The mapping

$$(x, Tx) \to x$$

is a linear transformation of $G(T)$ onto $D(T)$. It is bounded because

$$\|x\| \leq \|x\| + \|Tx\| = \|(x, Tx)\|.$$

Hence, by the open mapping theorem, the inverse mapping

$$x \to (x, Tx)$$

is bounded. Thus, there is an M for which

$$\|Tx\| \le \|Tx\| + \|x\| = \|(x, Tx)\| \le M\,\|x\|,$$

for all $x \in D(T)$. This proves the boundedness of T.

Proof of Open Mapping Theorem. We first prove the

LEMMA 1. If X and Y are complete metric spaces and F is a continuous mapping of X onto Y such that for every $r > 0$, there is a $k > 0$ such that for every $x \in X$ the closure of the image of the sphere, $\sigma(x, r)$, in X, of center x and radius r, contains the sphere $\sigma(F(x), k)$ in Y, then for every $\rho > r$ the image of $\sigma(x, \rho)$ contains $\sigma(F(x), k)$.

Proof. Let $\sum_{n=1}^{\infty} r_n$ be a convergent series of positive terms such that $r_1 = r$ and $\sum_{n=1}^{\infty} r_n = \rho$. For every n, there is a $k_n > 0$ such that the closure of the image of $\sigma(x, r_n)$ contains $\sigma(F(x), k_n)$. The k_n may be chosen so that $\lim_n k_n = 0$. For $x \in X$, let $y \in \sigma(F(x), k)$. We define a sequence $\{x_n\}$ such that, for every n, $x_n \in \sigma(x_{n-1}, r_n)$ and $F(x_n) \in \sigma(y, k_{n+1})$. Having chosen $x_1 = x$, $x_2, \ldots, x_{n-1}$ so that $F(x_i) \in \sigma(y, k_{i+1})$, $i = 1, \ldots, n-1$, we have $y \in \sigma(F(x_{n-1}), k_n)$. Since the closure of the image of $\sigma(x_{n-1}, r_n)$ contains $\sigma(F(x_{n-1}), k_n)$, there is an $x_n \in \sigma(x_{n-1}, r_n)$ such that $F(x_n) \in \sigma(y, k_{n+1})$. The sequence $\{x_n\}$ is evidently a Cauchy sequence and so it converges to a point x_0 which is contained in $\sigma(x, \rho)$. But $\{F(x_n)\}$ converges to $F(x_0)$ since F is continuous. Moreover, since $\lim_n k_n = 0$, it follows that $\lim_n F(x_n) = y$. Hence $y = F(x_0)$.

To prove the theorem, we need only prove that the closure of the image of every sphere in X, with center 0, contains a sphere in Y with center 0. For this, let $r > 0$ and let $S \subset X$ be the sphere of center 0 and radius r. For every $x \in X$, the sequence $\left\{\frac{1}{n} x\right\}$ converges to 0, so there is an n with $x \in nS$. Then $Y = \bigcup_{n=1}^{\infty} nT(S)$. Since Y is of the second category, there is an n for which the closure of $nT(S)$ contains a sphere. It follows that the closure of $T(S)$ contains a sphere, whose center y may be taken in $T(S)$. Let this sphere, $\sigma(y, k)$, have radius k. Now, let $y = T(x)$ and $y' = T(x')$ for $y' \in \sigma(y, k)$. Then $T(x - x') = y - y'$. As y' varies over the closure of $T(S)$, $y - y'$ covers the sphere $\sigma(0, k)$. But a set of these y', dense in $\sigma(y, k)$, are of the form $y' = T(x')$, $x' \in S$. Since x and x' are in S, $x - x' \in \sigma(0, 2r)$. Hence the closure of the image of $\sigma(0, 2r)$ contains $\sigma(0, k)$.

2.21 Application, Projections

In this section, we shall discuss the decomposition of a Banach space as the sum of two subspaces and the related question of the existence of operators which are projections onto subspaces. These ideas are essential to the analysis of the structure of a linear transformation (see, e.g., Lorch [1]). Although we shall not discuss spectral theory here, these results are of geometric interest, and also provide an illustration of the use of the closed graph theorem.

A vector space X is the **direct sum** of two of its subspaces M and N,

$$X = M \dotplus N,$$

if every $x \in X$ has a unique decomposition

$$x = y + z$$

with $y \in M$ and $z \in N$.

Observe that if $X = M \dotplus N$ then $M \cap N = (0)$.

If $X = M \dotplus N$ and we define a mapping P of X into itself by $Px = y$, where for every $x \in X$, $x = y + z$ with $y \in M$, $z \in N$, then P is a linear transformation and

(i) $Px = x$ if and only if $x \in M$,
(ii) $Px = 0$ if and only if $x \in N$,
(iii) $P^2 = P$, i.e., $P(Px) = Px$ for all $x \in X$.

It is reasonable to think of P as the operation of projecting X onto M along N. Conversely, if we have a linear transformation P which is idempotent, $P^2 = P$, then X is the direct sum of the subspaces

$$M = \text{range of } P = [x \in X : Px = x]$$

and

$$N = \text{nullspace of } P = [x \in X : Px = 0].$$

For, if $x \in X$, then

$$x = Px + (I - P)x,$$

where I denotes the identity operator in X, given by $Ix = x$. It is clear that $Px \in M$ and $(I - P)x \in N$, so that this equation gives a decomposition of x according to the subspaces M and N. But the decomposition is unique, since $x = y + z, y \in M, z \in N$ gives $Px = Py = y$ and $(I - P)x = x - Px = x - y = z$.

Thus in the purely algebraic setting, we see the connection between direct sum decompositions of a space and idempotent linear operators in that space.

If X is a Banach space, we are particularly interested in closed subspaces, on the one hand, and in continuous linear operators on the other. The term **projection** will be used to refer to a bounded, linear, idempotent operator in a Banach space X, while by a **direct summand** of X we shall mean a closed linear subspace M such that for some closed linear subspace N, $X = M \dotplus N$.

If $M \neq (0)$, $M \neq X$, is a direct summand, there are infinitely many closed subspaces N for which $X = M \dotplus N$. This is clear if X is the plane and M is a line, for then N may be chosen as any line, distinct from M, through the origin. The general case is left as an exercise.

If M is a finite dimensional subspace of X, then M is a direct summand of X. We shall see in Chapter 4 that if X is a Hilbert space (e.g., l_2), then any closed subspace is a direct summand. However, it has been shown in a variety of particular cases that a Banach space may contain closed subspaces which are not direct summands.

It is easy to see that a linear operator T is continuous if and only if its null space $[x : Tx = 0]$ is closed. Application of this to P and $I - P$ gives, in view of earlier remarks,

PROPOSITION 1. If P is a projection in X, and M and N are its range and null space, respectively, then M and N are closed. Since $X = M \dotplus N$, M and N are direct summands.

The converse follows from the closed graph theorem.

PROPOSITION 2. If M is a direct summand of X and N is a closed subspace with $X = M \dotplus N$, then P is a projection, where $Px = y$ for $x = y + z$, $y \in M$, $z \in N$.

Proof. Only the continuity of P requires proof. Since P has domain X and range M, both Banach spaces, we need only show that P is closed. Suppose therefore that $\lim_n x_n = x$ and $\lim_n Px_n = y$. We have

$$x_n = Px_n + (I - P)x_n$$

converges to x, and since Px_n converges to y, $(I - P)x_n$ must converge and its limit z must satisfy $x = y + z$. But $y \in M$ and $z \in N$ since these subspaces are closed. Hence $y = Px$.

2.22 Application, Schauder Expansion

We now give an application of the open mapping theorem. Let X be an infinite dimensional separable Banach space. By a **Schauder basis** in X, we mean a set $x_n \in X$, $\|x_n\| = 1$, $n = 1, 2, \ldots$, such that for every $x \in X$ there is a unique series $\sum_{n=1}^{\infty} a_n x_n$ such that

$$\lim_n \left\| x - \sum_{i=1}^{n} a_i x_i \right\| = 0.$$

For example, a Schauder basis is given, in l_2, by $x_n = (0, \ldots, 0, 1, 0, \ldots)$, $n = 1, 2, \ldots$, where 1 appears in the nth place.

We may write the Schauder expansion of x as $\sum_{n=1}^{\infty} a_n(x)x_n$, and this emphasizes that the coefficients $a_n(x)$ are functionals on X. That they are linear is obvious. We show that they are bounded.

We introduce the vector space Y of all sequences $(a_1, \ldots, a_n, \ldots)$ for which $\sum_{n=1}^{\infty} a_n x_n$ converges in X. The norm

$$\|y\| = \sup_n \left\| \sum_{i=1}^{n} a_i x_i \right\|$$

converts Y into a normed vector space. We show it is a Banach space. Let $y_m = \{a_n^{(m)}\}$, $m = 1, 2, \ldots$, be a Cauchy sequence in Y. Let $\epsilon > 0$. There is an N such that $m, k > N$ implies

$$\|y_m - y_k\| = \sup_n \left\| \sum_{i=1}^{n} (a_i^{(m)} - a_i^{(k)})x_i \right\| < \epsilon.$$

But this implies $\|a_n^{(m)} - a_n^{(k)}\| < 2\epsilon$ for every n. Hence, for every n, $\lim_m a_n^{(m)} = a_n$ exists.

It remains only to show that $y = (a_1, \ldots, a_n, \ldots) \in Y$ and $\lim_n y_n = y$ in Y. But these are computations of a standard type used in other completeness arguments in the text and the proof is left to the reader.

Consider the transformation $T: Y \to X$ for which $y = (a_1, a_2, \ldots) \in Y$ is taken into $T(y) = \sum_{n=1}^{\infty} a_n x_n \in X$. T is evidently linear, one-one, and onto. It is bounded since $\sup_n \left\| \sum_{i=1}^{n} a_i x_i \right\| \geq \lim_n \left\| \sum_{i=1}^{n} a_i x_i \right\|$.

By the open mapping theorem, the inverse T^{-1} of T is bounded. Now,

$$|a_n(x)| = |a_n| = \|a_n x_n\| = \left\| \sum_{i=1}^{n} a_i x_i - \sum_{i=1}^{n-1} a_i x_i \right\|$$

$$\leq 2 \sup_n \left\| \sum_{i=1}^{n} a_i x_i \right\| = 2\|y\| = 2\|T^{-1}x\| \leq 2\|T^{-1}\| \|x\|.$$

This proves the boundedness of the $a_n(x)$.

2.23 A Theorem on Operators in $C[0, 1]$

In the final section, we show that certain sequences $\{F_n\}$ of operators on $C[0, 1]$ into itself have the property that $\lim_n F_n f = f$ for every $f \in C$.

An operator F is called **positive** if $f \geq 0$ implies $Ff \geq 0$. We show that the sequence $\{F_n\}$ has the desired property if each F_n is linear, positive and if $\lim_n F_n f = f$ for the three functions $1, x, x^2$, where $1(t) = 1$, $x(t) = t$, and $x^2(t) = t^2$ for each $t \in [0, 1]$.

We need the

LEMMA 1. If $\{F_n\}$ are linear, $\lim_n F_n 1 = 1$, $\lim_n F_n x = x$, and $\lim_n F_n x^2 = x^2$, then if x_u^2 is the function $x_u^2(t) = (t - u)^2$, it follows that $\lim_n F_n x_u^2(u) = 0$ uniformly in $u \in [0, 1]$.

The proof is left to the reader.

We now prove the

THEOREM 1. If $\{F_n\}$ is a sequence of linear positive operators on $C[0, 1]$ into itself such that $\lim_n F_n f = f$, in the C norm for $f = 1, x, x^2$, then $\lim_n F_n f = f$ for every $f \in C$.

Proof. Let $f \in C$ and $\epsilon > 0$. There is a $\delta > 0$ such that $|t - u| < \delta$ implies $|f(t) - f(u)| < \epsilon$, and an M such that $\|f\| = \max |f(t)| = M$. For every $t \in [0, 1]$,

$$-\epsilon - \frac{2M}{\delta^2}(t - u)^2 \leq f(t) - f(u) \leq \epsilon + \frac{2M}{\delta^2}(t - u)^2.$$

For, if $|t - u| < \delta$, we have

$$-\epsilon \leq f(t) - f(u) \leq \epsilon$$

and if $|t - u| \geq \delta$ we have

$$-\frac{2M}{\delta^2}(t - u)^2 \leq -2M \leq f(t) - f(u) \leq 2M \leq \frac{2M}{\delta^2}(t - u)^2.$$

Consider u fixed. Then, for every n,

$$-\epsilon F_n 1 - \frac{2M}{\delta^2} F_n x_u^2 \leq F_n f - f(u) F_n 1 \leq \epsilon F_n 1 + \frac{2M}{\delta^2} F_n x_u^2.$$

By lemma 1 and the fact that $\lim_n F_n 1 = 1$, we have for sufficiently large n,

$$-2\epsilon \cdot 1 \leq F_n f - f \leq 2\epsilon \cdot 1.$$

It follows, since $\epsilon > 0$ is arbitrary, that $\lim_n F_n f = f$ in C.

EXERCISES

1.1 Show that $0 \cdot x = 0$ and $(-1)x = -x$ in a vector space.

1.2 Show that $\Sigma[X_\alpha : \alpha \in A]$ is a vector space and $\Sigma[X_\alpha : \alpha \in A] = \Pi[X_\alpha : \alpha \in A]$ if and only if A is finite.

1.3 Show that the functions on $[0, 1]$ for which

$$\int_0^1 (e^{|f(x)|} - 1)\, dx < \infty$$

do not form a vector space.

2.1 Show that (S) is the set of all finite linear combinations of points in S.

3.1 Give the details of the proof that X/Y is a vector space.

4.1 Show that a set S is linearly independent if and only if for each finite subset $x_1, x_2, \ldots, x_n \in S$, the only linear combination

$$a_1 x_1 + \ldots + a_n x_n$$

giving 0 is the one in which $a_1 = a_2 = \ldots = a_n = 0$.

4.2 Prove proposition 3.

4.3 Prove proposition 4.

4.4 Show that if Y is a subspace of X then X has a Hamel basis S which has a subset T which is a Hamel basis of Y.

5.1 Prove that for every vector space X with algebraic dual X^*, $\dim X^* \geq \dim X$.

5.2 Suppose $\dim X = \aleph_0$. What is $\dim X^*$?

5.3 Show that if X is infinite dimensional, then X^{**} is not isomorphic to X.

5.4 Show that if X is finite dimensional, the natural isomorphism of X into X^{**} is onto.

6.1 If S is convex, show that $x + S$ and aS are convex.

7.1 Show that the group G/H associated with the preordered group G is an ordered group.

7.2 Consider the abelian group of all real functions on $(-\infty, \infty)$, with f in the positive cone if $f(x) > 0$ for all x in some interval. Discuss the resulting preordered group and its associated ordered group.

7.3 Give details of the proof that every archimedean totally ordered group is isomorphic to a subgroup of the reals.

7.4 Give an example of a non-archimedean totally ordered group; of such a field.

8.1 Show directly that the set S of the example following theorem 1 does not have an interior point.

8.2 Complete the proof of theorem 2.

8.3 Prove theorem 3 using theorem 2.

9.1 Show that theorem 3, section 8, follows from the theorem of section 9.

10.1 Show that $p'(x) = \sup_j \underline{\lim} \frac{1}{k} \sum_{i=1}^{k} x_{n_i+j}$.

10.2 Prove that for $x \in m$

$$\underline{\lim}\, x_n \leq p'(x) \leq p(x) \leq \overline{\lim}\, x_n.$$

10.3 Show that the functional $\overline{\lim}\, x_n$ is subadditive on m.

10.4 If $\{x_n\}$ converges, show that $\left\{\frac{1}{n}(x_1 + \ldots + x_n)\right\}$ converges and has the same limit.

10.5 In the proof of proposition 5 give details of the proof that

$$p(x) = \inf_{y \in c} [p(y + x) - l(y)].$$

10.6 Show that the functional q does not satisfy proposition 3, by giving an example of a bounded sequence for which $q(x) < p(x)$.

11.1 Show that the norm is continuous on the metric space associated with a normed vector space.

11.2 Define the operations and the norm in the completion of a normed vector space so that it is a normed vector space.

11.3 Consider the class of all polynomials with

$$\|p\| = |a_0| + |a_1| + \ldots + |a_n|$$

if

$$p(t) = a_0 + a_1 t + \ldots + a_n t^n.$$

Show that this is a normed vector space but is not a Banach space. Discuss the completion.

11.4 Compare $P[0, 1]$ with the above norm and the norm of example (*b*).

11.5 Consider any norm in the plane. Show that the unit sphere $[x : \|x\| \leq 1]$ is a closed convex set which is symmetric with respect to the origin and contains the origin as an interior point. Conversely, if S is any set with these properties, then a norm is obtained by specifying

$$\|x\| = 1 \text{ if } x \text{ is on the boundary of } S,$$

$$\|x\| = a \text{ if } \frac{1}{a}x \text{ is on the boundary of } S,$$

$$\|0\| = 0.$$

Sketch the unit spheres for the norms $\|x\|_p$ for several values of p, $1 \leq p \leq \infty$.

11.6 Show that the sequences $x = \{x_n\}$ with $\sum_{n=1}^{\infty} |x_{n+1} - x_n| < \infty$ form a Banach space with norm

$$\|x\| = |x_1| + \sum_{n=1}^{\infty} |x_{n+1} - x_n|.$$

11.7 Show that c is a nowhere dense subspace of m.

11.8 Show that the space of all real sequences can be normed so as to become a Banach space.

11.9 Show that no norm in the space of all sequences has the property

$$s_n \geq t_n,\ n = 1, 2, \ldots, \text{ implies } \|s\| \geq \|t\|.$$

11.10 Show that

$$\|T\| = \sup [\|Tx\| : \|x\| \leq 1]$$
$$= \sup [\|Tx\| : \|x\| = 1].$$

11.11 A series $\sum_{n=1}^{\infty} x_n$ in a normed vector space is summable to x if

$$\lim_n \left\| x - \sum_{i=1}^{n} x_i \right\| = 0.$$

It is absolutely summable if $\sum_{n=1}^{\infty} \|x_n\| < \infty$. Show that a normed vector space is complete if and only if every absolutely summable series is summable.

12.1 If X is a Banach space and Y is a closed subspace, show that X/Y is a Banach space with the norm

$$\|\xi\| = \min [\|x\| : x \in \xi].$$

12.2 If X is a normed vector space and $Y \subset X$ is a Banach space, then if X/Y is a Banach space, show that X itself is a Banach space.

12.3 Let X be a complex vector space. Show that if F_1 is a linear functional on X considered as a real space, then

$$F(x) = F_1(x) - iF_1(ix)$$

is a linear functional on the complex space X.

12.4 Show directly that no countable set is a Hamel basis for $C[0, 1]$.

12.5 Consider the sequences of successive powers of a fixed $\xi \in (0, 1)$, $(\xi, \xi^2, \ldots, \xi^n, \ldots)$. Show that all such vectors form a linearly independent set in m.

12.6 Show that a finite dimensional subspace of a normed vector space is closed.

12.7 Show that a Banach space is finite dimensional if and only if every subspace is closed.

12.8 Show that a closed proper subspace of a normed vector space is nowhere dense.

12.9 Give a simple proof that a Hamel basis of an infinite dimensional Banach space is uncountable (without actually showing that its cardinality is at least c as in proposition 5).

13.1 Prove theorem 1′.

13.2 Prove that there exists a continuous function whose Fourier series diverges at all points except for those belonging to a set of the first category.

14.1 Prove that if X is finite dimensional and Y is a proper subspace, then there is a point on the unit sphere of X at distance 1 from Y.

14.2 Show that all norms on an n-dimensional vector space yield homeomorphic metric spaces.

14.3 Show that an infinite dimensional vector space has infinitely many norms, no two of which yield homeomorphic metric spaces.

14.4 Show that if f is of finite Baire type on $[0, a)$ and g is of finite Baire type on $[a, 1]$, then h is of finite Baire type on $[0, 1]$, where

$$h(x) = \begin{cases} f(x), & 0 \le x < a \\ g(x), & a \le x \le 1. \end{cases}$$

14.5 Give an example of a Banach space X and a decreasing sequence of non-empty bounded closed convex sets in X whose intersection is empty.

15.1 Show that $T^* \in B(Y', X')$ and $\|T^*\| = \|T\|$.

15.2 A Banach space X is called uniformly convex if $\|x_n\| = \|y_n\| = 1$, $n = 1, 2, \ldots$ and $\lim_n \|x_n + y_n\| = 2$ implies $\lim_n \|x_n - y_n\| = 0$. If X is uniformly convex and $K \subset X$ is a closed convex set, show that $\|x\|$ has a uniquely assumed minimum on K.

15.3 Show that a finite dimensional Banach space need not be uniformly convex.

16.1 Show that if X is a Banach space, $x_n' \in X'$, $n = 1, 2, \ldots$ and $\lim_n x_n'(x) = y(x)$ for each $x \in X$, then $y \in X'$.

16.2 Extend the result of the previous exercise to sequences of bounded linear transformations of one Banach space into another.

16.3 Prove that if $\{s_n^{(m)}\}$ is a sequence of sequences such that $\sum_{n=1}^{\infty} |s_n^{(m)}| = \infty$, $m = 1, 2, \ldots$, there is a $\{t_n\}$, converging to zero, such that all the series $\sum_{n=1}^{\infty} s_n^{(m)} t_n$, $m = 1, 2, \ldots$, diverge.

16.4 Prove that the spaces E_m, defined after lemma 1, are closed.

16.5 Apply theorem 1 to show that if $\mathcal{A}$ is regular, then there is a bounded sequence $x = \{x_n\}$ whose $\mathcal{A}$-limit does not exist.

17.1 Prove that a Banach space is either reflexive or its successive second duals X'', X^{iv}, . . . are all distinct.

17.2 If X is reflexive and $Y \subset X$ is a closed subspace, show that Y is reflexive.

18.1 Consider the plane under any norm. Describe the dual space and its norm.

18.2 Show that the dual of c is l_1, where c is the space of convergent sequences.

18.3 Identify the dual of the closed subspace c_0 of c, of sequences which converge to zero.

18.4 Let S be the vector space of all real sequences and let $x^m = (x_1^{(m)}, x_2^{(m)}, \ldots)$ converge to $x = (x_1, x_2, \ldots)$ if $\lim_m x_i^{(m)} = x_i$ for each $i = 1, 2, \ldots$. Show that every continuous linear functional on S is given by a sequence, all but a finite number of whose terms are zero.

18.5 Give an example of a Banach space which is not a dual. (Hint: Find example in the literature.)

19.1 Prove the inequality

$$\left|\int_a^b f\, dg\right| \leq \max\,[|f(x)| : x \in [a, b]] \cdot V(g).$$

19.2 Show that for any $g \in BV$ there is a unique $\bar{g} \in BV$, continuous from the right, such that

$$\int_a^b f\, d\bar{g} = \int_a^b f\, dg \text{ for all } f \in C \text{ and } V(\bar{g}) \leq V(g).$$

20.1 Prove that if $D(T) \subset X$ is closed and T is bounded, then T is closed.

20.2 Find a necessary and sufficient condition that a subspace G of $X \times Y$ be a graph of a linear transformation from X into Y.

20.3 If X and Y are Banach spaces and $T : X \to Y$ is a bounded linear transformation, show that either $T(X) = Y$ or is of the first category in Y.

20.4 Let X, Y and Z be Banach spaces. Let $T : X \to Z$ and $U : Y \to Z$ be bounded linear transformations. Suppose for every $x \in X$ the equation $Tx = Uy$ has a unique solution y. Show that the mapping $y = Vx$ so determined is linear and bounded.

20.5 Let $T : X \to Z$ be a bounded linear transformation. Suppose T is a composite $Tx = VUx$ for all $x \in X$, where $U : X \to Y$ is linear and $V : Y \to Z$ is one-one bounded and linear. Show that U is bounded.

20.6 Show that a linear operator T in a Banach space X is continuous if and only if its null space is closed.

21.1 Show that every finite dimensional subspace of a Banach space is a direct summand.

21.2 If X is a Banach space, M is a direct summand of X, $M \neq (0)$, $M \neq X$, then there are infinitely many distinct choices of the closed subspace N for which $M \dotplus N = X$.

22.1 Finish the proof of the completeness of Y.

22.2 Exhibit a Schauder basis in $C[0, 1]$.

22.3 Exhibit a Schauder basis in c.

23.1 Let C be the Banach space of continuous functions on $[0, 2\pi]$ with $f(0) = f(2\pi)$ and $\|f\| = \max\,[|f(t)| : t \in [0, 2\pi]]$. With 1, s, c defined by $1(t) = 1$, $s(t) = \sin t$, $c(t) = \cos t$, $t \in [0, 2\pi]$, show that if $\{F_n\}$ is a sequence of positive linear operators on C into itself such that $\lim_n F_n f = f$ for $f = 1, f = s$, and $f = c$, then $\lim_n F_n f = f$ for every $f \in C$.

23.2 Show that the Lagrange interpolation polynomials do not satisfy the conditions of theorem 1.

23.3 Show that the linear interpolation functions satisfy the conditions of theorem 1.

23.4 Let $F_n f$, $n = 1, 2, \ldots$ be the nth partial sum of the Fourier series of f. Show that the $\{F_n\}$ do not satisfy the conditions of exercise 23.1.

23.5 Let $\Phi_n = \frac{1}{n}(F_1 + \ldots + F_n)$, $n = 1, 2, \ldots$ where the F_n are those of exercise 23.4. Show that the $\{\Phi_n\}$ satisfy the conditions of exercise 23.1.

CHAPTER 3

MEASURE AND INTEGRATION L_p SPACES

3.1 Lebesgue Measure for Bounded Sets in E_n

Let E_n be euclidean n-space. An **open interval** I in E_n, given by $a_i < b_i$, $i = 1, 2, \ldots, n$, is the set of all $x = (x_1, \ldots, x_n) \in E_n$ for which $a_i < x_i < b_i$, $i = 1, \ldots, n$. By the (n-dimensional) **measure** of I, we understand the number

$$m(I) = \prod_{i=1}^{n} (b_i - a_i).$$

A **closed interval** is the set of all $x = (x_1, \ldots, x_n)$ for which $a_i \leq x_i \leq b_i$, $i = 1, \ldots, n$.

If $I_1, \ldots, I_k$ are pair-wise disjoint open intervals, and if $J = \bigcup_{j=1}^{k} I_j$ then by the **measure** of J we understand the number

$$m(J) = \sum_{j=1}^{k} m(I_j).$$

We shall designate as **elementary sets** those sets which are unions of finite numbers of pair-wise disjoint open intervals. Let U_n be the open unit n-cube which is composed of all $x = (x_1, \ldots, x_n)$ for which $0 < x_i < 1$, $i = 1, \ldots, n$. For convenience, we consider, for the time being, only subsets of U_n.

We may attach a number, called the exterior measure of S, to every subset $S \subset U_n$. For this purpose, we consider a covering of S by means of a countable set of open intervals

$$\mathfrak{J} = \{I_1, I_2, \ldots\},$$

where the I_n, $n = 1, 2, \ldots$, may overlap. Let

$$\psi(S, \mathfrak{J}) = \sum_{n=1}^{\infty} m(I_n).$$

By the **exterior measure** of S we mean the number

$$m_e(S) = \inf \psi(S, \mathfrak{J}),$$

where the infimum is taken for all coverings $\mathfrak{J}$ of S.

Let $\{S_n\}$ be a sequence of sets, and let $S = \bigcup_{n=1}^{\infty} S_n$. Then

$$m_e(S) \leq \sum_{n=1}^{\infty} m_e(S_n).$$

In order to prove this, let $\epsilon > 0$. For every $n = 1, 2, \ldots$, let $\mathfrak{J}_n$ be a covering of S_n such that

$$\psi(S_n, \mathfrak{J}_n) < m_e(S_n) + \frac{\epsilon}{2^n}.$$

Let $\mathfrak{J} = \bigcup_{n=1}^{\infty} \mathfrak{J}_n$. Then $\mathfrak{J}$ is a covering of S, and

$$m_e(S) \leq \psi(S, \mathfrak{J}) = \sum_{n=1}^{\infty} \psi(S_n, \mathfrak{J}_n) \leq \sum_{n=1}^{\infty} m_e(S_n) + \epsilon.$$

Since this holds for every $\epsilon > 0$, the statement is proved.

By an easy application of the Borel covering theorem, it can be shown that if J is an elementary set, then

$$m_e(J) = m(J).$$

For any $i = 1, \ldots, n$, let H be a hyperplane obtained by fixing the ith coordinate, so that H is the set of $x = \{x_1, \ldots, x_n\}$ for which $x_i = x_i^{(0)}$. It is then easy to show that $m_e(H) = 0$.

We leave these proofs, as well as the proof that $T \subset S$ implies $m_e(T) \leq m_e(S)$, to the reader.

We are now ready to give the main definition. A set $S \subset U_n$ will be called **measurable** if, for every $\epsilon > 0$ there are sets J, T_1 and T_2 in U_n such that

(i) J is an elementary set,

(ii) $T_1 \subset J$, $T_2 \subset U_n \sim J$,

(iii) $m_e(T_1) < \epsilon$, $m_e(T_2) < \epsilon$,

and

(iv) $S = (J \sim T_1) \cup T_2$.

PROPOSITION 1. If S is measurable, then $U_n \sim S$ is measurable.

Proof. Let $\epsilon > 0$. Then

$$S = (J \sim T_1) \cup T_2,$$

where J is an elementary set,

$$T_1 \subset J, T_2 \subset U_n \sim J, m_e(T_1) < \epsilon \quad \text{and} \quad m_e(T_2) < \epsilon.$$

Now

$$U_n \sim S = [(K \cup T_3) \sim (T_2 \cup T_3')] \cup T_1,$$

where K is an elementary set, T_3 is a subset of a finite set of hyperplanes such that $K \cup T_3 = U_n \sim J$, and $T_3' \subset T_3$. So,

$$U_n \sim S = (K \sim T_4) \cup T_5$$

where

$$T_4 \subset T_2 \cup T_3 \quad \text{and} \quad T_5 \subset T_1 \cup T_3.$$

But $m_e(T_2 \cup T_3) < \epsilon$ and $m_e(T_1 \cup T_3) < \epsilon$, so that the proposition is proved.

Proposition 2. Every open set is measurable.

Proof. We use the fact that every open set is the union of a sequence of closed intervals whose interiors are pair-wise disjoint. Let G be open. Let $J_1, J_2, \ldots$ be the interiors of closed intervals, with pair-wise disjoint interiors, whose union is G. Since $G \subset U_n$, $\sum_{k=1}^{n} m(J_k) \leq 1$, for every n, so that $\sum_{k=1}^{\infty} m(J_k) \leq 1$. Let $\epsilon > 0$. There is an N such that $\sum_{n=1}^{N} m(J_n) > \sum_{n=1}^{\infty} m(J_n) - \epsilon$. Now

$$G = \left(\bigcup_{n=1}^{N} J_n\right) \cup \left(\bigcup_{n=N+1}^{\infty} J_n \cup E\right),$$

where E is contained in a countable set of hyperplanes, so that $m_e(E) = 0$. It follows that $m_e\left(\bigcup_{n=N+1}^{\infty} J_n \cup E\right) < \epsilon$ and the proposition is proved.

Proposition 3. Every closed set is measurable.

Proof. By propositions 1 and 2.

Proposition 4. S is measurable if and only if, for every $\epsilon > 0$, there is an open set G such that $S \subset G$ and $m_e(G \sim S) < \epsilon$.

Proof. Suppose S is measurable. Let $\epsilon > 0$. There are sets J, T_1 and T_2 such that J is elementary, $m_e(T_1) < \epsilon/2$, $m_e(T_2) < \epsilon/2$, and

$$S = (J \sim T_1) \cup T_2.$$

There is an open set H such that $T_2 \subset H$ and $m_e(H) < \epsilon/2$. Let $G = J \cup H$. Then $S \subset G$ and $G \sim S \subset T_1 \cup H$. But $m_e(T_1 \cup H) < \epsilon$.

Suppose, for every $\epsilon > 0$, there is an open set G such that $S \subset G$ and $m_e(G \sim S) < \epsilon$. Now, $G = J \cup E$, where J is elementary and $m_e(E) < \epsilon$. Then

$$S = [J \sim (G \sim S) \cap J] \cup (S \cap E).$$

But $m_e[(G \sim S) \cap J] < \epsilon$ and $m_e(S \cap E) < \epsilon$. Hence S is measurable.

COROLLARY. S is measurable if and only if for every $\epsilon > 0$ there is a compact set F such that $F \subset S$ and $m_e(S \sim F) < \epsilon$.

The proof is immediate if "compact" is replaced by "closed." The required simple modification needed to complete the proof is left to the reader.

PROPOSITION 5. If $\{S_n\}$ is a sequence of measurable sets, then $S = \bigcup_{n=1}^{\infty} S_n$ is measurable.

Proof. Let $\epsilon > 0$. For every $n = 1, 2, \ldots$, there is an open set G_n such that $S_n \subset G_n$ and $m_e(G_n \sim S_n) < \epsilon/2^n$. Let $G = \bigcup_{n=1}^{\infty} G_n$. Now $G \sim S \subset \bigcup_{n=1}^{\infty} (G_n \sim S_n)$, so that $m_e(G \sim S) \leq \sum_{n=1}^{\infty} m_e(G_n \sim S_n) < \epsilon$. Hence, S is measurable.

PROPOSITION 6. If F_1 and F_2 are compact sets such that $F_1 \cap F_2 = 0$, then $m_e(F_1 \cup F_2) = m_e(F_1) + m_e(F_2)$.

Proof. We first observe that if I is an open interval and $\epsilon > 0$, then I may be covered by a finite set $I_1, \ldots, I_k$ of open intervals, each of diameter less than ϵ, such that $\sum_{j=1}^{k} m(I_j) < m(I) + \epsilon$. Let $d > 0$ be the distance between F_1 and F_2. Let $\{I_n\}$ be a covering of $F_1 \cup F_2$ such that $\sum_{n=1}^{\infty} m(I_n) < m_e(F_1 \cup F_2) + \epsilon$. By the above remark, there is a covering $\{J_n\}$ of $F_1 \cup F_2$ such that the diameter of each J_n is less than $d/2$ and $\sum_{n=1}^{\infty} m(J_n) < m_e(F_1 \cup F_2) + 2\epsilon$. Let $\{K_n\}$ be those intervals from among the J_n which contain points of F_1 and $\{L_n\}$ those which contain points of F_2. No J_n is both a K_i and an L_j. Then

$$m_e(F_1) + m_e(F_2) \leq \sum_{n=1}^{\infty} m(K_n) + \sum_{n=1}^{\infty} m(L_n) \leq \sum_{n=1}^{\infty} m(J_n) < m_e(F_1 \cup F_2) + 2\epsilon.$$

Thus, $m_e(F_1) + m_e(F_2) \leq m_e(F_1 \cup F_2)$. Since $m_e(F_1) + m_e(F_2) \geq m_e(F_1 \cup F_2)$, the proposition is proved.

PROPOSITION 7. If S_1 and S_2 are measurable sets and $S_1 \cap S_2 = 0$, then $m_e(S_1 \cup S_2) = m_e(S_1) + m_e(S_2)$.

Proof. Let $\epsilon > 0$. There are compact sets $F_1 \subset S_1$ and $F_2 \subset S_2$ such that $m_e(S_1 \sim F_1) < \epsilon$ and $m_e(S_2 \sim F_2) < \epsilon$. So,

$$\begin{aligned} m_e(S_1) + m_e(S_2) &< m_e(F_1) + m_e(F_2) + 2\epsilon \\ &= m_e(F_1 \cup F_2) + 2\epsilon \leq m_e(S_1 \cup S_2) + 2\epsilon. \end{aligned}$$

Thus, $m_e(S_1) + m_e(S_2) \leq m_e(S_1 \cup S_2)$. But, $m_e(S_1) + m_e(S_2) \geq m_e(S_1 \cup S_2)$, so that the proposition is proved.

PROPOSITION 8. If $\{S_n\}$ is a sequence of pair-wise disjoint measurable sets and $S = \bigcup_{n=1}^{\infty} S_n$, then $m_e(S) = \sum_{n=1}^{\infty} m_e(S_n)$.

Proof. By proposition 7,

$$m_e(S) \geq m_e\left(\bigcup_{k=1}^{n} S_k\right) = \sum_{k=1}^{n} m_e(S_k), \text{ for every } n = 1, 2, \ldots.$$

Hence,

$$m_e(S) \geq \sum_{n=1}^{\infty} m_e(S_n).$$

But,

$$m_e(S) \leq \sum_{n=1}^{\infty} m_e(S_n),$$

so that the proposition is proved.

We have now proved

THEOREM 1. The collection $\mathcal{M}$ of measurable sets is a closed system with respect to countable unions and complementation. On $\mathcal{M}$, the exterior measure is a countably additive non-negative set function, i.e., if $S_n \in \mathcal{M}$, $n = 1, 2, \ldots$ and $S_i \cap S_j = 0$ for $i \neq j$, then

$$m_e\left(\bigcup_{n=1}^{\infty} S_n\right) = \sum_{n=1}^{\infty} m_e(S_n).$$

For sets in $\mathcal{M}$, the exterior measure will be referred to as the **measure** and will be written as $m(S)$ rather than $m_e(S)$.

Finally, the term **almost everywhere** is used to mean "except for a set of measure zero."

3.2 Lebesgue Measure for Unbounded Sets

We now extend the definition of measure from subsets of U_n to subsets of E_n, including unbounded as well as bounded sets.

For every n-tuple $K = (k_1, \ldots, k_n)$ where the k_i, $i = 1, \ldots, n$, are integers, we consider the cube $U_n^{(K)}$, consisting of the points $x = (x_1, \ldots, x_n)$ for which $k_i < x_i < k_i + 1$, $i = 1, \ldots, n$. We may then define the set $\mathcal{M}_K$ of measurable subsets of $U_n^{(K)}$, and the measure on them, in a way analogous to that in which we defined $\mathcal{M}$. (Indeed, the sets in $\mathcal{M}_K$ are simply translations of the sets in $\mathcal{M}$.)

Now, we define a set $S \subset E_n$ to be measurable if, for every K, we have $S \cap U_n^{(K)} \in \mathcal{M}_K$. Let $\mathcal{S}$ be the collection of measurable subsets of E_n. It is an easy matter to see that the complement of a measurable set is measurable and that the union of a countable set of measurable sets is measurable.

For every $S \in \mathcal{S}$, we define the measure of S by

$$m(S) = \sum_K m(S \cap U_n^{(K)}).$$

Since all summands are non-negative, the order in which the series is summed does not matter. Moreover, there are sets $S \in \mathcal{S}$ for which $m(S) = +\infty$.

With the convention that for every $0 \leq a \leq +\infty$, $+\infty + a = +\infty$, $m(S)$ is a completely additive set function on $\mathcal{S}$.

3.3 Totally σ Finite Measures

We now say a few words about general measure theory. For this purpose, let S be a set and $\mathcal{S}$ a collection of subsets of S such that

(a) $S \in \mathcal{S}$,
(b) if $A \subset S$ and $A \in \mathcal{S}$ then $S \sim A \in \mathcal{S}$,
(c) if $A_n \subset S$ and $A_n \in \mathcal{S}$, $n = 1, 2, \ldots$, then $\bigcup_{n=1}^{\infty} A_n \in \mathcal{S}$.

Such a system of sets is called a **σ algebra.** Suppose now that there is a real-valued function μ on $\mathcal{S}$ such that

(α) $\mu(A) \geq 0$ for every $A \in \mathcal{S}$,
(β) $A_n \in \mathcal{S}$, $n = 1, 2, \ldots$ and $A_i \cap A_k = 0$, $i \neq k$, implies

$$\mu\left(\bigcup_{n=1}^{\infty} A_n\right) = \sum_{n=1}^{\infty} \mu(A_n).$$

Then μ is called a **measure** on $\mathcal{S}$ and the system $(S, \mathcal{S}, \mu)$ is called a **totally finite measure space.** Note that $S \in \mathcal{S}$ and $\mu(S) < \infty$.

Sometimes it is useful to make the further assumption

(γ) if $A \in \mathcal{S}$ and $\mu(A) = 0$ then, for every $B \subset A$, $B \in \mathcal{S}$.

It then follows, of course, that $\mu(B) = 0$.

If (γ) holds, the measure space is called **complete** (a work horse of a word which is perhaps overworked in this case).

The measure defined in Sec. 3.1 is totally finite and complete.

Now, let $\mathcal{S}$ be a σ algebra of subsets of a set S and let μ satisfy

(a′) $0 \leq \mu(A) \leq +\infty$ for every $A \in \mathcal{S}$,
(b′) if $A_n \in \mathcal{S}$, $n = 1, 2, \ldots$ and $A_i \cap A_j = 0$, $i \neq j$, then

$$\mu\left(\bigcup_{n=1}^{\infty} A_n\right) = \sum_{n=1}^{\infty} \mu(A_n),$$

(c′) there is a sequence T_n, $n = 1, 2, \ldots$ in $\mathcal{S}$ such that $S = \bigcup_{n=1}^{\infty} T_n$, and $\mu(T_n) < \infty$, $n = 1, 2, \ldots$.

Then μ is still called a measure on $\mathcal{S}$ but the measure space $(S, \mathcal{S}, \mu)$ is called **totally σ finite.**

The measure space discussed in Sec. 3.2 is totally σ finite and complete. It is called **Lebesgue measure.**

We now consider a special class of measure spaces. In each case, the set S will be the real line E_1.

Let f be a monotonically non-decreasing real-valued function on E_1. We define a measure μ on E_1 by means of the function f. For every $a \in E_1$, let $I_a = (-\infty, a]$. Define

$$\mu(I_a) = f(a).$$

Let $\{a_n\}$ be an increasing sequence which converges to a. Let

$$\mu(\{a\}) = \lim_{n\to\infty} [f(a) - f(a_n)].$$

It is clear that $\mu(\{a\})$ is independent of the choice of $\{a_n\}$. Then, for any open interval $I = (a, b)$, define

$$\mu(I) = \mu(I_b) - \mu(I_a) - \mu(\{b\}).$$

Now, let $J_n = (n, n + 1)$. Just as in the discussion of Sec. 3.1, $\mu(I)$ defined on the open subintervals of J_n determines an exterior measure for all sets in J_n. The measurable subsets of J_n are determined as before and on them, the exterior measure has the properties of a totally finite measure.

Now, a subset $A \subset E_1$ will be called measurable if $A \cap J_n$ is measurable for every n. Then the measure of A is defined as

$$\mu(A) = \sum_{n=-\infty}^{\infty} \mu(A \cap J_n) + \sum_{n=-\infty}^{\infty} \mu(A \cap \{n\}).$$

The measure space obtained in this way is totally σ finite and complete. It is totally finite if and only if $\lim_{x\to-\infty} f(x) > -\infty$ and $\lim_{x\to+\infty} f(x) < +\infty$.

General measure theory also deals with measures that are not totally σ finite. Such measures will not be of interest to us.

3.4 Measurable Functions, Egoroff Theorem

Let $(S, \mathcal{S}, \mu)$ be a totally σ finite measure space, which we assume to be complete for the sake of convenience.

A real function f on S is said to be **measurable** if, for every open set $G \subset E_1$, the set $f^{-1}(G)$ is measurable, i.e., $f^{-1}(G) \in \mathcal{S}$.

It is easy to see that f is measurable if and only if the inverse images of all Borel sets are measurable or, on the other hand, if and only if the inverse images of the open intervals (a, ∞) are measurable. It should also be clear that if f is measurable and $g(x) = f(x)$ almost everywhere, then g is measurable. We leave the easy proofs to the reader. If f and g are such that $f(x) = g(x)$ almost everywhere, we say that f is **equivalent** to g. The set of measurable functions equivalent to a given function will be called an **equivalence class** of measurable functions. We usually shall not distinguish between a function and its equivalence class, since there is little danger of confusion. Often we shall speak of an equivalence class as a function.

We shall also consider extended real-valued functions on S, i.e., functions which may assume the values $+\infty$ and $-\infty$, as well as real values. In this case, a measurable function f may be defined as one such that, for every real a, the inverse image of the interval (a, ∞) is measurable, and the set for which $f(x) = +\infty$ is measurable.

PROPOSITION 1. If f and g are extended real-valued measurable functions on a totally σ finite measure space $(S, \mathcal{S}, \mu)$, then the set $E = [x : f(x) > g(x)]$ is measurable.

Proof. For every rational r, let $E_r = [x : f(x) < r < g(x)]$. Now E_r, as the intersection of two measurable sets, is measurable. Morever,

$$E = \bigcup E_r$$

where the union is for all the rationals, and so E, as the union of a countable set of measurable sets, is measurable.

PROPOSITION 2. If f is measurable and a is a real number, then $f + a$ and af are measurable.

The easy proof is omitted.

In the next propositions, we assume that f is real-valued.

PROPOSITION 3. If f and g are measurable, then $f + g$ is measurable.

Proof. Let a be a real number. The set for which $f(x) + g(x) > a$ is the same as the set for which $f(x) > -g(x) + a$. But the function $-g + a$ is measurable, so that this set is measurable.

PROPOSITION 4. If f is measurable and a is real, then $|f|^a$ is measurable.

Proof. For $a = 0$, the proposition is trivially true. Let $a \neq 0$. The set for which $|f|^a$ exceeds a positive real number b is the union of the sets for which $f(x) > b^{1/a}$ and $f(x) < -b^{1/a}$ and so is measurable. This completes the proof.

PROPOSITION 5. If f and g are measurable, then fg is measurable.

Proof. $fg = \frac{1}{4}(f + g)^2 - \frac{1}{4}(f - g)^2$.

PROPOSITION 6. If f and g are measurable, then $|f|$, $\max(f, g)$ and $\min(f, g)$ are measurable.

Proof. That $|f|$ is measurable follows by proposition 4. Since

$$\max(f, g) = \tfrac{1}{2}(f + g) + \tfrac{1}{2}|f - g|$$

and

$$\min(f, g) = \tfrac{1}{2}(f + g) - \tfrac{1}{2}|f - g|,$$

these functions are measurable.

The set of measurable functions is thus closed with respect to addition, multiplication, and scalar multiplication. Moreover, every pair of measurable functions has a measurable greatest lower bound, the point-wise minimum, and a measurable least upper bound, the point-wise maximum.

We now consider sequences of measurable functions.

We first note that if $\{f_n\}$ is a monotonically non-decreasing sequence of extended real-valued functions, each of which is measurable, then the function f, defined by $f(x) = \lim_{n\to\infty} f_n(x)$, is also measurable. For, let a be any real number. Then $f(x) > a$ if and only if $f_n(x) > a$ for some n. So, the set of points for which $f(x) > a$, as the union of countably many measurable sets, is measurable. Thus, f is measurable.

We make the remark that if, for every n, g_n is equivalent to f_n, then $\{g_n\}$ converges almost everywhere to the function f. Indeed, in these considerations and others which follow, functions need only be defined almost everywhere.

PROPOSITION 7. If $\{f_n\}$ is a sequence of extended real-valued measurable functions, then $\lim_n \sup f_n$ and $\lim_n \inf f_n$ are measurable.

Proof. If $\{k_n\}$ is a sequence of extended real-valued measurable functions and, for every n, $g_n = \max(k_1, \ldots, k_n)$, then $\{g_n\}$ is monotonically non-decreasing and $\lim_n g_n$ is measurable. But $\lim_n g_n = \sup_n k_n$, so that we have shown that the supremum of a sequence of measurable functions is measurable. Now, for every n, let $h_n = \sup(f_n, f_{n+1}, \ldots)$. Then $\{h_n\}$ is a monotonically non-increasing sequence of measurable functions and $\lim_n h_n = \lim_n \sup f_n$. Thus $\lim_n \sup f_n$ is measurable. Similarly, $\lim_n \inf f_n$ is measurable.

COROLLARY. The limit of a convergent sequence of measurable functions is measurable.

We now consider only totally finite measure spaces. We show that convergent sequences of measurable functions on such spaces are "approximately" uniformly convergent.

THEOREM 1 (Egoroff). If $\{f_n\}$ is a sequence of measurable real functions defined on a totally finite measure space $(S, \mathcal{S}, \mu)$, and $\{f_n\}$ converges almost everywhere to a function f on S, then, for every $\epsilon > 0$, there is a set $E \in \mathcal{S}$ such that $\mu(E) > \mu(S) - \epsilon$ and $\{f_n\}$ converges uniformly to f on E.

Proof. Let $\epsilon > 0$. For every n, let E_n be the set of points $x \in S$ such that $|f(x) - f_k(x)| < \epsilon$ for every $k \geq n$. Then E_n, as the intersection of countably many measurable sets, is measurable. Moreover,

$$E_1 \subset E_2 \subset \ldots \subset E_n \subset \ldots$$

and, since $\{f_n\}$ converges to f almost everywhere,

$$\bigcup_{n=1}^{\infty} E_n = S \sim Z, \quad \text{where } \mu(Z) = 0.$$

Now,

$$\mu(S) = \mu(E_1) + \mu(E_2 \sim E_1) + \ldots + \mu(E_{n+1} \sim E_n) + \ldots,$$

so that there is an N such that

$$\mu(E_N) > \mu(S) - \epsilon.$$

There is a measurable set T_1, with $\mu(T_1) > \mu(S) - \epsilon/2$, and an n_1 such that, for all $k > n_1$ and all $x \in T_1$, $|f(x) - f_k(x)| < \epsilon/2$. There is a measurable set T_2, with $\mu(T_2) > \mu(S) - \epsilon/2^2$, and an $n_2 > n_1$ such that, for all $k > n_2$ and all $x \in T_2$, $|f(x) - f_k(x)| < \epsilon/2^2$. Continuing in this way, there is a sequence

$$n_1 < n_2 < \ldots < n_i < \ldots$$

and a sequence $\{T_i\}$ of measurable sets such that, for each i, for all $k > n_i$ and all $x \in T_i$, $|f(x) - f_k(x)| < \epsilon/2^i$. Let $E = \bigcap_{n=1}^{\infty} T_n$. Then it is easy to see that $\mu(E) > \mu(S) - \epsilon$, and $\{f_n\}$ converges uniformly to f on E.

This theorem is not always true for totally σ finite measure spaces.

3.5 Convergence in Measure

We now present a kind of convergence for sequences of measurable functions which is weaker than almost everywhere convergence and is of considerable importance in analysis and probability theory.

Let $(S, \mathcal{S}, \mu)$ be a totally finite measure space. A sequence $\{f_n\}$ of measurable functions on S is said to **converge in measure** to a function f if, for every $\epsilon > 0$, there is an N such that, for every $n > N$, the set E_n of points $x \in S$ for which $|f(x) - f_n(x)| > \epsilon$ has measure $\mu(E_n) < \epsilon$.

PROPOSITION 1. If $(S, \mathcal{S}, \mu)$ is a totally finite measure space and $\{f_n\}$ is a sequence of measurable functions on S which converges almost everywhere to a function f, then $\{f_n\}$ converges in measure to f.

Proof. Let $\epsilon > 0$. By theorem 1, Sec. 3.4, there is a set E such that $m(E) > m(S) - \epsilon$ and $\{f_n\}$ converges uniformly to f on E. There is an N such that $n > N$ and $x \in E$ implies $|f(x) - f_n(x)| < \epsilon$. This proves that $\{f_n\}$ converges in measure to f.

The converse to proposition 1 is false. For example, let S be the interval $(0, 1)$ and let μ be the measure defined in Sec. 3.1, i.e., Lebesgue measure. We consider the following sequence of functions:

$$f_1(x) = 1, \quad x \in (0, 1),$$

$$f_2(x) = \begin{cases} 1, & x \in (0, \frac{1}{2}) \\ 0, & x \in [\frac{1}{2}, 1), \end{cases}$$

$$f_3(x) = \begin{cases} 1, & x \in (\frac{1}{2}, 1) \\ 0, & x \in (0, \frac{1}{2}]. \end{cases}$$

Define the next four functions by

$$f_{3+i}(x) = \begin{cases} 1, & x \in \left(\dfrac{i-1}{4}, \dfrac{i}{4}\right), \ i = 1, \ldots, 4. \\ 0, & \text{elsewhere on } (0, 1) \end{cases}$$

We continue in a manner which should be clear. Now, for every $x \in (0, 1)$, except for diadic points (which form a set of measure zero), there is an infinite set of values of n for which $f_n(x) = 1$ and an infinite set of values of n for which $f_n(x) = 0$. Thus $\{f_n\}$ does not converge almost everywhere.

However, let $\epsilon > 0$. There is then an N such that, for every $n > N$, $f_n(x) = 0$ except on a set of measure less than ϵ. Hence, $\{f_n\}$ converges in measure to 0.

On the other hand, we have

PROPOSITION 2. If $(S, \mathcal{S}, \mu)$ is a totally finite measure space, and $\{f_n\}$ converges in measure to f, then $\{f_n\}$ has a subsequence which converges almost everywhere to f.

Proof. There is an n_1 such that the set E_1 of points $x \in S$ for which

$$|f(x) - f_{n_1}(x)| > 1$$

has measure $\mu(E_1) < 1/2$. There is an $n_2 > n_1$ such that the set E_2 of points $x \in S$ for which $|f(x) - f_{n_2}(x)| > 1/2$ has measure $\mu(E_2) < 1/2^2$. Proceeding in this way, there is a sequence

$$n_1 < n_2 < \ldots < n_i < \ldots$$

such that for every $i = 1, 2, \ldots$ the set E_i of points $x \in S$ for which

$$|f(x) - f_{n_i}(x)| > 1/i$$

has measure $\mu(E_i) < 1/2^i$. We show that the sequence $\{f_{n_i}\}$ converges almost everywhere to f.

Let $\epsilon > 0$. There is an N such that $\sum_{i=N+1}^{\infty} \frac{1}{2^i} < \epsilon$. Hence

$$\mu(E_{N+1} \cup E_{N+2} \cup \ldots) < \epsilon.$$

Let

$$S_N = S \sim \bigcup_{i=N+1}^{\infty} E_i.$$

Then $\{f_{n_i}\}$ converges uniformly to f on S_N. It follows that $\{f_{n_i}\}$ converges to f on $T = \bigcup_{N=1}^{\infty} S_N$ and $\mu(S \sim T) = 0$.

It is now easy to prove the following: If $(S, \mathcal{S}, \mu)$ is a totally finite measure space, then a sequence $\{f_n\}$ of measurable real functions on S converges in measure to a function f if and only if every subsequence of $\{f_n\}$ has a subsequence which converges almost everywhere to f. We leave the proof to the reader.

3.6. Summable Functions

We now consider an important subset of the set of measurable functions, the so-called summable functions.

Let $(S, \mathcal{S}, \mu)$ be a totally σ finite measure space. Let $A_1, \ldots, A_n$ be a finite set of pair-wise disjoint sets belonging to $\mathcal{S}$, each of finite measure. We use the notation

$$s = (a_1, A_1; a_2, A_2; \ldots ; a_n, A_n)$$

to represent the function which assumes the value a_i for all $x \in A_i$, $i = 1, \ldots, n$, and the value 0 on $S \sim \bigcup_{i=1}^{n} A_i$. This function is measurable and is called a **step function.** We define the **integral** of the step function s as

$$\int_S s \, d\mu = \sum_{i=1}^{n} a_i \mu(A_i).$$

The following simple facts are easy to prove:

If s is a step function and a is a real number, then as is a step function and $\int_S as \, d\mu = a \int_S s \, d\mu$.

If s and t are step functions and $s(x) \geq t(x)$, for every $x \in S$, then $\int_S s \, d\mu \geq \int_S t \, d\mu$. In particular, if s is non-negative, then $\int_S s \, d\mu \geq 0$.

The proofs will be omitted. We do prove

PROPOSITION 1. If s and t are step functions then $s + t$ is a step function and

$$\int_S (s + t)\, d\mu = \int_S s\, d\mu + \int_S t\, d\mu.$$

Proof. Let $s = (a_1, A_1; a_2, A_2; \dots ; a_n, A_n)$ and $t = (b_1, B_1; b_2, B_2; \dots ; b_m, B_m)$. Then

$$s + t = \Big(a_1 + b_1, A_1 \cap B_1; \dots ; a_i + b_j, A_i \cap B_j; \dots;$$
$$a_n + b_m, A_n \cap B_m; \dots ; a_i, A_i \sim \bigcup_{j=1}^{m} B_j; \dots ; b_j, B_j \sim \bigcup_{i=1}^{n} A_i \dots\Big).$$

Then

$$\begin{aligned}
\int_S (s + t)\, d\mu &= \sum_{i=1}^{n} \sum_{j=1}^{m} (a_i + b_j)\mu(A_i \cap B_j) \\
&\quad + \sum_{i=1}^{n} a_i\mu\Big(A_i \sim \bigcup_{j=1}^{m} B_j\Big) + \sum_{j=1}^{m} b_j\Big(B_j \sim \bigcup_{i=1}^{n} A_i\Big) \\
&= \sum_{i=1}^{n} \sum_{j=1}^{m} a_i\mu(A_i \cap B_j) + \sum_{i=1}^{n} a_i\mu\Big(A_i \sim \bigcup_{j=1}^{m} B_j\Big) \\
&\quad + \sum_{j=1}^{m} \sum_{i=1}^{n} b_j\mu(A_i \cap B_j) + \sum_{j=1}^{m} b_j\mu\Big(B_j \sim \bigcup_{i=1}^{n} A_i\Big) \\
&= \sum_{i=1}^{n} a_i\mu(A_i) + \sum_{j=1}^{m} b_j\mu(B_j) \\
&= \int_S s\, d\mu + \int_S t\, d\mu.
\end{aligned}$$

We proceed to extend the definition of integral to measurable functions which are not step functions. For this purpose, we need

PROPOSITION 2. If f is non-negative and measurable, there is a non-decreasing sequence $\{s_n\}$ of step functions which converges everywhere to f.

Proof. Let $\{A_n\}$ be an increasing sequence of sets of finite measure such that $S = \bigcup_{n=1}^{\infty} A_n$. Let

$$s_n(x) = \begin{cases} \dfrac{k}{2^n} \text{ if } x \in A_n \text{ and } \dfrac{k}{2^n} \le f(x) < \dfrac{k+1}{2^n},\ k = 0, 1, \dots, n \cdot 2^n - 1, \\ n \ \text{ if } x \in A_n, f(x) \ge n \\ 0 \ \text{ if } x \notin A_n. \end{cases}$$

The sequence $\{s_n\}$ is easily seen to have the desired property.

We observe that for every non-decreasing sequence $\{s_n\}$ of step functions, the sequence

$$\left\{\int_S s_n \, d\mu\right\}$$

is a non-decreasing sequence of real numbers, so that it converges to a real number or to $+\infty$. The next fact is crucial to our discussion.

Proposition 3. If f is a non-negative measurable function and $\{s_n\}$ and $\{t_n\}$ are non-decreasing sequences of step functions converging to f, then

$$\lim_{n\to\infty} \int_S s_n \, d\mu = \lim_{n\to\infty} \int_S t_n \, d\mu.$$

Proof. Fix N. Let $s_N = (a_1, A_1; a_2, A_2; \ldots; a_k, A_k)$. Let $\epsilon > 0$ and $M = \max(a_1, \ldots, a_k)$. Now,

$$\lim_{n\to\infty} t_n(x) = f(x) \geq s_N(x)$$

for every x. It follows that the sets

$$E_n = \left[x : t_n(x) < s_N(x) - \frac{\epsilon}{2\sum_{i=1}^{k} \mu(A_i)}\right]$$

satisfy $\lim_{n\to\infty} \mu(E_n) = 0$. Choose n so that $\mu(E_n) < \dfrac{\epsilon}{2M}$. Then

$$\int_S t_n \, d\mu > \int_S s_N \, d\mu - \left(\frac{\epsilon}{2\sum_{i=1}^{k} \mu(A_i)} \sum_{i=1}^{k} \mu(A_i) + \frac{\epsilon}{2M} M\right)$$

$$= \int_S s_N \, d\mu - \epsilon.$$

Thus, $\lim_{n\to\infty} \int_S t_n \, d\mu \geq \int_S s_N \, d\mu$. Since this holds for every N, we have $\lim_{n\to\infty} \int_S t_n \, d\mu \geq \lim_{n\to\infty} \int_S s_n \, d\mu$.

Propositions 2 and 3 allow us to define the integral of any non-negative measurable function on S. Thus, if f is measurable and non-negative on S, let $\{s_n\}$ be a non-decreasing sequence of step functions which converges to f. Define the **integral** of f as

$$\int_S f \, d\mu = \lim_{n\to\infty} \int_S s_n \, d\mu,$$

where the value $+\infty$ is allowed for the integral.

We now prove

PROPOSITION 4. If f and g are non-negative measurable functions on S, then

$$\int_S (f + g)\, d\mu = \int_S f\, d\mu + \int_S g\, d\mu.$$

Proof. Suppose that $\int_S f\, d\mu$ and $\int_S g\, d\mu$ are both finite. Let $\{s_n\}$ be a non-decreasing sequence of step functions which converges to f and $\{t_n\}$ a non-decreasing sequence of step functions which converges to g. The result follows from the facts that

$$\int_S f\, d\mu = \lim_{n\to\infty} \int_S s_n\, d\mu, \quad \int_S g\, d\mu = \lim_{n\to\infty} \int_S t_n\, d\mu,$$

and

$$\int_S (s_n + t_n)\, d\mu = \int_S s_n\, d\mu + \int_S t_n\, d\mu \quad \text{for } n = 1, 2, \ldots .$$

The case where one of the integrals is infinite is trivial.

The following facts, whose proofs are easy and will be omitted, also hold:

If f and g are non-negative and $f(x) \geq g(x)$ for every $x \in S$, then $\int_S f\, d\mu \geq \int_S g\, d\mu$.

If f is a non-negative measurable function and $a \geq 0$, then

$$\int_S af\, d\mu = a \int_S f\, d\mu.$$

We now extend the definition of integral to functions which assume both positive and negative values. Let f, accordingly, be a measurable real function on S. We consider the positive and negative parts of f defined as

$$f^+(x) = \begin{cases} f(x) & \text{if } f(x) > 0 \\ 0 & \text{if } f(x) \leq 0, \end{cases}$$

and

$$f^-(x) = \begin{cases} -f(x) & \text{if } f(x) < 0 \\ 0 & \text{if } f(x) \geq 0. \end{cases}$$

It is clear that f^+ and f^- are non-negative measurable functions and that

$$f = f^+ - f^-.$$

Moreover,

$$|f| = f^+ + f^-.$$

A measurable function f is said to be **summable** if both $\int_S f^+\, d\mu < \infty$ and $\int_S f^-\, d\mu < \infty$.

If f is summable, then the integral of f is defined as

$$\int_S f\, d\mu = \int_S f^+\, d\mu - \int_S f^-\, d\mu.$$

Otherwise, f is said to be non-summable. Sometimes functions are called **integrable** if at most one of the two integrals $\int_S f^+ \, d\mu$ and $\int_S f^- \, d\mu$ is infinite.

If $\int_S f^+ \, d\mu = +\infty$ and $\int_S f^- \, d\mu < +\infty$, then we say

$$\int_S f \, d\mu = +\infty.$$

If $\int_S f^+ \, d\mu < +\infty$ and $\int_S f^- \, d\mu = +\infty$, then we say

$$\int_S f \, d\mu = -\infty.$$

If both $\int_S f^+ \, d\mu = +\infty$ and $\int_S f^- \, d\mu = +\infty$, then f is non-integrable as well as non-summable.

Now, let f and g both be summable. Then

$$f + g = (f^+ + g^+) - (f^- + g^-).$$

Clearly, the function $f^+ + g^+ \geq f + g$. But $(f + g)^+$, as $\max(f + g, 0)$, is the smallest non-negative function which exceeds $f + g$. Therefore,

$$f^+ + g^+ = (f + g)^+ + h,$$

where h is non-negative. So

$$\int_S (f^+ + g^+) \, d\mu = \int_S (f + g)^+ \, d\mu + \int_S h \, d\mu.$$

Also,

$$f^- + g^- = (f + g)^- + h,$$

since

$$(f^+ + g^+) - (f^- + g^-) = (f + g)^+ - (f + g)^-,$$

so that

$$\int_S (f^- + g^-) \, d\mu = \int_S (f + g)^- \, d\mu + \int_S h \, d\mu.$$

Thus,

$$\int_S (f + g)^+ \, d\mu < \infty \quad \text{and} \quad \int_S (f + g)^- \, d\mu < \infty,$$

so that $f + g$ is summable. Moreover,

$$\begin{aligned}\int_S (f + g) \, d\mu &= \int_S (f + g)^+ \, d\mu - \int_S (f + g)^- \, d\mu \\ &= \int_S (f^+ + g^+) \, d\mu - \int_S h \, d\mu - \int_S (f^- + g^-) \, d\mu + \int_S h \, d\mu \\ &= \int_S f^+ \, d\mu - \int_S f^- \, d\mu + \int_S g^+ \, d\mu - \int_S g^- \, d\mu = \int_S f \, d\mu + \int_S g \, d\mu.\end{aligned}$$

We have thus proved

THEOREM 1. If f and g are summable, then $f + g$ is summable and

$$\int_S (f + g) \, d\mu = \int_S f \, d\mu + \int_S g \, d\mu.$$

It is also true that if f is summable and c is a real number, then cf is summable and

$$\int_S cf\,d\mu = c\int_S f\,d\mu.$$

3.7 Fatou and Lebesgue Dominated Convergence Theorems

We now prove some facts about sequences of summable functions.

PROPOSITION 1. If $\{f_n\}$ is a non-decreasing sequence of non-negative summable functions and f is the point-wise limit of $\{f_n\}$, then

$$\int_S f\,d\mu = \lim_{n\to\infty}\int_S f_n\,d\mu,$$

where possibly $\int_S f\,d\mu = +\infty$.

Proof. For every n, let $\{s_{nm}\}$ be a non-decreasing sequence of step functions which converges to f_n, and let

$$t_n = \max\,[s_{ij} : i, j \le n].$$

Then $t_n(x) \le f_n(x)$, for every $x \in S$, so that

$$\int_S t_n\,d\mu \le \int_S f_n\,d\mu, \text{ and } \lim_{n\to\infty}\int_S t_n\,d\mu \le \lim_{n\to\infty}\int_S f_n\,d\mu,$$

where the limits exist since $\{t_n\}$ and $\{f_n\}$ are non-decreasing, so that $\left\{\int_S t_n\,d\mu\right\}$ and $\left\{\int_S f_n\,d\mu\right\}$ are non-decreasing.

For every n, m for all $k \ge \max(m, n)$, $t_k(x) \ge s_{nm}(x)$, for every $x \in S$, so that

$$\lim_{k\to\infty}\int_S t_k\,d\mu \ge \lim_{m\to\infty}\int_S s_{nm}\,d\mu = \int_S f_n\,d\mu.$$

Hence,

$$\lim_{n\to\infty}\int_S t_n\,d\mu = \lim_{n\to\infty}\int_S f_n\,d\mu.$$

We have thus shown that

$$\lim_{n\to\infty}\int_S t_n\,d\mu = \lim_{n\to\infty}\int_S f_n\,d\mu.$$

Now, $\lim_{k\to\infty} t_k(x) \ge f_n(x)$ for every n and $x \in S$, and $t_k(x) \le f(x)$ for every k and $x \in S$. Hence $f(x) = \lim_{k\to\infty} t_k(x)$ for every x. But, by definition, $\int_S f\,d\mu = \lim_{n\to\infty}\int_S t_n\,d\mu$. Hence $\int_S f\,d\mu = \lim_{n\to\infty}\int_S f_n\,d\mu$.

COROLLARY. If $\{f_n\}$ is a non-decreasing sequence of summable functions which converges to f, then

$$\lim_{n\to\infty}\int_S f_n\,d\mu = \int_S f\,d\mu.$$

Proof. Apply proposition 1 to the sequence $\{f_n - f_1\}$ and the limit function $f - f_1$.

It is possible for a sequence $\{f_n\}$ to converge to a function f, but for the integrals of the functions not to converge to the integral of f. We give examples for which this fails in different ways.

EXAMPLE 1. Let S be the open interval (0, 1) and let μ be Lebesgue measure. (In this case, and in others, we shall write $\int f\,dx$, or $\int_0^1 f(x)\,dx$, or $\int f$, or other variants, instead of $\int_S f\,d\mu$.) For every $n = 1, 2, \ldots$, let

$$f_n(x) = \begin{cases} 2k(k+1) & \text{if } x \in \left(\dfrac{1}{k+1}, \dfrac{2k+1}{2k(k+1)}\right) \\ -2k(k+1) & \text{if } x \in \left(\dfrac{2k+1}{2k(k+1)}, \dfrac{1}{k}\right) \qquad k = 1, \ldots, n \\ 0 & \text{elsewhere.} \end{cases}$$

Then f_n is summable, for every $n = 1, 2, \ldots$. Indeed, $\int f_n = 0$. But $\{f_n\}$ converges to the function f on (0, 1) defined by

$$(x) = \begin{cases} 2k(k+1) & \text{if } x \in \left(\dfrac{1}{k+1}, \dfrac{2k+1}{2k(k+1)}\right) \\ -2k(k+1) & \text{if } x \in \left(\dfrac{2k+1}{2k(k+1)}, \dfrac{1}{k}\right) \\ & k = 1, 2, \ldots. \end{cases}$$

But $\int f^+ = +\infty$ and $\int f^- = +\infty$, so that f is not summable.

EXAMPLE 2. Let S be the open interval (0, 1) and let μ be Lebesgue measure. For every $n = 1, 2, \ldots$, let

$$f_n(x) = \begin{cases} n(n+1), & x \in \left(\dfrac{1}{n+1}, \dfrac{1}{n}\right) \\ 0 & \text{elsewhere.} \end{cases}$$

Then $\{f_n\}$ converges on (0, 1) to the function f which is identically zero. But $\int f_n = 1$, $n = 1, 2, \ldots$, and $\int f = 0$.

On the positive side, we already have proposition 1. We prove the basic

THEOREM 1 (Fatou). If $(S, \mathcal{S}, \mu)$ is a totally σ finite measure space and $\{f_n\}$ is a sequence of non-negative summable functions on S, then

$$\int_S \left[\liminf_{n\to\infty} f_n\right] d\mu \leq \liminf_{n\to\infty} \int_S f_n\,d\mu.$$

Proof. For every $n = 1, 2, \ldots$, let

$$g_n = \inf [f_n, f_{n+1}, \ldots].$$

Then $\{g_n\}$ is a non-decreasing sequence of summable functions, and

$$\lim_{n\to\infty} g_n(x) = \liminf_{n\to\infty} f_n(x), \quad \text{for every } x \in S.$$

Hence,

$$\int_S \left[\liminf_{n\to\infty} f_n\right] d\mu = \int_S \left[\lim_{n\to\infty} g_n\right] d\mu$$
$$= \lim_{n\to\infty} \int_S g_n \, d\mu.$$

But $g_n(x) \leq f_n(x)$ for every $n = 1, 2, \ldots$, and $x \in S$, so that

$$\int_S g_n \, d\mu \leq \int_S f_n(x) \, d\mu \quad \text{for every } n = 1, 2, \ldots.$$

Thus,

$$\int_S \left[\liminf_{n\to\infty} f_n\right] d\mu = \lim_{n\to\infty} \int_S g_n \, d\mu \leq \liminf_{n\to\infty} \int_S f_n \, d\mu.$$

COROLLARY. If $\{f_n\}$ is a sequence of non-positive summable functions then

$$\int_S \left[\limsup_{n\to\infty} f_n\right] d\mu \geq \limsup_{n\to\infty} \int_S f_n \, d\mu.$$

The proof is left to the reader.

We now prove the so-called dominated convergence theorem.

THEOREM 2 (Lebesgue). If $(S, \mathcal{S}, \mu)$ is a totally σ finite measure space and $\{f_n\}$ is a convergent sequence of summable functions on S such that there is a summable g for which $|f_n(x)| \leq g(x)$, for every $n = 1, 2, \ldots$ and $x \in S$, then

$$\lim_{n\to\infty} \int_S f_n \, d\mu = \int_S \left[\lim_{n\to\infty} f_n\right] d\mu.$$

Proof. The functions in the sequence $\{g + f_n\}$ are non-negative and summable, so that, by theorem 1,

$$\int_S \left[\liminf_{n\to\infty} (g + f_n)\right] d\mu \leq \liminf_{n\to\infty} \int_S (g + f_n) \, d\mu.$$

But,

$$\int_S \left[\liminf_{n\to\infty} (g + f_n)\right] d\mu = \int_S g \, d\mu + \int_S \left[\liminf_{n\to\infty} f_n\right] d\mu$$

and

$$\liminf_{n\to\infty} \int_S (g + f_n) \, d\mu = \int_S g \, d\mu + \liminf_{n\to\infty} \int_S f_n \, d\mu.$$

Hence,

$$\int_S \left[\liminf_{n\to\infty} f_n\right] d\mu \le \liminf_{n\to\infty} \int_S f_n\, d\mu.$$

Similarly, by using the corollary to theorem 1,

$$\int_S \left[\limsup_{n\to\infty} f_n\right] d\mu \ge \limsup_{n\to\infty} \int_S f_n\, d\mu.$$

Accordingly,

$$\liminf_{n\to\infty} \int_S f_n\, d\mu \ge \int_S \left[\lim_{n\to\infty} f_n\right] d\mu \ge \limsup_{n\to\infty} \int_S f_n\, d\mu,$$

so that $\lim_{n\to\infty} \int_S f_n\, d\mu$ exists and equals $\int_S \left[\lim_{n\to\infty} f_n\right] d\mu$.

3.8 Integral as a Set Function

Let $(S, \mathcal{S}, \mu)$ be a totally σ finite measure space, and let f be a non-negative summable function on S. We show, in this section, that f determines a measure on S which is totally finite.

For every $E \in \mathcal{S}$, we define the integral of f on E as

$$\int_E f\, d\mu = \int_S f \cdot \chi_E\, d\mu,$$

where $\chi_E = \begin{cases} 1, & x \in E \\ 0, & x \notin E \end{cases}$ is the characteristic function of E.

Since, for every $x \in S$,

$$0 \le (f \cdot \chi_E)(x) \le f(x),$$

it follows that $f \cdot \chi_E$ is summable and

$$0 \le \int_E f\, d\mu \le \int_S f\, d\mu.$$

Let

$$\nu(E) = \int_E f\, d\mu.$$

Then ν is a non-negative function on $\mathcal{S}$. We show it is a measure.

Suppose $E_1, E_2 \in \mathcal{S}$ and $E_1 \cap E_2 = 0$. Then,

$$\begin{aligned} \nu(E_1 \cup E_2) &= \int_{E_1 \cup E_2} f\, d\mu = \int_S f \cdot \chi_{E_1 \cup E_2}\, d\mu \\ &= \int_S f \cdot (\chi_{E_1} + \chi_{E_2})\, d\mu = \int_S f\chi_{E_1}\, d\mu + \int_S f\chi_{E_2}\, d\mu \\ &= \int_{E_1} f\, d\mu + \int_{E_2} f\, d\mu = \nu(E_1) + \nu(E_2). \end{aligned}$$

This shows that the set function ν is additive. Now, we show it is completely additive. For this purpose, let $E_n \in \mathcal{S}$, $n = 1, 2, \ldots$, where $E_i \cap E_j = 0$, if $i \ne j$, and let $E = \bigcup_{n=1}^{\infty} E_n$. Moreover, let $F_n = \bigcup_{k=1}^{n} E_k$, $n = 1, 2, \ldots$.

Then $\{f \cdot \chi_{F_n}\}$ is a non-decreasing sequence of non-negative functions which converges to the function $f \cdot \chi_E$. It follows that

$$\int_S f\chi_E \, d\mu = \lim_{n\to\infty} \int_S f\chi_{F_n} \, d\mu$$
$$= \sum_{n=1}^{\infty} \int_S f\chi_{E_n} \, d\mu.$$

In other words, $\nu(E) = \sum_{n=1}^{\infty} \nu(E_n)$.

This proves that ν is a measure. Since $\nu(S) = \int_S f \, d\mu < \infty$, the measure $(S, \mathcal{S}, \nu)$ is totally finite.

Suppose, however, that f is summable but not non-negative. We shall see that it again generates a set function ν, which is no longer non-negative. This leads to the notion of a signed measure.

3.9 Signed Measure, Decomposition into Measures

Let S be a set and $\mathcal{S}$ a σ algebra of subsets of S. Then we have $S \in \mathcal{S}$; the empty set $0 \in \mathcal{S}$; for every $E \in \mathcal{S}$, the complement $S \sim E \in \mathcal{S}$; and for every $E_n \in \mathcal{S}$, $n = 1, 2, \ldots$, the union $\bigcup_{n=1}^{\infty} E_n \in \mathcal{S}$.

Let μ be a real valued function on $\mathcal{S}$ such that if $E_n \in \mathcal{S}$, $n = 1, 2, \ldots$, and $E_i \cap E_j = 0$, whenever $i \neq j$, then

$$\mu\left(\bigcup_{n=1}^{\infty} E_n\right) = \sum_{n=1}^{\infty} \mu(E_n).$$

Such a function μ is called a **finite signed measure** on $\mathcal{S}$, and we write $(S, \mathcal{S}, \mu)$ for the signed measure.

PROPOSITION 1. If $(S, \mathcal{S}, \mu)$ is a finite signed measure, there is an M such that $|\mu(E)| < M$ for every $E \in \mathcal{S}$.

Proof. Suppose the assertion is false. Then

$$\sup\,[|\mu(E)| : E \in \mathcal{S}] = +\infty.$$

Since $\mu(S)$ is finite, there is then a $T \in \mathcal{S}$ such that

$$|\mu(T)| \geq |\mu(S)| + 1.$$

If

$$\sup\,[|\mu(E)| : E \in \mathcal{S},\, E \subset T] = +\infty,$$

let $S_1 = T$; otherwise, let $S_1 = S \sim T$. In either case, $|\mu(S_1)| \geq 1$ and

$$\sup\,[|\mu(E)| : E \in \mathcal{S},\, E \subset S_1] = +\infty.$$

By induction, we obtain a decreasing sequence

$$S_1 \supset S_2 \supset \ldots \supset S_n \supset \ldots$$

such that $|\mu(S_n)| \geq n$, and

$$\sup [|\mu(E)| : E \in \mathcal{S}, E \subset S_n] = +\infty,$$

for every $n = 1, 2, \ldots$. Let

$$R = \bigcap_{n=1}^{\infty} S_n.$$

It is easily seen from the countable additivity of μ that

$$\mu(R) = \lim_{n\to\infty} \mu(S_n).$$

Hence

$$|\mu(R)| = +\infty$$

in contradiction with the hypothesis.

In particular, let $(S, \mathcal{S}, \mu)$ be a totally σ finite measure space and let f be a real valued summable function on S. For every $E \in \mathcal{S}$, let

$$\nu(E) = \int_E f\, d\mu = \int_S f \cdot \chi_E\, d\mu.$$

Since f is summable, the functions $f^+ = \max(f, 0)$ and $f^- = -\min(f, 0)$ are non-negative summable functions, and the corresponding set functions ν^+ and ν^-, defined by

$$\nu^+(E) = \int_E f^+\, d\mu$$

and

$$\nu^-(E) = \int_E f^-\, d\mu,$$

are completely additive non-negative set functions, so that they are measures. Moreover, it is clear that

$$\nu(E) = \nu^+(E) - \nu^-(E)$$

and it readily follows that ν is a finite signed measure.

Every signed measure behaves essentially like the one obtained above, and this is the meaning of the next few results.

Let $(S, \mathcal{S}, \mu)$ be a finite signed measure. We shall show that there are non-negative totally finite measures μ^+, μ^-, and $|\mu|$ such that, for every $E \in \mathcal{S}$,

$$\mu(E) = \mu^+(E) - \mu^-(E)$$

and

$$|\mu|(E) = \mu^+(E) + \mu^-(E).$$

Indeed, we define μ^+ and μ^- by

$$\mu^+(E) = \sup [\mu(T) : T \in \mathcal{S}, T \subset E]$$

and

$$\mu^-(E) = -\inf [\mu(T) : T \in \mathcal{S}, T \subset E].$$

It is almost immediately evident that μ^+ and μ^- are completely additive and non-negative. We show that for every $E \in \mathcal{S}$,

$$\mu(E) = \mu^+(E) - \mu^-(E).$$

Let $T \subset E$, $T \in \mathcal{S}$. Then

$$\mu(T) = \mu(E) - \mu(E \sim T).$$

Since $\mu^+(E) \geq \mu(E \sim T)$, it follows that

$$\mu(T) \geq \mu(E) - \mu^+(E).$$

This holds for every $T \subset E$, $T \in \mathcal{S}$, so that

$$-\mu^-(E) \geq \mu(E) - \mu^+(E),$$

and

$$\mu^+(E) - \mu^-(E) \geq \mu(E).$$

A similar computation shows that

$$\mu^+(E) - \mu^-(E) \leq \mu(E).$$

Since μ^+ and μ^- are measures, $|\mu| = \mu^+ + \mu^-$ is also a measure. It is called the **total variation** of the measure μ. Indeed, it is easy to show that, for every $E \in \mathcal{S}$,

$$|\mu|\,(E) = \sup \sum_{i=1}^{k} |\mu(E_i)|,$$

where the supremum is taken for all partitions $E = \bigcup_{i=1}^{k} E_i$, $E_i \cap E_j = 0$, $i \neq j$. We leave the proof for the reader.

Now let $(S, \mathcal{S}, \mu)$ be a finite signed measure. We show that there are sets $A \in \mathcal{S}$, $B \in \mathcal{S}$ such that $A \cup B = S$, $A \cap B = 0$, and such that $\mu(E) \geq 0$ whenever $E \subset A$, $E \in \mathcal{S}$, and $\mu(E) \leq 0$, whenever $E \subset B$, $E \in \mathcal{S}$. This follows from

LEMMA 1. If $(S, \mathcal{S}, \mu)$ is a finite signed measure, there is an $E \in \mathcal{S}$ such that

$$\mu(E) = \sup\,[\mu(T) : T \in \mathcal{S}].$$

Proof. Let $m = \sup\,[\mu(T) : T \in \mathcal{S}]$. There is a set $E_1 \in \mathcal{S}$ such that $\mu(E_1) > m - 1/2$. There is a set $E_2 \in \mathcal{S}$ such that $E_2 = (E_1 \sim R_1) \cup S_1$, where $|\mu(R_1)| < 1/2$, $|\mu(S_1)| < 1/2$ and $\mu(E_2) > m - 1/2^2$. Proceeding in this way, we obtain a sequence $E_n \in \mathcal{S}$, $n = 1, 2, \ldots$, such that

$$E_{n+1} = (E_n \sim R_n) \cup S_n,$$

where $|\mu(R_n)| < 1/2^n$, $|\mu(S_n)| < 1/2^n$, and $\mu(E_n) > m - 1/2^n$, for every $n = 1, 2, \ldots$. Let

$$E = \bigcup_{k=1}^{\infty} \bigcap_{n=k}^{\infty} E_n.$$

It is easily seen that

$$\mu(E) > \mu(E_n) - \frac{1}{2^{n-1}} > m - \frac{1}{2^{n-2}},$$

for every n, so that $\mu(E) = m$.

Let $A = E$, $B = S \sim E$. If A has a subset $T \in \mathcal{S}$ such that $\mu(T) < 0$, then $\mu(A \sim T) = \mu(A) - \mu(T) > m$, which is impossible. Also, if B had a subset $T \in \mathcal{S}$ such that $\mu(T) > 0$, then $\mu(A \cup T) = m + \mu(T) > m$, which is impossible. We may now state

THEOREM 1. If $(S, \mathcal{S}, \mu)$ is a finite signed measure, there are sets $A \in \mathcal{S}$, $B \in \mathcal{S}$ such that $A \cup B = S$, $A \cap B = 0$, $\mu(T) \geq 0$ if $T \in \mathcal{S}$, $T \subset A$, and $\mu(T) \leq 0$ if $T \in \mathcal{S}$, $T \subset B$.

The set functions $\mu^+(E) = \mu(E \cap A)$ and $\mu^-(E) = -\mu(E \cap B)$ are measures, and $\mu = \mu^+ - \mu^-$, $|\mu| = \mu^+ + \mu^-$.

3.10 Absolute Continuity and Singularity of Measures

Let $(S, \mathcal{S}, \mu)$ be a totally finite measure space, and f a summable function on S. Then the set function ν given by

$$\nu(E) = \int_E f\, d\mu$$

defines a finite signed measure $(S, \mathcal{S}, \nu)$.

Let $\epsilon > 0$. Then, by the definition of summability, there is an n such that if

$$A = [x : f(x) > n] \quad \text{and} \quad B = [x : f(x) < -n]$$

then

$$\int_A f\, d\mu < \frac{\epsilon}{4} \quad \text{and} \quad \int_B -f\, d\mu < \frac{\epsilon}{4}.$$

Now, let $C = S \sim (A \cup B)$, let $\delta = \epsilon/2n$, and let $E \in \mathcal{S}$ with $\mu(E) < \delta$. Then

$$|\nu|\,(E) = \int_E |f|\, d\mu = \int_{C \cap E} |f|\, d\mu + \int_{A \cap E} |f|\, d\mu + \int_{B \cap E} |f|\, d\mu$$
$$\leq \delta \cdot n + \frac{\epsilon}{4} + \frac{\epsilon}{4} = \epsilon.$$

We consider the following definition. If $(S, \mathcal{S}, \mu)$ and $(S, \mathcal{S}, \nu)$ are finite signed measures, ν is said to be **absolutely continuous** with respect to μ if $|\mu|\,(E) = 0$ implies $|\nu|\,(E) = 0$.

The main fact regarding absolute continuity is the Radon-Nikodym theorem below, which by the above analysis implies that if ν is absolutely continuous with respect to μ, where μ is a measure, then for every $\epsilon > 0$ there is a $\delta > 0$ such that $\mu(E) < \delta$ implies $|\nu|\,(E) < \epsilon$.

THEOREM 1. If $(S, \mathcal{S}, \mu)$ is a totally finite measure space and $(S, \mathcal{S}, \nu)$ is a finite signed measure, then if ν is absolutely continuous with respect to μ, there is a summable f on S such that, for every $E \in \mathcal{S}$,

$$\nu(E) = \int_E f \, d\mu.$$

Proof. We suppose first that ν is non-negative and obtain a non-negative summable function with the desired property. In order to obtain such a function, we let $\mathcal{M}$ be the set of non-negative summable functions on S such that, for every $E \in \mathcal{S}$,

$$\int_E f \, d\mu \leq \nu(E).$$

The set $\mathcal{M}$ is non-empty since $0 \in \mathcal{M}$. We note that if $f \in \mathcal{M}$ and $g \in \mathcal{M}$, then $\max(f, g) \in \mathcal{M}$. For, if $E \in \mathcal{S}$, let

$$E_1 = [x : x \in E, f(x) \geq g(x)] \quad \text{and} \quad E_2 = E \sim E_1.$$

Then

$$\int_E \max(f, g) \, d\mu = \int_{E_1} f \, d\mu + \int_{E_2} g \, d\mu$$
$$\leq \nu(E_1) + \nu(E_2) = \nu(E).$$

Now, let

$$m = \sup \left[\int_S f \, d\mu : f \in \mathcal{M}\right].$$

There is a sequence $f_n \in \mathcal{M}$, $n = 1, 2, \ldots$ such that

$$\lim_{n \to \infty} \int_S f_n \, d\mu = m.$$

For every n, let

$$g_n = \max(f_1, f_2, \ldots, f_n).$$

Then $g_n \in \mathcal{M}$, $n = 1, 2, \ldots$, is a non-decreasing sequence, and

$$\lim_{n \to \infty} \int_S g_n \, d\mu = m.$$

Let $g = \lim_{n \to \infty} g_n$. Since

$$\int_E g \, d\mu = \lim_{n \to \infty} \int_E g_n \, d\mu,$$

for every $E \in \mathcal{S}$, it follows that $g \in \mathcal{M}$ and $\int_S g \, d\mu = m$.

We now define a measure ω by

$$\omega(E) = \nu(E) - \int_E g \, d\mu.$$

Since $g \in \mathcal{M}$, ω is non-negative. We show it is identically zero. Suppose then that there is an $E \in \mathcal{S}$ with $\omega(E) > 0$. There is then a $k > 0$ such that $\omega(E) > k\mu(E)$, i.e.,

$$(\omega - k\mu)(E) > 0.$$

There is then a subset $A \subset E$, $A \in \mathcal{S}$, such that

$$(\omega - k\mu)(A) > 0,$$

and for every $T \subset A$, $T \in \mathcal{S}$,

$$(\omega - k\mu)(T) \geq 0.$$

It is evident that $\omega - k\mu$ is absolutely continuous with respect to μ, and it follows that $\mu(A) > 0$.

We next note that

$$g + k\chi_A \in \mathcal{M}.$$

For every $E \in \mathcal{S}$,

$$\int_E (g + k\chi_A)\, d\mu = \int_{E \sim A} g\, d\mu + \int_{E \cap A} (g + k\chi_A)\, d\mu$$
$$\leq \nu(E \sim A) + \nu(E \cap A) = \nu(E).$$

But,

$$\int_S (g + k\chi_A)\, d\mu = m + k\mu(A) > m,$$

which is a contradiction. Thus, for every $E \in \mathcal{S}$,

$$\nu(E) = \int_E g\, d\mu.$$

The general case follows by letting $\nu = \nu^+ - \nu^-$ and finding the measurable functions g and h which correspond to ν^+ and ν^-, respectively. Then for every $E \in \mathcal{S}$,

$$\nu(E) = \int_E (g - h)\, d\mu.$$

A companion notion to absolute continuity is that of singularity. If $(S, \mathcal{S}, \mu)$ and $(S, \mathcal{S}, \nu)$ are finite signed measures, then ν is **singular** with respect to μ if there are $A \in \mathcal{S}$, $B \in \mathcal{S}$ such that $A \cup B = S$ and $A \cap B = 0$, and $\mu(A) = 0$, $\nu(B) = 0$. Clearly, ν is singular with respect to μ if and only if μ is singular with respect to ν. The next theorem will be stated and proved only for the case of totally finite measures.

THEOREM 2. If $(S, \mathcal{S}, \mu)$ and $(S, \mathcal{S}, \nu)$ are totally finite measures, there are measures α and β, which are singular with respect to each other, such that α is absolutely continuous with respect to μ, β is singular with respect to μ, and $\nu = \alpha + \beta$. There is then a summable f, with respect to μ, such that, for every $E \in \mathcal{S}$,

$$\nu(E) = \int_E f\, d\mu + \beta(E).$$

Proof. Let

$$\mathcal{A} = [E : E \in \mathcal{S},\ \mu(E) = 0],$$

and let

$$m = \sup\,[\nu(E) : E \in \mathcal{A}].$$

For every n, there is an $E_n \in \mathcal{A}$ such that $\nu(E_n) > m - 1/n$. Let

$$B = \bigcup_{n=1}^{\infty} E_n.$$

Then $\mu(B) = 0$, so that $B \in \mathcal{A}$, and $\nu(B) = m$. Let $A = S \sim B$. We now let

$$\alpha(E) = \nu(E \cap A) \quad \text{and} \quad \beta(E) = \nu(E \cap B),$$

for every $E \in \mathcal{S}$. Then it is clear that α and β are measures which are singular with respect to each other and that β is singular with respect to μ. Moreover, $\nu = \alpha + \beta$. We show that α is absolutely continuous with respect to μ. Otherwise, there would be an $E \subset A$, $E \in \mathcal{S}$, such that $\mu(E) = 0$ and

$$\nu(E) > 0.$$

Then $\mu(E \cup B) = 0$ and $\nu(E \cup B) = \nu(E) + m > m$, which is impossible.

3.11 The L_p Spaces, Completeness

In this section, we introduce an important class of Banach spaces, the L_p spaces. Let $(S, \mathcal{S}, \mu)$ be a totally σ finite measure space, and let $p \geq 1$. A measurable real function f on S is said to be in $L_p = L_p(S, \mathcal{S}, \mu)$ if

$$\int_S |f|^p \, d\mu < \infty.$$

We first note that L_p is a vector space. If $f \in L_p$, $a \in R$, then

$$\int_S |af|^p \, d\mu = |a|^p \int_S |f|^p \, d\mu < \infty,$$

so that $af \in L_p$. If $f \in L_p$, $g \in L_p$,

$$A = [x : |f(x)| \geq |g(x)|] \quad \text{and} \quad B = S \sim A,$$

then

$$\begin{aligned}\int_S |f + g|^p \, d\mu &= \int_A |f + g|^p \, d\mu + \int_B |f + g|^p \, d\mu \\ &\leq 2^p \int_A |f|^p \, d\mu + 2^p \int_B |g|^p \, d\mu \\ &\leq 2^p \Big[\int_S |f|^p \, d\mu + \int_S |g|^p \, d\mu\Big] < \infty.\end{aligned}$$

Hence, L_p is a vector space.

The vector space L_p has a "natural" norm for which it is a Banach space. We consider the case $p = 1$ first, and let

$$\|f\| = \int_S |f| \, d\mu$$

for $f \in L_1$. Then $\|f\| \geq 0$, and $\|f\| = 0$ if and only if f is zero almost everywhere. It is accordingly clear that the objects we are considering are not functions but are equivalence classes of functions. The objects of L_p, $p > 1$, will also be equivalence classes of functions. We use the function notation for these objects. That we have a norm in L_1 now follows since

$$\|af\| = \int_S |af|\, d\mu = |a| \int_S |f|\, d\mu = |a|\, \|f\|,$$

and

$$\|f + g\| = \int_S |f + g|\, d\mu \leq \int_S |f|\, d\mu + \int_S |g|\, d\mu$$
$$= \|f\| + \|g\|.$$

Thus, with this norm, L_1 is a normed vector space.

For $p > 1$, the norm is taken as

$$\|f\| = \left[\int_S |f|^p\, d\mu\right]^{1/p}.$$

Again, $\|f\| \geq 0$, and $\|f\| = 0$ if and only if f is zero almost everywhere. Moreover, it is trivial that

$$\|af\| = |a|\, \|f\|.$$

The proof that $\|f + g\| \leq \|f\| + \|g\|$ involves the Hölder and Minkowski inequalities. Since the proofs differ little from those given in Chapter 1, we leave the minor changes needed for the proofs to the reader. Having conceded this much, we know that L_p, $p > 1$ is a normed vector space. We now prove

THEOREM 1. If $(S, \mathcal{S}, \mu)$ is a totally σ finite measure space and $p \geq 1$, then the normed vector space $L_p = L_p(S, \mathcal{S}, \mu)$ is complete.

Proof. Let $\{f_n\}$ be a Cauchy sequence in L_p. This implies that, for every $\epsilon > 0$, there is an N such that $m, n > N$ implies

$$\int_S |f_n - f_m|^p\, d\mu < \epsilon.$$

Now, $\{f_n\}$ converges in measure since $\int_S |f_n - f_m|^p\, d\mu < \epsilon$ implies

$$\mu[x : |f_n(x) - f_m(x)| > \epsilon^{1/2p}] < \epsilon^{1/2}.$$

It follows that $\{f_n\}$ has a subsequence $\{f_{n_k}\}$ which converges almost everywhere to a function f.

Now, $\{|f_{n_k}|^p\}$ converges almost everywhere to $|f|^p$, and it follows that

$$\int_S |f|^p\, d\mu \leq \liminf_{k \to \infty} \int_S |f_{n_k}|^p\, d\mu < \infty,$$

whereby $f \in L_p$.

Since, for every k, the sequence $\{|f_{n_r} - f_{n_k}|^p\}$ converges almost everywhere to $|f - f_{n_k}|^p$, we have

$$\int_S |f - f_{n_k}|^p\, d\mu \leq \liminf_{r \to \infty} \int_S |f_{n_r} - f_{n_k}|^p\, d\mu.$$

It follows that, for every $\epsilon > 0$, there is an N, such that $k > N$ implies $\|f - f_{n_k}\| < \epsilon$. Thus $\{f_{n_k}\}$ converges in L_p to f and, since $\{f_n\}$ is a Cauchy sequence, $\{f_n\}$ converges in L_p to f.

The spaces $L_p = L_p(S, \mathcal{S}, \mu)$, $p \geq 1$, are thus Banach spaces.

We now consider the case where $(S, \mathcal{S}, \mu)$ is one dimensional Lebesgue measure and $S = [0, 1]$. We show that in this case the L_p spaces are separable.

LEMMA 1. Let S_i, $i = 1, \ldots, n$, be a partition of S into measurable sets which are pair-wise disjoint and such that $S = \bigcup_{i=1}^{n} S_i$. Then, for every $\epsilon > 0$, there are elementary sets J_i, $i = 1, \ldots, n$, which are pair-wise disjoint and such that

$$S \sim \left(\bigcup_{i=1}^{n} J_i\right)$$

is finite, and

$$\mu(S_i \sim J_i) < \epsilon, \quad i = 1, \ldots, n.$$

Proof. This is a routine application of the definition of measurable set, and the proof is left to the reader.

We shall call a function a **stair** function if there is a partition $0 = a_0 < a_1 < \ldots < a_n = 1$, on each interval of which the function is constant.

LEMMA 2. If f is a bounded measurable function on S, then for every $\epsilon > 0$ there is a stair function g, with the same bound as f, and such that

$$|f(x) - g(x)| < \epsilon$$

except on a set of measure less than ϵ.

Proof. This is an easy application of lemma 1 and the details are left to the reader.

COROLLARY. If f is a bounded measurable function on S, then for every $\epsilon > 0$, there is a continuous function h, with the same bound as f, and such that

$$|f(x) - h(x)| < \epsilon$$

except on a set of measure less than ϵ.

Proof. By a modification of the function g of lemma 2.

PROPOSITION 1. If $p \geq 1$, the continuous functions are dense in $L_p = L_p(S, \mathcal{S}, \mu)$.

Proof. Let $f \in L_p$, and $\epsilon > 0$. There is a bounded g such that $\|f - g\| < \epsilon/2$. But, by the corollary to lemma 2, there is a continuous h such that $\|g - h\| < \epsilon/2$.

COROLLARY. The spaces $L_p = L_p(S, \mathcal{S}, \mu)$ are separable.

Proof. Let $f \in L_p$ and $\epsilon > 0$. There is a continuous g such that $\|f - g\| < \epsilon/2$. By the Weierstrass approximation theorem, there is a polynomial p, with rational coefficients, such that $\|g - p\| < \epsilon/2$. Since the set of polynomials with rational coefficients is countable, the result follows.

3.12 Approximation and Smoothing Operations

We next discuss the approximation of functions in L_p by means of special functions in a more systematic way.

As a first example, suppose for every $n = 1, 2, \ldots,$ we divide $S = [0, 1]$ into n equal intervals

$$S_1 = \left[0, \frac{1}{n}\right], \quad S_i = \left(\frac{i-1}{n}, \frac{i}{n}\right], \quad i = 2, \ldots, n.$$

Let $p > 1$. For every n, and $f \in L_p$, let

$$f_n(x) = n \int_{S_i} f(x)\, dx, \quad x \in S_i, \quad i = 1, \ldots, n.$$

(We shall write $\int f\, d\mu$ or $\int f(x)\, dx$ for the integral.)

Then f_n is constant on each S_i, the constant being the mean value of f on S_i. We first show that the norm of f_n, in the space L_p, is not greater than that of f.

$$\begin{aligned}
\int_S |f_n|^p\, d\mu &= \sum_{i=1}^{n} \int_{S_i} |f_n|^p\, d\mu \\
&= \sum_{i=1}^{n} \int_{S_i} \left| n \int_{S_i} f(x)\, dx \right|^p dt \\
&= \sum_{i=1}^{n} n^p \int_{S_i} \left| \int_{S_i} f(x)\, dx \right|^p dt \\
&\leq \sum_{i=1}^{n} n^p \int_{S_i} \left\{ \int_{S_i} |f(x)|\, dx \right\}^p dt \\
&\leq \sum_{i=1}^{n} n^p \int_{S_i} \left(\int_{S_i} |f(x)|^p\, dx \right) \left(\int_{S_i} |1|^q\, dx \right)^{p/q} dt,
\end{aligned}$$

where $1/p + 1/q = 1$, and the Hölder inequality is applied in each term to the function pair f, 1. Then,

$$\begin{aligned}
\int_S |f_n|^p\, d\mu &\leq \sum_{i=1}^{n} n^p \int_{S_i} |f|^p\, d\mu \cdot \left(\frac{1}{n}\right)^{1+p/q} \\
&= \sum_{i=1}^{n} \int_{S_i} |f|^p\, d\mu = \int_S |f|^p\, d\mu.
\end{aligned}$$

It follows that $\|f_n\| \leq \|f\|$.

The proof for the case $p = 1$, which is easier, is left to the reader. We now prove

PROPOSITION 1. For every $p \geq 1$, and $f \in L_p$, the sequence $\{f_n\}$ converges to f in the L_p norm.

Proof. Let $\epsilon > 0$. There is a continuous g such that

$$\|f - g\| < \frac{\epsilon}{3}.$$

We show that $\{g_n\}$ converges to g uniformly; hence, in the L_p norm. Let $\eta > 0$. There is a $\delta > 0$ such that $|x - y| < \delta$ implies $|g(x) - g(y)| < \eta$. Choose N so that $1/N < \delta$. Then $n > N$ implies $|g(x) - g_n(x)| < \eta$ for all $x \in S$.

Now, suppose η chosen so small that $n > N$ implies

$$\|g - g_n\| < \frac{\epsilon}{3}.$$

Then,

$$\|f - f_n\| \leq \|f - g\| + \|g - g_n\| + \|g_n - f_n\|.$$

But,

$$\|g_n - f_n\| = \|(g - f)_n\| \leq \|g - f\|,$$

so that

$$\|f - f_n\| \leq \frac{\epsilon}{3} + \frac{\epsilon}{3} + \frac{\epsilon}{3} = \epsilon, \quad \text{for every } n > N.$$

Hence $\{f_n\}$ converges to f in the L_p norm.

Instead of taking the mean values on intervals, as above, we may take a sliding average. Let $S = [0, 1]$ and let μ be Lebesgue measure. Then, for every $f \in L_p$, extend the domain of f so that it is defined for all reals and is zero outside of S. For every $h > 0$, let

$$f_h(x) = \frac{1}{2h} \int_{x-h}^{x+h} f(t)\, dt, \quad 0 \leq x \leq 1.$$

We shall need

LEMMA 3. For every totally finite measure space $(S, \mathcal{S}, \mu)$, and every $p \geq 1$, $L_1 \supset L_p$.

Proof. Let $f \in L_p$, and let

$$E = [x : |f(x)| > 1], \quad \text{and} \quad F = S \sim E.$$

Then,

$$\int_S |f|\, d\mu = \int_F |f|\, d\mu + \int_E |f|\, d\mu$$
$$\leq \int_F |f|\, d\mu + \int_E |f|^p\, d\mu < \infty.$$

Hence, $f \in L_1$.

PROPOSITION 2. For every $f \in L_1$, and $h > 0$, the function f_h is continuous.

Proof. For every $\epsilon > 0$, there is a $\delta > 0$, such that $\mu(E) < \delta$ implies $\int_E |f(t)|\, dt < \epsilon h$. Now, $|x - y| < \delta$ implies

$$|f_h(x) - f_h(y)| = \frac{1}{2h}\left| \int_{x-h}^{x+h} f(t)\, dt - \int_{y-h}^{y+h} f(t)\, dt \right|$$
$$= \frac{1}{2h}\left| \int_{x-h}^{y-h} f(t)\, dt - \int_{y+h}^{x+h} f(t)\, dt \right| < \epsilon.$$

PROPOSITION 3. If $p \geq 1, f \in L_p$, and $h > 0$, then

$$\|f_h\| \leq \|f\|.$$

Proof. We first suppose $p = 1$. Suppose f is non-negative. Then

$$\int_0^1 f_h(x)\, dx = \int_0^1 \left\{\frac{1}{2h}\int_{x-h}^{x+h} f(t)\, dt\right\} dx$$
$$= \frac{1}{2h}\int_{-h}^{h} dx \int_x^{1+x} f(t)\, dt \leq \int_0^1 f(t)\, dt,$$

since

$$\int_x^{1+x} f(t)\, dt \leq \int_0^1 f(t)\, dt \text{ for every } x \in S.$$

(We have used Fubini's theorem, whose proof has been relegated to the exercises.)

Now, consider any $f \in L_1$. Then, for every $x \in S$,

$$|f_h(x)| = \left|\frac{1}{2h}\int_{x-h}^{x+h} f(t)\, dt\right| \leq \frac{1}{2h}\int_{x-h}^{x+h} |f(t)|\, dt$$
$$= |f|_h(x).$$

Then,

$$\int_0^1 |f_h(t)|\, dt \leq \int_0^1 |f|_h(t)\, dt \leq \int_0^1 |f(t)|\, dt.$$

Suppose $p > 1$. Let $f \in L_p$ and $h > 0$. By the Hölder inequality,

$$\left|\int_{x-h}^{x+h} f(t)\, dt\right| \leq \left(\int_{x-h}^{x+h} |f|^p\, d\mu\right)^{1/p}\left(\int_{x-h}^{x+h} d\mu\right)^{1/q},$$

whereby

$$\left|\int_{x-h}^{x+h} f(t)\, dt\right|^p \leq \int_{x-h}^{x+h} |f|^p\, d\mu \cdot (2h)^{p/q},$$

and it follows that

$$|f_h(x)|^p \leq \frac{1}{2h}\int_{x-h}^{x+h} |f|^p\, d\mu = \{|f|^p\}_h(x).$$

So,

$$\int_0^1 |f_h|^p\, d\mu \leq \int_0^1 \{|f|^p\}_h\, d\mu.$$

But,

$$\int_0^1 \{|f|^p\}_h \, d\mu \le \int_0^1 |f|^p \, d\mu,$$

so that

$$\|f_h\| \le \|f\|.$$

THEOREM 1. For every $f \in L_p$, $p \ge 1$,

$$\lim_{h\to 0} \|f - f_h\| = 0.$$

Proof. Suppose g is continuous. Then it is easy to see that the g_h are uniformly bounded and converge uniformly to g on every compact subset of $(0, 1)$. Hence,

$$\lim_{h\to 0} \|g - g_n\| = 0.$$

Let $f \in L_p$ and $\epsilon > 0$. There is a continuous g such that $\|f - g\| < \epsilon/3$. Let $\delta > 0$ be such that $0 < h < \delta$ implies $\|g - g_h\| < \epsilon/3$. Then,

$$\|f - f_h\| \le \|f - g\| + \|g - g_h\| + \|g_h - f_h\|$$

and

$$\|g_h - f_h\| = \|(g - f)_h\| \le \|g - f\|$$

imply that $\|f - f_h\| < \epsilon$, and the theorem is proved.

There are other interesting ways in which this theorem may be proved, and various generalizations which we leave as exercises.

Using the approximating functions f_h, we may obtain an interesting characterization of compact sets in L_p, $p > 1$.

THEOREM 2. If $S = [0, 1]$ and μ is Lebesgue measure, then for every $p > 1$, a set $A \subset L_p$ is compact if and only if it is closed, bounded, and

$$\lim_{h\to 0} \|f - f_h\| = 0$$

uniformly on A.

Proof. We first show that if $\{f_n\}$ is a Cauchy sequence in L_p, then

$$\lim_{h\to 0} \|f_n - f_{n,h}\| = 0$$

and the convergence is uniform in n.

Let $\epsilon > 0$. There is an N such that $n > N$ implies $\|f_n - f_N\| < \epsilon/3$. There is a $\delta_1 > 0$ such that $0 < h < \delta_1$ implies $\|f_N - f_{N,h}\| < \epsilon/3$. Then, for every $n > N$,

$$\|f_n - f_{n,h}\| \le \|f_n - f_N\| + \|f_N - f_{N,h}\| + \|f_{N,h} - f_{n,h}\|.$$

But,

$$\|f_{N,h} - f_{n,h}\| = \|(f_N - f_n)_h\| \le \|f_N - f_n\|,$$

so that

$$\|f_n - f_{n,h}\| < \epsilon.$$

There is a $\delta_2 > 0$ such that $0 < h < \delta_2$ and $n \leq N$ implies $\|f_n - f_{n,h}\| < \epsilon$. Let $\delta = \min(\delta_1, \delta_2)$. Then $0 < h < \delta$ implies

$$\|f_n - f_{n,h}\| < \epsilon, \text{ for all } n.$$

We assume $A \subset L_p$ is compact. Then A is closed and bounded. Suppose $\|f - f_h\|$ does not converge uniformly to 0 on A. Then there is a sequence $\{h_n\}$ converging to 0 and $\{f_n\}, f_n \in A$, and a $k > 0$ such that

$$\|f_n - f_{n,h_n}\| > k, \quad n = 1, 2, \ldots .$$

Since A is compact, the sequence $\{f_n\}$ may be assumed to be convergent. But this contradicts the assertion proved above. Thus, the conditions are necessary.

Suppose now that $A \subset L_p$ is closed, bounded, and that $\lim_{h\to 0} \|f - f_h\| = 0$ uniformly on A. In order to show that A is compact, we need only show that it is totally bounded. We note that we will know this as soon as we know that for every $h > 0$ the set

$$[f_h : f \in A]$$

is totally bounded, for if $\epsilon > 0$ is prescribed, there is a $\delta > 0$ so that $0 < h < \delta$ implies

$$\|f - f_h\| < \epsilon$$

for every $f \in A$. Hence, if we choose a finite set $g_1, \ldots, g_n$ such that for every f_h there is a g_i with $\|f_h - g_i\| < \epsilon$, then $\|f - g_i\| < 2\epsilon$.

But the functions

$$[f_h : f \in A]$$

are continuous and their total boundedness follows from uniform boundedness and equicontinuity, which we now prove.

There is an M such that $\|f\| \leq M$ for every $f \in A$. Let $h > 0$ and $f \in A$. Then for every $x \in [0, 1]$,

$$|f_h(x)| \leq \frac{1}{2h}\left(\int_{x-h}^{x+h} |f|^p \, d\mu\right)^{1/p}\left(\int_{x-h}^{x+h} d\mu\right)^{1/q} \leq \frac{M}{(2h)^{1/p}}.$$

This shows that $[f_h : f \in A]$ is uniformly bounded.

Finally, if $0 \leq x < y \leq 1$, the Hölder inequality implies

$$|f_h(y) - f_h(x)| < \frac{M}{h}|y - x|,$$

so that $[f_h : f \in A]$ is equicontinuous. This completes the proof.

3.13. The Dual of L_p, $p > 1$

We now show that if $p > 1$, the dual of L_p is L_q, where $1/p + 1/q = 1$. It is convenient, in certain parts of the proof, to assume that $(S, \mathcal{S}, \mu)$ is totally finite, and we make this assumption. The necessary changes for the totally

σ finite case are cumbersome but minor. We first consider some preliminary material.

PROPOSITION 1. If $f \in L_p$, $p > 1$, then

$$\|f\| = \max \left[\int_S |fg| \, d\mu : g \in L_q, \|g\| = 1 \right].$$

Proof. By Hölder's inequality,

$$\int_S |fg| \, d\mu \leq \|f\| \, \|g\| \leq \|f\|, \text{ if } \|g\| = 1.$$

Hence,

$$\|f\| \geq \sup \left[\int_S |fg| \, d\mu : g \in L_q, \|g\| = 1 \right].$$

Let

$$g = \operatorname{sgn} f \cdot |f|^{p-1} \, \|f\|^{-p/q},$$

where

$$\operatorname{sgn} f(x) = \begin{cases} +1 & \text{if } f(x) \geq 0 \\ -1 & \text{if } f(x) < 0. \end{cases}$$

Then,

$$\int_S |g|^q \, d\mu = \int_S |f|^{(p-1)q} \, \|f\|^{-p} \, d\mu = 1,$$

so that $\|g\| = 1$. But

$$\int_S |fg| \, d\mu = \int_S |f|^p \, d\mu \cdot \|f\|^{-p/q} = \|f\|^{p-p/q} = \|f\|.$$

PROPOSITION 2. If $f \notin L_p$, $p > 1$, then

$$\sup \left[\int_S |fg| \, d\mu : g \in L_q, \|g\| = 1 \right] = \infty.$$

Proof. Let

$$f_n(x) = \begin{cases} n & \text{if } f(x) > n \\ f(x) & \text{if } |f(x)| \leq n \\ -n & \text{if } f(x) < -n. \end{cases}$$

Then $\{\|f_n\|\}$ is an unbounded increasing sequence. Now,

$$\begin{aligned} \sup \left[\int_S |fg| \, d\mu : g \in L_q, \|g\| = 1 \right] & \\ &\geq \lim_{n \to \infty} \max \left[\int_S |f_n g| \, d\mu : g \in L_q, \|g\| = 1 \right] \\ &= \lim_{n \to \infty} \|f_n\| = \infty. \end{aligned}$$

COROLLARY. If $f \notin L_p$, there is $g \in L_q$ with $\int_S fg \, d\mu = \infty$.

Proof. Let $\epsilon_n > 0$, $n = 1, 2, \ldots$ and $\sum_{n=1}^{\infty} \epsilon_n < \infty$. By proposition 2, there are $g_n \in L_q$, $n = 1, 2, \ldots$ such that fg_n is non-negative, $\|g_n\| = \epsilon_n$ and

$\int_S fg_n \, d\mu > 1$. The function $g = \sum_{n=1}^{\infty} g_n$ is easily seen to have the desired property.

Let $(S, \mathcal{S}, \mu)$ be a totally finite measure space, and let $g \in L_q$, $q > 1$.

PROPOSITION 3. The functional

$$\varphi(f) = \int_S fg \, d\mu$$

is linear and continuous on L_p, and

$$\|\varphi\| = \|g\|.$$

Proof. The functional is linear since for $f_1, f_2 \in L_p$ and $a_1, a_2 \in R$,

$$\varphi(a_1 f_1 + a_2 f_2) = \int_S (a_1 f_1 + a_2 f_2) g \, d\mu = a_1 \int_S f_1 g \, d\mu + a_2 \int_S f_2 g \, d\mu$$
$$= a_1 \varphi(f_1) + a_2 \varphi(f_2).$$

By proposition 1, with the roles of p and q interchanged,

$$\max [|\varphi(f)| : f \in L_p, \quad \|f\| = 1] = \|g\|.$$

This completes the proof.

We shall prove that for every continuous linear functional φ on L_p, $p > 1$, there is a $g \in L_q$ such that

$$\varphi(f) = \int_S fg \, d\mu$$

for every $f \in L_p$. Thus, let φ be a continuous linear functional on L_p. We define a function g as follows:

For every $E \in \mathcal{S}$, let

$$\nu(E) = \varphi(\chi_E).$$

Then ν is a signed measure. Indeed, that it is finite and additive follows from the linearity of φ. Let $\{E_n\}$ be a sequence of pair-wise disjoint sets in $\mathcal{S}$. Let $F_n = \bigcup_{k=1}^{n} E_k$, $n = 1, 2, \ldots$, and let $E = \bigcup_{n=1}^{\infty} E_n$. Then χ_E is the limit of $\{\chi_{F_n}\}$ in the L_p norm so that, since φ is continuous, $\nu(E) = \lim_{n \to \infty} \nu(F_n)$. Hence, ν is a signed measure. Moreover, ν is absolutely continuous with respect to μ. By the Radon-Nikodym theorem, there is a summable g such that

$$\nu(E) = \int_E g \, d\mu$$

for every $E \in \mathcal{S}$. In other words,

$$\varphi(\chi_E) = \nu(E) = \int_E g \, d\mu = \int_S \chi_E g \, d\mu.$$

It follows from the linearity of φ and of the integral that, for every step function f,

$$\varphi(f) = \int_S fg \, d\mu.$$

Let f be a bounded measurable function. There is a sequence $\{f_n\}$ of step functions, which converges uniformly to f, so that $\{f_n g\}$ converges boundedly to fg. Hence,

$$\varphi(f) = \lim_{n\to\infty} \varphi(f_n) = \lim_{n\to\infty} \int_S f_n g \, d\mu = \int_S fg \, d\mu.$$

We next show that the function g is in the space L_q. Suppose $f \in L_p$ and, for every n, let

$$f_n(x) = \begin{cases} |f(x)| \operatorname{sgn} g(x) & \text{if } |f(x)| \le n \\ 0 & \text{if } |f(x)| > n. \end{cases}$$

Since $\|f_n\| \le \|f\|$, we have

$$|\varphi(f_n)| \le \|\varphi\| \, \|f_n\| \le \|\varphi\| \, \|f\|.$$

Since $\{|f_n g|\}$ converges to $|fg|$,

$$\begin{aligned} \int_S |fg| \, d\mu &\le \liminf_{n\to\infty} \int_S |f_n g| \, d\mu \\ &= \liminf_{n\to\infty} \int_S f_n g \, d\mu = \liminf_{n\to\infty} |\varphi(f_n)| \\ &\le \|\varphi\| \, \|f\|. \end{aligned}$$

Thus, $\int_S fg \, d\mu < \infty$, for every $f \in L_p$. By the corollary to proposition 2, it follows that $g \in L_q$.

Now, let $f \in L_p$ and, for every n, let

$$f_n(x) = \begin{cases} n & \text{if } f(x) > n \\ f(x) & \text{if } |f(x)| \le n \\ -n & \text{if } f(x) < -n. \end{cases}$$

Then $\{f_n\}$ converges to f in the L_p norm, so that $\varphi(f) = \lim_{n\to\infty} \varphi(f_n)$. Moreover, $\{f_n g\}$ converges to fg, and $\{|f_n g|\}$ is dominated by $|fg|$, so that

$$\int_S fg \, d\mu = \lim_{n\to\infty} \int_S f_n g \, d\mu.$$

Since $\varphi(f_n) = \int_S f_n g \, d\mu$, we have shown that $\varphi(f) = \int_S fg \, d\mu$. This completes the proof of

THEOREM 1. If $(S, \mathcal{S}, \mu)$ is a totally finite measure space and φ is a continuous linear functional on $L_p = L_p(S, \mathcal{S}, \mu)$, $p > 1$, there is a $g \in L_q$ such that

$$\varphi(f) = \int_S fg \, d\mu$$

for every $f \in L_p$, and $\|\varphi\| = \|g\|$.

Thus, the dual $(L_p)'$ of L_p is isomorphic, as a Banach space, with L_q.

3.14 The Dual of L_1

We now consider the case $p = 1$. We show that the dual of $L_1 = L_1(S, \mathcal{S}, \mu)$, where $(S, \mathcal{S}, \mu)$ is totally finite, is the space M of bounded measurable functions with

$$\|f\| = \text{ess sup}\,[|f(x)| : x \in S],$$

where

$$\text{ess sup}\,[|f(x)| : x \in S] = \inf\,[y : \mu\{x : |f(x)| > y\} = 0].$$

We obtain

(a) If $f \in L_1$, then

$$\|f\| = \max\left[\int_S |fg|\,d\mu : g \in M,\ \|g\| = 1\right].$$

The proof of (a) is easy, and is left to the reader.

(b) If $f \notin L_1$, then

$$\sup\left[\int_S |fg|\,d\mu : g \in M,\ \|g\| = 1\right] = \infty.$$

The proof of (b) is also easy.

(c) If $f \in M$, then

$$\|f\| = \sup\left[\int_S |fg|\,d\mu : g \in L_1,\ \|g\| = 1\right].$$

That $\|f\| \geq \int_S |fg|\,d\mu$, for every $g \in L_1$, $\|g\| = 1$, is obvious. Suppose $\|f\| > 0$. Let $\epsilon > 0$. Let $E \in \mathcal{S}$, $\mu(E) > 0$, be such that $|f(x)| > \|f\| - \epsilon$ for every $x \in E$. Define g so that

$$f(x) = \begin{cases} \dfrac{1}{\mu(E)}\,\text{sgn}\,f(x) & \text{if } x \in E \\ 0 & \text{if } x \notin E. \end{cases}$$

Then,

$$\int_S fg\,d\mu \geq \|f\| - \epsilon$$

and $\|g\| = 1$ in the L_1 space.

(d) If $f \notin M$, then

$$\sup\left[\int_S |fg|\,d\mu : g \in L_1,\ \|g\| = 1\right] = \infty.$$

The proof is like that of proposition 2, Sec. 3.13.

(e) If $f \notin M$, there is $g \in L_1$ with $\int_S fg\,d\mu = \infty$. This follows from (d) in the same way as the corollary follows from proposition 2, Sec. 3.13.

(f) If $f \notin L_1$, there is $g \in M$ with $\int_S fg\,d\mu = \infty$. The function $g = \text{sgn}\,f$ does the job.

PROPOSITION 1. If $g \in M$, then the functional

$$\varphi(f) = \int_S fg\, d\mu$$

is continuous and linear on $L_1 = L_1(S, \mathcal{S}, \mu)$ and $\|\varphi\| = \|g\|$. $(S, \mathcal{S}, \mu)$ is again restricted to being totally finite.

Proof. The proof differs little from that of proposition 3, Sec. 3.13. The details are left to the reader.

Conversely, for every continuous linear φ on L_1, there is a $g \in M$ such that

$$\varphi(f) = \int_S fg\, d\mu,$$

for every $f \in L_1$.

However, there exist continuous linear functionals φ on M such that there is no $g \in L_1$ for which $\varphi(f) = \int_S fg\, d\mu$ for all $f \in M$. We discuss these facts.

Let φ be a continuous linear functional on L_1. Then

$$\nu(E) = \varphi(\chi_E)$$

is easily seen to be a finite signed measure on $\mathcal{S}$.

(The proof breaks down at this point in the case of a continuous linear functional on M.)

ν is absolutely continuous with respect to μ. There is, accordingly, a summable g such that

$$\nu(E) = \varphi(\chi_E) = \int_S \chi_E \cdot g\, d\mu.$$

The extension of this equality to the bounded measurable functions, the proof that g is essentially bounded, and the proof that

$$\varphi(f) = \int_S fg\, d\mu$$

for all $f \in L_1$, all proceed in much the same way as for L_p, $p > 1$. The details are omitted. We then obtain

THEOREM 1. If $(S, \mathcal{S}, \mu)$ is a totally finite measure space, and φ is a continuous linear functional on $L_1 = L_1(S, \mathcal{S}, \mu)$, there is a $g \in M$ such that

$$\varphi(f) = \int_S fg\, d\mu$$

for every $f \in L_1$ and such that $\|\varphi\| = \|g\|$. Thus, the dual $(L_1)'$ of L_1 is isomorphic with M as a Banach space.

Let S be the interval $[0, 1]$ and μ Lebesgue measure. We determine a continuous linear functional φ on $M = M(S, \mathcal{S}, \mu)$ as follows: For every continuous f on $[0, 1]$, let $\varphi(f) = f(1)$. Then φ is continuous and linear on the subspace of M composed of continuous functions. By the Hahn-Banach theorem, φ may be extended so as to be continuous and linear on M. For every $n = 1, 2, \ldots$, let

$$f_n(x) = \begin{cases} 0 & \text{if } 0 \leq x \leq 1 - \dfrac{1}{n} \\ nx - n + 1 & \text{if } 1 - \dfrac{1}{n} \leq x \leq 1. \end{cases}$$

Then $\varphi(f_n) = 1$. But for every summable g,

$$\lim_{n \to \infty} \int_S f_n g \, d\mu = 0.$$

Thus, there is no summable g such that

$$\varphi(f) = \int_S fg \, d\mu$$

for every $f \in M$.

Another way of proving this is by noting that M is not separable. It is shown in Chapter 2 that if a Banach space is not separable, then its dual is also not separable. Since L_1 is separable, it cannot be the dual of M.

We have also proved that the spaces L_p, $p > 1$ are reflexive and that L_1 is not reflexive.

3.15 The Individual Ergodic Theorem

In the remaining sections, we present a sampling of the many interesting further developments of the material of this chapter.

The ergodic theorem is concerned with measure preserving transformations, and is considered to be important because of an old theorem of Liouville which says that certain transformations which arise in the space of sets of coordinates and velocities of a finite system of particles are measure preserving. There are two types of ergodic theorems, individual and mean. We consider the individual ergodic theorem here. Many mathematicians have written proofs of this theorem since the original one given by G. D. Birkhoff in 1933. The proof presented here, which is relatively simple, is due to F. Riesz. We start with

LEMMA 1. If $a_1, a_2, \ldots, a_n$ is an ordered set of real numbers, if $m < n$, and if $a_i \in S_m$ whenever $a_i + a_{i+1} + \ldots + a_{i+p-1} \geq 0$ for some $p \leq m$, then

$$\sum [a_i : a_i \in S_m] \geq 0.$$

The proof is left as an exercise for the reader. For convenience, the members of S_m are called m-favorable.

Let $(S, \mathcal{S}, \mu)$ be a totally finite measure space, and let T be a one-one measure preserving transformation of S onto itself. Then

$$\mu(T(E)) = \mu(E), \quad \text{for every } E \in \mathcal{S}.$$

For every $x \in S$, we consider the sequence

$$x, Tx, T^2x = T(Tx), \ldots, T^nx = T(T^{n-1}x), \ldots.$$

PROPOSITION 1. If $f \in L_1$ and E is the set of points x for which

$$f(x) + f(Tx) + \ldots + f(T^nx) \geq 0$$

for some $n = 0, 1, 2, \ldots$, then

$$\int_E f\, d\mu \geq 0.$$

Proof. For every m, let E_m be the set of points x such that

$$f(x) + f(Tx) + \ldots + f(T^kx) \geq 0$$

for some $k \leq m$. It is enough to show that $\int_{E_m} f\, d\mu \geq 0$, for every m.

For every x, consider the ordered set

$$f(x), f(Tx), \ldots, f(T^{n+m-1}x)$$

where n is fixed but arbitrary. Let F_k be the set of points x for which $f(T^kx)$ is m-favorable. By lemma 1,

$$\sum_{k=0}^{n+m-1} \int_{F_k} f(T^kx)\, d\mu \geq 0.$$

But, it is evident that $TF_k = F_{k-1}$ for every $k \leq n - 1$ and that $F_0 = E_m$. Hence, the last inequality reduces to

$$n \int_{E_m} f\, d\mu + \sum_{k=n}^{n+m-1} \int_{F_k} f(T^kx)\, d\mu \geq 0.$$

This yields,

$$n \int_{E_m} f\, d\mu + m \int_S |f|\, d\mu \geq 0.$$

Since this holds for every n, it follows that $\int_{E_m} f\, d\mu \geq 0$ and the proposition is proved.

We now prove the individual ergodic theorem for totally finite measures.

THEOREM 1. If T is measure preserving and $f \in L_1$, then if

$$\varphi_n(x) = \frac{1}{n}\{f(x) + f(Tx) + \ldots + f(T^{n-1}x)\},$$

$\lim_{n\to\infty} \varphi_n(x)$ exists for almost every x.

Proof. Let $a < b$ be rational numbers, and let A be the set of points x for which

$$\liminf_{n\to\infty} \varphi_n(x) < a < b < \limsup_{n\to\infty} \varphi_n(x).$$

It is clearly sufficient to show that $\mu(A) = 0$. The definition of A readily implies that $TA = A$. Using A as our space, which is permissible since it is invariant under T, proposition 1 yields

$$\int_A (f - b)\, d\mu \geq 0 \text{ and } \int_A (a - f)\, d\mu \geq 0.$$

It follows that $\int_A (a - b)\, d\mu \geq 0$. Since $a - b < 0$, this implies $\mu(A) = 0$ and the theorem is proved.

3.16 L_p Convergence of Fourier Series

In the last section we gave a proof of the ergodic theorem due to F. Riesz. In this section, we present a theorem on Fourier series due to his brother M. Riesz. Not all details in the proof will be given; the reader is referred to the books of Bari [1] and Zygmund [1].

Let $f \in L_p(-\pi, \pi)$, $p > 1$, extend f by periodicity, of period 2π to the real line, and let

$$\frac{a_0}{2} + \sum_{n=1}^{\infty} (a_n \cos nx + b_n \sin nx)$$

be the Fourier series of f.

There is a function $\tilde{f}$ defined by

$$\begin{aligned}\tilde{f}(x) &= -\frac{1}{\pi}\int_0^\pi \frac{f(x+t) - f(x-t)}{2 \tan t/2}\, dt \\ &= \lim_{\varepsilon \to 0} \left\{-\frac{1}{\pi}\int_\varepsilon^\pi \frac{f(x+t) - f(x-t)}{2 \tan t/2}\, dt\right\}.\end{aligned}$$

We omit the proof of the existence, and also that f and $\tilde{f}$ are boundary functions of conjugate harmonic functions. To be precise, there is an analytic $F(z)$, $|z| < 1$, with

$$\begin{aligned}F(z) &= u(z) + iv(z) \\ &= u(re^{i\theta}) + iv(re^{i\theta})\end{aligned}$$

and

$$\lim_{r \to 1} u(re^{i\theta}) = f(\theta), \ \lim_{r \to 1} v(re^{i\theta}) = \tilde{f}(\theta)$$

almost everywhere. Moreover, $0 < r < 1$ implies

$$\|u(re^{i\theta})\| \leq \|f\|,$$

and $f(\theta) \geq 0$, not identically zero, implies $u(z) > 0$, $|z| < 1$.

The Fourier series of $\tilde{f}$ is

$$\sum_{n=1}^{\infty} (-b_n \cos nx + a_n \sin nx).$$

(These are the only major facts whose proofs are omitted.)

We shall show that there is a constant A, depending only on p, such that $\|\bar{f}\| \leq A \|f\|$. In other words, the linear operator which takes each function in L_p into its conjugate function is a bounded operator on L_p to L_p. We need

LEMMA 1. If $x \in [-\pi/2, \pi/2]$, $1 < p \leq 2$, then

$$|\sin x|^p \leq a |\cos x|^p - b \cos px,$$

where a and b depend only on p.

This is an elementary computation and is left to the reader.

PROPOSITION 1. With the above notation, and the additional hypothesis that $u(z) > 0$ for $|z| < 1$, $v(0) = 0$, we have

$$\|v(re^{i\theta})\| \leq A\|u(re^{i\theta})\|,$$

where A depends only on p, and $0 \leq r < 1$.

Proof. Let $u = R \cos \varphi$, $v = R \sin \varphi$. We first show that

$$\int_0^{2\pi} R^p \cos p\varphi \, dx > 0.$$

Since $u(z) > 0$, $F(z) \neq 0$, so that F^p is analytic for $|z| < 1$. Then

$$\frac{1}{2\pi} \int_0^{2\pi} R^p \cos p\varphi \, dx = \text{Re} \left[\frac{1}{2\pi i} \int \frac{F(z)^p}{z} \, dz \right] = \text{Re} \, [F(0)^p]$$

$$= u(0)^p > 0.$$

Multiplying the inequality of lemma 1 by R^p, and integrating,

$$\int_0^{2\pi} |v(re^{i\theta})|^p \, d\theta \leq a \int_0^{2\pi} |u(re^{i\theta})|^p \, d\theta - b \int_0^{2\pi} R^p \cos p\varphi \, d\theta$$

and so

$$\|v(re^{i\theta})\| \leq A \|u(re^{i\theta})\|,$$

where $1 < p \leq 2$.

We next show how to obtain this inequality for q, having it for p, where $1/p + 1/q = 1$.

For every trigonometric polynomial g, with p norm $\|g\| \leq 1$, and, considering the q norms of u and v, we have

$$\int_0^{2\pi} |u\bar{g}| \, dx \leq \|u\| \, \|\bar{g}\| \leq \|u\| \, A \, \|g\| \leq A \, \|u\|,$$

and

$$\int_0^{2\pi} |vg| \, dx \leq A \, \|u\|, \text{ since } \int_0^{2\pi} vg \, dx = -\int_0^{2\pi} u\bar{g} \, dx,$$

by the Parseval equality (see Chapter 4), which applies since all functions involved are in L_2. But

$$\sup \left[\int_0^{2\pi} |vg| \, dx : \|g\| = 1 \right] = \|v\|,$$

since the trigonometric polynomials are dense in L_p, whereby

$$\|v\| \leq A \|u\|.$$

We now prove

THEOREM 1. For every $f \in L_p$, $p > 1$,

$$\|\bar{f}\| \leq A \|f\|.$$

Proof. Suppose $f \geq 0$. Then by the Fatou theorem,

$$\|\bar{f}\| \leq \limsup_{r \to 1} \|v(re^{i\theta})\|.$$

But

$$\limsup_{r \to 1} \|u(re^{i\theta})\| \leq \|f\|,$$

so that

$$\|\bar{f}\| \leq A \|f\|.$$

For f arbitrary, let

$$f_1 = \max(f, 0)$$
$$f_2 = f - f_1.$$

Then,

$$\|\bar{f}\| \leq \|\bar{f}_1\| + \|\bar{f}_2\| \leq A[\|f_1\| + \|f_2\|] \leq 2A \|f\|.$$

We shall use this theorem to show that if $f \in L_p$, $p > 1$, then the Fourier series of f converges to f in the L_p norm.

We introduce the sequence $\{s_n^*\}$ defined by

$$s_n^*(x) = \frac{1}{\pi} \int_{-\pi}^{\pi} \frac{f(x+t) \sin nt}{2 \tan t/2}\, dt.$$

Then

$$s_n^*(x) = \cos nx \cdot \frac{1}{\pi} \int_{-\pi}^{\pi} \frac{f(x+t) \sin n(t-x)}{2 \tan t/2}\, dt - \sin nx \cdot \frac{1}{\pi} \int_{-\pi}^{\pi} \frac{f(x+t) \cos n(t-x)}{2 \tan t/2}\, dt.$$

Let

$$f_1(x) = f(x) \sin nx, \quad f_2(x) = f(x) \cos nx,$$

then

$$s_n^*(x) = \cos nx\, \bar{f}_1(x) - \sin nx\, \bar{f}_2(x),$$

and it follows that

$$\|s_n^*\| \leq \|\bar{f}_1\| + \|\bar{f}_2\| \leq A[\|f_1\| + \|f_2\|] \leq 2A \|f\|.$$

Since the partial sum s_n of the Fourier series of f satisfies

$$s_n(x) = s_n^*(x) + \frac{1}{2\pi} \int_{-\pi}^{\pi} f(x+t) \cos nt\, dt,$$

we have

$$\|s_n\| \leq \|s_n^*\| + \|f\| \leq 2(A+1)\,\|f\|.$$

Thus the sequence of linear operators $\{s_n\}$ on L_p to L_p is uniformly bounded.

Let T be a trigonometric polynomial such that, for a prescribed $\epsilon > 0$, $\|f - T\| < \epsilon$. $\left(\text{The averages } \frac{1}{n+1}(s_0 + s_1 + \ldots + s_n) \text{ of the partial sums of the Fourier series of } f \in L_p,\ p > 1, \text{ converge to } f \text{ in the } L_p \text{ norm.}\right)$ Now,

$$\begin{aligned} f - s_n(f) &= (f - T) + (T - s_n(f)) \\ &= f - T + s_n(T - f), \end{aligned}$$

where n is greater than the degree of T. But then

$$\|f - s_n\| < \epsilon + 2(A+1)\epsilon.$$

This proves

THEOREM 2. If $f \in L_p$, then the Fourier series of f converges to f in the L_p norm.

3.17 Functions Whose Fourier Series Diverge Almost Everywhere

Let X be a Banach space, and let M be the space of equivalence classes of measurable functions on a subset S of the real line, of finite measure. Then M is a vector space. We shall show in Chapter 5 that M is a metric space with distance

$$d(f, g) = \int_S \frac{|f(t) - g(t)|}{1 + |f(t) - g(t)|}\, dt.$$

We prove

LEMMA 1. Let X be a Banach space, and $\{U_n\}$ a sequence of continuous linear operators on X into M. Let $H \subset X$ be of the second category. Suppose that, for every $x \in H$, there is a set $A_x \subset S$, of measure greater than $\alpha > 0$, such that

$$\limsup_{n \to \infty} |U_n(x)(t)| < \infty$$

for every $t \in A_x$. Let $0 < \epsilon < \alpha$. Then there is a set $A \subset S$ of measure greater than $\alpha - \epsilon$ such that, for every $x \in X$,

$$\limsup_{n \to \infty} |U_n(x)(t)| < \infty$$

almost everywhere on A.

Proof. We first recall that we have shown in exercise 3.3 that the equivalence classes of measurable subsets of S form a metric space with distance

$$d(E, F) = \mu(E \sim F) + \mu(F \sim E).$$

This metric space is separable in the present case. Let $\mathcal{A}$ be a countable dense set in this metric space. Let $A_1, A_2, \ldots$ be those sets in $\mathcal{A}$ whose measure exceeds $\alpha - \epsilon/2$. Let $H_{km} \subset X$ consist of those x for which there is an $R(x)$ such that

(a) $|U_n(x)(t)| \leq m$, for every n and $t \in R(x)$,

and

(b) $\mu(A_k \sim R(x)) < \epsilon/2$.

Then

$$H \subset \bigcup H_{km}$$

and at least one of the sets in the union, say $H_{k_1m_1}$, is of the second category in X. Moreover, since the operators U_n are continuous, $H_{k_1m_1}$ is closed, and so it contains a sphere K.

By linearity,

$$\limsup_{n\to\infty} |U_n(x)(t)| < \infty,$$

for every $x \in X$ and $t \in A_{k_1} \cap R(x)$.

Designate A_{k_1} by $A^{(1)}$ and $A_{k_1} \cap R(x)$ by $R^{(1)}(x)$. By applying the above argument to $A^{(1)}$, we obtain $R^{(2)}(x) \subset A^{(1)}$, for every $x \in X$, such that

$$\limsup_{n\to\infty} |U_n(x)(t)| < \infty$$

for every $t \in R^{(2)}(x)$, where $m(A^{(2)} \sim R^{(2)}(x)) < \epsilon/4$ and $A^{(2)} \subset A^{(1)}$, $m(A^{(2)}) \geq \alpha - \frac{3}{4}\epsilon$.

By continuing in this way, we obtain a sequence

$$A^{(1)} \supset A^{(2)} \supset \ldots,$$

and for every $x \in X$, $R^{(k)}(x) \subset A^{(k)}$, with $m(A^{(k)} \sim R^{(k)}(x)) < \epsilon/2^k$ and $m(A^{(k)}) > \alpha - (1 - 1/2^k)\epsilon$.

Let $A = \bigcap_{k=1}^{\infty} A^{(k)}$. It is an easy matter to verify that A satisfies the requirements of the lemma.

Proposition 1. Let $\{u_n(x, t)\} = \{U_n(x)(t)\}$. There is an $A \subset S$ such that

$$\limsup_{n\to\infty} |u_n(x, t)| < \infty$$

for almost all $t \in A$, for every $x \in X$, and

$$\limsup_{n\to\infty} |u_n(x, t)| = \infty$$

for almost all $t \notin A$, for every $x \in X$, except for a set of the first category.

Proof. Let β be the supremum of all α for which there is an $H(\alpha) \subset X$, of the second category, such that, for every $x \in H(\alpha)$,

$$\limsup_{n\to\infty} |u_n(x, t)| < \infty$$

on a set of measure α. If $\beta = 0$, the proposition holds. Suppose $\beta > 0$.

By lemma 1, for every p, there is an $A_p \subset S$, with $m(A_p) \geq \beta - 1/p$, such that, for every $x \in X$,

$$\limsup_{n\to\infty} |u_n(x)(t)| < \infty.$$

The set $A = \bigcap A_p$ is then seen to have the desired property without too much difficulty.

This proposition has an interesting application to Fourier series.

Let $X = L_1[-\pi, \pi]$, and for every n, $x \in L_1$, $t \in [-\pi, \pi]$, let $u_n(x, t)$ be the nth partial sum of the Fourier series of x, evaluated at t. It is a deep fact, proved by Kolmogoroff, that there is an $x \in L_1$ such that

$$\limsup_{n\to\infty} |u_n(x, t)| = \infty$$

for almost all t. (The proof of this theorem is given in Zygmund [1] and Hardy and Rogosinski [1].)

It follows that, for this case, the set A of proposition 1 is empty. In other words, the set of functions in L_1 whose Fourier series diverge almost everywhere is all of L_1 except for a set of the first category.

3.18 Continuous Functions Which Differ from All Those Having a Given Modulus

In the last section, we gave an example in which we showed how the existence of one function of a certain type implied, with the help of functional analysis, the existence of many functions of this type. In most applications of functional analysis to real variable theory, the existence itself is proved and the analysis is not nearly so deep.

We give one example which seems interesting. We shall need the Lebesgue density theorem, which we have not discussed in this text. We shall simply define **metric density** and state the theorem. The proof can be found in many places; in particular, in Goffman [1].

Let $S \subset [0, 1]$ be measurable. For every interval $I \subset [0, 1]$ we define the relative measure of S in I by

$$\frac{\mu(S \cap I)}{\mu(I)}.$$

The metric density is said to exist at a point $x \in (0, 1)$ and equal d if for every $\epsilon > 0$ there is a $\delta > 0$ such that if I is an interval, with $x \in I$ and

$\mu(I) < \delta$, then

$$\left|\frac{\mu(S \cap I)}{\mu(I)} - d\right| < \epsilon.$$

Clearly, if the metric density exists at a point, its value is between 0 and 1.

The **Lebesgue density theorem** asserts that if S is measurable, then the metric density of S exists and is equal to 1 almost everywhere on S.

We shall deal with the space $C[0, 1]$ of continuous functions on $[0, 1]$. We recall that this is a Banach space with norm

$$\|f\| = \max \{|f(x)| : x \in [0, 1]\}.$$

A function σ will be called a **modulus of continuity** if σ is defined for positive reals, is increasing, and

$$\lim_{x \to 0} \sigma(x) = 0.$$

A function $f \in C[0, 1]$ will be said to have σ as its modulus of continuity, and **belong to $C(\sigma)$**, if $x, y \in [0, 1]$ implies

$$|f(x) - f(y)| \leq \sigma(|x - y|).$$

It follows readily from the definition of continuity that every $f \in C[0, 1]$ is in $C(\sigma)$ for some σ.

What we shall show is that for every modulus of continuity σ there is an $f \in C[0, 1]$ such that for every $g \in C(\sigma)$

$$\mu\{x : f(x) = g(x)\} = 0.$$

We start with

LEMMA 1. Let ϵ and n be given, where $1 > \epsilon > 0$ and n is a positive integer. There are δ and η, where $1/n > \delta > 0$ and $\eta > 0$, and a continuous function f, with $\|f\| \leq \epsilon$, such that for every $x \in [0, 1 - 1/n]$ and every g, with $\|f - g\| < \eta$, we have either

$$|g(x) - g(y)| > \sigma(|x - y|) \text{ for every } y \in \left[x - \frac{\delta}{2}, x - \frac{\delta}{4}\right]$$

or

$$|g(x) - g(y)| > \sigma(|x - y|) \text{ for every } y \in \left[x + \frac{\delta}{4}, x + \frac{\delta}{2}\right].$$

Proof. Choose $\delta < 1/n$, so that

$$\sigma(\delta) < \frac{\epsilon}{8}.$$

Let f be continuous, with graph composed of a finite set of straight line segments, such that

$$f(0) = 0$$

$$0 \leq f(x) \leq \epsilon \text{ for all } x \in [0, 1],$$

and such that the line segments which form the graph of f have slopes $\pm\epsilon/\delta$, and all but the last has length equal to $(\epsilon^2 + \delta^2)^{1/2}$. There is a positive integer k such that $k\delta < 1 \leq (k + 1)\delta$. Then $[0, k\delta] \supset [0, 1 - 1/n]$.

For every $x \in [0, k\delta]$, it is true that $(y, f(y))$ is on the same line segment of the graph of f as is $(x, f(x))$ either for all $y \in \left[x - \frac{\delta}{2}, x - \frac{\delta}{4}\right]$ or for all $y \in \left[x + \frac{\delta}{4}, x + \frac{\delta}{2}\right]$. For all such y,

$$\begin{aligned} |f(x) - f(y)| &= \frac{\epsilon}{\delta}|x - y| \\ &> 8\sigma(|x - y|) \cdot \frac{|x - y|}{\delta} \\ &\geq 2\sigma(|x - y|), \end{aligned}$$

since $\sigma(|x - y|) < \sigma(\delta) < \epsilon/8$ and $|x - y| \geq \delta/4$. Let

$$\eta = \frac{1}{2}\sigma\left(\frac{\delta}{4}\right).$$

Suppose $\|f - g\| < \eta$. Then for x and y as above

$$\begin{aligned} |g(x) - g(y)| &> |f(x) - f(y)| - 2\eta \\ &> 2\sigma(|x - y|) - \sigma\left(\frac{\delta}{4}\right) \\ &\geq 2\sigma(|x - y|) - \sigma(|x - y|) \\ &= \sigma(|x - y|), \end{aligned}$$

since $\sigma(|x - y|) \geq \sigma(\delta/4)$.

LEMMA 2. For every positive integer n, the set $E_n \subset C[0, 1]$, of functions f for which there is a δ, with $0 < \delta < 1/n$, depending on f, such that, for every $x \in \left[0, 1 - \frac{1}{n}\right]$,

$$|f(x) - f(y)| > \sigma(|x - y|)$$

either for every $y \in \left[x - \frac{\delta}{2}, x - \frac{\delta}{4}\right]$ or for every $y \in \left[x + \frac{\delta}{4}, x + \frac{\delta}{2}\right]$, contains a dense open set in $C[0, 1]$.

Proof. Let $g \in C[0, 1]$ and ζ such that $0 < \zeta < 1$. There is a polynomial p such that

$$\|p - g\| < \frac{\zeta}{2}.$$

Let

$$M = \max\{|p'(x)| : x \in [0, 1]\}.$$

Letting the roles of ϵ and σ in lemma 1 be played by $\zeta/2$ and the function ω defined by

$$\omega(x) = \sigma(x) + Mx,$$

there are δ and η, where $0 < \delta < 1/n$ and $\eta > 0$, and a continuous function h, with $\|h\| \leq \zeta/2$, such that $\|k - h\| < \eta$ implies that, for every $x \in \left[0, 1 - \frac{1}{n}\right]$,

$$|k(x) - k(y)| > \omega(|x - y|)$$

either for every $y \in \left[x - \frac{\delta}{2}, x - \frac{\delta}{4}\right]$ or for every $y \in \left[x + \frac{\delta}{4}, x + \frac{\delta}{2}\right]$. Then, for all such x and y,

$$\begin{aligned} |(p + k)(x) - (p + k)(y)| &\geq |k(x) - k(y)| - |p(x) - p(y)| \\ &> \omega(|x - y|) - M\,|x - y| \\ &= \sigma(|x - y|). \end{aligned}$$

Since

$$\|g - (p + h)\| \leq \|g - p\| + \|h\| < \zeta,$$

the sphere of center g and radius ζ contains an open subset of E_n. Since $g \in C[0, 1]$ and $\zeta > 0$ are arbitrary, E_n contains a dense, open subset of $C[0, 1]$.

We may now prove

THEOREM 1. For every modulus of continuity σ, there exist functions $f \in C[0, 1]$ such that, for every $g \in C(\sigma)$,

$$\mu\{x : f(x) = g(x)\} = 0.$$

Moreover, the set of functions which do not have this property is of the first category.

Proof. Let E_n, $n = 1, 2, \ldots$, be as defined in lemma 2, and let

$$E = \bigcap_{n=1}^{\infty} E_n.$$

Then the set E is residual in $C[0, 1]$, i.e., its complement is of the first category in $C[0, 1]$.

Let $f \in E$. Then for every n, there is a δ_n, with $0 < \delta_n < 1/n$, such that for every $x \in \left[0, 1 - \frac{1}{n}\right]$, we have

$$|f(x) - f(y)| > \sigma(|x - y|),$$

either for every $y \in \left[x - \frac{\delta_n}{2}, x - \frac{\delta_n}{4}\right]$ or for every $y \in \left[x + \frac{\delta_n}{4}, x + \frac{\delta_n}{2}\right]$.

Now, let $g \in C(\sigma)$, and suppose the set

$$A = \{x : f(x) = g(x)\}$$

has positive measure. Let $x \in (0, 1)$ be a point in A at which the metric density of A is 1. Then the set

$$B = \{y : |f(x) - f(y)| > \sigma(|x - y|)\}$$

has metric density 0 at x. Choose n_0 so that $x < 1 - \frac{1}{n_0}$. Then, for every $n \geq n_0$, since $f \in E_n$,

$$|f(x) - f(y)| > \sigma(|x - y|)$$

on a subset of $\left[x - \frac{\delta_n}{2}, x + \frac{\delta_n}{2}\right]$ of relative measure $\frac{1}{4}$. Since $\lim_{n\to\infty} \delta_n = 0$, this contradicts the assertion that B has metric density 0 at x.

EXERCISES

1.1 Show that $S \subset T$ implies $m_e(S) \leq m_e(T)$.

1.2 If J is an elementary set, show that $m_e(J) = m(J)$.

1.3 Show that if $H \subset E_n$ is a hyperplane, then $m_e(H) = 0$.

1.4 Show that every open set in E_n is the union of a countable set of intervals whose interiors are pair-wise disjoint.

1.5 Give the details of the proof of the corollary to proposition 4 which says that a subset $S \subset U$ is measurable if and only if, for every $\epsilon > 0$, there is a compact $F \subset S$ such that $m_e(S \sim F) < \epsilon$.

1.6 Prove that there is a nowhere dense measurable set in $[0, 1]$ whose intersection with every open set is either empty or of positive measure.

1.7 Prove that there is a measurable set S in $[0, 1]$ such that, for every open set $G \subset [0, 1]$, both $m(S \cap G) > 0$ and $m(G \cap CS) > 0$.

1.8 Let S be a measurable subset of $[0, 1]$ with the property that if $x \in S$ and the decimal expansion of x is changed in finitely many places to yield y, then $y \in S$. Show that $m(S)$ is 0 or 1.

1.9 Discuss the measurability and exterior measure of the subset of $[0, 1]$ of points whose decimal expansions do not contain the digit 5.

1.10 Show that $S \subset U_n$ is measurable if and only if, for every $A \subset U_n$,

$$m_e(S) = m_e(S \cap A) + m_e(S \cap CA).$$

1.11 Given any set Z of measure 0, show that there is a continuous monotonically increasing function whose derivative is $+\infty$ at every point of Z.

2.1 Give an example of an unbounded connected open set of finite measure in E_2.

2.2 Give an example of an unbounded everywhere dense connected open set of finite measure in E_2.

2.3 Show that for every measurable S in E_n there is a set A, which is the union of an increasing sequence of compact sets, such that $A \subset S$ and $m(S \sim A) = 0$.

2.4 Give an example of a homeomorphic image of the unit circle $x^2 + y^2 = 1$ in E_2 whose measure in E_2 is positive.

3.1 Define a class of measures on E_n analogous to the ones defined in the text on E_1.

3.2 Give an example of a measure space which is not σ finite.

3.3 If $(S, \mathcal{S}, \mu)$ is a totally finite measure space, let

$$d(A, B) = \mu(A \sim B) + \mu(B \sim A),$$

for $A, B \in \mathcal{S}$. Show that the equivalence classes of sets in $\mathcal{S}$ form a metric space, where A is equivalent to B if $d(A, B) = 0$.

3.4 Show that the metric space of exercise 3.3 is complete.

3.5 A totally finite measure space is called separable if its associated metric space is separable. Show that the measure space of Section 3.1 is separable.

3.6 A totally finite measure space $(S, \mathcal{S}, \mu)$ is called non-atomic if for every $A \in \mathcal{S}$, $\mu(A) > 0$, there is $B \in \mathcal{S}$, $B \subset A$, $0 < \mu(B) < \mu(A)$. It is called normal if $\mu(S) = 1$. Show that if $(S, \mathcal{S}, \mu)$ and $(T, \mathcal{T}, \nu)$ are separable, non-atomic, and normal, there is a one-one mapping φ between their equivalence classes of sets such that $\nu(\varphi(A)) = \mu(A)$, $\varphi(A \cup B) = \varphi(A) \cup \varphi(B)$ and $\varphi(S \sim A) = T \sim \varphi(A)$.

4.1 Using the definition in the text, show that a function f is measurable if and only if the inverse image of every Borel set is measurable.

4.2 Using the definition in the text, show that a function f is measurable if and only if the inverse image of $[a, \infty)$ is measurable for every a.

4.3 Show, by example, that the measurability of the inverse image of (a, ∞) for every a does not imply the measurability of f.

4.4 If f is measurable on the unit interval $[0, 1]$, show that for every $\epsilon > 0$ there is a continuous g on $[0, 1]$ such that $|f(x) - g(x)| < \epsilon$, except on a set of measure less than ϵ.

4.5 Show, accordingly, that there is a sequence of continuous functions which converges almost everywhere to f.

4.6 However, using exercise 1.7, show that there is a measurable function which is not equivalent to any Baire 1 function.

4.7 Nevertheless, show that every measurable function is equivalent to a Baire 2 function.

4.8 If f is measurable on $[0, 1]$, show that, for every $\epsilon > 0$, there is a continuous g on $[0, 1]$ such that $f(x) = g(x)$, except on a set of measure less than ϵ.

4.9 If $(S, \mathcal{S}, \mu)$ is a totally finite measure space and we order equivalence classes of measurable sets by $S \geq T$ if $\mu(T \sim S) = 0$, then every collection of equivalence classes has a least upper bound.

4.10 If equivalence classes of measurable functions on a totally finite measure space are ordered so that $f \geq g$ if $f(x) \geq g(x)$ almost everywhere, show that every set of equivalence classes which has an upper bound has a least upper bound.

4.11 Give an example of a totally σ finite measure space in which theorem 1 fails.

5.1 If $\{f_n\}$ converges in measure to f and $\{g_n\}$ converges in measure to g, show that $\{f_n + g_n\}$ converges in measure to $f + g$.

5.2 If $\{f_n\}$ converges in measure to f and $\{g_n\}$ converges in measure to g, show that $\{f_n g_n\}$ converges in measure to fg.

5.3 If $(S, \mathcal{S}, \mu)$ is a totally finite measure space, show that a sequence $\{f_n\}$ of measurable real functions on S converges in measure to f if and only if every subsequence of $\{f_n\}$ has a subsequence which converges almost everywhere to f.

6.1 Let $(S, \mathcal{S}, \mu)$ be a totally σ finite measure space, and let A be the set of step functions on S. Show that with

$$\|s\| = \int_S |s| \, d\mu,$$

A is a normed vector space.

6.2 Show that A is dense in the space of summable functions with this norm.

6.3 Show that if $E \subset [0, 1] \times [0, 1]$ is measurable, and if, for every $x_0 \in [0, 1]$,

$$I_{x_0} = \{(x_0, y) : y \in [0, 1]\},$$

then $E \cap I_x$ is measurable for almost all x, and

$$\mu_2(E) = \int_0^1 \mu_1(E \cap I_x) \, dx;$$

where μ_k indicates k-dimensional Lebesgue measure.

6.4 Use the result of exercise 6.3 to prove that if f is summable on E_2, then $f(x, y)$ is summable as a function of each variable for almost all values of the other variable, and that

$$\int_{E_2} f \, d\mu_2 = \int_{-\infty}^{\infty} dy \left\{ \int_{-\infty}^{\infty} f(x, y) \, dx \right\} = \int_{-\infty}^{\infty} dx \left\{ \int_{-\infty}^{\infty} f(x, y) \, dy \right\}.$$

This is called Fubini's theorem.

6.5 Generalize Fubini's theorem to E_k.

7.1 Prove the corollary to theorem 1.

7.2 Give an example where f, g are summable, but fg is not summable.

7.3 For f, g summable on E_1, with respect to Lebesgue measure, define

$$(f * g)(t) = \int_{-\infty}^{\infty} f(t - u) g(u) \, du.$$

Show that $f * g$ is summable.

7.4 If f is summable on E_1, with respect to Lebesgue measure, show that

$$\lim_{t \to 0} \int_{-\infty}^{\infty} |f(x + t) - f(x)| \, dt = 0.$$

7.5 Show that if $(S, \mathcal{S}, \mu)$ is totally finite and $\{f_n\}$ converges to f in the sense that

$$\lim_{n\to\infty} \int_S |f_n - f|\, d\mu = 0,$$

then $\{f_n\}$ converges in measure to f.

7.6 Show that convergence in the sense of exercise 7.5 does not always imply almost everywhere convergence.

7.7 Show that almost everywhere convergence does not always imply convergence in the sense of exercise 7.5.

7.8 If $\{a_n\}$ is a sequence of real numbers, and $b_n = \inf(a_n, a_{n+1}, \ldots)$ for every n, show that

$$\lim_{n\to\infty} b_n = \liminf_{n\to\infty} a_n.$$

9.1 If $(S, \mathcal{S}, \mu)$ is a finite signed measure and

$$\mu^+(E) = \sup\,[\mu(T) : T \in \mathcal{S},\ T \subset E],$$

give details of the proof that μ^+ is completely additive and non-negative.

9.2 Having defined μ^+ as above and μ^- in similar fashion, as in the text, and $|\mu| = \mu^+ + \mu^-$, show that

$$|\mu|\,(E) = \sup \sum_{i=1}^{k} |\mu(E_i)|$$

for all partitions of E, for every $E \in \mathcal{S}$.

10.1 Prove the Radon-Nikodym theorem for the totally σ finite case.

10.2 Construct an example of a measure space (not totally σ finite) in which the Radon-Nikodym theorem fails to hold.

11.1 Prove the Hölder and Minkowski inequalities in the context of this chapter.

11.2 Prove that if $(S, \mathcal{S}, \mu)$ is a separable measure space, then $L_p = L_p(S, \mathcal{S}, \mu)$ is a separable metric space for every $p > 1$.

11.3 Show that for every $p_1 \geq 1$, $p_2 \geq 1$, and totally σ finite $(S, \mathcal{S}, \mu)$, the set $L_{p_1} \cap L_{p_2}$ is dense in the space L_{p_1}.

11.4 If $(S, \mathcal{S}, \mu)$ is a measure space, not necessarily totally σ finite, show that, for every $p \geq 1$, every function in L_p vanishes outside of a totally σ finite subspace.

11.5 For $(S, \mathcal{S}, \mu)$ totally σ finite, but not totally finite, $p_1 \geq 1$, $p_2 \geq 1$, $p_1 \neq p_2$, show that neither L_{p_1} nor L_{p_2} is a subset of the other.

11.6 If $p_1 > p_2 \geq 1$ and $(S, \mathcal{S}, \mu)$ is totally finite, show that $L_{p_1} \subset L_{p_2}$.

11.7 If $(S, \mathcal{S}, \mu)$ is totally finite and $p > 1$, show that convergence in the L_p norm implies convergence in measure.

11.8 If $(S, \mathcal{S}, \mu)$ is totally finite, we say that $\{f_n\}$ converges asymptotically in the L_p norm to f if for every $\epsilon > 0$ there is an $E \in \mathcal{S}$, $\mu(S \sim E) < \epsilon$ such that $\{f_n\}$ converges to f in the L_p norm on E. Is asymptotic convergence in the L_p norm implied by convergence in measure? Prove or give a counter example.

12.1 Prove that the mapping which takes each $f \in L_1[0, 1]$ into the stair function f_n is norm decreasing.

12.2 Give an example of a space, not an L_p space, for which proposition 1 holds.

12.3 If $(S, \mathcal{S}, \mu)$ is a separable, non-atomic measure space of norm 1, show that an analog of proposition 1 holds.

12.4 If $(S, \mathcal{S}, \mu)$ is non-separable, show that an analog of proposition 1 does not hold.

12.5 If M is the space of equivalence classes of bounded measurable functions on $[0, 1]$ with

$$\|f\| = \inf\{y : \mu[x : f(x) > y] = 0\},$$

show that proposition 1 does not hold for M.

12.6 Let $\{f_n\}$ be a sequence of continuous, non-negative functions on E_1 such that, for every n, $f_n(x) = 0$ if $|x| \geq 1/n$ and $\int_{E_1} f_n(x)\, dx = 1$. For every $f \in L_1$, which vanishes off a compact set, let

$$F_n(x) = \int_{-\infty}^{\infty} f(x - t) f_n(t)\, dt.$$

Show that the functions F_n are continuous and that

$$\lim_{n \to \infty} \|f - F_n\| = 0,$$

where we are using the L_1 norm.

12.7 If $f \in L_p$, $p > 1$, show that

$$\lim_{n \to \infty} \|f - F_n\| = 0$$

for the L_p norm.

12.8 Give an example of a Banach function space X, not an L_p space, such that $f \in X$ implies

$$\lim_{n \to \infty} \|f - F_n\| = 0$$

in the norm of X.

12.9 Give an example of a Banach function space, such that the $\{F_n\}$ as defined above do not converge to f in the space.

12.10 Show that if the $\{f_n\}$ of exercise 12.6 are of class C^∞, then so are the $\{F_n\}$.

14.1 Give the details of the proof that the dual of L_1 is M for the totally finite case.

14.2 Prove that the dual of L_1 is M also for the totally σ finite case. Is this restriction on the measure space necessary?

14.3 Prove the existence of a continuous linear functional on M for which the associated set function

$$\nu(E) = \varphi(\chi_E)$$

is not completely additive.

14.4 Give the details of the construction which proves (e).

15.1 Prove that if $a_1, a_2, \ldots, a_n$ is an ordered set of real numbers, if $m \leq n$, and if $a_i \in S_m$ whenever $a_i + a_{i+1} + \ldots + a_{i+p-1} \geq 0$, for some $p \leq m$, then

$$\sum [a_i : a_i \in S_m] \geq 0.$$

16.1 Prove the lemma that if $x \in [-\pi/2, \pi/2]$, $1 < p \leq 2$, then

$$|\sin x|^p \leq a\,|\cos x|^p - b \cos px$$

where a and b depend only on p.

16.2 Prove that the trigonometric polynomials are dense in $L_p[0, 1]$ from the fact that the algebraic polynomials have this property.

16.3 Prove the fact that the trigonometric polynomials are dense in L_p by considering the averages of the partial sums of Fourier series and then applying a modified, but still valid, version of exercise 12.6.

18.1 If σ and τ are moduli of continuity, and $\lim\limits_{n \to 0} \dfrac{\sigma(x)}{\tau(x)} = \infty$, show that there is a function in $C(\sigma)$ which is not in $C(\tau)$ on any interval.

18.2 Given any set Z of measure 0, show that there is a measurable set S whose metric density does not exist at any point of Z.

18.3 Give an example of a measurable set whose metric density exists and is equal to $\frac{1}{2}$ at a point x.

CHAPTER 4

HILBERT SPACE

4.1 Inner Product, Hilbert Space

A Hilbert space is a Banach space in which the norm is derived from a scalar-valued function called an inner product. We shall define this concept and show that linear spaces with an inner product retain many geometric properties of finite dimensional euclidean spaces.

Let X be a vector space over the field F (real or complex). A mapping of $X \times X$ into F which takes each ordered pair $\{x, y\} \in X \times X$ into the number $(x, y) \in F$ is called an **inner product** in X if

(i) $(x, y) = \overline{(y, x)}$,
(ii) $(ax_1 + bx_2, y) = a(x_1, y) + b(x_2, y)$,
(iii) $(x, x) \geq 0$ and $(x, x) = 0$ if and only if $x = 0$.

Condition (i) clearly reduces to $(x, y) = (y, x)$ if X is a real vector space. In general, we confine our discussion to the complex case. However, the real case will also be considered when natural.

From (i) and (ii), we obtain

(iv) $(x, cy_1 + dy_2) = \bar{c}(x, y_1) + \bar{d}(x, y_2)$.

We shall show that the quantity

$$\|x\| = (x, x)^{1/2}$$

is a norm in the space X. The only property which is not obvious is the triangle inequality and this follows directly from the fundamental

Proposition 1 (Cauchy-Schwarz inequality). For every $x, y \in X$, we have

$$|(x, y)| \leq \|x\| \, \|y\|.$$

Proof. We may suppose that $x \neq 0, y \neq 0$. For any a, $\|x + ay\|^2 \geq 0$ by (iii). Thus, using (ii) and (iv), and then (i),

$$\begin{aligned} 0 \leq (x + ay, x + ay) &= \|x\|^2 + a(y, x) + \bar{a}(x, y) + |a|^2 \, \|y\|^2 \\ &= \|x\|^2 + 2 \operatorname{Re}(a(y, x)) + |a|^2 \, \|y\|^2. \end{aligned}$$

Choosing the argument of a in such a way that $a(y, x) \leq 0$, we may write,

$$2\,|a|\,|(x, y)| \leq \|x\|^2 + |a|^2\,\|y\|^2,$$

and the choice

$$|a| = \frac{\|x\|}{\|y\|}$$

reduces this to the desired inequality.

The proof of the triangle inequality is now obtained by

$$\begin{aligned}\|x + y\|^2 &= \|x\|^2 + (x, y) + (y, x) + \|y\|^2 \\ &= \|x\|^2 + 2\,\mathrm{Re}\,(x, y) + \|y\|^2 \\ &\leq \|x\|^2 + 2\,|(x, y)| + \|y\|^2 \\ &\leq \|x\|^2 + 2\,\|x\|\,\|y\| + \|y\|^2 \\ &= (\|x\| + \|y\|)^2.\end{aligned}$$

A vector space X, together with an inner product in X, is called an **inner product space** and is, as we have seen, a special kind of normed vector space. If X is complete under the norm obtained from its inner product, then X is called a **Hilbert space.**

The reader will verify without difficulty that

(a) n-space under

$$(x, y) = \sum_{i=1}^{n} x_i \bar{y}_i$$

is a Hilbert space. (In the complex case this space is called n dimensional **unitary** space; in the real case, euclidean n-space.)

(b) l_2 is a Hilbert space with

$$(x, y) = \sum_{i=1}^{\infty} x_i \bar{y}_i.$$

(c) $L_2[0, 1]$ is a Hilbert space with

$$(x, y) = \int_0^1 x(t)\,\overline{y(t)}\,dt.$$

(d) More generally, if $(S, \mathcal{S}, \mu)$ is any measure space, then $L_2(S, \mathcal{S}, \mu)$ is a Hilbert space with

$$(x, y) = \int_S x\bar{y}\,d\mu.$$

(e) An inner product space, not complete, is the vector space $P[0, 1]$ of real valued polynomials on $[0, 1]$ with

$$(p, q) = \int_0^1 p(t)q(t)\,dt.$$

That this is not complete follows since its Hamel basis is countable.

A more interesting example, along these lines, is the set X of real-valued functions on $R \cup C$, where R is a domain in the uv-plane and its boundary C is a smooth simple closed curve, which are continuous on $R \cup C$ and have continuous second partial derivatives in R. Define (x, y) by

$$(x, y) = \int_R (x_u y_u + x_v y_v)\, du\, dv + \int_C xy\, ds.$$

The Cauchy-Schwarz inequality shows that the inner product is a continuous function on $X \times X$ into F, where the norm of $\{x, y\} \in X \times X$ is $\|x\| + \|y\|$. That is,

$$\lim_n x_n = x \text{ and } \lim_n y_n = y \text{ implies } \lim_n (x_n, y_n) = (x, y).$$

A consequence of this fact is that the completion of an inner product space is again an inner product space, hence a Hilbert space.

In euclidean 3 space, the inner product

$$(x, y) = x_1y_1 + x_2y_2 + x_3y_3$$

is used to express the angle between two non-zero vectors by means of the formula

$$\cos\theta = \frac{(x, y)}{\|x\|\,\|y\|}, \quad 0 \le \theta \le \pi.$$

In particular, orthogonality ($\theta = \pi/2$) of x and y is characterized by $(x, y) = 0$, if we accept the convention that the vector 0 is orthogonal to every vector. In a general inner product space we define x and y to be **orthogonal,** written $x \perp y$, if $(x, y) = 0$.

The **Pythagorean theorem** can be stated as

$$x \perp y \text{ implies } \|x\|^2 + \|y\|^2 = \|x + y\|^2$$

and is seen to be valid in any inner product space, by direct computation.

Similarly, it is easy to verify directly that the **parallelogram law** holds in an inner product space (the sum of the squares of the diagonals of a parallelogram equals the sum of the squares of the sides):

$$\|x + y\|^2 + \|x - y\|^2 = 2\,\|x\|^2 + 2\,\|y\|^2.$$

The converse is also valid. Thus, a Banach space in which the norm satisfies the parallelogram law is necessarily a Hilbert space. We consider the real case, and suppose the parallelogram law holds in a Banach space X. We define an inner product in X by

$$(x, y) = \frac{1}{4}\,[\|x + y\|^2 - \|x - y\|^2].$$

Then $(x, x) \ge 0$ and $(x, x) = 0$ if and only if $x = 0$. Moreover, $(x, x) = \|x\|^2$ and $(x, y) = (y, x)$. It is only necessary to show that

$$(x_1 + x_2, y) = (x_1, y) + (x_2, y), \text{ and } (ax, y) = a(x, y).$$

First,

$$\|u + v + w\|^2 + \|u + v - w\|^2 = 2\,\|u + v\|^2 + 2\,\|w\|^2$$

and

$$\|u - v + w\|^2 + \|u - v - w\|^2 = 2\,\|u - v\|^2 + 2\,\|w\|^2$$

so that

$$\|u + v + w\|^2 + \|u + v - w\|^2 - \|u - v + w\|^2 - \|u - v - w\|^2 = 2\,\|u + v\|^2 - 2\,\|u - v\|^2$$

or

$$(u + w, v) + (u - w, v) = 2\,(u, v).$$

Setting $u = w$, this implies immediately that

$$(2u, v) = 2(u, v).$$

Now, let $x_1 = u + w$, $x_2 = u - w$, and $y = v$ to obtain

$$(x_1, y) + (x_2, y) = (x_1 + x_2, y).$$

We leave it to the reader to show that $(ax, y) = a(x, y)$.

We thus have

PROPOSITION 2. A Banach space is a Hilbert space if and only if the parallelogram law holds.

It follows that a real Banach space is a Hilbert space if and only if every two-dimensional subspace is euclidean.

The identity

$$(x, y) = \frac{1}{4}\,[\|x + y\|^2 - \|x - y\|^2]$$

used in the proof of proposition 2 is called the **polarization identity.** In complex Hilbert space it has the form

$$(x, y) = \frac{1}{4}\,[\|x + y\|^2 - \|x - y\|^2 + i\,\|x + iy\|^2 - i\,\|x - iy\|^2].$$

It may be established by direct computation.

The next section presents further special aspects of Hilbert spaces which set them apart from general Banach spaces.

4.2 Basic Lemma, Projection Theorem, Dual

We shall show that any closed subspace M of a Hilbert space X is a direct summand of X. Indeed we let

$$M^{\perp} = [z \in X : z \perp y \text{ for all } y \in M].$$

It is immediate that $M^\perp$ is a closed subspace of X. We shall show that $X = M \dotplus M^\perp$. We first show that $M \neq X$ implies $M^\perp \neq (0)$. For this purpose, we prove

LEMMA 1. If K is a closed, convex set in X and $x_0 \in X \sim K$, there is a unique $y_0 \in K$ such that

$$\|x_0 - y_0\| = \inf[\|x_0 - y\| : y \in K].$$

Proof. Let $d = \inf[\|x_0 - y\| : y \in K]$. Choose $y_1, y_2, \ldots$ in K so that

$$\lim_{n\to\infty} \|x_0 - y_n\| = d.$$

By the parallelogram law,

$$\|y_m - y_n\|^2 = 2\,\|y_m - x_0\|^2 + 2\,\|y_n - x_0\|^2 - \|(y_m - x_0) + (y_n - x_0)\|^2$$
$$= 2\,\|y_m - x_0\|^2 + 2\,\|y_n - x_0\|^2 - 4\|\frac{y_m + y_n}{2} - x_0\|^2.$$

Since K is convex, $\left\|\dfrac{y_m + y_n}{2} - x_0\right\| \geq d$. Hence,

$$\|y_m - y_n\|^2 \leq 2\,\|y_m - x_0\|^2 + 2\,\|y_n - x_0\|^2 - 4\,d^2$$

from which $\{y_n\}$ is a Cauchy sequence. Let $y_0 = \lim_n y_n$. Then $y_0 \in K$ and $\|x_0 - y_0\| = d$.

For the uniqueness, suppose $z_0 \in K$ and $\|x_0 - z_0\| = d$. Then

$$\|y_0 - z_0\|^2 = 2\,\|y_0 - x_0\|^2 + 2\,\|x_0 - z_0\|^2 - \|y_0 + z_0 - 2x_0\|^2$$
$$= 4d^2 - 4\left\|\frac{y_0 + z_0}{2} - x_0\right\|^2 \leq 0.$$

Hence, $z_0 = y_0$.

Apply lemma 1 to the closed convex set M. It associates a unique $y_0 \in M$ with every $x_0 \in X \sim M$. We show that $x_0 - y_0 \in M^\perp$.

If $y \in M$ and a is a scalar, then $y_0 + ay \in M$, so that

$$\|x_0 - (y_0 + ay)\|^2 \geq \|y_0 - x_0\|^2$$

and

$$-\bar{a}(x_0 - y_0, y) - a(y, x_0 - y_0) + |a|^2\,\|y\|^2 \geq 0.$$

With $a = \epsilon$, $\epsilon > 0$, this becomes

$$2\,\mathrm{Re}\,(x_0 - y_0, y) \leq \epsilon\,\|y\|^2$$

and with $a = i\epsilon$, it becomes

$$2\,\mathrm{Im}\,(x_0 - y_0, y) \leq \epsilon\,\|y\|^2.$$

Since $\epsilon > 0$ is arbitrary, it follows that $(x_0 - y_0, y) = 0$ and so $x_0 - y_0 \in M^\perp$.

Now since $M \cap M^\perp = (0)$ and any $x_0 \in X$ can be written as

$$x_0 = y_0 + (x_0 - y_0),$$

where y_0 is the vector in M at minimum distance from x_0, we see that

$$X = M \dotplus M^{\perp}.$$

The mapping P of X onto M given by $Px_0 = y_0$ is a projection operator with the special property that its range and null space are mutually orthogonal subspaces of X. For this reason it is called the orthogonal projection on M.

Our results so far are summarized in

THEOREM 1 (Projection theorem). If M is a closed subspace of a Hilbert space X, then every $x \in X$ has a unique decomposition

$$x = y + z, \qquad y \in M, z \in M^{\perp}.$$

The operator $x \to Px = y$ is a bounded linear idempotent (a projection), such that $M = PX$ and $M^{\perp} = (I - P)X$ are mutually orthogonal closed subspaces with

$$X = M \dotplus M^{\perp}.$$

For each $x \in X$, Px is the unique element of M which minimizes the distance from x to M.

We may use this result to identify the dual space of a Hilbert space, as follows.

If $y_0 \in X$, then (x, y_0) is a linear functional (in x) on X. The Cauchy-Schwarz inequality gives

$$\frac{|(x, y_0)|}{\|x\|} \leq \|y_0\|, \quad x \neq 0$$

and leads immediately to the observation that for each $y_0 \in X$,

$$x \to (x, y_0)$$

is a bounded linear functional on X with norm $\|y_0\|$.

We thus have a natural, norm preserving mapping φ on X into X'. It is not linear (unless X is real) but has the property

$$\varphi(ax + by) = \bar{a}\varphi(x) + \bar{b}\varphi(y).$$

We shall show that φ is onto, thus establishing a natural identification of a Hilbert space with its own dual.

THEOREM 2. If x' is a bounded linear functional on a Hilbert space X, there is a unique $y_0 \in X$ such that

$$x'(x) = (x, y_0), x \in X.$$

Proof. If $x' = 0$, take $y_0 = 0$. Suppose $x' \neq 0$. The null space N of x' is a closed subspace of X and $N \neq X$. Consequently $N^{\perp} \neq (0)$. Let $x_0 \in N^{\perp}$, $x_0 \neq 0$.

We choose $y_0 = ax_0$, where a is determined so that $x'(x_0) = (x_0, y_0)$, that is, $x'(x_0) = a \|x_0\|^2$, giving

$$a = \frac{\overline{x'(x_0)}}{\|x_0\|^2}.$$

To verify that y_0 has the desired property, let $x \in X$ and put $b = x'(x)/x'(x_0)$. Then $x - bx_0 \in N$, since $x'(x - bx_0) = 0$. Hence

$$(x, y_0) = (x - bx_0, y_0) + (bx_0, y_0) = b(x_0, y_0)$$

since $y_0 \perp N$. But

$$b(x_0, y_0) = bx'(x_0) = x'(x).$$

Thus, for any $x \in X$,

$$(x, y_0) = x'(x)$$

and the proof is complete.

4.3 Application, Mean Ergodic Theorem

The lemma of the preceding section is a form of variational principle which has several applications in analysis. We present the mean ergodic theorem as an example.

If $(S, \mathcal{S}, \mu)$ is a totally σ finite measure space and T is a one-one measure preserving transformation of S into itself, then for any function f defined on S, we consider the means φ_n defined by

$$\varphi_n(x) = \frac{1}{n}\,[f(x) + f(Tx) + \ldots + f(T^{n-1}x)],\ x \in S, \quad n = 1, 2, \ldots,$$

and seek a limiting function for $\{\varphi_n\}$.

The individual ergodic theorem establishes the existence of an almost everywhere limit in case $f \in L_1$ (see Sec. 3.15). The mean ergodic theorem establishes the existence of a limit in the mean, i.e., in the sense of L_2 convergence, in case $f \in L_2(S)$.

The transition to a problem in abstract Hilbert space comes about through the observation that if $f \in L_2$ then $f \to Vf$, where

$$Vf(x) = f(Tx),\ x \in S,$$

defines a linear transformation of $L_2(S)$ into itself, which is norm preserving;

$$\|Vf\| = \|f\|,\ f \in L_2.$$

The proof of this fact is left to the reader.

The mean ergodic theorem is thus a consequence of

PROPOSITION 1. Let V be a bounded linear operator on a Hilbert space X with $\|V\| \leq 1$. Let $f \in X$ and put

$$\varphi_n = \frac{1}{n}[f + Vf + \dots + V^{n-1}f], \quad n = 1, 2, \dots.$$

There is then a $\varphi \in X$ such that $\lim_n \varphi_n = \varphi$ in X.

Proof. Let K be the set of all finite convex combinations of the elements

$$f, Vf, V^2f, \dots,$$

i.e., all g of the form (taking $V^0 f = f$)

$$g = \sum_{i=0}^{m-1} C_i V^i f, \quad C_i \geq 0, \quad \sum_{i=0}^{m-1} C_i = 1.$$

Clearly K is convex. Its closure $\bar{K}$ is convex and lemma 1, Sec. 4.2, assures the existence of a unique $\varphi \in \bar{K}$ realizing the distance from 0 to $\bar{K}$. Then

$$\|\varphi\| = \inf [\|g\| : g \in \bar{K}].$$

To show that $\lim_n \varphi_n = \varphi$, it suffices to show that $\{\varphi_n\}$ is a minimizing sequence, i.e., for every $\epsilon > 0$ there is an N such that $n > N$ implies

$$\|\varphi_n\| < \|\varphi\| + \epsilon.$$

We may choose $g \in K$ so that

$$\|g\| < \|\varphi\| + \frac{\epsilon}{2}.$$

Putting

$$\psi_n = \frac{1}{n}[g + Vg + \dots + V^{n-1}g],$$

$$\begin{aligned}
\|\varphi_n\| &\leq \|\varphi_n - \psi_n\| + \|\psi_n\| \\
&\leq \|\varphi_n - \psi_n\| + \frac{1}{n}\sum_{i=0}^{n-1} \|V^i g\| \\
&\leq \|\varphi_n - \psi_n\| + \frac{1}{n}\sum_{i=0}^{n-1} \|g\| = \|\varphi_n - \psi_n\| + \|g\| \\
&< \|\varphi_n - \psi_n\| + \|\varphi\| + \frac{\epsilon}{2},
\end{aligned}$$

where we have used the fact that $\|V\| \leq 1$.

Now, we must show that $\|\varphi_n - \psi_n\| < \epsilon/2$ for all n sufficiently large. Since $g \in K$, we have

$$g = \sum_{j=0}^{m-1} C_j V^j f, \quad C_j \geq 0, \quad \sum_{j=0}^{m-1} C_j = 1.$$

Thus, for $n \geq m$,

$$\psi_n = \frac{1}{n} \sum_{i=0}^{n-1} \sum_{j=0}^{m-1} C_j V^{i+j} f$$

$$= \frac{1}{n} \sum_{j=0}^{m-1} C_j \sum_{i=0}^{n-1} V^{i+j} f.$$

Also,

$$\varphi_n = \frac{1}{n} \sum_{i=0}^{n-1} V^i f = \frac{1}{n} \sum_{j=0}^{m-1} C_j \sum_{i=0}^{n-1} V^i f$$

and so

$$\psi_n - \varphi_n = \frac{1}{n} \sum_{j=0}^{m-1} C_j \sum_{i=0}^{n-1} (V^{i+j} f - V^i f).$$

Cancellations occur in the inner sum, leaving $2j$ terms of the form $\pm V^k f$. Hence, applying the triangle inequality and the assumption on V,

$$\|\psi_n - \varphi_n\| \leq \frac{1}{n} \sum_{j=0}^{m-1} C_j 2j \,\|f\|$$

$$\leq \frac{2(m-1)}{n} \|f\| \sum_{j=0}^{m-1} C_j = \frac{2(m-1)}{n} \|f\|,$$

and the result follows.

4.4 Orthonormal Sets, Fourier Expansion

A set S of elements of an inner product space X is an **orthogonal set** if $x \perp y$ whenever $x \in S$, $y \in S$ and $x \neq y$. If, in addition, each $x \in S$ has norm one, S is called **orthonormal.**

$$(x, y) = \begin{cases} 0 \text{ if } x \neq y \\ 1 \text{ if } x = y \end{cases}, \quad x, y \in S.$$

A set S is **complete** in X if no non-zero $x \in X$ is orthogonal to S (i.e., to every element of S). Since the orthonormal sets in an $X \neq (0)$ form a non-empty class partially ordered by inclusion, and the complete orthonormal sets are the maximal elements, it follows by Zorn's lemma that complete orthonormal sets exist in X.

We shall show that every $x \in X$ has a unique series expansion in terms of a complete orthonormal set in X, but first we discuss a few concrete examples.

(i) The set $e_1 = (1, 0, 0, \ldots)$, $e_2 = (0, 1, 0, \ldots)$, $\ldots$ is clearly a complete orthonormal set in l_2. It is also clear that any $x = (x_1, x_2, \ldots) \in l_2$ is a sum $x = \sum_{i=1}^{\infty} x_i e_i$, where the partial sums converge in the l_2 norm and $x_i = (x, e_i)$.

(ii) In the complex space $L_2(0, 2\pi)$, the sequence

$$\frac{1}{\sqrt{2\pi}} e^{ikt}, \quad k = 0, \pm 1, \pm 2, \ldots$$

is immediately seen to be orthonormal. We show it is complete. Indeed, we show that for any $f \in L_1 \supset L_2$,

$$\int_0^{2\pi} f(t) e^{ikt}\, dt = 0, \quad k = 0, \pm 1, \pm 2, \ldots$$

implies $f = 0$.

Put

$$F(t) = \int_0^t f(u)\, du.$$

For any constant a, by partial integration,

$$\int_0^{2\pi} [F(t) - a] e^{ikt}\, dt = 0, \quad k = \pm 1, \pm 2, \ldots,$$

and a may be chosen so that this holds also for $k = 0$.

Since $F - a$ is periodic of period 2π (because $\int_0^{2\pi} f(t)\, dt = 0$), there is a trigonometric polynomial

$$T(t) = \sum_{k=-n}^{n} c_k e^{ikt},$$

given $\epsilon > 0$, such that

$$\max\,[|F(t) - a - T(t)| : t \in [0, 2\pi]] < \epsilon.$$

This follows from the fact that $F(t)$ is continuous, by the Weierstrass theorem. Now,

$$\begin{aligned}\int_0^{2\pi} |F(t) - a|^2\, dt &= \int_0^{2\pi} (F(t) - a)(\overline{F(t)} - \bar{a} - T(t))\, dt \\ &\le \epsilon \int_0^{2\pi} |F(t) - a|\, dt \\ &\le \epsilon \left[\int_0^{2\pi} |F(t) - a|^2\, dt\right]^{1/2} \left[\int_0^{2\pi} dt\right]^{1/2}.\end{aligned}$$

Hence

$$\int_0^{2\pi} |F(t) - a|^2\, dt \le 2\pi\epsilon^2,$$

so that $F(t)$ is constant. Thus $f(t)$ is zero almost everywhere.

The corresponding system for real $L_2(0, 2\pi)$ is the sequence

$$\frac{1}{\sqrt{2\pi}}, \frac{1}{\sqrt{\pi}} \cos nt, \frac{1}{\sqrt{\pi}} \sin nt, \quad n = 1, 2, 3, \ldots,$$

and the series for these systems are the usual Fourier series.

(iii) Consider the collection X of functions on $-\infty < t < \infty$ representable in the form

$$x(t) = \sum_{k=1}^{n} a_k e^{i\lambda_k t},$$

for arbitrary n, real numbers $\lambda_1, \lambda_2, \ldots, \lambda_n$, and complex coefficients $a_1, a_2, \ldots, a_n$.

X is a vector space and an inner product is defined in X by

$$(x, y) = \lim_{T\to\infty} \frac{1}{2T} \int_{-T}^{T} x(t)\overline{y(t)}\, dt.$$

In this space, the uncountable set $[e^{i\lambda t} : -\infty < \lambda < \infty]$ forms a complete orthonormal set, as direct computation shows.

(iv) The functions holomorphic on the unit disk $|z| < 1$ in the complex z plane and having finite Dirichlet integral

$$\iint_{|z|<1} |f(z)|^2\, dx\, dy < \infty$$

form an inner product space under

$$(f, g) = \iint_{|z|<1} f\bar{g}\, dx\, dy.$$

An orthonormal sequence is given by

$$\varphi_n(z) = \sqrt{\frac{n}{\pi}}\, z^{n-1}, \quad n = 1, 2, 3, \ldots.$$

Some additional examples appear in the exercises and in later sections.

We are interested in expansions of the form $x = \Sigma\, a_\alpha x_\alpha$, for $x \in X$ and $\{x_\alpha\}$ an orthonormal family in X, possibly uncountable. The meaning to be given to such a sum will be described below. First we note formally that

$$(x, x_\beta) = \sum a_\alpha(x_\alpha, x_\beta) = a_\beta,$$

so that the coefficients of interest are the numbers (x, x_β), called the **Fourier coefficients** of x with respect to $\{x_\alpha\}$.

PROPOSITION 1. If $\{x_1, x_2, \ldots, x_n\}$ is an orthonormal set, then for any $x \in X$,

$$\sum_{i=1}^{n} |(x, x_i)|^2 \le \|x\|^2.$$

Proof.

$$\left\| x - \sum_{i=1}^{n} (x, x_i)x_i \right\|^2 = \|x\|^2 - \left(x, \sum_{i=1}^{n} (x, x_i)x_i\right) - \left(\sum_{i=1}^{n} (x, x_i)x_i, x\right) + \left\| \sum_{i=1}^{n} (x, x_i)x_i \right\|^2 \ge 0.$$

But

$$\left(x, \sum_{i=1}^{n} (x, x_i)x_i\right) = \sum_{i=1}^{n} \overline{(x, x_i)}(x, x_i) = \sum_{i=1}^{n} |(x, x_i)|^2,$$

$$\left(\sum_{i=1}^{n} (x, x_i)x_i, x\right) = \sum_{i=1}^{n} (x, x_i)\overline{(x, x_i)} = \sum_{i=1}^{n} |(x, x_i)|^2$$

and, by the pythagorean relation,

$$\left\| \sum_{i=1}^{n} (x, x_i)x_i \right\|^2 = \sum_{i=1}^{n} |(x, x_i)|^2 \, \|x_i\|^2 = \sum_{i=1}^{n} |x, x_i|^2.$$

It follows that

$$\|x\|^2 \geq \sum_{i=1}^{n} |(x, x_i)|^2.$$

Now we let $S = [x_\alpha : \alpha \in A]$ be an orthonormal set in X and define the sum

$$\sum_{\alpha \in A} (x, x_\alpha)x_\alpha$$

for any $x \in X$.

First, by proposition 1, the number of x_α for which $|(x, x_\alpha)| > 1/k$ is finite for each $k = 1, 2, \ldots$. Thus, for each $x \in X$ the set of Fourier coefficients of x which do not vanish is countable. The sum

$$\sum_{\alpha \in A} (x, x_\alpha)x_\alpha$$

is thus a countable sum.

With x fixed, arrange the countable set of x_α for which $(x, x_\alpha) \neq 0$ as a sequence $x_1, x_2, \ldots$.

By proposition 1, the series $\sum_{i=1}^{\infty} |(x, x_i)|^2$ converges, since its partial sums do not exceed $\|x\|^2$. Since

$$\left\| \sum_{i=n}^{n+k} (x, x_i)x_i \right\|^2 = \left(\sum_{i=n}^{n+k} (x, x_i)x_i, \sum_{j=n}^{n+k} (x, x_j)x_j \right)$$

$$= \sum_{i=n}^{n+k} \sum_{j=n}^{n+k} (x, x_i)\overline{(x, x_j)}(x_i, x_j) = \sum_{i=n}^{n+k} |(x, x_i)|^2,$$

it follows that the series $\sum_{i=1}^{\infty} (x, x_i)x_i$ converges. Moreover, from a similar computation the sum is independent of the arrangement of the $\{x_i\}$. This value is the sum of the series

$$\sum_{\alpha \in A} (x, x_\alpha)x_\alpha.$$

We have also proved

Proposition 2 (Bessel's inequality). If X is a Hilbert space, $S = [x_\alpha : \alpha \in A]$ is an orthonormal set in X and $x \in X$, then

$$\sum_{\alpha \in A} |(x, x_\alpha)|^2 \leq \|x\|^2.$$

Fixing the Hilbert space X and the orthonormal set S as above, we say that S is a **basis** (orthonormal basis; also called a closed orthonormal set) in X if the Fourier series representation

$$x = \sum_{\alpha \in A} (x, x_\alpha)x_\alpha$$

is valid for each $x \in X$.

We have two theorems.

THEOREM 1. S is a basis if and only if it is complete in X.

THEOREM 2 (Parseval's formula). S is a basis if and only if equality holds in Bessel's inequality

$$\|x\|^2 = \sum_{\alpha \in A} |(x, x_\alpha)|^2, \quad x \in X$$

or, equivalently,

$$(x, y) = \sum_{\alpha \in A} (x, x_\alpha)\overline{(y, x_\alpha)}, \quad x, y \in X.$$

Proofs. Suppose S is a basis, then if $x \in X$ satisfies $(x, x_\alpha) = 0$, $\alpha \in A$, the definition of sum gives

$$x = \sum_{\alpha \in A} (x, x_\alpha)x_\alpha = 0.$$

Thus, S is complete.

Moreover,

$$\|x\|^2 = \left(\sum_{\alpha \in A} (x, x_\alpha)x_\alpha, \ \sum_{\beta \in A} (x, x_\beta)x_\beta\right)$$
$$= \sum_{\alpha \in A} |(x, x_\alpha)|^2.$$

The equivalence with the second form of Parseval's formula is left as an exercise.

That Parseval's formula implies completeness is obvious, so we need only show that the completeness of S implies S is a basis. Let $\beta \in A$. Then for any $x \in X$,

$$\left(x - \sum_{\alpha \in A} (x, x_\alpha)x_\alpha, x_\beta\right) = (x, x_\beta) - \sum_{\alpha \in A} (x, x_\alpha)(x_\alpha, x_\beta)$$
$$= (x, x_\beta) - (x, x_\beta) = 0,$$

and completeness yields

$$x = \sum_{\alpha \in A} (x, x_\alpha)x_\alpha.$$

To conclude this section, we describe a constructive procedure, the **Gramm-Schmidt process,** for orthonormalizing a given countable linearly independent set of vectors U in an inner product space X. The process is inductive. It will suffice to indicate a few steps.

Choose any $u_1 \in U$. The first member of the proposed orthonormal set $\{x_n\}$ is $x_1 = u_1/\|u_1\|$. Choose $u_2 \in U \sim \{u_1\}$. Then

$$v_2 = u_2 - (u_2, x_1)\, x_1$$

is non-zero, by linear independence, and is orthogonal to x_1. Put $x_2 = v_2/\|v_2\|$. Choose $u_3 \in U \sim \{u_1, u_2\}$ and put

$$v_3 = u_3 - [(u_3, x_1)x_1 + (u_3, x_2)x_2] \quad \text{and} \quad x_3 = v_3/\|v_3\|.$$

Continue in this way.

A linearly independent set of elements of X is a complete set in X if and only if the set of finite linear combinations of its elements is dense in X. We leave the proof to the reader.

4.5 Application, Isoperimetric Theorem

The Parseval formula for the real trigonometric system is

$$a_0^2 + \sum_{n=1}^{\infty} (a_n^2 + b_n^2) = \int_0^{2\pi} |f(t)|^2\, dt,$$

where

$$\frac{a_0}{2} + \sum_{n=1}^{\infty} (a_n \cos nt + b_n \sin nt)$$

is the Fourier series of $f \in L_2\,(0, 2\pi)$. This may be applied to prove the isoperimetric theorem, in the following form:

THEOREM 1. Among all simple, closed, piecewise smooth curves of length L in the plane, the circle encloses the maximum area.

Proof. Let $x = x(s)$, $y = y(s)$, $0 \leq s \leq L$, be a parametric representation of such a curve with arc length as parameter. Let A be the area enclosed by this curve. Introduce the parameter $t = 2\pi s/L$, $0 \leq t \leq 2\pi$, and let the Fourier coefficients of $x(t)$ be a_n and b_n, while denoting those of $y(t)$ by c_n and d_n. Then the Fourier coefficients of dx/dt and dy/dt are, respectively, nb_n, $-na_n$ and nd_n, $-nc_n$.

Now,

$$\left(\frac{dx}{dt}\right)^2 + \left(\frac{dy}{dt}\right)^2 = \left(\frac{L}{2\pi}\right)^2 \left[\left(\frac{dx}{ds}\right)^2 + \left(\frac{dy}{ds}\right)^2\right] = \left(\frac{L}{2\pi}\right)^2,$$

so that

$$2\pi\left(\frac{L}{2\pi}\right)^2 = \int_0^{2\pi} \left[\left(\frac{dx}{dt}\right)^2 + \left(\frac{dy}{dt}\right)^2\right] dt = \sum_{n=1}^{\infty} n^2(a_n^2 + b_n^2 + c_n^2 + d_n^2).$$

Moreover, by Green's theorem,

$$A = \int_0^{2\pi} x \frac{dy}{dt}\, dt = \sum_{n=1}^{\infty} n(a_n d_n - b_n c_n).$$

Thus,

$$L^2 - 4\pi A = 2\pi \sum_{n=1}^{\infty} [(na_n - d_n)^2 + (nb_n + c_n)^2 + (n^2 - 1)(c_n^2 + d_n^2)] \geq 0.$$

This establishes the inequality

$$L^2 \geq 4\pi A$$

with equality only if

$$a_1 = d_1,\ b_1 = -c_1 \quad \text{and} \quad a_n = b_n = c_n = d_n = 0 \quad \text{for } n = 2, 3, \ldots .$$

Since the maximum enclosed area occurs in the case of equality, the curve which realizes it is given by the circle

$$x(t) = \frac{a_0}{2} + a_1 \cos t + b_1 \sin t$$

$$y(t) = \frac{b_0}{2} - b_1 \cos t + a_1 \sin t.$$

4.6 Müntz Theorem

Let $x_1, x_2, \ldots, x_n \in L_2[0, 1]$. The **Gramm determinant** of $x_1, x_2, \ldots, x_n$ is

$$G = G(x_1, x_2, \ldots, x_n) = \begin{vmatrix} (x_1, x_1) & (x_1, x_2) & \ldots & (x_1, x_n) \\ (x_2, x_1) & (x_2, x_2) & \ldots & (x_2, x_n) \\ \cdot & \cdot & & \cdot \\ \cdot & \cdot & & \cdot \\ \cdot & \cdot & & \cdot \\ (x_n, x_1) & (x_n, x_2) & \ldots & (x_n, x_n) \end{vmatrix}.$$

We leave to the reader the proof of

Proposition 1. A necessary and sufficient condition for $(x_1, x_2, \ldots, x_n)$ to be linearly independent is that $G \neq 0$.

Now if $x_1, x_2, \ldots, x_n$ are linearly independent and if $y \in L_2[0, 1]$, then the minimum distance d from y to the subspace generated by $x_1, x_2, \ldots, x_n$ is realized by the projection

$$Py = \sum_{i=1}^{n} a_i x_i$$

of y on that subspace. We wish to evaluate the coefficients a_i and the minimal distance d.

Since $y - Py \perp x_j$, $j = 1, 2, \ldots, n$, we obtain a system of equations for the coefficients:

$$(y, x_j) - \sum_{i=1}^{n} a_i(x_i, x_j) = 0, \quad j = 1, 2, \ldots, n.$$

The determinant of coefficients is just G, so a unique solution exists and is given by

$$a_i = \frac{G^{(i)}}{G}, \quad i = 1, \ldots, n,$$

where $G^{(i)}$ is obtained from G by replacing the ith column by the constants (y, x_j).

Now,

$$\begin{aligned} d^2 = \|y - Py\|^2 &= (y, y - Py) - (Py, y - Py) \\ &= (y, y - Py) \\ &= \|y\|^2 - \sum_{i=1}^{n} a_i(y, x_i). \end{aligned}$$

Let G^+ be the Gramm determinant of the set $y, x_1, x_2, \ldots, x_n$. We show that

$$\frac{G^+}{G} = \|y\|^2 - \sum_{i=1}^{n} a_i(y, x_i) = d^2.$$

Indeed,

$$\frac{G^+}{G} = \frac{1}{G}\begin{vmatrix} (y, y) & (y, x_1) & \ldots & (y, x_n) \\ (x_1, y) & (x_1, x_1) & \ldots & (x_1, x_n) \\ \vdots & \vdots & & \vdots \\ (x_n, y) & (x_n, x_1) & \ldots & (x_n, x_n) \end{vmatrix}$$

$$= \frac{(y, y)G - (y, x_1)M_1 + \ldots + (-1)^n(y, x_n)M_n}{G},$$

where M_i is the ith minor in the expansion of the determinant by its first row. But, it is clear that $M_i = (-1)^{i-1}G^{(i)}$. Hence,

$$\begin{aligned} \frac{G^+}{G} &= \|y\|^2 \\ &+ \frac{(-1)(y, x_1)G^{(1)} + (-1)^3(y, x_2)G^{(2)} + \ldots + (-1)^{2n-1}(y, x_n)G^{(n)}}{G} \\ &= \|y\|^2 - \sum_{i=1}^{n}\left[\frac{G^{(i)}}{G}\right](y, x_i) = d^2. \end{aligned}$$

We shall make use of these observations to prove a remarkable result known as Müntz's theorem.

The set of functions

$$1, t, t^2, t^3, \ldots$$

is a total set in $C[0, 1]$ by the Weierstrass theorem. It is also total (complete) in $L_2[0, 1]$, since the polynomials are dense in that space as well. Müntz's theorem gives necessary and sufficient conditions that the set

$$1, t^{n_1}, t^{n_2}, \ldots, 1 \leq n_1 < n_2 < \ldots$$

enjoy the same properties.

Let $x \in C[0, 1]$. The inequality

$$\left[\int_0^1 \left| x(t) - \sum_{i=1}^n a_i t^{n_i} \right|^2 dt\right]^{1/2} \leq \max \left| x(t) - \sum_{i=1}^n a_i t^{n_i} \right|$$

shows that the sequence is complete in L_2 if it is total in $C[0, 1]$. Conversely, to show that the sequence is total in $C[0, 1]$ if it is complete in L_2, it is enough to show that an inequality in the reverse direction holds for the functions t^m, $m = 1, 2, \ldots$. We have

$$\begin{aligned} \left| t^m - \sum_{i=1}^n a_i t^{n_i} \right| &= m \left| \int_0^t \left[t^{m-1} - \sum_{i=1}^n b_i t^{n_i - 1} \right] dt \right| \\ &\leq m \int_0^1 \left| t^{m-1} - \sum_{i=1}^n b_i t^{n_i - 1} \right| dt \\ &\leq m \left[\int_0^1 \left| t^{m-1} - \sum_{i=1}^n b_i t^{n_i - 1} \right|^2 dt \right]^{1/2}, \end{aligned}$$

fulfilling the requirement.

Thus the theorem, which we now state, may be regarded as a generalization of the Weierstrass theorem as well as an L_2 theorem.

THEOREM 1. A necessary and sufficient condition for the set

$$t^{n_1}, t^{n_2}, \ldots, 1 \leq n_1 < n_2 < \ldots$$

to be complete in L_2 is that

$$\sum_{i=1}^{\infty} \frac{1}{n_i} = \infty.$$

REMARK. The function 1 must be added in the case of $C[0, 1]$ but is redundant for L_2.

Proof. The completeness holds if and only if for each $m \geq 1$, with $m \neq n_i$, $i = 1, 2, \ldots$, the minimal distance d_k of t^m from the subspace generated by $t^{m_1}, \ldots, t^{m_k}$ approaches zero as k goes to infinity.

In view of the previous observations, this condition may be stated as

$$\lim_{k \to \infty} \frac{G(t^m, t^{n_1}, \ldots, t^{n_k})}{G(t^{n_1}, \ldots, t^{n_k})} = \lim_{k \to \infty} d_k^2 = 0.$$

Computing a typical element of such a determinant requires only the formula

$$(t^p, t^q) = \int_0^1 t^{p+q}\, dt = \frac{1}{p+q+1}.$$

The determinants themselves can then be explicitly evaluated (see the exercises for an outline of the computation). The result is

$$d_k^2 = \frac{\prod_{i=1}^{k} (n_i - m)^2}{(2m + 1)^2 \prod_{i=1}^{k} (m + n_i + 1)^2}.$$

In view of this, the condition becomes

$$\lim_{k\to\infty} \left[\sum_{i=1}^{k} \left(\log \left(1 - \frac{m}{n_i}\right) - \log \left(1 + \frac{m+1}{n_i}\right)\right)\right] = -\infty.$$

Now the series $\sum_{i=1}^{\infty} \log (1 + a_i)$ and the series $\sum_{i=1}^{\infty} a_i$ converge or diverge simultaneously, since

$$\lim_{x\to 0} \frac{\log (1 + x)}{x} = \lim_{x\to 0} \frac{1}{1 + x} = 1,$$

and so, for any $\epsilon > 0$,

$$(1 - \epsilon)a_i < \log (1 + a_i) < (1 + \epsilon)a_i$$

if i is sufficiently large.

Thus the convergence of

$$\sum_{i=1}^{\infty} \left(\log \left(1 - \frac{m}{n_i}\right) - \log \left(1 + \frac{m+1}{n_i}\right)\right)$$

occurs simultaneously with the convergence of

$$\sum_{i=1}^{\infty} \frac{1}{n_i}$$

which establishes the theorem.

4.7 Dimension, Riesz-Fischer Theorem

Let $S = [x_\alpha : \alpha \in A]$ and $T = [y_\beta : \beta \in B]$ be two bases for the Hilbert space X, and denote by $|A|$ and $|B|$ their cardinal numbers. Since, for each $\alpha \in A$,

$$x_\alpha = \sum_{\beta\in B} (x_\alpha, y_\beta) y_\beta,$$

the subset $B_\alpha \subset B$ of indices for which $(x_\alpha, y_\beta) \neq 0$ is countable. Moreover,

$$B = \bigcup_{\alpha\in A} B_\alpha,$$

since otherwise some y_β would be orthogonal to the complete set S, which is impossible. Hence, $|B| \leq \aleph_0 |A|$ and, by symmetry, $|A| \leq \aleph_0 |B|$.

If A and B are infinite sets, this proves the following proposition, which is well known from linear algebra in case A or B is finite.

PROPOSITION 1. The cardinality is the same for each basis of a given Hilbert space.

In view of this fact, we define the (orthogonal) **dimension** of a Hilbert space to be the cardinality of its bases.

Now we show

PROPOSITION 2. X is separable if and only if there is a countable basis for X, i.e., the dimension of X does not exceed $\aleph_0$.

Proof. If X is separable and $(x_1, x_2, \ldots)$ is a dense set in S, then by an inductive procedure we can construct an orthonormal set of linear combinations of the x_i's. The procedure differs from the Gramm-Schmidt procedure only in that at each stage the next x_i may be linearly dependent on the preceding, in which case it is skipped. The resulting orthonormal set is complete since it is a total set in X.

Conversely, if $(x_1, x_2, \ldots)$ is a basis for X, then the linear combinations with rational coefficients form a countable dense set.

Now, suppose that X and Y are two Hilbert spaces of the same dimension. Let S be a basis for X and let T be a basis for Y. Let φ be a one-one map of S onto T. Extend φ to X as follows: If $x \in X$, $x = \sum_{\alpha \in A} (x, x_\alpha)x_\alpha$, where $S = [x_\alpha : \alpha \in A]$, put

$$\varphi(x) = \sum_{\alpha \in A} (x, x_\alpha)\varphi(x_\alpha).$$

The latter series converges because the former does and each convergence is equivalent to

$$\sum_{\alpha \in A} |(x, x_\alpha)|^2 < \infty.$$

Now φ is clearly a linear transformation, which is one-one since $\varphi(x) = 0$ implies $(x, x_\alpha) = 0$ for all $\alpha \in A$, so that $x = 0$. Moreover, φ maps X onto Y since, if $y \in Y$, then

$$y = \sum_{\alpha \in A} (y, \varphi(x_\alpha))\varphi(x_\alpha)$$

and we may put

$$x = \sum_{\alpha \in A} (y, \varphi(x_\alpha))x_\alpha$$

to obtain $(x, x_\alpha) = (y, \varphi(x_\alpha))$, $\alpha \in A$, and

$$\varphi(x) = \sum_{\alpha \in A} (x, x_\alpha)\varphi(x_\alpha) = \sum_{\alpha \in A} (y, \varphi(x_\alpha))\varphi(x_\alpha) = y.$$

Finally, the Parseval formula implies that φ is norm preserving and so preserves inner product:

$$\|\varphi(x)\| = \|x\| \text{ and } (\varphi(x), \varphi(x')) = (x, x').$$

We have exhibited a mapping φ which is an isomorphism of the Hilbert spaces X and Y in the sense of being one-one and preserving all the Hilbert space structure. Thus we have proved

PROPOSITION 3. Two Hilbert spaces are isomorphic if they have the same dimension.

The converse is obvious.

We have seen that both l_2 and $L_2(0, 2\pi)$ are separable. Hence they are isomorphic. The isomorphism φ is simply the mapping which associates a function f with its sequence of Fourier coefficients.

The deep part of this result is the classical Riesz-Fischer theorem in the theory of Fourier series:

THEOREM 1. If $\sum_{n=-\infty}^{\infty} |c_n|^2 < \infty$, then there is an $f \in L_2(0, 2\pi)$ such that $\sum_{n=-\infty}^{\infty} c_n e^{inx}$ is the Fourier series of f and converges to f in the sense of L_2.

Clearly, the essential part of this theorem is the completeness of L_2, and so the latter assertion is often called the Riesz-Fischer theorem.

The space of example (iii) in Sec. 4.4 generates, upon completion, a Hilbert space which is non-separable.

4.8 Reproducing Kernel

The introduction of a Banach or Hilbert space in a problem in analysis often involves the step of completing a class of functions on a set S with respect to a norm appropriate to the problem. The functions of the class are usually defined everywhere in S, and there is some relation between the norm and the functional values at points of S. In general, all this is lost in the abstract process of completion, i.e., by imbedding in a space of equivalence classes of Cauchy sequences. For this reason, a more concrete completion is to be preferred if it is available. In particular, a completion by the adjunction of functions is desired. This problem was studied by Aronszajn and Smith [1]. The simple case of completing the class of continuous functions on [0, 1] under the norm of $L_p[0, 1]$ already shows that one cannot expect, in general, to obtain functions defined everywhere in S for the completion, but rather classes of equivalent functions in the sense of being defined and equal except on certain exceptional sets in S (the sets of measure zero in the example, where $L_p[0, 1]$ is the completion).

Under adequate conditions relating the norm and the functional values, however, this phenomenon does not occur. It is this case which we shall discuss here.

A vector space X of functions on a set S, together with a norm in X, is called a **proper functional space** if for every $s \in S$ the evaluation functional at s is continuous, i.e., there is an M_s such that

$$|x(s)| \leq M_s \|x\|, \ x \in X.$$

A **proper functional completion** of X is a proper functional space $\bar{X}$ on the same basic set S such that $\bar{X}$ is complete and X is a dense subspace of $\bar{X}$.

Since the abstract completion is unique up to isomorphism and since if $\bar{X}$ exists then the function values of its elements are well determined by the continuous extension there of the evaluation functionals, it is clear that at most one proper functional completion of X can exist.

We have

PROPOSITION 1. A proper functional space X has a proper functional completion if and only if for each Cauchy sequence $\{x_n\}$ in X,

$$\lim_n x_n(s) = 0 \text{ for all } s \in S \text{ implies } \lim_n \|x_n\| = 0.$$

Proof. Suppose $\bar{X}$ exists. If $\{x_n\}$ is a Cauchy sequence, $\lim_n \|x_n\|$ exists and $\|\bar{x}\| = \lim_n \|x_n\|$, if $\bar{x}$ is the limit in X of $\{x_n\}$. Suppose $\|\bar{x}\| > 0$. Then $\bar{x}(s) \neq 0$ for some $s \in S$. But $\bar{x}(s) = \lim_n x_n(s) = 0$ by assumption and the continuity of evaluation at s. This contradiction establishes the condition.

Conversely, assuming the condition, let $\bar{X}$ consist of all functions on S defined by

$$\bar{x}(s) = \lim_n x_n(s), \quad s \in S,$$

where $\{x_n\}$ is any Cauchy sequence in X (the limit exists since $|x_n(s) - x_m(s)| \leq M_s \|x_n - x_m\|$). In addition, let

$$\|\bar{x}\| = \lim_n \|x_n\|.$$

This choice is independent of the sequence defining $\bar{x}$, since if

$$\bar{x}(s) = \lim_n y_n(s)$$

also, then $\|x_n - y_n\|$ has limit zero by the condition, and so

$$\lim_n | \|x_n\| - \|y_n\| | \leq \lim_n \|x_n - y_n\| = 0.$$

Since the constant sequence $(x, x, \ldots)$ defines $x \in X$ in the above way, we have $X \subset \bar{X}$ with agreement of norms.

Let $\bar{x} \in \bar{X}$ and $\{x_n\}$ define $\bar{x}$. Then

$$\lim_n \|\bar{x} - x_n\| = \lim_k \lim_n \|x_k - x_n\| = 0,$$

since $\{x_n\}$ is a Cauchy sequence. Hence any defining sequence for $\bar{x}$ converges to $\bar{x}$ in $\bar{X}$. In particular, X is dense in $\bar{X}$.

Now, for $s \in S$,

$$|\bar{x}(s)| = |\lim_n x_n(s)| = \lim_n |x_n(s)| \leq M_s \lim_n \|x_n\| = M_s \|\bar{x}\|.$$

Thus $\bar{X}$ is a proper functional space.

Finally, $\bar{X}$ is complete. Let $\{\bar{x}_k\}$ be a Cauchy sequence in $\bar{X}$ and, for each k, let $\{x_{k,n}\}$ define $\bar{x}_k$,

$$\bar{x}_k(s) = \lim_n x_{k,n}(s), \quad s \in S \quad \text{and} \quad \bar{x}_k = \lim_n x_{k,n} \text{ in } \bar{X}.$$

Choose $1 < N(1) < N(2) < \ldots$ so that

$$\|\bar{x}_k - x_{k,N(k)}\| < \frac{1}{2^k}.$$

The sequence $\{x_{k,N(k)}\}$ is Cauchy in X, so the limit

$$\bar{x}(s) = \lim_k x_{k,N(k)}(s), \quad s \in S$$

exists by the proper functional space property. That $\bar{x} = \lim_k \bar{x}_k$ in $\bar{X}$ follows from

$$\|\bar{x}_k - \bar{x}\| \leq \|\bar{x}_k - x_{k,N(k)}\| + \|x_{k,N(k)} - \bar{x}\|$$

and the fact that in $\bar{X}$

$$\bar{x} = \lim_k x_{k,N(k)}.$$

If X is a proper functional Hilbert space, then for each $t \in S$ the evaluation functional is represented by an element, K_t, of X. Then,

$$x(t) = (x, K_t), \qquad x \in X, t \in S.$$

Denote by $K(s, t)$ the function on $S \times S$ given by

$$K(s, t) = K_t(s) = (K_t, K_s)$$

and adopt the notation $K(\cdot, t)$ for the element $K_t \in X$.

A Hilbert space of functions on a set S is said to have a **reproducing kernel** if there is a function $K(s, t)$ on $S \times S$ with the properties

(i) $K(\cdot, t) \in X$, $t \in S$

(ii) (reproducing property) $x(t) = (x, K(\cdot, t))$, $x \in X$, $t \in S$.

Thus, any proper functional Hilbert space has a reproducing kernel. It is immediately seen to be unique. On the other hand, if X has a reproducing kernel, then

$$|x(t)| = |(x, K(\cdot, t))| \leq \|K(\cdot, t)\| \|x\|, \qquad x \in X, t \in S,$$

and X is a proper functional space.

In our next remarks, we shall characterize those functions on a set $S \times S$ which are reproducing kernels, and indicate how the proper functional space can be constructed from the kernel function.

A function $K(s, t)$ on $S \times S$ is a **positive matrix** if for each $n = 1, 2, \ldots$ and each choice of points $t_1, t_2, \ldots, t_n$ the quadratic form

$$\sum_{i,j=1}^{n} K(t_i, t_j)\xi_i\bar{\xi}_j$$

in $\xi_1, \xi_2, \ldots, \xi_n$ is non-negative.

If K is the reproducing kernel of a space X, this expression is easily seen to be just $\left\| \sum_{i=1}^{n} K(\cdot\,, t_i)\xi_i \right\|^2$. Thus each reproducing kernel is a positive matrix. Conversely, if K is a positive matrix, then the class of all functions on S representable in the form $\sum_{i=1}^{n} K(s, t_i)\xi_i$ for some $n, t_1, t_2, \ldots, t_n \in S$ and scalars $\xi_1, \xi_2, \ldots, \xi_n$, is a proper functional inner product space under the norm

$$\left\| \sum_{i=1}^{n} K(\cdot\,, t_i)\xi_i \right\|^2 = \sum_{i,j=1}^{n} K(t_i, t_j)\xi_i\bar{\xi}_j.$$

The proper functional completion X of this space has reproducing kernel K. (The condition for existence of a proper functional completion is clearly satisfied.)

If X is a proper functional Hilbert space with $K(s, t)$ as reproducing kernel and if $[x_\alpha : \alpha \in A]$ is a complete orthonormal set in X, then

$$K(\cdot\,, t) = \sum_{\alpha \in A} (K(\cdot\,, t), x_\alpha)x_\alpha = \sum_{\alpha \in A} \overline{x_\alpha(t)}x_\alpha, \quad t \in S,$$

or

$$K(s, t) = \sum_{\alpha \in A} x_\alpha(s)\overline{x_\alpha(t)}.$$

This expansion makes it possible to give an explicit representation of the reproducing kernel when a complete orthonormal set for X is known.

At first we only have the convergence of this expansion in the sense that, for each t, only countably many terms of $\sum_{\alpha \in A} \overline{x_\alpha(t)}x_\alpha$ are non-zero and this series converges in X to $K(\cdot\,, t)$.

However, the convergence is actually point-wise in S for each t since, if $\{x_n\}$ converges in X to x, then, for each $s \in S$,

$$|x_n(s) - x(s)| = |(x_n - x, K(\cdot\,, s))| \le \|x_n - x\| \, \|K(\cdot\,, s)\|.$$

4.9 Application, Bergman Kernel

Let D be a bounded domain in the $z = x + iy$ plane whose boundary consists of a finite number of smooth simple closed curves.

Consider the class $L_2(D)$ of all holomorphic functions in D for which the Dirichlet integral exists

$$\iint_D |f(z)|^2 \, dx \, dy < \infty.$$

This integral is to be understood in the sense of

$$\lim_{n} \iint_{K_n} |f(z)|^2 \, dx \, dy,$$

where K_n is a non-decreasing sequence of compact subsets of D whose union is D.

We shall show that $L_2(D)$, with $\|f\|^2$ taken as the Dirichlet integral, is a proper functional Hilbert space and illustrate the importance of its reproducing kernel K_D, called the Bergman kernel of D, by an application to conformal mapping.

We need the mean value theorem for holomorphic functions. If f is holomorphic in a disk $|z - z_0| < r$, then

$$f(z_0) = \frac{1}{\pi r^2} \iint_{|z-z_0|<r} f(z) \, dx \, dy.$$

This follows from the identity

$$\iint_D f(z)\overline{g'(z)} \, dx \, dy = \frac{1}{2i} \int_C f(z)\overline{g(z)} \, dz,$$

a consequence of Green's theorem in the plane, because

$$\begin{aligned} f(z_0) &= \frac{1}{2\pi i} \int_{|z-z_0|=r} \frac{f(z)}{z - z_0} \, dz \\ &= \frac{1}{2\pi i r^2} \int_{|z-z_0|=r} f(z)\overline{(z - z_0)} \, dz \\ &= \frac{1}{\pi r^2} \iint_{|z-z_0|<r} f(z) \, dx \, dy. \end{aligned}$$

If we apply the Cauchy-Schwarz inequality in the mean value theorem, we obtain

$$|f(z_0)| \leq \frac{1}{\sqrt{\pi r}} \|f\|, \quad z_0 \in D, \quad f \in L_2(D),$$

where r is chosen so that the disk $|z - z_0| < r$ is contained in D. Thus, $L_2(D)$ is a proper functional space.

Next, we show that $L_2(D)$ is complete. If K is any compact subset of D, then a single R may be found such that for any $z_0 \in K$

$$|f(z_0)| \leq \frac{1}{\sqrt{\pi R}} \|f\|, \quad f \in L_2(D).$$

Thus convergence in $L_2(D)$ of a sequence $\{f_n\}$ implies convergence in D, uniformly on compact subsets of D. By a standard theorem of Weierstrass, such convergence yields a holomorphic limit function. Thus, if $\{f_n\}$ is a Cauchy sequence in $L_2(D)$, it converges point-wise (uniformly on compact sets) to a holomorphic function f on D. We show that $f \in L_2(D)$.

Let $K \subset D$ be compact and choose N so that

$$|f(z) - f_N(z)| < 1, \; z \in K,$$

and

$$|\, \|f_N\| - \lim_n \|f_n\| \,| < 1.$$

Thus, if m denotes planar measure,

$$\begin{aligned} \left[\iint_K |f(z)|^2 \,dx\,dy\right]^{1/2} &\le \left[\iint_K |f(z) - f_N(z)|^2 \,dx\,dy\right]^{1/2} + \left[\iint_K |f_N(z)|^2 \,dx\,dy\right]^{1/2} \\ &< \sqrt{m(K)} + \|f_N\| \\ &< \sqrt{m(D)} + \lim_n \|f_n\| + 1. \end{aligned}$$

Since the final bound is independent of K, we have $f \in L_2(D)$.

It remains for us to show that $\{f_n\}$ converges to f in $L_2(D)$. Let $\epsilon > 0$. Choose N so that $m, n \ge N$ implies $\|f_n - f_m\| < \epsilon$. Next choose a compact set $K \subset D$ so that both

$$\|f\chi_K - f\| < \epsilon \text{ and } \|f_N\chi_K - f_N\| < \epsilon,$$

where the norm sign here indicates the norm in the Hilbert space of all square summable functions in D, the characteristic function of K being non-analytic. That there exists such a compact set K follows since

$$\|f\|^2 = \lim_n \iint_{K_n} |f|^2 dx\,dy$$

and similarly for f_N.

Next, by the uniform convergence of f_n to f on K, we may choose $N' > N$ such that

$$|f_{N'}(z) - f(z)|^2 < \frac{\epsilon^2}{m(K)}, \quad z \in K,$$

and hence such that

$$\begin{aligned} \|(f_{N'} - f)\chi_K\| &= \left[\iint_K |f_{N'}(z) - f(z)|^2 \,dx\,dy\right]^{1/2} \\ &< \left[\frac{\epsilon^2}{m(K)} \cdot m(K)\right]^{1/2} = \epsilon. \end{aligned}$$

Now, for $n > N'$,

$$\begin{aligned} \|f_n - f\| \le \|f_n - f_N\| + \|f_N - f_N\chi_K\| + \|(f_N - f_{N'})\chi_K\| \\ + \|(f_{N'} - f)\chi_K\| + \|f\chi_K - f\| < 5\epsilon. \end{aligned}$$

We recall the celebrated Riemann mapping theorem which asserts that if D is a simply connected domain having more than one boundary point, then there exists a holomorphic function in D which maps D one-one onto the unit disk. We assume, as above, that D is bounded. Moreover, if $\xi \in D$ there is a unique mapping function $f(z) = f(z, \xi)$ for which $f(\xi) = 0$ and $f'(\xi) > 0$.

If $K = K_D$ denotes the Bergman kernel of D, we have

THEOREM 1. The mapping function f is expressed in terms of K by the formula

$$f'(z) = \sqrt{\frac{\pi}{K(\xi, \xi)}}\, K(z, \xi).$$

Proof. Let D_r denote the subdomain of D which is mapped by f onto the disk $|w| < r$, where $r < 1$ and $w = f(z)$. Denote the boundary of D_r by C_r.

If $g \in L_2(D)$, then $g(z)/f(z)$ is meromorphic in D_r with a single pole at $z = \xi$. The residue at this pole is obtained from

$$\lim_{z \to \xi} \frac{(z - \xi)g(z)}{f(z)} = \frac{g(\xi)}{f'(\xi)}.$$

Thus, by the residue theorem,

$$\frac{g(\xi)}{f'(\xi)} = \frac{1}{2\pi i} \int_{C_r} \frac{g(z)}{f(z)}\, dz = \frac{1}{2\pi i r^2} \int_{C_r} \overline{f(z)} g(z)\, dz,$$

since $|f(z)|^2 = r^2$ for $z \in C_r$. Applying the identity (consequence of Green's theorem) mentioned at the beginning of this section, we obtain

$$\frac{g(\xi)}{f'(\xi)} = \frac{1}{\pi r^2} \iint_{D_r} \overline{f'(z)} g(z)\, dx\, dy.$$

Letting r converge to 1, we get

$$g(\xi) = \iint_D \frac{\overline{f'(z)}\, \overline{f'(\xi)}}{\pi}\, g(z)\, dx\, dy.$$

In other words, the function

$$K(z, \xi) = \frac{f'(z) \overline{f'(\xi)}}{\pi}$$

has the reproducing property for $L_2(D)$. Since reproducing kernels are unique, it follows that $K(z, \xi)$ is the Bergman kernel of D.

In case $\xi = z$,

$$[f'(\xi)]^2 = \pi K(\xi, \xi)$$

and substitution for $f'(\xi)$ in the formula for K gives the desired result.

We conclude with the remark that if a complete orthonormal set for $L_2(D)$ is known, K may be written in the form

$$K(z, \xi) = \sum_{n=1}^{\infty} \varphi_n(z)\overline{\varphi_n(\xi)}$$

and so the mapping function can be obtained.

We refer the reader to Nehari [1] for additional interesting applications of Bergman kernels.

4.10 Examples of Complete Orthonormal Sets

In this section, we shall discuss a few of the many important examples of complete orthonormal sets.

First, we consider the sequence

$$1, z, z^2, z^3, \ldots$$

in the space $L_2(D)$. This set is complete for a variety of domains D, each leading to a set of orthonormal polynomials. We shall give the proof only in case D is the unit disk $|z| < 1$.

In this case, the orthonormal set is $\varphi_n(z) = \sqrt{\frac{n}{\pi}}\, z^{n-1}$, $n = 1, 2, 3, \ldots$.

Thus, if $f \in L_2(D)$, the Fourier coefficients are given by

$$\begin{aligned} a_n &= \sqrt{\frac{n}{\pi}} \iint_{|z|<1} f(z)\bar{z}^{n-1}\, dx\, dy \\ &= \lim_{r\to 1} \sqrt{\frac{n}{\pi}} \iint_{|z|<r} f(z)\bar{z}^{n-1}\, dx\, dy \\ &= \lim_{r\to 1} \frac{1}{2i} \sqrt{\frac{n}{\pi}} \int_{|z|=r} f(z)\frac{\bar{z}^n}{n}\, dz, \end{aligned}$$

where we have applied the complex Green's formula of the preceding section.

Since $|z|^2 = r^2$, we have $\bar{z} = r^2 z^{-1}$ and so

$$a_n = \lim_{r\to 1} \frac{1}{\sqrt{\pi n}} \frac{r^{2n}}{2i} \int_{|z|=r} \frac{f(z)}{z^n}\, dz.$$

Now, if

$$f(z) = b_0 + b_1 z + b_2 z^2 + \ldots, \quad |z| < 1$$

is the power series expansion for f, then

$$b_{n-1} = \frac{1}{2\pi i} \int_{|z|=r} \frac{f(z)}{z^n}\, dz.$$

Hence,

$$a_n = \lim_{r\to 1} \sqrt{\frac{\pi}{n}}\, r^{2n} b_{n-1} = \sqrt{\frac{\pi}{n}}\, b_{n-1}, \quad n = 1, 2, \ldots.$$

We proceed to verify Parseval's formula,

$$\iint\limits_{|z|<1} |f(z)|^2\, dx\, dy = \sum_{n=1}^{\infty} |a_n|^2 = \pi \sum_{n=1}^{\infty} \frac{|b_{n-1}|^2}{n},$$

thereby establishing the completeness. For this,

$$\begin{aligned}\iint\limits_{|z|<1} |f(z)|^2\, dx\, dy &= \int_0^1 \int_0^{2\pi} |f(re^{i\theta})|^2 r\, dr\, d\theta \\ &= \int_0^1 \int_0^{2\pi} \left(\sum_{n=0}^{\infty} b_n r^n e^{in\theta}\right)\left(\sum_{n=0}^{\infty} \bar{b}_n r^n e^{-in\theta}\right) r\, dr\, d\theta \\ &= \int_0^1 \int_0^{2\pi} \sum_{n=0}^{\infty} \sum_{m=0}^{\infty} b_n \bar{b}_m r^{n+m} e^{i(n-m)\theta} r\, dr\, d\theta \\ &= \int_0^1 \sum_{n=0}^{\infty} \sum_{m=0}^{\infty} b_n \bar{b}_m \int_0^{2\pi} e^{i(n-m)\theta}\, d\theta\, r^{n+m+1}\, dr,\end{aligned}$$

where the term by term integration is valid because the power series converges uniformly on $|z| \leq r$ for $r < 1$. Then,

$$\begin{aligned}\iint\limits_{|z|<1} |f(z)|^2\, dx\, dy &= \int_0^1 2\pi \sum_{n=0}^{\infty} |b_n|^2 r^{2n+1}\, dr \\ &= \pi \sum_{n=0}^{\infty} \frac{|b_n|^2}{n+1} = \pi \sum_{n=1}^{\infty} \frac{|b_{n-1}|^2}{n}.\end{aligned}$$

With this result as a basis, it is not hard to establish a complete orthonormal system for $L_2(D)$, in case D is a simply connected domain with at least two boundary points, in terms of any mapping function $w = f(z)$ which maps D conformally on the unit disk $|w| < 1$. Indeed,

$$\varphi_n(z) = \sqrt{\frac{n}{\pi}}\, [w(z)]^{n-1} w'(z), \quad n = 1, 2, \ldots$$

is such a system.

A complete orthonormal system for the space $L_2(0, \infty)$ is given by the Laguerre functions

$$\varphi_n(x) = \frac{1}{n!}\, e^{-x/2} L_n(x), \quad n = 0, 1, 2, \ldots,$$

where $L_n(x)$ is the Laguerre polynomial, defined as the coefficient of e^{-x} in the nth derivative of $x^n e^{-x}$:

$$\begin{aligned}L_n(x) &= e^x \frac{d^n}{dx^n} (x^n e^{-x}) \\ &= \sum_{k=0}^{n} (-1)^k \binom{n}{k} n(n-1) \ldots (k+1) x^k.\end{aligned}$$

For the orthogonality,

$$\int_0^{\infty} e^{-x} L_n(x) L_m(x)\, dx = 0, \quad n > m,$$

we compute, for $k < n$,

$$\int_0^\infty e^{-x}x^k L_n(x)\,dx = \int_0^\infty x^k \frac{d^n}{dx^n}(x^n e^{-x})\,dx$$

$$= (-1)^k k! \int_0^\infty \frac{d^{n-k}}{dx^{n-k}}(x^n e^{-x})\,dx = 0,$$

by repeated integration by parts. Also,

$$\int_0^\infty e^{-x}L_n^2(x)\,dx = \int_0^\infty \frac{d^n}{dx^n}(x^n e^{-x})\sum_{k=0}^{n}(-1)^k\binom{n}{k}n(n-1)\ldots(k+1)x^k\,dx$$

$$= \int_0^\infty (-1)^n x^n \frac{d^n}{dx^n}(x^n e^{-x})\,dx$$

$$= n!\int_0^\infty x^n e^{-x}\,dx = (n!)^2$$

which shows that $\{\varphi_n\}$ is orthonormal.

We show that the Laguerre functions are complete in $L_2(0, \infty)$. Thus, we show that if $f \in L_2(0, \infty)$ and

$$\int_0^\infty f(x)e^{-x/2}L_n(x)\,dx = 0, \quad n = 0, 1, 2, \ldots,$$

then f is zero almost everywhere. Let

$$g(x) = f(x)e^{-x/2}.$$

Then we need only show that

$$\int_0^\infty g(x)x^n\,dx = 0, \quad n = 0, 1, 2, \ldots$$

implies $g(x) = 0$ almost everywhere for $g \in L_1(0, \infty)$, since $f \in L_2$, $e^{-x/2} \in L_2$ implies $g \in L_1$.

Now consider

$$\Phi(s) = \int_0^\infty e^{-st}g(t)\,dt.$$

Since $g \in L_1$, Φ is defined for all $s = \sigma + i\tau$, $\sigma \geq 0$. Moreover, Φ is regular for all $s = \sigma + i\tau$, $\sigma > 0$ (see Widder, [1]).

We consider the series

$$\sum_{n=0}^{\infty} s^n \cdot \frac{1}{n!}\int_0^\infty g(t)t^n\,dt$$

for real s. An easy computation using the fact that

$$\int_0^\infty e^{-x/2}x^n\,dx = 2^{n+1}n!$$

shows that this series converges for $0 \leq s < \frac{1}{4}$ to the function Φ. Thus Φ is zero for all real $s \geq 0$.

But

$$\Phi(s) = \int_0^1 t^{s-1}g(-\log t)\,dt = 0, \quad s \geq 0$$

implies, as the reader may verify, that

$$g(-\log t) = 0 \text{ a.e. in } (0, 1)$$

so that

$$g(x) = 0 \text{ a.e. in } (0, \infty).$$

4.11 Systems of Haar, Rademacher, Walsh; Applications

We now consider the Haar system in $L_2[0, 1]$. Let

$$\varphi_0^{(0)}(x) = 1, \quad x \in [0, 1]$$

$$\varphi_1^{(0)}(x) = \begin{cases} 1, & x \in [0, \tfrac{1}{2}) \\ -1, & x \in (\tfrac{1}{2}, 1] \\ 0, & x = \tfrac{1}{2} \end{cases}$$

and for $m = 1, 2, \ldots ; k = 1, \ldots, 2^m$

$$\varphi_m^{(k)}(x) = \begin{cases} \sqrt{2^m}, & x \in \left(\dfrac{k-1}{2^m}, \dfrac{k-1/2}{2^m}\right) \\ -\sqrt{2^m}, & x \in \left(\dfrac{k-1/2}{2^m}, \dfrac{k}{2^m}\right) \\ 0, & x \in [0, 1] \sim \left[\dfrac{k-1}{2^m}, \dfrac{k}{2^m}\right] \end{cases}$$

and at that finite set of points at which $\varphi_m^{(k)}(x)$ has not yet been defined, let $\varphi_m^{(k)}(x)$ be the average of the left and right limits of $\varphi_m^{(k)}(x)$ as x approaches the point in question. At 0 and 1, let $\varphi_m^{(k)}(x)$ assume the value of the one-sided limit. The set of functions

$$\{\varphi_0^{(0)}, \varphi_1^{(0)}, \varphi_m^{(k)}, m = 1, 2, \ldots ; k = 1, \ldots, 2^m\}$$

is known as the **Haar system.**

PROPOSITION 1. The Haar system is orthonormal in $L_2[0, 1]$.

Proof. If $m = n$, then $\varphi_m^{(k)}(x) \cdot \varphi_n^{(l)}(x) = 0$, $k \neq l$, except possibly at one point, so that

$$\int_0^1 \varphi_m^{(k)}(x)\varphi_n^{(l)}(x)\, dx = 0.$$

If $m \neq n$, then

$$\int_0^1 \varphi_m^{(k)}(x) \cdot \varphi_n^{(l)}(x)\, dx = \int_{\frac{l-1}{2^n}}^{\frac{l}{2^n}} \varphi_m^{(k)}(x)\varphi_n^{(l)}(x)\, dx$$

$$= \sqrt{2^n} \int_{\frac{l-1}{2^n}}^{\frac{l-1/2}{2^n}} \varphi_m^{(k)}\, dx - \sqrt{2^n} \int_{\frac{l-1/2}{2^n}}^{\frac{l}{2^n}} \varphi_m^{(k)}\, dx = 0,$$

since both integrals vanish.

For normality,

$$\int_0^1 (\varphi_m^{(k)}(x))^2\,dx = 2\left((\sqrt{2^m})^2 \cdot \frac{1}{2^{m+1}}\right) = 1.$$

We leave it to the reader to show that the Haar functions are complete in $L_2[0, 1]$. We show that they have a deeper property.

The **Haar expansion** of a function $f \in L_1$ is the series

$$a_0^{(0)}\varphi_0^{(0)} + a_1^{(0)}\varphi_1^{(0)} + \sum_{m=1}^{\infty}\left(\sum_{k=1}^{2^m} a_m^{(k)}\varphi_m^{(k)}\right),$$

where $a_m^{(k)} = \int_0^1 \varphi_m^{(k)}(x)f(x)\,dx$, and the terms are added in the order indicated.

We shall need the fact that if f is summable and F is defined by $F(x) = \int_0^x f(t)\,dt$, then F' exists almost everywhere and $F'(x) = f(x)$ almost everywhere. For a proof see, for example, Goffman [1].

THEOREM 1. If $f \in L_1$, then the Haar expansion of f converges to f almost everywhere.

Proof. Note that $a_m^{(k)}\varphi_m^{(k)}(x) = \int_0^1 \varphi_m^{(k)}(x)\varphi_m^{(k)}(t)f(t)\,dt$. The partial sums

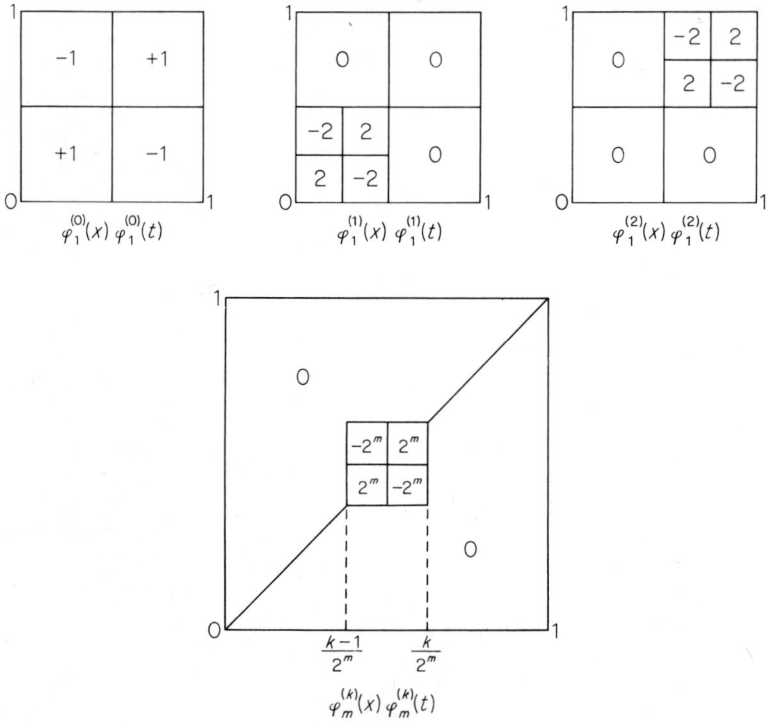

Figure 3

$$s_{m_0}^{(k_0)}(x) = a_0^{(0)}\varphi_0^{(0)}(x) + a_1^{(0)}\varphi_1^{(0)}(x) + \sum_{m=1}^{m_0-1}\left(\sum_{k=1}^{2^m} a_m^{(k)}\varphi_m^{(k)}(x)\right) + \sum_{k=1}^{k_0} a_{m_0}^{(k)}\varphi_{m_0}^{(k)}(x)$$

will be abbreviated by defining the kernel

$$K_{m_0}^{(k_0)}(x, t) = \varphi_0^{(0)}(x)\varphi_0^{(0)}(t) + \ldots + \varphi_m^{(k)}(x)\varphi_m^{(k)}(t) + \ldots + \ldots + \varphi_{m_0}^{(k_0)}(x)\varphi_{m_0}^{(k_0)}(t).$$

Thus,

$$s_{m_0}^{(k_0)}(x) = \int_0^1 f(t)K_{m_0}^{(k_0)}(x, t)\,dt.$$

Consider now the products $\varphi_m^{(k)}(x)\varphi_m^{(k)}(t)$ on the unit square.

$\varphi_0^{(0)}(x)\varphi_0^{(0)}(t) = 1$ on the unit square. The others will be given by diagram (Figure 3) for the sake of clarity. Since the values on the bounding lines do not matter in this discussion, they are omitted.

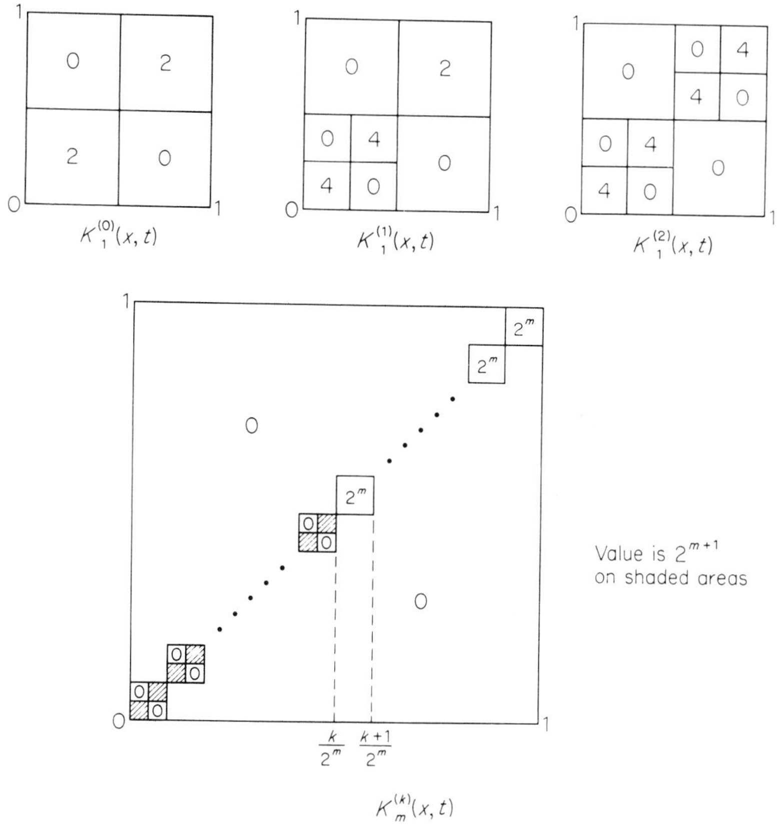

Figure 4

The kernels then take on the following values. $K_0^{(0)}(x, t) = 1$ on the unit square and the others are as in Figure 4.

Note that the value of the kernel on each diagonally situated square is the reciprocal of the length of the side of that square. Let $x \in [0, 1]$ not be of the form $p/2^n$ for any non-negative integers p and n. Then

$$s_m^{(k)}(x) = \int_0^1 K_m^{(k)}(x, t) f(t)\, dt$$
$$= \frac{1}{m(I)} \int_I f(t)\, dt,$$

where I contains x and has length either $1/2^m$ or $1/2^{m+1}$. But if $F(x) = \int_0^x f(t)\, dt$, then clearly $\lim s_m^{(k)}(x) = F'(x) = f(x)$ almost everywhere.

A system closely related to the Haar system is the **Rademacher system:**

$$r_0(x) = \varphi_0^{(0)}(x)$$

$$r_1(x) = \varphi_1^{(0)}(x)$$

$$r_n(x) = \sqrt{2^{-n}} \sum_{k=1}^{2^n} \varphi_n^{(k)}(x), \quad n = 1, 2, \ldots .$$

It is clear that the Rademacher functions may be defined as follows: If $x \in [0, 1]$ has a unique binary expansion $0 \cdot a_1 a_2 \ldots$, then

$$r_n(x) = \begin{cases} 1, & a_n = 0 \\ -1, & a_n = 1. \end{cases}$$

If $x \in [0, 1]$ has two expansions, $0 \cdot a_1 a_2 \ldots$ and $0 \cdot b_1 b_2 \ldots$, then

$$r_n(x) = \begin{cases} 1 & \text{if } a_n = b_n = 0 \\ 0 & \text{if } a_n \neq b_n \\ -1 & \text{if } a_n = b_n = 1. \end{cases}$$

Proposition 2. The Rademacher system is orthonormal in $L_2[0, 1]$. The proof is left to the reader.

Moreover, the Rademacher system is not complete. By symmetry considerations, $f(x) = \cos 2\pi x$ is orthogonal to all the Rademacher functions. The details are left to the reader.

Proposition 3. If $\sum_{n=0}^{\infty} C_n^2 < \infty$, then $\sum_{n=0}^{\infty} C_n r_n(x)$ converges almost everywhere.

Proof. Let $C_n^{(k)} = C_n/\sqrt{2^n}$, $k = 1, \ldots, 2^n$; $n = 1, 2, \ldots$. So

$$\sum_{n=1}^{\infty} C_n r_n(x) = \sum_{n=1}^{\infty}\sum_{k=1}^{2^n} \sqrt{2^{-n}}C_n \varphi_n^{(k)}(x) = \sum_{n=1}^{\infty}\sum_{k=1}^{2^n} C_n^{(k)}\varphi_n^{(k)}(x),$$

which is the Haar expansion of some function in $L_1 \supset L_2$, by the Riesz-Fischer theorem, since

$$\sum_{n=1}^{\infty}\sum_{k=1}^{2^n} (C_n^{(k)})^2 = \sum_{n=1}^{\infty} C_n^2 < \infty.$$

Hence, by theorem 1, $\sum_{n=0}^{\infty} C_n r_n(x)$ converges almost everywhere.

Corollary 1. If $\sum_{n=1}^{\infty} C_n^2 < \infty$, then $\sum_{n=1}^{\infty} \pm C_n$ converges for almost all choices of signs.

Proof. "Almost all" is taken in the sense that to each sequence $s_1, s_2, \ldots$ of signs corresponds the point $0 \cdot a_1 a_2 \ldots \in [0, 1]$, where

$$a_i = 1 \quad \text{if } s_i \text{ is a } + \text{ sign,}$$
$$a_i = 0 \quad \text{if } s_i \text{ is a } - \text{ sign,}$$

and the measure of a set of sequences of signs is the Lebesgue measure of the corresponding set of points in [0, 1]. This mating is one-one, except for a countable set.

The result follows by considering $\sum_{n=1}^{\infty} C_n r_n(x)$ at each $x \in [0, 1]$.

Corollary 2. If $\{\varphi_n\}$ is any orthonormal system in $L_2[0, 1]$ and

$$\sum_{n=1}^{\infty} C_n^2 < \infty, \quad \text{then} \quad \sum_{n=1}^{\infty} \pm C_n \varphi_n$$

converges almost everywhere for almost all choices of signs.

Proof. Since the system is normal,

$$\sum_{n=1}^{\infty} C_n^2 = \sum_{n=1}^{\infty} \int_0^1 C_n^2 \varphi_n^2(x)\, dx < \infty.$$

So,

$$\left\{\int_0^1 \sum_{n=1}^{m} C_n^2 \varphi_n^2(x)\, dx\right\}$$

is a bounded increasing sequence, and it follows that $\sum_{n=1}^{\infty} C_n^2\varphi_n^2(x) < \infty$ for almost all x. By proposition 3, it follows that

$$\sum_{n=1}^{\infty} C_n\varphi_n(x)r_n(t)$$

converges for almost all values of t for almost all choices of x.

But the set of pairs (x, t) for which this series converges is measurable. Thus its planar measure is 1. It follows that for almost all choices of t, $\sum_{n=1}^{\infty} C_n\varphi_n(x)r_n(t)$ converges almost everywhere in x. Then, just as in corollary 1, $\sum_{n=1}^{\infty} \pm C_n\varphi_n(x)$ converges almost everywhere in x for almost all choices of signs.

We shall need the following lemma, whose proof we leave to the reader.

Lemma. If at least two of the integers $k_1, k_2, \ldots, k_n$ are distinct, then $\int_0^1 r_{k_1}(x) \ldots r_{k_n}(x)\, dx = 0$.

Proposition 4. If $\sum_{n=0}^{\infty} C_n^2 = \infty$, then $\sum_{n=0}^{\infty} C_n r_n(x)$ diverges almost everywhere.

Proof. Suppose the series $\sum_{n=0}^{\infty} C_n r_n(x)$ converges on a set of positive measure. Then by Egoroff's theorem, it converges uniformly on a set E of positive measure. Let

$$S_n(x) = \sum_{k=0}^{n} C_k r_k(x), \quad n = 0, 1, 2, \ldots .$$

Let M be a positive integer and n such that $|S_m(x) - S_n(x)| < M$ for all $m > n$ and $x \in E$. Then, for every $m > n$,

$$M^2 m(E) > \int_E \left[\sum_{k=n+1}^{m} C_k r_k(x)\right]^2 dx$$

$$= m(E) \sum_{k=n+1}^{m} C_k^2 + 2 \sum_{k=n+1}^{m-1} \sum_{l=k+1}^{m} C_k C_l \int_E r_k(x) r_l(x)\, dx.$$

By the Cauchy-Schwarz inequality,

$$\left| \sum_{k=n+1}^{m-1} \sum_{l=k+1}^{m} C_k C_l \int_E r_k(x) r_l(x)\, dx \right|$$

$$\leq \left[\sum_{k=n+1}^{m} \sum_{l=n+1}^{m} C_k^2 C_l^2\right]^{1/2} \left[\sum_{k=n+1}^{\infty} \sum_{l=k+1}^{\infty} \left(\int_E r_k(x) r_l(x)\, dx\right)^2\right]^{1/2}.$$

The functions $f_{kl} = r_k \cdot r_l$ form an orthonormal system, by the lemma, so we may expand in terms of them. The kl Fourier coefficient of χ_E is given by

$$\int_0 \chi_E(x) r_k(x) r_l(x)\, dx = \int_E r_k(x) r_l(x)\, dx.$$

By Bessel's inequality,

$$\sum_{k=0}^{\infty} \sum_{l=0}^{\infty} \left(\int_E r_k(x) r_l(x)\, dx\right)^2 \leq \int_0^1 \chi_E^2(x)\, dx = m(E).$$

Hence for sufficiently large n,

$$\sum_{k=n+1}^{\infty} \sum_{l=k+1}^{\infty} \left(\int_E r_k(x) r_l(x)\, dx\right)^2 < \frac{1}{9} m(E)^2.$$

Moreover,

$$\left[\sum_{k=n+1}^{m} \sum_{l=n+1}^{m} C_k^2 C_l^2\right]^{1/2} = \sum_{k=n+1}^{m} C_k^2.$$

Hence,

$$M^2 m(E) \geq m(E) \sum_{k=n+1}^{m} C_k^2 - \frac{2}{3} m(E) \sum_{k=n+1}^{\infty} C_k^2,$$

so that $\sum_{k=n+1}^{m} C_k^2 \leq 3M^2$ for every $m > n$. Therefore, $\sum_{k=0}^{\infty} C_k^2 < \infty$, a contradiction.

The Rademacher system has an extension to a complete orthonormal system, the **Walsh system,** given by

$$w_0 = 1$$

$$w_1 = r_1$$

$$\cdots$$

$$w_n = r_{\nu_1+1} \cdots r_{\nu_p+1}, \text{ for } n \geq 1,$$

where $\nu_1 < \nu_2 < \ldots < \nu_p$ are determined from the binary expansion of $n = 2^{\nu_1} + \ldots + 2^{\nu_p}$.

Observe that for $n = 2^p$, $w = r_n$, so that the Walsh functions include the Rademacher functions.

THEOREM 2. The Walsh system is a complete orthonormal set in L_2 [0, 1].

Proof. The orthogonality follows by the lemma. The normality is easy to verify.

To prove completeness, take any $f \in L_2[0, 1]$, or even $L_1[0, 1]$, and define $F(x) = \int_0^x f(t)\, dt$. Suppose $\int_0^1 f(x) w_n(x)\, dx = 0$, $n = 0, 1, 2, \ldots$. f will be shown equal to zero almost everywhere by proving $F(x) = 0$ on a dense set in [0, 1]. Since F is continuous, it must then be identically zero. Since $F'(x) = f(x)$ almost everywhere, it follows that $f(x) = 0$ almost everywhere.

Now, $F(0) = 0$.

$$0 = \int_0^1 f(x)w_0(x)\,dx = F(1).$$

$$0 = \int_0^1 f(x)w_1(x)dx = \left[F\left(\frac{1}{2}\right) - F(0)\right] - \left[F(1) - F\left(\frac{1}{2}\right)\right] = 2F\left(\frac{1}{2}\right).$$

$$\begin{aligned} 0 &= \int_0^1 f(x)w_2(x)\,dx \\ &= \left[F\left(\frac{1}{4}\right) - F(0)\right] - \left[F\left(\frac{1}{2}\right) - F\left(\frac{1}{4}\right)\right] \\ &\quad + \left[F\left(\frac{3}{4}\right) - F\left(\frac{1}{2}\right)\right] - \left[F(1) - F\left(\frac{3}{4}\right)\right] \\ &= 2\left[F\left(\frac{1}{4}\right) + F\left(\frac{3}{4}\right)\right] \end{aligned}$$

and

$$0 = \int_0^1 f(x)w_3(x)\,dx = 2\left[F\left(\frac{1}{4}\right) - F\left(\frac{3}{4}\right)\right]$$

so that

$$F\left(\frac{1}{4}\right) = F\left(\frac{3}{4}\right) = 0.$$

We leave it to the reader to show that $F(x) = 0$, $x = k/2^m$, for all $m = 0, 1, 2, \ldots, k = 1, \ldots, 2^m$.

EXERCISES

1.1 Show that equality holds in the Cauchy-Schwarz inequality if and only if x and y are proportional.

1.2 Derive conditions for equality in the triangle inequality.

1.3 Verify the pythagorean theorem and the parallelogram law.

1.4 Let $x_1, x_2, \ldots, x_n$ satisfy $x_i \neq 0$ and $x_i \perp x_j$ if $i \neq j$, $i, j = 1, 2, \ldots, n$. Show that the x_i's are linearly independent and extend the pythagorean theorem.

1.5 Verify the polarization identities in both the real and complex cases.

1.6 Give an example of a Schauder basis in a separable Hilbert space which is not a complete orthonormal set.

2.1 Give an example of a Banach space, not a Hilbert space, in which lemma 1 holds.

2.2 Give an example of a Banach space in which lemma 1 fails to hold.

2.3 Show that the minimizing point y_0 in lemma 1 is characterized by

$$\text{Re}\,(y_0 - x_0, y - y_0) \geq 0 \text{ for all } y \in K.$$

2.4 Let $f \in L_2(0, 1)$. Show that for each $n = 1, 2, \ldots$, there is a unique polynomial of degree n, or less, which is the best approximant to f in the sense of L_2.

2.5 Show that if M and N are closed subspaces of a Hilbert space X, then $M \dot{+} N$ is closed provided $x \perp y$ for all $x \in M$, $y \in N$.

2.6 If S is a subset of a Hilbert space X, show that $S^{\perp} = [x \in X : x \perp y$ for all $y \in S]$ is a closed subspace of X and that $(S^{\perp})^{\perp}$ is the closed linear span of X.

2.7 Show that a projection P is an orthogonal projection if and only if $(Px, y) = (x, Py)$, $x, y \in X$.

2.8 A sequence $\{x_n\}$ in a Hilbert space X is said to be weakly convergent if $\lim_n (x_n, y)$ exists for each $y \in X$. We say $\{x_n\}$ converges weakly to $x \in X$, written $x_n \rightharpoonup x$, if $\lim_n (x_n, y) = (x, y)$ for every $y \in X$. Show that if $\{x_n\}$ converges weakly, then there is an x for which $x_n \rightharpoonup x$.

2.9 If $\|x_n\| \leq 1$, $n = 1, 2, \ldots$ in separable Hilbert space, show that a subsequence of $\{x_n\}$ converges weakly.

2.10 Show that $e_n = (0, \ldots, 0, 1, 0, \ldots)$, where 1 is in the nth place, converges weakly to $(0, 0, \ldots)$ in l_2.

2.11 Show that $\{x_n\}$ converges to x in the Hilbert space norm (called strong convergence) if and only if $x_n \rightharpoonup x$ and $\lim_n \|x_n\| = \|x\|$.

2.12 Let X be separable and let $\{\varphi_m\}$ be a complete orthonormal sequence in X. Show that $\{x_n\}$ converges weakly to x if and only if it is bounded and $\{(x_n, \varphi_m)\}$ converges to (x, φ_m) for each $m = 1, 2, \ldots$.

2.13 Show that if $x_n \rightharpoonup x$, there is a subsequence $\{x_{n_k}\}$ such that $\left\{\frac{1}{m} \sum_{i=1}^{m} x_{n_i}\right\}$ converges strongly to x.

3.1 Show that V is norm preserving, i.e.,

$$\int_S |f(x)|^2 \, d\mu = \int_S |f(Tx)|^2 \, d\mu, \quad f \in L_2.$$

4.1 Show that for the functions in example (iii),

$$(x, y) = \lim_{T \to \infty} \frac{1}{2T} \int_{-T}^{T} x(t) y(t) \, dt$$

exists. Show that $\{e^{i\lambda t} : -\infty < \lambda < \infty\}$ is a complete orthonormal set.

4.2 Prove that $\varphi_n(z) = \sqrt{\frac{n}{\pi}}\, z^{n-1}$, $n = 1, 2, \ldots$, is orthonormal with

$$(f, g) = \iint_{|z|<1} f\bar{g} \, dx \, dy.$$

4.3 Show that the two forms of Parseval's formula are equivalent.

4.4 Show that if $S = [x_\alpha : \alpha \in A]$ is orthonormal, then $\sum_{\alpha \in A} (x, x_\alpha) x_\alpha$ is the projection of x on the closed subspace spanned by S.

4.5 Let $x_1, x_2, \ldots, x_n$ be orthonormal in X and let $x \in X$. Show that for all sums of the form $\sum_{i=1}^{n} a_i x_i$, the distance (mean square error)

$$\|x - \sum_{i=1}^{n} a_i x_i\|$$

is a minimum when the a_i's are the Fourier coefficients of x.

4.6 Apply the preceding exercise to prove theorem 2.

4.7 Let $f \in L_2[-1, 1]$. Give an expression for the polynomial of degree n or less which best approximates to f in mean square.

4.8 Show that a linearly independent set in X is complete if and only if it is total.

4.9 Apply the Gramm-Schmidt process to the functions $1, t, t^2, \ldots$ in $L_2[-1, 1]$. Show that the resulting orthonormal set consists of $\sqrt{n + \frac{1}{2}}\, P_n(t)$, where

$$P_n(t) = \frac{1}{2^n n!} \frac{d^n}{dt^n} (t^2 - 1)^n$$

is the nth Legendre polynomial.

4.10 Prove completeness for the set in exercise 4.9.

4.11 Show that the trigonometric functions are complete in $L_2[0, 2\pi]$ by showing that if f is continuously differentiable, then its Fourier series converges uniformly to f.

4.12 Show that $\{\varphi_n\}$ is complete for $L_2[a, b]$ if and only if

$$\sum_{n=1}^{\infty} \left(\int_a^x \varphi_n(t)\, dt \right)^2 = x - a$$

for every $x \in [a, b]$.

4.13 Show that $\{\varphi_n\}$ is complete for $L_2[a, b]$ if and only if

$$\sum_{n=1}^{\infty} \int_a^b \left[\int_a^x \varphi_n(t)\, dt \right]^2 dx = \frac{(b - a)^2}{2}.$$

6.1 Let $x_1, x_2, \ldots, x_n \in X$ and let

$$\begin{aligned} y_1 &= c_{11}x_1 \\ y_2 &= c_{21}x_1 + c_{22}x_2 \\ &\ldots \\ y_n &= c_{n1}x_1 + c_{n2}x_2 + \ldots + c_{nn}x_n \end{aligned}$$

be obtained by the Gramm-Schmidt process from $x_1, x_2, \ldots, x_n$. Put

$$D_n = \begin{vmatrix} c_{11} & 0 & 0 & \ldots & 0 \\ c_{21} & c_{22} & 0 & \ldots & 0 \\ \cdot & \cdot & & & \cdot \\ \cdot & \cdot & & & \cdot \\ \cdot & \cdot & & & \cdot \\ c_{n1} & c_{n2} & & \ldots & c_{nn} \end{vmatrix}.$$

The determinant

$$G_n = \det(x_i, x_j)$$

is called the Gramm determinant of the set $x_1, x_2, \ldots, x_n$. Show that

$$D_n G_n \bar{D}_n = 1.$$

6.2 Prove that $x_1, x_2, \ldots, x_n$ are linearly independent if and only if $G_n \neq 0$.

6.3 Let

$$\Delta_n = \begin{vmatrix} \dfrac{1}{a_1 + b_1} & \dfrac{1}{a_1 + b_2} & \cdots & \dfrac{1}{a_1 + b_n} \\ \vdots & \vdots & & \vdots \\ \dfrac{1}{a_n + b_1} & \dfrac{1}{a_n + b_2} & \cdots & \dfrac{1}{a_n + b_n} \end{vmatrix}.$$

By subtracting the last row from each of the others, removing common factors, subtracting the last column and again removing common factors, show that

$$\Delta_n = \frac{\prod_{i=1}^{n-1} (a_n - a_i)(b_n - b_i)}{\prod_{i=1}^{n} (a_n + b_i) \prod_{i=1}^{n-1} (a_i + b_n)} \begin{vmatrix} & & & 1 \\ & \Delta_{n-1} & & 1 \\ & & & 1 \\ & & & \vdots \\ 0 & 0 & \cdots \; 0 & 1 \end{vmatrix}$$

and thus evaluate Δ_n.

6.4 Apply the above to verify the value of $d^2_{m,k}$ given in the text.

6.5 Show that if $\{\varphi_n\}$ is complete for $L_2[0, 1]$, then $1, \varphi_n, n = 1, 2, \ldots$ is total for $C[0, 1]$.

6.6 Show that Müntz's theorem is valid for every $L_p[0, 1]$, $1 \leq p < \infty$.

7.1 Let $\{x_k\}$ be a complete orthonormal system in X (separable). Suppose $\{y_k\}$ satisfies

$$\sum_{k=1}^{\infty} \|x_k - y_k\|^2 < 1.$$

Show that $\{y_k\}$ is complete.

7.2 Let $\{x_n\}$ be a complete sequence in a separable Hilbert space X. Find necessary and sufficient conditions on $y \in X$ in order that

$$y, x_2, x_3, \ldots$$

be a complete sequence.

7.3 Give the details of the proof of the Riesz-Fischer theorem.

8.1 Determine whether l_2 is a proper functional space. If it is, find its reproducing kernel.

8.2 Prove that a reproducing kernel, if it exists, is unique.

8.3 Let S be a metric space and X a proper functional Hilbert space of functions on S with reproducing kernel $K(s, t)$. Show that the mapping

$$t \to K(\cdot\,, t)$$

is continuous if and only if the spheres $[f \in X : \|f\| < M]$ in X are equicontinuous.

8.4 Suppose X, with reproducing kernel K, is a closed subspace of a Hilbert space Y. Show that if P is the orthogonal projection of Y on X, then $Py(t) = (y, K(\cdot, t)), y \in Y$.

8.5 If Y is a closed subspace of X, where X has reproducing kernel K, then Y has a reproducing kernel. The kernels K' and K'' of Y and $Y^{\perp}$ satisfy $K = K' + K''$.

8.6 Suppose $S_1 \subset S$ and X is a proper functional Hilbert space on X with reproducing kernel K. Show that the restriction of K to $S_1 \times S_1$ is the reproducing kernel K_1 of the space X_1, where X_1 consists of all restrictions to S_1 of functions in X, and the norm in X_1 is

$$\|x_1\| = \min \|x\|,$$

the minimum being taken over all $x \in X$ whose restriction to S_1 is x_1.

8.7 Give details for the construction of X given the positive matrix K on S.

9.1 Derive the identity

$$\iint_D f(z)\overline{g'(z)}\, dx\, dy = \frac{1}{2i} \int_C f(z)\overline{g(z)}\, dz$$

from Green's theorem.

9.2 Verify the conditions for proper functional completion in the case of $L_2(D)$.

9.3 Find the mapping function $f(z)$ which maps the unit circle onto itself and takes ζ into 0 with $f'(\zeta) > 0$. Use the fact that a complete orthonormal set in the unit circle is given by

$$\varphi_n(z) = \sqrt{\frac{n}{\pi}}\, z^{n-1}, \quad n = 1, 2, \ldots .$$

10.1 Prove that

$$\varphi_n(z) = \sqrt{\frac{n}{\pi}}\, [w(z)]^{n-1} w'(z), \quad n = 1, 2, \ldots$$

is a complete orthonormal set for $L_2(D)$, where D satisfies the conditions of the Riemann mapping theorem and w is a conformal mapping of D on the unit disk.

10.2 Prove the identity

$$\sum_{n=0}^{\infty} \frac{L_n(x)}{n!}\, t^n = \frac{e^{-xt/1-t}}{1 - t}.$$

11.1 Show that the Haar functions are complete in $L_2[0, 1]$.

11.2 Show that the Haar functions are a Schauder basis for $L_p[0, 1], p \geq 1$.

11.3 Show that the set of (x, t) for which $\sum_{n=1}^{\infty} C_n \varphi_n(x) r_n(t)$ converges is measurable.

CHAPTER 5

TOPOLOGICAL VECTOR SPACES

5.1 Topology

A **topological space** $(X, \mathcal{G})$ consists of a set X together with a collection $\mathcal{G} = [G]$ of subsets of X, called **open** sets, such that

(a) $X \in \mathcal{G}$, and the empty set $0 \in \mathcal{G}$,
(b) if $G_\alpha \in \mathcal{G}$, $\alpha \in A$, then $\bigcup [G_\alpha : \alpha \in A] \in \mathcal{G}$,
(c) if $G_1, G_2 \in \mathcal{G}$, then $G_1 \cap G_2 \in \mathcal{G}$.

If Y is a subset of X, $(X, \mathcal{G})$ is a topological space, and if $\mathcal{H} = [Y \cap G : G \in \mathcal{G}]$, then $(Y, \mathcal{H})$ is easily seen to be a topological space. This topology in Y is called the **topology induced by the topology in *X*.**

Every set X can be topologized in two trivial ways.

(i) Let $\mathcal{G}$ consist of the two sets X and 0.
(ii) Let $\mathcal{G}$ consist of all subsets of X.

If $(X, \mathcal{G})$ and $(X, \mathcal{H})$ are topological spaces, with the same set X, then the topology given by $\mathcal{G}$ is said to be **finer** than the one given by $\mathcal{H}$ if $\mathcal{G} \supset \mathcal{H}$. The topology given by $\mathcal{H}$ is then said to be **coarser** than that given by $\mathcal{G}$.

The topology (i) above is the coarsest among all the topologies possible for X; the topology (ii) is the finest.

If $(X, \mathcal{G})$ is a topological space and $\mathcal{B} \subset \mathcal{G}$, then $\mathcal{B}$ is called a **base** for the topology if every $G \in \mathcal{G}$ is the union of sets in $\mathcal{B}$. The reader may verify with ease that $\mathcal{B}$ is a base if and only if, for every $x \in X$ and $G \in \mathcal{G}$ such that $x \in G$, there is an $H \in \mathcal{B}$ such that $x \in H$ and $H \subset G$.

For fixed $x \in X$, a set $\mathcal{B}_x \subset \mathcal{G}$ is called a **base at *x*** for the topology if, for every $G \in \mathcal{G}$ such that $x \in G$, there is an $H \in \mathcal{B}_x$ such that $x \in H$ and $H \subset G$. Moreover, $x \in H$ for every $H \in \mathcal{B}_x$.

A subset $\mathcal{S} \subset \mathcal{G}$ is called a **subbase** for the topology if there is a base $\mathcal{B}$ for the topology such that, for every $G \in \mathcal{B}$, there is a finite set in $\mathcal{S}$, G_i, $i = 1, \ldots, n$, such that $G = \bigcap_{i=1}^{n} G_i$.

Finally, a set $\mathcal{S}_x \subset \mathcal{G}$ is called a **subbase at *x*,** $x \in X$, for the topology, if there is a base $\mathcal{B}_x$ at x such that, for every $G \in \mathcal{B}_x$, there is a finite set in $\mathcal{S}_x$, G_i, $i = 1, \ldots, n$, such that $G = \bigcap_{i=1}^{n} G_i$.

A topological space is associated in a unique way with every metric space. Let X be a metric space with metric d. Let $\mathcal{B}$ consist of all open spheres in X, and let $\mathcal{G}$ be the set of all unions of subsets of $\mathcal{B}$. It is a routine matter to show that $(X, \mathcal{G})$ is a topological space and that, for $x \in X$, $x_n \in X$, $n = 1, 2, \ldots$, $\lim_{n\to\infty} d(x, x_n) = 0$ if and only if, for every $G \in \mathcal{G}$ with $x \in G$, $x_n \in G$ for all but finitely many values of n.

A topological space $(X, \mathcal{G})$ is said to be **metrizable** if there is a metric d for X such that the topological space corresponding, as above, to this metric space, is $(X, \mathcal{G})$.

A topological space $(X, \mathcal{G})$ is said to be a **Hausdorff space** if, for every x, $y \in X$, $x \neq y$, there are G, $H \in \mathcal{G}$ such that $x \in G$, $y \in H$, and $G \cap H = 0$.

In particular, (ii) is a Hausdorff space, (i) is not a Hausdorff space. On the other hand, every metrizable space is a Hausdorff space.

Let $(X, \mathcal{G})$ and $(Y, \mathcal{H})$ be topological spaces and let f be a mapping of X into Y. Then f is said to be **continuous at x** $\in X$ if, for every open set H with $f(x) \in H$, there is an open set G, with $x \in G$, such that $f(G) \subset H$. The mapping f is said to be **continuous** if it is continuous at every $x \in X$. We prove the following statement.

f is continuous if and only if the inverse image of every open set in Y is an open set in X.

Proof. Suppose the inverse image of every open set in Y is open. Let $x \in X$ and let H be an open set in Y with $f(x) \in H$. Then $f^{-1}(H)$ is open, $f[f^{-1}(H)] \subset H$, and $x \in f^{-1}(H)$, so that f is continuous.

Suppose f is continuous. Let H be open and let $x \in f^{-1}(H)$. Then H is an open set with $f(x) \in H$. There is, accordingly, an open set G, with $x \in G$ and $f(G) \subset H$. Then $G \subset f^{-1}(H)$, and it follows that $f^{-1}(H)$ is open.

As a special case, let X be a set with topologies $\mathcal{G}$ and $\mathcal{H}$, where $\mathcal{G}$ is finer than $\mathcal{H}$. The identity mapping

$$i : (X, \mathcal{G}) \to (X, \mathcal{H})$$

is continuous.

5.2 Tychonoff Theorem, Application in Banach Space

If X and Y are topological spaces, the space $X \times Y$ is defined as follows:

(a) $X \times Y = [(x, y) : x \in X, y \in Y]$,

(b) the open sets in $X \times Y$ are all the unions of sets of the form $G \times H$, where G is open in X and H is open in Y.

We may define the topological product of an arbitrary set X_α, $\alpha \in A$, of topological spaces. Let

$$X = \Pi[X_\alpha : \alpha \in A]$$

be the set of functions $[x_\alpha]$ such that for every $\alpha \in A$, $x_\alpha \in X_\alpha$. We topologize the space by defining a subbase for the topology. For each $\alpha \in A$, and open set $G_\alpha \subset X_\alpha$, let $U(\alpha, G_\alpha)$ be the set of $[x_\beta] \in X$ such that $x_\alpha \in G_\alpha$. We let the set $\mathcal{U}$ of all $U(\alpha, G_\alpha)$ be a subbase for the topology.

It is easy to see that a base for the topology is given by the sets

$$U(\alpha_1, \ldots, \alpha_n; G_{\alpha_1}, \ldots, G_{\alpha_n})$$

of elements $[x_\alpha] \in X$ for which $x_{\alpha_i} \in G_{\alpha_i}$, $i = 1, \ldots, n$, for all finite sets $\{\alpha_1, \ldots, \alpha_n\} \subset A$ and open sets $G_{\alpha_i} \subset X_{\alpha_i}$, $i = 1, \ldots, n$.

Certain properties of topological spaces are preserved by the product operation. We present the most important one of these properties.

We first recall that the closed sets in a topological space are merely the complements of the open sets. Thus, in a topological space X, the set X and the empty set are closed. The intersection of any collection of closed sets is closed. For every $S \subset X$, the intersection of all closed sets containing S is called the closure $\bar{S}$ of S. It is easy to see that $\bar{S}$ is closed and that $x \in \bar{S}$ if and only if, for every open set G such that $x \in G$, the set $G \cap S \neq 0$.

A topological space X is said to be **compact** if for every family $\mathcal{G}$ of open sets which covers X (i.e., for every $x \in X$ there is a $G \in \mathcal{G}$ such that $x \in G$), there is a finite subset of $\mathcal{G}$ which covers X. For example, a bounded closed set in the reals is a compact space, with the usual topology, but a non-empty open set is not compact.

It is an immediate consequence of the definition that a space X is compact if and only if every collection $\mathcal{F}$ of closed sets in X with the property that every finite subset of $\mathcal{F}$ has non-empty intersection is such that the intersection of all the sets in $\mathcal{F}$ is non-empty.

We have shown in Chapter 1 that a metric space is compact if and only if every infinite set in X has a limit point in X. Moreover, every closed subset of a compact Hausdorff space is easily seen to be compact with the induced topology.

We now state what is perhaps the main theorem of general topology.

THEOREM 1. If X_α, $\alpha \in A$, are compact spaces, then $X = \Pi[X_\alpha : \alpha \in A]$ is compact.

Proof. The proof is subtle but simple. A collection of sets in a topological space is said to have the finite intersection property if the intersection of any finite number of sets in the collection is non-empty. The compactness of X then follows from

(α) If $\mathcal{F}$ is a collection of sets in X, with the finite intersection property, then

$$\bigcap[\bar{F} : F \in \mathcal{F}] \neq 0.$$

In order to prove (α) we observe that if the family of collections of sets in X with the finite intersection property is ordered by inclusion, then every chain of such collections has an upper bound; indeed, the union of the members of the chain is in the family. Thus, by Zorn's lemma, every collection of sets in X with the finite intersection property is contained in a maximal collection of the same type. Thus, in order to prove the theorem, it remains only to prove

(β) If $\mathcal{F}$ is a maximal collection of sets in X, with the finite intersection property, then

$$\bigcap[\bar{F} : F \in \mathcal{F}] \neq 0.$$

Now, let $\mathcal{F}$ be a maximal collection of sets in X with the finite intersection property. For each $F \in \mathcal{F}$ and $\alpha \in A$, let F_α be the projection of F in X_α i.e.,

$$F_\alpha = \{x_\alpha : [x_\beta] \in F\}.$$

Then the collection $\{F_\alpha : F \in \mathcal{F}\}$ evidently has the finite intersection property. Since X_α is compact, there is an $x_\alpha \in \bigcap \{\bar{F}_\alpha : F \in \mathcal{F}\}$. Consider a point $[x_\beta] \in X$ such that for each $\alpha \in A$, $x_\alpha \in \bigcap \{\bar{F}_\alpha : F \in \mathcal{F}\}$. It remains only to show that, for every $F \in \mathcal{F}$, we have $[x_\alpha] \in \bar{F}$. For this purpose, let $\alpha \in A$ and let G_α be an open set in X_α, with $x_\alpha \in G_\alpha$. Then let G be the set of $[y_\beta] \in X$ such that $y_\alpha \in G_\alpha$. Then the union of $\mathcal{F}$ with the single set G continues to have the finite intersection property. Since $\mathcal{F}$ is maximal, $G \in \mathcal{F}$. Moreover, every finite intersection of such sets G also belongs to $\mathcal{F}$. But these finite intersections form a base for the topology in X at the point $[x_\alpha]$. This implies that every $F \in \mathcal{F}$ meets every open set in X to which $[x_\alpha]$ belongs. Thus, $[x_\alpha] \in \bar{F}$.

This theorem has many important applications. We now give one of them. Let X be a Banach space. The closed unit ball in X (i.e., the set for which $\|x\| \leq 1$) may not be compact. For example, consider the space l_2 of sequences $\{x_n\}$ of real numbers for which $\sum_{n=1}^{\infty} x_n^2 < \infty$. The closed unit ball in this space is not compact (see Chapter 1).

Now the dual X' of a Banach space is also a Banach space with the usual norm. But X' also has the **weak topology** defined as follows:

For each $x \in X$, and open $G \subset R$, let

$$U(x, G) = [x' \in X' : x'(x) \in G].$$

Let the sets $U(x, G)$ be a subbase for the topology in X'. This topology is called the weak topology in X' determined by X. (It is sometimes called the weak-star topology to distinguish it from the weak topology in X' determined by X''.)

For each $x \in X$, let R_x be the set of real numbers. The space $\Pi[R_x : x \in X]$ evidently contains X', and the weak topology in X' is the one induced by the topology in $\Pi[R_x : x \in X]$. Let K be the subset of $\Pi[R_x : x \in X]$ of points whose x-coordinate has absolute value not greater than $\|x\|$, for every $x \in X$. By theorem 1, K is compact. We show that the closed unit ball $B \subset X'$ is a weakly closed subset of K.

Let $\psi \in \bar{B}$, the weak closure of B in K. Then $\psi \in K$. We show that ψ is linear. For this, let $x, y, x + y \in X$. Let $\epsilon > 0$. By the definition of the topology $\Pi[R_x : x \in X]$, there is an $x' \in X'$ such that

$$|x'(x) - \psi(x)| < \epsilon, \; |x'(y) - \psi(y)| < \epsilon,$$

and $|x'(x + y) - \psi(x + y)| < \epsilon$. Since $x'(x + y) = x'(x) + x'(y)$, it follows that $|\psi(x + y) - \psi(x) - \psi(y)| < 3\epsilon$. Since this holds for every $\epsilon > 0$, $\psi(x + y) = \psi(x) + \psi(y)$. It is just as easy to show that for every $x \in X$ and $a \in R$, $\psi(ax) = a\psi(x)$. Since $|\psi(x)| \leq \|x\|$, for every $x \in X$, it follows that $\psi \in B$. Hence B is closed and we have proved

THEOREM 2. If X is a Banach space, the closed unit ball $B \subset X'$ is compact in the weak topology.

5.3 Topological Vector Space

A **topological vector space** is a set X which is:

(a) A vector space.

(b) A topological space.

(c) The operations $(x, y) \to x + y$ of $X \times X$ into X and $(a, x) \to ax$ of $R \times X$ into X are continuous.

We shall also suppose:

(d) If $x \neq 0$, there is an open set U such that $0 \in U$ and $x \notin U$.

The condition (d) is not always assumed by writers on the subject, but it is satisfied by all interesting examples.

PROPOSITION 1. If X is a topological vector space, then for every $x \in X$, the mapping $f_x : X \to X$, where $f_x(y) = x + y$, is a homeomorphism.

Proof. For every $y \in X$, $f_x(y - x) = (y - x) + x = y$, so that f_x is onto. If $y \neq z$, then $f_x(y) \neq f_x(z)$, since $y + x \neq z + x$. Hence f_x is one-one. The first part of condition (c) implies the continuity of f_x and of its inverse.

Proposition 1 implies that the open sets G_x containing x are the translations $x + G = [x + y : y \in G]$ of the open sets G containing 0. Thus, the topology in X is completely determined by a base for the open sets containing 0 (i.e., for the neighborhoods of 0). (Axioms for a topological vector space can be given in terms of a neighborhood base of 0, but we shall not do this here.)

5.4 Normable Space

If X is a Banach space, then its dual X', with the weak topology, is a topological vector space. In order to show this, one needs only make the easy verification that the vector space operations are continuous. We leave the details for the reader.

It is also easy to show that a normed vector space is a topological vector space. In this case, a base for the open sets containing 0 is given by the sets

$$U_a = [x : \|x\| < a],$$

for all $a > 0$.

A topological vector space is said to be **normable** if its topology may be given in terms of a norm.

It is of interest to know which topological vector spaces are normable.

For this purpose, we need the notion of a bounded set in a topological vector space. A set $A \subset X$ is said to be **bounded** if for every neighborhood U of 0 there is an a such that $A \subset aU$. In the particular case of a normed space, this simply means that the set $[\|x\| : x \in A]$ is bounded, which coincides with previous convention. We recall that a set $A \subset X$ is **convex** if for every $x, y \in A$ and $0 \leq a \leq 1$, $ax + (1 - a)y \in A$.

THEOREM 1. A topological vector space X is normable if and only if there is a non-empty $A \subset X$ which is open, bounded, and convex.

Proof. Let X be normable, and let $\| \ \|$ be a norm in X which yields the given topology. Let $U = [x : \|x\| < 1]$. Then U is non-empty and open. Let G be a neighborhood of 0. Then G contains the set $V = [x : \|x\| < a]$ for some $a > 0$. Then $\frac{1}{a} V \supset U$, and U is bounded. Finally, let $x, y \in U$ and $0 \leq a \leq 1$. Then $\|x\| < 1$, $\|y\| < 1$. It follows that $\|ax + (1 - a)y\| \leq a \|x\| + (1 - a) \|y\| < a + (1 - a) = 1$. Thus U is convex.

Conversely, suppose X contains a non-empty, open, bounded, convex set H. Let $x \in H$. Then the set $U = H - x = [y : y = z - x, z \in H]$ is also non-empty and open, and is easily seen to be convex and bounded. Moreover, the set $V = U \cap (-U)$ is also non-empty, open, bounded, convex and is also such that $x \in V$ implies $-x \in V$. We define a norm in X as follows:

$$\|x\| = 0 \quad \text{if } x = 0$$

and

$$\|x\| = \sup\,[a : a \geq 0, x \notin aV] \quad \text{if } x \neq 0.$$

Let $x \neq 0$. There is a neighborhood G of 0 such that $x \notin G$. There is an $a > 0$ such that $aV \subset G$, since V is bounded. Thus $x \notin aV$ and $\|x\| \geq a > 0$.

Let $b \neq 0$, $x \neq 0$. Then $x \in aV$ if and only if $bx \in |b|\, aV$, since $x \in V$ implies $-x \in V$. Hence $\|bx\| = |b|\, \|x\|$.

Finally, let $x \in aV$, $y \in bV$, so that $\|x\| \leq a$, $\|y\| \leq b$. Then $x + y \in (a + b)V$, so that $\|x + y\| \leq a + b$. Hence $\|x + y\| \leq \|x\| + \|y\|$. Thus, the defined $\| \;\|$ is indeed a norm.

We note that the topology defined by this norm agrees with the given topology in X. For, if G is any neighborhood of 0, there is an $a > 0$ such that $aV \subset G$, since G is bounded. This completes the proof.

5.5 Space of Measurable Functions

We now consider a special topological vector space. Let M be the vector space of equivalence classes of measurable functions on [0, 1]. We shall define a topology on this space in terms of a metric. For every f, $g \in M$, let

$$d(f, g) = \int_0^1 \frac{|f(t) - g(t)|}{1 + |f(t) - g(t)|}\, dt.$$

It is evident that $d(f, g) \geq 0$ and that $d(f, g) = 0$ if and only if $f(t) = g(t)$ almost everywhere. Moreover, $d(f, g) = d(g, f)$. In order to show that $d(f, g) + d(g, h) \geq d(f, h)$ it is only necessary to show that for any real numbers a, b

$$\frac{|a + b|}{1 + |a + b|} \leq \frac{|a|}{1 + |a|} + \frac{|b|}{1 + |b|}\,.$$

This is a routine calculation which we leave to the reader.

The metric d is an invariant metric, i.e., $d(f, g) = d(f + h, g + h)$ for every $f, g, h \in M$. Thus, in order to show that M is a topological vector space it is only necessary to show that if $\{f_n\}$ and $\{g_n\}$ converge to 0, then $\{f_n + g_n\}$ converges to 0, and if $\{f_n\}$ converges to 0 and $\{a_n\}$ converges, then $\{a_n f_n\}$ converges to 0.

In order to prove this, we consider an equivalent metric on M. Thus, for every $k > 0$, let

$$E_k = [x : |f(x)| \geq k],$$

and let

$$\delta(f, 0) = \inf\, [k : m(E_k) < k].$$

Now let

$$\delta(f, g) = \delta(f - g, 0).$$

We leave it as an exercise for the reader to show that $\lim_{n \to \infty} \delta(f_n, 0) = 0$ if and only if $\lim_{n \to \infty} d(f_n, 0) = 0$. Now, it is an easy matter to show that if $\delta(f_n, 0)$ and $\delta(g_n, 0)$ converge to 0, then $\delta(f_n + g_n, 0)$ converges to 0, and that if $\delta(f_n, 0)$ converges to 0 and $\{a_n\}$ is bounded, then $\delta(a_n f_n, 0)$ converges to 0. We leave these details to the reader as well.

The space M is separable. Let $f \in M$. Then, for every $\epsilon > 0$, there is a continuous g such that

$$|f(x) - g(x)| < \frac{\epsilon}{2}$$

except on a set of measure less than $\epsilon/2$. But there is a polynomial p, with rational coefficients, such that

$$|g(x) - p(x)| < \frac{\epsilon}{2}$$

everywhere. Hence, $\delta(f, p) < \epsilon$. Thus, the polynomials with rational coefficients are dense in M. But the set of such polynomials is countable, so that the separability of M is proved.

We remark that the topology in M is the topology of convergence in measure. Suppose that $\{f_n\}$ converges in measure to f. Then, for every $\epsilon > 0$, there is an N such that $n > N$ implies

$$|f_n(x) - f(x)| < \epsilon$$

except on a set of measure less than ϵ, so that $\delta(f, f_n) < \epsilon$. The converse, that convergence in M implies convergence in measure, is shown in analogous fashion.

In particular, it follows that every convergent sequence in M has a subsequence which converges almost everywhere.

PROPOSITION 1. The only continuous linear functional φ on M is the trivial one, $\varphi(f) = 0$.

Proof. Let φ be a linear functional on M which is not identically zero. Then there is an $f \in M$ such that $\varphi(f) \neq 0$. Let

$$J_1 = \left[0, \frac{1}{2}\right], \quad J_2 = \left[\frac{1}{2}, 1\right],$$

and let

$$g_1 = f\chi_{J_1}, \qquad g_2 = f\chi_{J_2}.$$

Since $f = g_1 + g_2$, either $\varphi(g_1) \neq 0$ or $\varphi(g_2) \neq 0$. Let f_1 be one of the g_1, g_2 for which $\varphi(f_1) \neq 0$. Then $m[x : f_1(x) \neq 0] \leq \frac{1}{2}$. It should be clear that, by proceeding in this way, we obtain a sequence $\{f_n\}$ such that $\varphi(f_n) \neq 0$ and

$$m[x : f_n(x) \neq 0] \leq \frac{1}{2^n}, \quad n = 2, 3, \ldots.$$

For every n, let

$$F_n = \frac{1}{\varphi(f_n)} f_n.$$

Then $\varphi(F_n) = 1$, $n = 1, 2, \ldots$, and $\{F_n\}$ converges to 0 in M. Thus φ is not continuous on M.

PROPOSITION 2. Let $\{f_n\}$ be a countable set of functions in M such that the finite linear combinations of the $\{f_n\}$ are dense in M. Let X be the closure in M of the finite linear combinations of $\{f_2, f_3, \ldots\}$. Then every $f \in M$ is of the form $f = af_1 + g$, where $g \in X$ and $a \in R$.

Proof. There are $g_n \in X$, $a_n \in R$, $n = 1, 2, \ldots$ such that

$$f = \lim_{n\to\infty} (a_n f_1 + g_n).$$

Consider first the case where $\{a_n\}$ is unbounded. It suffices to assume that $\lim_{n\to\infty} a_n = +\infty$. Then

$$\lim_{n\to\infty} \left(f_1 + \frac{1}{a_n} g_n\right) = 0,$$

so that

$$f_1 = -\lim_{n\to\infty} \frac{1}{a_n} g_n$$

and $f_1 \in X$. Thus, $a_n f_1 + g_n \in X$, $n = 1, 2, \ldots$, and, since X is closed, $f \in X$.

Suppose then that $\{a_n\}$ is bounded. We may assume that $\{a_n\}$ converges. Let $a = \lim_{n\to\infty} a_n$. Now

$$f = \lim_{n\to\infty} (a_n f_1 + g_n) = af_1 + g,$$

where $g = \lim_{n\to\infty} g_n$ exists, since $\lim_{n\to\infty} a_n f_1$ exists.

The simple observations made in propositions 1 and 2 have some surprising consequences.

Let X be a separable metrizable topological vector space. We say that a countable set $A \subset X$ is **total** in X if the finite linear combinations of elements of A are dense in X. A total set A is said to be **minimal** if no proper subset of A is total. Many Banach spaces are known to have minimal total sets, and there is no known example of a separable Banach space which does not have a minimal total set. On the other hand, the space M has no minimal total set. Indeed, the following stronger fact holds.

THEOREM 1. If A is a total set for M and B is a subset of A obtained by discarding a finite subset of A, then B is a total set for M.

Proof. It is only necessary to show that, if $\{f_1, f_2, \ldots\}$ is total, then $\{f_2, f_3, \ldots\}$ is also total. Let X be the closure of the set of finite linear combinations of $\{f_2, f_3, \ldots\}$. Then $\{f_2, f_3, \ldots\}$ is total for X. Suppose $f_1 \notin X$. Define a linear functional φ on M by letting $\varphi(f) = a$, where

$$f = af_1 + g,\ g \in X.$$

Then φ is a non-trivial continuous linear functional on M, in contradiction with proposition 1. Hence, $f_1 \in M$ and $X = M$.

We have the following corollary to theorem 1.

COROLLARY. If A is total for M, there is an infinite subset $B \subset A$ such that $A \sim B$ is total for M.

Proof. Let $A = \{f_1, f_2, \ldots\}$ be total for M and $\{\epsilon_n\}$ a sequence of positive numbers which converges to 0. Delete f_1 from A. There is a finite linear combination

$$a_{2,2}f_2 + \ldots + a_{2,n_2}f_{n_2}$$

such that

$$d(f_1, a_{2,2}f_2 + \ldots + a_{2,n_2}f_{n_2}) < \epsilon_1.$$

Delete f_{n_2+1} from A. There are finite linear combinations

$$a_{3,i,n_2+2}f_{n_2+2} + \ldots + a_{3,i,n_3}f_{n_3}, \quad i = 1, 2$$

such that

$$d(f_i, a_{3,i,n_2+2}f_{n_2+2} + \ldots + a_{3,i,n_3}f_{n_3}) < \epsilon_2, \quad i = 1, 2.$$

Delete f_{n_3+1} from A. By continuing in this way, we delete an infinite subset $B \subset A$ from A such that the finite linear combinations of elements of $A \sim B$ are dense in B. Thus, they are dense in M.

A series $\sum_{n=1}^{\infty} a_n f_n$ is said to be **universal** in a space X if, for every $x \in X$, a subsequence of the sequence of partial sums of the series converges to x in the space X.

THEOREM 2. If $A = \{f_1, f_2, \ldots\}$ is total for M, there is a sequence $\{a_n\}$ such that $\sum_{n=1}^{\infty} a_n f_n$ is a universal series for M.

Proof. Let $\{g_n\}$ be a countable dense subset of M and $\{\epsilon_n\}$ a sequence of positive real numbers which converges to 0. There is a linear combination $a_1 f_1 + \ldots + a_{n_1} f_{n_1}$ such that

$$d(g_1, a_1 f_1 + \ldots + a_{n_1} f_{n_1}) < \epsilon_1.$$

There is then a linear combination $a_{n_1+1} f_{n_1+1} + \ldots + a_{n_2} f_{n_2}$ such that

$$d(g_1 - a_1 f_1 - \ldots - a_{n_1} f_{n_1}, a_{n_1+1} f_{n_1+1} + \ldots + a_{n_2} f_{n_2}) < \epsilon_2.$$

There is then a linear combination $a_{n_2+1} f_{n_2+1} + \ldots + a_{n_3} f_{n_3}$ such that

$$d(g_2 - a_1 f_1 - \ldots - a_{n_2} f_{n_2}, a_{n_2+1} f_{n_2+1} + \ldots + a_{n_3} f_{n_3}) < \epsilon_2.$$

By continuing in a way which should be clear to the reader, we obtain a series $\sum_{n=1}^{\infty} a_n f_n$ whose sequence of partial sums has, for every n, a subsequence which converges in M to g_n. It thus has a subsequence converging to any prescribed $f \in M$.

Consider now a Banach space X of equivalence classes of measurable functions defined on $[0, 1]$. Then $X \subset M$. For every measurable $G \subset [0, 1]$, with $m(G) > 0$, let X_G be the set of restrictions of the functions in X to the set G. Suppose X_G is normed so as to be a Banach space, and the following conditions hold.

(a) If $\{g_n\}$ converges to g in X, then $\{g_n\}$ converges to g in X_G.
(b) The set of bounded measurable functions is a dense subset of X.
(c) For every G, uniform convergence on G implies convergence in X_G, and convergence in X_G implies convergence in measure on G.

It follows from (a) and (b) that the set of bounded measurable functions is a dense subset of X_G for every G.

THEOREM 3. With the above set-up, if $A = \{f_1, f_2, \ldots\}$ is total for X, and $\epsilon > 0$, there is a measurable $G \subset [0, 1]$, with $m(G) > 1 - \epsilon$, such that $\{f_2, f_3, \ldots\}$ is total for X_G.

Proof. Let $\{g_1, g_2, \ldots\}$ be dense in X. Since $\{f_1, f_2, \ldots\}$ is total for X, every bounded measurable function is, by (b), a limit in X of finite linear combinations of $\{f_1, f_2, \ldots\}$; hence, by (c), in M. Since the bounded functions are dense in M, $\{f_1, f_2, \ldots\}$ is total for M. By theorem 1, $\{f_2, f_3, \ldots\}$ is total for M. Fix g_n. There is a sequence $\{\varphi_1, \varphi_2, \ldots\}$ of finite linear combinations of $\{f_2, f_3, \ldots\}$ which converges in measure to g_n. It has a subsequence $\{\psi_1, \psi_2, \ldots\}$ which converges uniformly to g_n on a measurable set G_n, with $m(G_n) > 1 - \dfrac{\epsilon}{2^n}$. Let $G = \bigcap_{n=1}^{\infty} G_n$.
Since uniform convergence on G implies convergence in X_G and since $\{g_1, g_2, \ldots\}$ is dense in X_G, it follows that $\{f_2, f_3, \ldots\}$ is total for X_G.

COROLLARY. If $\{f_1, f_2, \ldots\}$ is complete for $L_2[0, 1]$, and $\epsilon > 0$, there is a measurable $G \subset [0, 1]$, with $m(G) > 1 - \epsilon$, such that $\{f_2, f_3, \ldots\}$ is complete for $L_2(G)$.

As a companion to this corollary, we have a related phenomenon discovered by Boas and Pollard.

THEOREM 4. Let $\{f_1, f_2, \ldots\}$ be a complete orthonormal set for $L_2[a, b]$. There is a bounded g such that $\{gf_2, gf_3, \ldots\}$ is complete for $L_2[a, b]$.

Proof. Choose g so that $g(x) > 0$, for all x, g is bounded, and $f_1 g^{-1} \notin L_2$. Let $F \in L_2$. Suppose

$$\int_a^b g f_n F = 0, \quad n = 2, 3, \ldots.$$

Then $gF = cf_1$. Since $f_1 g^{-1} \notin L_2$ and $F \in L_2$, it follows that $c = 0$, and so $F = 0$. Thus $\{gf_2, \ldots, gf_n, \ldots\}$ is complete.

Indeed, Boas and Pollard proved the above theorem for the case where any finite number of functions is discarded from $\{f_1, f_2, \ldots\}$, but we shall not give the proof.

5.6 Locally Convex Space

An important class of topological vector spaces is the set of **locally convex** spaces. In this case, every open set containing 0 contains a convex open set containing 0. It then follows that the topology is given by a set of semi-norms.

Recall that a **semi-norm** p on a vector space X is a non-negative real function on X such that $p(x + y) \leq p(x) + p(y)$, for every $x, y \in X$ and $p(ax) = |a|\, p(x)$ for every $a \in R$ and $x \in X$.

Now, let U be a convex open set containing 0. Then $V = U \cap (-U)$ is also a convex open set containing 0. It is easy to see that for every $x \in X$ there is an $a \in R$ such that $x \in aV$. Moreover, $x \in aV$ if and only if $-x \in aV$. Let

$$p(x) = \sup\,[a : x \notin aV,\ a \geq 0],\ \text{if } x \neq 0,$$
$$p(0) = 0.$$

It is a routine matter to verify that p is a semi-norm and that the sets

$$U_{p,r} = [x : p(x) < r],$$

for all p obtained in this way, and all $r > 0$, form a base for the topology in X at 0.

Thus, in a locally convex topological vector space, the topology is given by a set p_α, $\alpha \in A$, of semi-norms. The requirement that for every $x \neq 0$ there is an open set $G \subset X$ such that $0 \in G$ and $x \notin G$ is translated into the requirement that for every $x \neq 0$ there is an $\alpha \in A$ such that $p_\alpha(x) \neq 0$.

In contrast with the example of Sec. 5.5, in a locally convex space X, the dual X' is non-trivial. Indeed, the Hahn-Banach theorem holds here, and it assures the existence of many continuous linear functionals on X. The proof is quite the same as for normed spaces and will not be given here.

Let X^* be the algebraic dual of X, i.e., the set of all linear functionals on X, continuous or not. An $x' \in X^*$ is continuous on X if and only if there is an open set containing 0 on which it is bounded. It is only necessary to show that if there is such a set U, then x' is continuous. Let $\epsilon > 0$ and suppose $|x'(x)| < M$ if $x \in U$. Let $a > 0$ and $aM < \epsilon$. Then $|x'(x)| < \epsilon$ if $x \in aU$

and aU is an open set containing 0. Hence x' is continuous. This result implies that x' is continuous if and only if there is an $\alpha \in A$ and an M such that

$$|x'(x)| \leq Mp_\alpha(x), \text{ for every } x \in X.$$

This observation allows us to penetrate into the nature of the topological dual X' of a locally convex topological vector space X. Let X be a vector space, without topology. Let p be any semi-norm on X and $M > 0$. Let

$$S_{p,M} = [x' \in X^* : |x'(x)| \leq Mp(x) \text{ for all } x \in X].$$

Then, let

$$S_p = \bigcup [S_{p,M} : \text{for all } M > 0].$$

S_p will be called the **semi-norm set** of p. It is clearly a vector subspace of X^*.

Now, let X be a locally convex topological vector space where the topology is given by a collection p_α, $\alpha \in A$, of semi-norms in the sense that the sets

$$U_{p_\alpha, r} = [x : p_\alpha(x) < r]$$

for all $\alpha \in A$ and $r > 0$ form a base for the topology at 0. The dual X' of X is then given by

$$X' = \bigcup [S_{p_\alpha} : \alpha \in A].$$

We start over again, let X be a vector space, and observe that semi-norms in X may be defined by means of certain subsets $A \subset X^*$. For any $A \subset X^*$, let

$$p_A(x) = \sup [|x'(x)| : x' \in A],$$

for each $x \in X$. It is almost immediate that p_A has all the properties of a semi-norm except that it might take on the value $+\infty$. We thus restrict A so that it is point-wise bounded, i.e.,

$$\sup [|x'(x)| : x' \in A] < \infty$$

for each $x \in X$. These are precisely the sets A for which p_A is a semi-norm.

Now, X^* as a space of functions, may be given the product topology. Point-wise boundedness is the same as boundedness in this topology. We shall call a subset $A \subset X^*$ **distinguished** if it is bounded and closed in the product topology, if it is convex, and if $x' \in A$, $|a| \leq 1$, implies $ax' \in A$.

LEMMA 1. For every semi-norm p on a vector space X, the set $A_p \subset X^*$ of functionals x', such that $p(x) \leq 1$ implies $|x'(x)| \leq 1$ is distinguished. Conversely, if A is a distinguished subset of X^*, there is a semi-norm p such that $A = A_p$.

Proof. The first part of the lemma consists of a direct and simple verification. For the converse, let

$$p(x) = \sup [|x'(x)| : x' \in A].$$

Then p is a semi-norm. If $x' \in A$, $x \in X$, and $p(x) \leq 1$, then $|x'(x)| \leq 1$.

Suppose then that $x' \notin A$. By the Hahn-Banach theorem, applied to X^* with the weak topology induced by X, there is an $x \in X$ such that $|y'(x)| \leq 1$ for all $y' \in A$ and $x'(x) > 1$. Thus $p(x) \leq 1$, but $x'(x) > 1$.

Now, let $X' \subset X^*$ be a subspace of X^*. Using lemma 1, we are able to find semi-norms on X whose semi-norm sets are contained in X'. Indeed, the lemma tells us that every distinguished $A \subset X'$ produces such a semi-norm. We show that every locally convex topology on X, with respect to which X' is the dual, is given by means of such semi-norms.

Indeed, it is now obvious that if A_α is a collection of distinguished sets which are all subsets of X', and whose union is X', then X' is the dual of the locally convex space given by the semi-norms p_{A_α}. (Such a collection of distinguished sets are the sets $[ax' : |a| \leq 1]$ for all $x' \in X'$.)

Suppose, conversely, that we have a locally convex topology in X and that X' is the dual. Let p be one of the defining semi-norms for the topology. The set A_p of $x' \in X^*$ such that $p(x) \leq 1$ implies $|x'(x)| \leq 1$ is a distinguished subset of X^*. But A_p, as a subset of the semi-norm set of p, is a subset of X'. Moreover, $p = p_{A_p}$, by use of the Hahn-Banach theorem.

THEOREM 1. If X' is a subspace of X^*, every locally convex topology on X, for which X' is the dual, is determined by the semi-norms associated with a system of distinguished subsets of X^* whose union is X'. The finest topology exists and is given by the system of all distinguished subsets of X'.

If among all the locally convex topologies on X, for which X' is the dual of X, there happens to be one for which X is a Banach space, then it is the finest locally convex topology on X for which X' is the dual. We prove this by using the principle of uniform boundedness. Suppose, then, that there is a norm $\| \ \|$ for which X is a Banach space and X' is the dual. Let A be a distinguished set in X^* which is a subset of X'. Since A is point-wise bounded, it is norm bounded by the principle of uniform boundedness. Thus, there is an M such that $|x'(x)| \leq M \|x\|$ for every $x' \in A$ and $x \in X$. Let p be the semi-norm in X determined by A. Then $p(x) \leq M \|x\|$, for every $x \in X$. This means that if X is topologized in any way so as to be locally convex and have X' as its dual, then the Banach topology is finer. This proves

THEOREM 2. If X is a vector space and X' is a subspace of X^*, then X can be normed in at most one way (within topological equivalence) so as to be a Banach space and have X' as its dual.

5.7 Metrizable Space, Space of Entire Functions

An important class of locally convex topological vector spaces consists of those which are metrizable. Since a metrizable space is such that, at each point in the space, a base for the topology at the point is countable, it is evident that the topology for a metrizable locally convex topological vector space can be given in terms of countably many semi-norms.

We show that, conversely, if X is a locally convex topological vector space, in which the topology is given by countably many semi-norms, $\{p_n\}$, then X is metrizable. Indeed, we consider the number

$$d(x, y) = \sum_{n=1}^{\infty} \frac{1}{2^n} \frac{p_n(x-y)}{1 + p_n(x-y)}.$$

This is easily seen to be an invariant metric. We show that the topology given by this metric is the same as the one given by the semi-norms $\{p_n\}$.

Let $\{x_n\}$ be a sequence which converges to 0 in the locally convex space. Then

$$\lim_{n\to\infty} p_m(x_n) = 0, \quad m = 1, 2, \ldots.$$

Let $\epsilon > 0$. Choose N' so that $\sum_{n=N'}^{\infty} \frac{1}{2^n} < \frac{\epsilon}{2}$. Choose N so that $n > N$, $m < N'$ implies $p_m(x_n) < \epsilon/2$. Now, for $n > N$,

$$\begin{aligned} d(x_n, 0) &= \sum_{m=1}^{N'-1} \frac{1}{2^m} \frac{p_m(x_n)}{1 + p_m(x_n)} + \sum_{m=N'}^{\infty} \frac{1}{2^m} \frac{p_m(x_n)}{1 + p_m(x_n)} \\ &\leq \sum_{m=1}^{N'-1} \frac{1}{2^m} \cdot \frac{\epsilon}{2} + \sum_{m=N'}^{\infty} \frac{1}{2^m} < \epsilon. \end{aligned}$$

Thus $\{x_n\}$ converges to 0 in the metric.

The converse is trivial.

An interesting example is given by the space E of entire functions. This is a vector space over the complex numbers. The functions in E are given by power series

$$f(z) = \sum_{n=0}^{\infty} a_n z^n,$$

for which

$$\lim_{n\to\infty} \sqrt[n]{|a_n|} = 0.$$

If

$$f(z) = \sum_{n=0}^{\infty} a_n z^n \quad \text{and} \quad g(z) = \sum_{n=0}^{\infty} b_n z^n$$

are entire functions, let

$$d(f, g) = \sup\,[|a_0 - b_0|, \sqrt[n]{|a_n - b_n|} : n = 1, 2, \ldots].$$

PROPOSITION 1. $\{f_n\}$ converges to f in the space E if and only if it converges uniformly to f on every compact set.

Proof. Suppose $\{f_n\}$ converges to f uniformly on every compact set. Let

$$f(z) = \sum_{m=0}^{\infty} a_m z^m, \quad f_n(z) = \sum_{m=0}^{\infty} a_m^{(n)} z^m, \quad n = 1, 2, \ldots.$$

Let $\epsilon > 0$. Choose $R > 1/\epsilon$. Then, there is an N such that $n > N$ implies

$$|a_0^{(n)} - a_0| < \epsilon$$

and, by the Cauchy inequalities applied to the circle of radius R,

$$|a_m^{(n)} - a_m|\, R^m \leq 1, \quad m = 1, 2, \ldots,$$

so that

$$|a_m^{(n)} - a_m|^{1/m} < \epsilon.$$

Hence, we have convergence with respect to the metric.

Conversely, suppose $\{f_n\}$ converges to f in the metric. Choose R and $\epsilon > 0$. There is an N such that $m > N$ implies

$$|a_0^{(m)} - a_0| < \epsilon, \quad |a_n^{(m)} - a_n|^{1/n} < \epsilon, \quad n = 1, 2, \ldots.$$

It follows that $|z| = R$ implies

$$|f(z) - f_m(z)| \leq |a_0 - a_0^{(m)}| + \sum_{n=1}^{\infty} |a_n^{(m)} - a_n|\, R^n$$
$$\leq \epsilon + \sum_{n=1}^{\infty} \epsilon^n R^n.$$

Since, for fixed R, the right-hand side converges to 0 as ϵ converges to 0, the proposition follows by the maximum modulus principle.

We consider the following semi-norms in E. For every $n = 1, 2, \ldots$ let

$$p_n(f) = \max\,[|f(z)| : |z| \leq n].$$

The topology given E by this set of semi-norms is the same as that of uniform convergence on compact sets. In Chapter 1, we observed that the metric space E is complete.

We examine the dual of E. For this purpose we need

Lemma 1. The series $\sum_{n=0}^{\infty} a_n b_n$ converges for every $\{a_n\}$ for which

$$\lim_{n\to\infty} \sqrt[n]{|a_n|} = 0$$

if and only if $\{\sqrt[n]{|b_n|}\}$ is bounded.

Proof. Suppose $|b_0| \leq M$, $|b_n| \leq M^n$, $n = 1, 2, \ldots$. Let $\{a_n\}$ be such that $\lim_{n\to\infty} \sqrt[n]{|a_n|} = 0$. There is an N such that $n > N$ implies $|a_n| \leq 1/(2^n M^n)$. Then, clearly $\sum_{n=0}^{\infty} |a_n b_n| < \infty$.

For the converse, suppose $\{|b_n|^{1/n}\}$ is not bounded. For every k, there is an n_k with $|b_{n_k}| > k^{n_k}$. Let $a_{n_k} = 1/k^{n_k}$, and $a_n = 0$ otherwise. Then $\lim_{n\to\infty} \sqrt[n]{|a_n|} = 0$, but $\sum_{n=0}^{\infty} a_n b_n$ does not converge.

THEOREM 1. Every continuous linear functional φ on E is of the form

$$\varphi(f) = \sum_{n=0}^{\infty} b_n a_n,$$

where $f(z) = \sum_{n=0}^{\infty} a_n z^n$ and $\{b_n\}$ is a fixed sequence for which $\{|b_n|^{1/n}\}$ is bounded, and for every such $\{b_n\}$ the corresponding φ, defined as above, is a continuous linear functional on E.

Proof. Suppose $\{|b_n|^{1/n}\}$ is bounded. Let

$$\varphi(f) = \sum_{n=0}^{\infty} a_n b_n.$$

Since the series on the right converges for every $f \in E$, φ is defined on E. It is clear that φ is linear. Suppose $\{f_m\}$ converges to 0 in E, where

$$f_m(z) = \sum_{n=0}^{\infty} a_n^{(m)} z^n, \quad m = 1, 2, \ldots .$$

Let

$$M = \sup \{|b_0|, |b_n|^{1/n} : n = 1, 2, \ldots\}.$$

Let $\epsilon > 0$. There is an N such that $m > N$ implies

$$|a_0^{(m)}| < \epsilon, \quad |a_n^{(m)}|^{1/n} < \epsilon, \quad n = 1, 2, \ldots .$$

Then

$$|\varphi(f_m)| = \left| \sum_{n=0}^{\infty} a_n^{(m)} b_n \right| \le \sum_{n=0}^{\infty} |a_n^{(m)} b_n|$$
$$\le \epsilon M + \sum_{n=1}^{\infty} (\epsilon M)^n.$$

But the right-hand side converges to 0 as ϵ converges to 0. Hence

$$\lim_{m \to \infty} \varphi(f_m) = 0.$$

Conversely, suppose φ is a continuous linear functional on E. Let

$$b_n = \varphi(z^n), \quad n = 0, 1, 2, \ldots .$$

Now, let

$$f(z) = \sum_{n=0}^{\infty} a_n z^n$$

be in E, and let

$$f_n(z) = \sum_{k=0}^{n} a_k z^k, \quad n = 0, 1, 2, \ldots .$$

Then $\{f_n\}$ converges in E to f, so that

$$\varphi(f) = \lim_{n \to \infty} \varphi(f_n).$$

But

$$\varphi(f_n) = \sum_{k=0}^{n} a_k b_k, \quad n = 1, 2, \ldots ,$$

so that

$$\varphi(f) = \sum_{n=0}^{\infty} a_n b_n.$$

Moreover, since for every $\{a_n\}$ for which $\lim_{n\to\infty} \sqrt[n]{|a_n|} = 0$, the series

$$\sum_{n=0}^{\infty} a_n b_n$$

converges, it follows that $\{\sqrt[n]{|b_n|}\}$ is bounded.

REMARK. A power series $\sum_{n=0}^{\infty} b_n z^n$ has positive radius of convergence if and only if $\{\sqrt[n]{|b_n|}\}$ is bounded. The dual of E may accordingly be identified with the function elements at 0 (or at any other point on the Riemann sphere).

We now use theorem 1 to obtain a simple but interesting condition for a set of functions to form a total set in the space E of entire functions. We first note a general criterion for a set to form a total set. Let $A \subset E$, and let X be the closure of the vector space generated by A. If $X \neq E$, by the Hahn-Banach theorem, for every $f \in E \sim X$, there is a continuous linear functional φ on E such that $\varphi(f) = 1$ and $\varphi(g) = 0$ for every $g \in X$. It follows that $X = E$ if and only if every continuous linear functional which vanishes on A is identically zero on E. In other words, a necessary and sufficient condition that A be total in E is that the zero functional is the only continuous linear functional on E which vanishes on A.

Now, suppose that

$$f(z) = \sum_{n=0}^{\infty} a_n z^n \in E$$

and that none of the coefficients a_n, $n = 0, 1, 2, \ldots$ are zero. Let S be a set of complex numbers which has at least one finite limit point. For every $\zeta \in S$, let

$$f_\zeta(z) = \sum_{n=0}^{\infty} a_n (\zeta z)^n.$$

Then $f_\zeta \in E$. Let

$$A = [f_\zeta : \zeta \in S].$$

PROPOSITION 2. *A is total in E.*

Proof. Suppose φ is a continuous linear functional on E which vanishes on A. There is a sequence $\{b_n\}$, with $\{|b_n|^{1/n}\}$ bounded, such that

$$\varphi(g) = \sum_{n=0}^{\infty} c_n b_n$$

for every $g(z) = \sum_{n=0}^{\infty} c_n z^n \in E$. Then, for every $\zeta \in S$,

$$\varphi(f_\zeta) = \sum_{n=0}^{\infty} a_n b_n \zeta^n = 0.$$

Consider the function given by

$$h(z) = \sum_{n=0}^{\infty} a_n b_n z^n.$$

Since $\lim_{n\to\infty} \sqrt[n]{|a_n b_n|} = 0$, $h \in E$. But $h(\zeta) = 0$ for every $\zeta \in S$, so that $h(z) = 0$, since S has a finite limit point. Thus $a_n b_n = 0$ for every $n = 0, 1, 2, \ldots$. Since no a_n is 0, it follows that $b_n = 0$ for $n = 0, 1, 2, \ldots$ and φ is identically zero.

5.8 FK Spaces

The space E discussed above is typical of a wide class of spaces, the *FK* spaces. An *FK* **space** X is:

(a) A vector space, over the real numbers (or complex numbers), whose elements are sequences of real numbers (or complex numbers).

(b) X is a locally convex metrizable topological vector space in which the topology is, accordingly, given by a countable set $\{p_n\}$ of semi-norms.

(c) The metric space X is complete.

(d) If we use the notation

$$x = (a_1(x), a_2(x), \ldots)$$

for $x \in X$, the linear functionals $a_n(x)$, $n = 1, 2, \ldots$, are continuous on X.

The space E, discussed in Sec. 5.7, may be interpreted as being composed of those sequences $\{a_n\}$ of complex numbers for which $\lim_{n\to\infty} \sqrt[n]{|a_n|} = 0$. This is a vector space, over the complex numbers, with semi-norms

$$p_n(f) = \sup\left[\left|\sum_{n=0}^{\infty} a_n(f) z^n\right| : |z| = n\right], \quad n = 0, 1, 2, \ldots.$$

E is a complete metric space. If

$$f(z) = \sum_{n=0}^{\infty} a_n(f) z^n, \quad f \in E,$$

the Cauchy inequalities imply that $a_n(f)$ is a continuous linear functional on E for every $n = 0, 1, 2, \ldots$.

A complete metrizable locally convex topological vector space is called a **Fréchet space.** Fréchet spaces have many properties in common with Banach spaces. In particular, the closed graph theorem holds, the proof being the same as for Banach spaces. We shall see that this implies the following uniqueness result:

Let X be a vector space whose elements are sequences of numbers. If X may be topologized in such a way as to be an *FK* space, then this may be done in only one way.

Indeed, a more general fact holds:

If X and Y are *FK* spaces, and $X \subset Y$, then the identity mapping of X into Y is continuous. In other words, the topology induced in X by the *FK* topology in Y is coarser than the *FK* topology in X.

PROPOSITION 1. Let X and Y be *FK* spaces, with $X \subset Y$. The identity mapping

$$I : X \to Y$$

is continuous.

Proof. We need only show that the graph of I is closed in $X \times Y$. Let $\{x_m, x_m\}$ be a Cauchy sequence in the graph of I. Let

$$x_m = (a_1^{(m)}, a_2^{(m)}, \ldots), \quad m = 1, 2, \ldots,$$

converge to

$$x = (a_1, a_2, \ldots)$$

in X, and to

$$y = (b_1, b_2, \ldots)$$

in Y. By continuity of the coordinate functions in an *FK* space, we have

$$a_n = \lim_{m\to\infty} a_n^{(m)} \quad \text{and} \quad b_n = \lim_{m\to\infty} a_n^{(m)}, \quad n = 1, 2, \ldots.$$

Hence, $a_n = b_n$, for every n, and $x = y$. Hence, $\lim_{m\to\infty} (x_m, x_m) = (x, x)$ is on the graph of I, and the graph of I is closed. By the closed graph theorem, I is continuous.

COROLLARY. Let X be a vector space of sequences of real or complex numbers. If there are two sets of semi-norms $\{p_n\}$ and $\{q_n\}$, for each of which X is an *FK* space, then the corrresponding topologies are the same.

Proof. Let t_1 and t_2 be the corresponding topologies. By proposition 1, the identity mapping of X, with either topology, onto X, with the other topology, is continuous. Hence, the topologies are the same.

Thus, a vector space of sequences either is an *FK* space or it is not an *FK* space. If it is an *FK* space, the *FK* topology that it carries is unique.

Moreover, larger *FK* spaces have coarser topologies. Precisely, if $X \subset Y$ are *FK* spaces, the topology in X, induced by the *FK* topology in Y, is coarser than the *FK* topology in X.

We give some examples of *FK* spaces. In the first few examples, the sequences of numbers are either real or complex.

(a) The space of all sequences. This is an *FK* space with semi-norms

$$p_n(x) = |a_n(x)|, \quad n = 1, 2, \ldots,$$

where $x = (a_1(x), a_2(x), \ldots)$.

The p_n are evidently semi-norms. Convergence in this space is coordinatewise convergence, and it follows easily that the space is complete. Moreover, it is clear that the functionals $a_n(x)$, $n = 1, 2, \ldots$, are continuous and linear.

(b) The space of bounded sequences with the single semi-norm

$$p(x) = \sup_n |a_n(x)|.$$

The confirmation that this is an *FK* space is routine.

(c) For every $p \geq 1$, the space l_p of sequences

$$x = (a_1(x), a_2(x), \ldots),$$

for which

$$\sum_{n=1}^{\infty} |a_n(x)|^p < \infty,$$

with the semi-norm

$$p(x) = \left[\sum_{n=1}^{\infty} |a_n(x)|^p\right]^{1/p}.$$

We have only to show that the $a_n(x)$ are continuous. But

$$|a_n(x)|^p \leq \sum_{n=1}^{\infty} |a_n(x)|^p,$$

for every n, so that $|a_n(x)| \leq p(x)$.

(d) Let X be the vector space of sequences $\{a_n(x)\}$ such that

$$\sum_{n=1}^{\infty} |a_n(x)|^p < \infty$$

for all $p > 1$. We first note that $p > p'$ implies $l_p \supset l_{p'}$. Hence

$$X = \bigcap_{n=1}^{\infty} l_{1+1/n}, \quad n = 1, 2, \ldots$$

Thus, X is the intersection of a properly decreasing sequence of *FK* spaces. Let X have as its set of semi-norms, the semi-norms of the spaces $l_{1+1/n}$, $n = 1, 2, \ldots$, i.e., the semi-norms

$$q_n(x) = \left[\sum_{k=1}^{\infty} |a_k(x)|^{1+1/n}\right]^{n/n+1}, \quad n = 1, 2, \ldots.$$

We show that X is an *FK* space. It is necessary only to show that X is complete and that the $a_n(x)$ are continuous on X.

In order to show that X is complete, let $\{x_n\}$ be a Cauchy sequence in X. This implies that $\{q_m(x_n)\}$ is a Cauchy sequence of numbers for every $m = 1, 2, \ldots$. Accordingly, $\{x_n\}$ is a Cauchy sequence in each of the spaces $l_{1+1/m}$, $m = 1, 2, \ldots$. We next note that the limit of $\{x_n\}$, in each $l_{1+1/m}$, is the same sequence of numbers. This is true because the $l_{1+1/m}$ are all *FK* spaces so that convergence implies coordinate-wise convergence. Let x be this common limit. Then, since for every m,

$$q_m(x) = \lim_{n\to\infty} q_m(x_n),$$

x is also the limit of $\{x_n\}$ in X. Hence, X is complete.

It is implicit in the above argument that convergence in X implies coordinate-wise convergence.

We next note that there are vector spaces of sequences which are not *FK* spaces. Indeed, the union of any strictly increasing sequence of *FK* spaces is not an *FK* space. In order to prove this, we need a fact from the general theory of Fréchet spaces.

PROPOSITION 2. If X and Y are Fréchet spaces and f is a continuous linear mapping of X into Y, then $f(X)$ is either all of Y or is of the first category in Y.

Proof. We do not give all the details of the proof, but point out that it is similar to that of the open mapping theorem for Banach spaces. Just as in the proof of that theorem, if the image of the unit sphere in X is dense in a sphere in Y, then it contains a sphere in Y. Thus $f(X)$ is of the first category in Y or else $f(X) = Y$.

PROPOSITION 3. If $\{X_n\}$ is a sequence of *FK* spaces, $X_n \subset X_{n+1}$, $X_n \neq X_{n+1}$, $n = 1, 2, \ldots$, then $X = \bigcup_{n=1}^{\infty} X_n$ is not an *FK* space.

Proof. Suppose X were an *FK* space. Then, by proposition 1, for every n, the identity mapping of X_n into X would be continuous. Since $X \neq X_n$, X_n would be of the first category in X. Then X, as the union of a countable set of subsets of the first category, would be of the first category in itself. But an *FK* space is a complete metric space and so is of the second category.

In contrast with this fact, we have

PROPOSITION 4. If X_n, $n = 1, 2, \ldots$, is a sequence of *FK* spaces, then $X = \bigcap_{n=1}^{\infty} X_n$ is an *FK* space.

The proof of this theorem follows the lines of the special case given in example (d) above, and will be omitted.

5.9 Application to Summability Methods

We shall apply FK spaces to the theory of limitation of divergent sequences. In this regard, we consider sequence-to-sequence transformations given by infinite matrices. A more complete discussion than the one given in Chapter 2 will be given here. Accordingly, let

$$A = (a_{mn}) = \begin{pmatrix} a_{11} & a_{12} & \cdots & a_{1n} & \cdots \\ a_{21} & a_{22} & \cdots & a_{2n} & \cdots \\ & & \cdots & & \\ a_{m1} & a_{m2} & \cdots & a_{mn} & \cdots \\ & & \cdots & & \end{pmatrix}$$

be an infinite matrix.

Let $E(A)$ be the set of sequences $\{x_n\}$ for which all the series

$$\sum_{n=1}^{\infty} a_{mn}x_n, \quad m = 1, 2, \ldots$$

converge. Then A acts as a linear transformation on the set $E(A)$ to the vector space of all sequences, where the image of $\{x_n\} \in E(A)$ is the sequence $\left\{\sum_{n=1}^{\infty} a_{mn}x_n\right\}$. $E(A)$ is evidently a vector space.

We consider two vector subspaces of $E(A)$, the space $C(A)$ of all $\{x_n\} \in E(A)$ for which $\left\{\sum_{n=1}^{\infty} a_{mn}x_n\right\}$ converges, and the subspace $P(A)$ of $C(A)$ of sequences $\{x_n\}$ for which $\{x_n\}$ converges and

$$\lim_{m\to\infty} \sum_{n=1}^{\infty} a_{mn}x_n = \lim_{n\to\infty} x_n.$$

We recall that if $P(A)$ is precisely the set of convergent sequences, then A is said to be **regular.** The main fact in this subject is the following theorem which was proved in Chapter 2, and for which the following proof is also of interest.

THEOREM 1. *A is regular if and only if*

(a) $\sum_{n=1}^{\infty} |a_{mn}| < M$ *for some M and all m.*

(b) $\lim_{m\to\infty} a_{mn} = 0$ *for every n.*

(c) $\lim_{m\to\infty} \sum_{n=1}^{\infty} a_{mn} = 1.$

Proof. Suppose A is regular. Let c be the space of convergent sequences. Since $\sum_{n=1}^{\infty} a_{mn}x_n$ converges for every $\{x_n\} \in c$, for every m, it follows that

$\{a_{mn}\} \in l_1$, $m = 1, 2, \ldots$, since l_1 is the dual of c. But this sequence of linear functionals is bounded for every $\{x_n\} \in c$. By the principle of uniform boundedness, its sequence of norms is bounded in l_1. This proves that (a) must hold. The necessity of (b) and (c) is not as deep. For (b), consider the sequence which is 1 in the nth place and 0 everywhere else. This sequence is taken by the matrix A into the sequence $\{a_{mn}\}$. Thus we must have $\lim_{m\to\infty} a_{mn} = 0$ for every n. In order to prove that (c) holds, it is only necessary to consider the transform of the sequence $\{1, 1, \ldots, 1, \ldots\}$.

The sufficiency of the conditions (a), (b), (c) may be proved by a direct computation as follows:

Let $\{x_n\} \in c$ and suppose $\lim_{n\to\infty} x_n = s$. Then

$$\lim_{m\to\infty} \left| \sum_{n=1}^{\infty} a_{mn}x_n - s \right|$$
$$= \lim_{m\to\infty} \left| \sum_{n=1}^{\infty} a_{mn}(x_n - s) \right| \le \lim_{m\to\infty} \sum_{n=1}^{\infty} |a_{mn}|\,|x_n - s|$$
$$= \lim_{m\to\infty} \left[\sum_{n=1}^{N} |a_{mn}|\,|x_n - s| + \sum_{n=N+1}^{\infty} |a_{mn}|\,|x_n - s| \right], \text{ for every } N.$$

Now, let $\epsilon > 0$. Choose N so that $n > N$ implies $|x_n - s| < \epsilon/M$. Since $\lim_{m\to\infty} \sum_{n=1}^{N} |a_{mn}|\,|x_n - s| = 0$, we have $\lim_{m\to\infty} \left| \sum_{n=1}^{\infty} a_{mn}x_n - s \right| < \epsilon$, for every $\epsilon > 0$.

The following fact will be of central importance to the remaining considerations of this section.

PROPOSITION 1. Let X be an FK space with semi-norms $\{p_n\}$, Y an FK space with semi-norms $\{q_n\}$, and $\{f_n\}$ a sequence of continuous linear functionals on X. The set H of elements of X, for which $\{f_n(x)\} \in Y$, is an FK space with semi-norms

$$\{p_n(x)\},\ \{q_n(\{f_m(x)\})\}.$$

Proof. For every $x \in X$, the sequence

$$\{f_1(x), f_2(x), \ldots\}$$

will be called the transform of x. H is clearly a vector space. H has countably many semi-norms. Since the topology in H is finer than that induced in H by X, the coordinate functionals are continuous. It remains only to prove that H is complete. Accordingly, let $\{x_m\}$ be a Cauchy sequence in H. Then, for every n, the sequence $\{p_n(x_m)\}$ converges, and the sequence $\{q_n(y_m)\}$ converges, where y_m is the transform of x_m. By the completeness of X and Y, the sequence $\{x_m\}$ converges to an $x \in X$ and the sequence $\{y_m\}$ converges to a $y \in Y$. Now, by coordinate-wise convergence in Y, and the continuity of the f_n, the nth coordinate of y is given by

$$\lim_{m\to\infty} f_n(x_m) = f_n\left(\lim_{m\to\infty} x_m\right) = f_n(x).$$

Thus, y is the transform of x. This means that $\{x_m\}$ converges to x in H so that H is complete.

COROLLARY 1. If $\{a_n\}$ is a sequence of real numbers, the set H of sequences $x = \{x_n\}$, for which $\sum_{n=1}^{\infty} a_n x_n$ converges, is an *FK* space with semi-norms

$$|x_n|, \quad n = 1, 2, \ldots$$

and

$$\sup_n \left| \sum_{k=1}^{n} a_k x_k \right| .$$

Proof. Let X be the *FK* space of all sequences. Then the determining semi-norms for X are

$$p_n(x) = |x_n|, \quad n = 1, 2, \ldots$$

for $x = (x_1, x_2, \ldots)$. Let

$$f_n(x) = \sum_{k=1}^{n} a_k x_k, \quad n = 1, 2, \ldots .$$

Let Y be the *FK* space of convergent sequences. The determining semi-norm for Y is

$$q(y) = \sup_n |y_n|$$

for $y = (y_1, y_2, \ldots)$. The conclusion is obtained by substitution in proposition 1.

As an immediate consequence of this corollary, we have

PROPOSITION 2. For every matrix $A = (a_{mn})$, the set $E(A)$ is an *FK* space with semi-norms

$$p_n(x) = |x_n|, \quad n = 1, 2, \ldots$$

$$q_m(x) = \sup_n \left| \sum_{k=1}^{n} a_{mk} x_k \right|, \quad m = 1, 2, \ldots .$$

Proof. By corollary 1 and the fact that the intersection of a countable set of *FK* spaces is an *FK* space with all the semi-norms of the factor spaces as the set of determining semi-norms.

Now, let A be an infinite matrix and consider the *FK* space $E(A)$. For every m, let

$$f_m(x) = \sum_{n=1}^{\infty} a_{mn} x_n .$$

Since

$$\left|\sum_{n=1}^{\infty} a_{mn}x_n\right| \leq \sup_n \left|\sum_{k=1}^{n} a_{mk}x_k\right|,$$

the functionals f_m are continuous on $E(A)$. By proposition 1, we obtain

THEOREM 2. For every A, the set $C(A)$ is an FK space with semi-norms

$$\sup_n \left|\sum_{k=1}^{n} a_{mk}x_k\right|, \quad m = 1, 2, \ldots,$$

$$|x_n|, \quad n = 1, 2, \ldots,$$

$$\sup_m \left|\sum_{n=1}^{\infty} a_{mn}x_n\right|.$$

The set $C(A)$ is called the **convergence field** of a matrix A. Thus, every convergence field is an FK space. We shall see that there are FK spaces, however, which are not convergence fields.

We shall consider, briefly, a special collection of regular matrix methods, the Cesaro methods. For every $\alpha > 0$, consider the matrix

$$a_{mn} = \begin{cases} \dfrac{\dbinom{m+n+\alpha-1}{m-n}}{\dbinom{m+\alpha}{m}}, & n \leq m \\ 0 & n > m, \end{cases}$$

for $m, n = 0, 1, 2, \ldots$.

This method is designated the (C, α) method.

The following hold but will not be proved here (see Hardy [1] and Zeller [1]).

(a) For every $\alpha > 0$, the (C, α) method is regular.

(b) For every $\alpha, \beta > 0$, the (C, α) and (C, β) methods are consistent, i.e., if a sequence is in the convergence fields of both methods, its transformed sequences have the same limit.

(c) If $\alpha > \beta$, then (C, α) is strictly stronger than (C, β), i.e., the convergence field of (C, α) contains that of (C, β) as a proper subset.

Let E_α be the convergence field of (C, α). Then E_α is an FK space. It has the property:

(d) For every $x = (x_1, x_2, \ldots)$ in E_α, the sequence $x^n = (x_1, \ldots, x_n, 0, \ldots)$, $n = 1, 2, \ldots$, converges to x in E_α.

Let H consist of those sequences all of whose terms, except for a finite number, are zero.

PROPOSITION 3. If $\{A_n\}$ is a sequence of matrices such that, for every n, the convergence field E_n of A_n contains H and has property (d), and if

$E_{n+1} \subset E_n$, $E_{n+1} \neq E_n$, $n = 1, 2, \ldots$, then $E = \bigcap_{n=1}^{\infty} E_n$ is not the convergence field for any matrix, even though it is an *FK* space.

Proof. Let A be a matrix whose convergence field F contains E. We may then take sets of determining semi-norms for F and E such that the former is a subset of the latter. In particular,

$$q(x) = \sup_m \left| \sum_{n=1}^{\infty} a_{mn} x_n \right|$$

may be taken as one of the semi-norms for F. Since each E_i has a determining set of semi-norms $p_{i1}, p_{i2}, \ldots$, the totality p_{ij}, $i, j = 1, 2, \ldots$, is a determining set of semi-norms for E. It follows that

$$q(x) \leq M \sum_{k=1}^{n} p_{i_k j_k}(x)$$

for some M and n. Since the E_i are decreasing, for sufficiently large m,

$$q(x) \leq M \sum_{k=1}^{m} p_{i_n k}(x).$$

Thus A maps E, with the semi-norms $p_{i1}, p_{i2}, \ldots$, continuously into the space of convergent sequences. Since $E \supset H$, and E_i has the property (d), it follows that this mapping can be extended to E_i. Thus $F \supset E_i$, so that E is not the convergence field of A.

We may now state for the Cesaro methods

PROPOSITION 4. $\bigcup_{\alpha>0} E_\alpha$ is not an *FK* space and so it is not a matrix convergence field. $\bigcap_{\alpha>0} E_\alpha$ is an *FK* space but it is not a matrix convergence field.

5.10 Ordered Vector Spaces

Vector spaces of real functions have a natural order relation and there is an interplay between this order relation and topologies on such spaces.

It is just as easy to work in a more general setting. Let X be a vector space as well as an ordered set. By an **ordered set** X we understand that X has an order relation $\geq$ defined for some pairs in X such that

(i) $x \geq y$, $y \geq z$ implies $x \geq z$
(ii) $x \geq y$, $y \geq x$ implies $x = y$.

Then, X is said to be an **ordered vector space** if

(a) X is a vector space and an ordered set, and
(b) $x \geq y$ implies $x + z \geq y + z$ for every $z \in X$; $x \geq 0$ and $a \geq 0$ implies $ax \geq 0$.

An ordered vector space is said to be a **vector lattice** if for every $x, y \in X$, $\sup(x, y)$ and $\inf(x, y)$ exist.

We give some examples of ordered vector spaces.

(a) The vector space $C(X)$ of continuous functions, each having compact support, on a locally compact Hausdorff space X, with the order relation $x \geq y$ if $x(t) \geq y(t)$ for every $t \in X$. $C(X)$ is easily seen to be a vector lattice.

(b) The vector space D of differentiable real functions, defined on the reals with $x \geq y$ if $x(t) \geq y(t)$, for every real t, is an ordered vector space. It is not a vector lattice since the pair of functions $t, -t$ does not have a least upper bound in D.

(c) Let $(X, \mathcal{S}, \mu)$ be a measure space and $p \geq 1$. The corresponding L_p space is a vector lattice if, for equivalence classes x and y, $x \geq y$, if $x(t) \geq y(t)$ almost everywhere for every representative of x and of y.

Although some of the most important ordered vector spaces of functions are not vector lattices, we shall consider only the vector lattice case.

Let X be a vector lattice. For every $x \in X$, let $x^+ = \sup(x, 0)$ and $x^- = -\inf(x, 0)$. Since $y \geq z$ implies $x + y \geq x + z$, it follows easily that for every $x, y, z \in X$,

$$\sup(x + y, x + z) = x + \sup(y, z).$$

Then

$$\begin{aligned} x^+ - x &= \sup(x, 0) - x = \sup(x - x, -x) \\ &= \sup(0, -x) = -\inf(0, x) = x^-. \end{aligned}$$

Thus, every $x \in X$ has the decomposition

$$x = x^+ - x^-.$$

We define the **absolute value** of x by

$$|x| = x^+ + x^-.$$

We shall be interested in linear functionals on a vector lattice.

A linear functional x' on X is said to be **positive** if $x \geq 0$ implies $x'(x) \geq 0$.

A linear functional x' on X is said to be **bounded** if for every $x \in X$, x' is bounded on the set of y for which $|y| \leq |x|$.

We shall call the set X^ω of bounded linear functionals on X the **order dual** of X. The set X^ω is easily seen to be a vector space, a subspace of the algebraic dual X^* of X. If x' is positive, then

$$|y| \leq |x| \text{ implies } x'(|y|) \leq x'(|x|).$$

But

$$\begin{aligned} |x'(y)| &= |x'(y^+ - y^-)| = |x'(y^+) - x'(y^-)| \\ &\leq |x'(y^+)| + |x'(y^-)| = x'(y^+) + x'(y^-) \\ &= x'(|y|). \end{aligned}$$

Hence x' is bounded.

The main fact here is that every bounded linear functional is the difference between positive ones. This fact closely resembles the theorem on decomposition of signed measures.

We need

LEMMA 1. If $x_1, x_2, y_1, y_2 \geq 0$ and $x_1 + x_2 = y_1 + y_2$, there are $u, v, r, s \geq 0$ such that $x_1 = u + v$, $x_2 = r + s$, $y_1 = u + r$, $y_2 = v + s$.

Proof. Let $u = (x_1 - y_2)^+$, $v = x_1 - u$, $r = y_1 - u$, $s = u - (x_1 - y_2)$. It is easy to see that $u, v, r, s \geq 0$. The rest is trivial.

COROLLARY 1. If $x_1, x_2 \geq 0$ and $0 \leq y \leq x_1 + x_2$, there are $0 \leq y_1 \leq x_1$, $0 \leq y_2 \leq x_2$ such that $y = y_1 + y_2$.

Proof. Apply lemma 1 to $x_1, x_2, y, x_1 + x_2 - y$. There are $y_1, y_2, z_1, z_2 \geq 0$, with $x_1 = y_1 + z_1$, $x_2 = y_2 + z_2$, $y = y_1 + y_2$, $x_1 + x_2 - y = z_1 + z_2$.

We are now ready to prove the main theorem.

THEOREM 1. If X is a vector lattice, and f is a bounded linear functional on X, there are positive linear functionals g, h on X such that $f = g - h$.

Proof. Let $x \geq 0$. Define

$$g(x) = \sup [f(y) : 0 \leq y \leq x].$$

Now, let $x_1, x_2 \geq 0$. We show that

$$g(x_1) + g(x_2) = g(x_1 + x_2).$$

In the first place,

$$\begin{aligned} g(x_1) + g(x_2) &= \sup [f(y) : 0 \leq y \leq x_1] \\ &\quad + \sup [f(y) : 0 \leq y \leq x_2] \\ &= \sup [f(y_1 + y_2) : 0 \leq y_1 \leq x_1, 0 \leq y_2 \leq x_2] \\ &\leq g(x_1 + x_2). \end{aligned}$$

Conversely, let $0 \leq z \leq x_1 + x_2$. By the corollary 1, there are $0 \leq y_1 \leq x_1$, $0 \leq y_2 \leq x_2$ such that $y_1 + y_2 = z$. Then

$$f(z) = f(y_1) + f(y_2) \leq g(x_1) + g(x_2).$$

Since this holds for every $0 \leq z \leq x_1 + x_2$,

$$g(x_1 + x_2) \leq g(x_1) + g(x_2).$$

Now, for arbitrary $x \in X$, $x = x^+ - x^-$. Define

$$g(x) = g(x^+) - g(x^-).$$

Then,

$$g(x_1 + x_2) = g(x_1) + g(x_2)$$

for every $x_1, x_2 \in X$. That $g(ax) = ag(x)$ is evident.

Thus, g is a positive linear functional on X. Moreover, $g(x) \geq f(x)$ for every $x \geq 0$. So, $h = g - f$ is positive on X.

We remark that if we endow X^ω with the order relation $f \geq g$ if $f - g$ is positive, then X^ω is a vector lattice.

5.11 Banach Lattice

We now allow a vector space X to have both an order relation and a topology. To prevent any confusion we shall avoid using the term bounded to refer to continuous linear functionals in this discussion. Let X be a vector lattice. A semi-norm p in the vector space X is said to be **compatible** with the order relation in X if

$$|x| \geq |y| \text{ implies } p(x) \geq p(y).$$

A locally convex topology in X turns X into a **locally convex topological vector lattice** if it has a determining set of semi-norms compatible with the order relation in X. Now, a locally convex topological vector lattice has a topological dual X' and an order dual X^ω.

PROPOSITION 1. $X' \subset X^\omega$.

Proof. It is only necessary to show that if p is a semi-norm compatible with the order relation in X, then the semi-norm set of p is a subset of X^ω. Accordingly, let $f \in X^*$ be such that

$$|f(x)| \leq Mp(x)$$

for some M and all $x \in X$. Now, let $0 \leq y$. For $|z| \leq y$,

$$p(z) \leq p(y),$$

so that

$$|f(z)| \leq Mp(z) \leq Mp(y),$$

and $f \in X^\omega$.

On the other hand, we have

PROPOSITION 2. For every vector lattice X there is a locally convex topology on X such that X is a locally convex topological vector lattice for which $X' = X^\omega$.

Proof. Let $f \in X^\omega$ be positive and let p_f be defined by

$$p_f(x) = f(|x|)$$

for every $x \in X$. Then p_f is easily seen to be a semi-norm compatible with the order relation in X. But

$$\begin{aligned} |f(x)| &= |f(x^+) - f(x^-)| \le f(x^+) + f(x^-) \\ &= f(|x|) = p_f(x), \end{aligned}$$

so that $f \in X'$, where X' is the dual of X topologized by the semi-norms $[p_f : f \in X^\omega]$. Since every positive $f \in X^\omega$ is in X', it follows that $X^\omega \subset X'$.

Suppose now that X is a vector lattice and that there is a norm in X, which is compatible with the order relation, for which X is a Banach space. Then X is called a **Banach lattice.** We shall show that in a Banach lattice, $X' = X^\omega$. We first prove

LEMMA 1. If X is a Banach lattice, if $0 \le x_1 \le x_2 \le \ldots$ and

$$\lim_{n \to \infty} \|x - x_n\| = 0,$$

then $x_n \le x$, for every n.

Proof. Suppose $(x_n - x)^+ > 0$ for some n. For every $m > n$,

$$(x_m - x)^+ \ge (x_n - x)^+.$$

But,

$$|x_m - x| \ge (x_m - x)^+,$$

so that

$$\|x_m - x\| \ge \|(x_n - x)^+\|,$$

and the sequence $\{x_n\}$ does not converge to x.

PROPOSITION 3. If X is a Banach lattice, then $X' = X^w$.

Proof. Suppose, on the contrary, that f is a positive linear functional on X which is not continuous. Then, for every M, there is an $x \in X$ such that $\|x\| \le 1$ and $|f(x)| \ge M$. Since $\| \, |x| \, \| = \|x\|$ and since

$$\begin{aligned} f(|x|) &= f(x^+ + x^-) \\ &\ge |f(x^+ - x^-)| = |f(x)|, \end{aligned}$$

there is an $x > 0$ for which $\|x\| \le 1$ and $f(x) \ge M$.

Now, let $\{x_n\}$ be a sequence of positive elements in X such that, for every n,

$$\|x_n\| \le 1 \quad \text{and} \quad f(x_n) \ge 2^{2n}.$$

Let

$$y_n = \frac{1}{2} x_1 + \frac{1}{2^2} x_2 + \ldots + \frac{1}{2^n} x_n,$$

for every $n = 1, 2, \ldots$. Then $\{y_n\}$ is an increasing sequence of positive elements. But, for every n and k,

$$\|y_{n+k} - y_n\| = \left\| \frac{1}{2^{n+1}} x_{n+1} + \ldots + \frac{1}{2^{n+k}} x_{n+k} \right\|$$
$$\leq \frac{1}{2^{n+1}} + \ldots + \frac{1}{2^{n+k}} < \frac{1}{2^n}.$$

Thus, $\{y_n\}$ is a Cauchy sequence in X. Let $y = \lim_{n\to\infty} y_n$. By lemma 1, $y > y_n$, for every n. Hence,

$$f(y) > f(y_n) > \frac{1}{2^n} f(x_n) \geq 2^n, \text{ for every } n.$$

But this is impossible, so that f is continuous, and the proposition is proved.

We may now prove

THEOREM 1. If a vector lattice X can be normed as a Banach lattice, it can be done in only one way to within topological equivalence.

Proof. Since X^ω is a subspace of X^*, there is at most one norm on X, within topological equivalence, for which X is a Banach space and X^ω is the dual. But, for every compatible norm on X, for which X is a Banach space, X^ω is the dual. This proves the theorem.

We give some examples.

(a) Let S be a compact Hausdorff space, and let $C(S)$ be the vector lattice of continuous functions on S with the natural order relation $x \geq y$ if $x(t) \geq y(t)$ for every $t \in S$. Then the only norm, within topological equivalence, for which $|x(t)| \geq |y(t)|$, for every $t \in S$, implies $\|x\| \geq \|y\|$ and $C(S)$ is a Banach space, is the sup norm

$$\|x\| = \max\,[|x(t)| : t \in S].$$

(b) If $(S, \mathcal{S}, \mu)$ is a measure space, then the L_p norm is the only one, within topological equivalence, for the pth power integrable functions, $p \geq 1$, for which it is a Banach space in which $|x(t)| \geq |y(t)|$ almost everywhere implies $\|x\| \geq \|y\|$.

Vector lattices also play a role in the theory of integration. Let S be a compact Hausdorff space, and let $C(S)$ be the set of continuous real functions on S. Then, $C(S)$ is a Banach lattice with norm

$$\|x\| = \max\,[|x(t)| : t \in S]$$

and the natural order relation for functions. The **Radon measures** on S are, by definition, the continuous linear functionals on $C(S)$. But we have already seen that these are precisely the bounded linear functionals on $C(S)$. The

Radon measures on S may thus be defined either in terms of the topology or the order relation in $C(S)$.

More generally, if S is locally compact and $C(S)$ is the set of continuous functions with compact support on S, then a Radon measure on S is defined as a linear functional on $C(S)$, whose restriction to $C(K)$ is in the dual of the Banach space $C(K)$, for every compact $K \subset S$. There is a locally convex topology on $C(S)$ such that the Radon measures are the dual of $C(S)$ with this topology, but we shall not discuss it here. Moreover, this dual is again the same as the order dual of $C(S)$.

5.12 Köthe Spaces

We consider now a special class of locally convex topological vector lattices, the so-called Köthe spaces.

As a setting for this subject, we consider a totally σ finite measure space $(S, \mathcal{S}, \mu)$, and fix a sequence $\{S_n\}$ of sets in $\mathcal{S}$ such that $\mu(S_n) < \infty$, $n = 1, 2, \ldots$, and $S = \bigcup_{n=1}^{\infty} S_n$.

A real function f on S is said to be **locally summable** if the restriction of f to S_n is summable for every $n = 1, 2, \ldots$. (As usual, we do not discriminate between functions and equivalence classes of functions unless a special need arises.)

Let F be the set of all locally summable functions on S. All of the spaces of interest here will be subspaces of F.

Let $A \subset F$. We associate a subset $A^* \subset F$ with A, where $f \in A^*$ if and only if $f \in F$ and

$$\int_S |f(t)g(t)|\, dt < \infty$$

for every $g \in A$.

PROPOSITION 1. For every $A \subset F$, A^* is a vector lattice.

Proof. $\int_S |f(t)g(t)|\, dt < \infty$ implies $\int_S |af(t)g(t)|\, dt < \infty$ for every real a. If $\int_S |f_1(t)g(t)|\, dt < \infty$ and $\int_S |f_2(t)g(t)|\, dt < \infty$, then

$$\int_S |(f_1(t) + f_2(t))g(t)|\, dt < \infty, \quad \text{and} \quad \int_S |\max(f_1(t), f_2(t))g(t)|\, dt < \infty.$$

PROPOSITION 2. For every $A \subset F$, $A^{***} = A^*$, where $A^{**} = (A^*)^*$ and $A^{***} = (A^{**})^*$.

Proof. Let $f \in A$. Then $\int_S |f(t)g(t)|\, dt < \infty$ for every $g \in A^*$, so that $f \in A^{**}$. Thus $A \subset A^{**}$. In particular, $A^* \subset A^{***}$. Conversely, let $f \in A^{***}$. Then, for every $g \in A^{**}$, $\int_S |f(t)g(t)|\, dt < \infty$. Then, for every $g \in A$, $\int_S |f(t)g(t)|\, dt < \infty$. Hence $f \in A^*$. It follows that $A^* \supset A^{***}$.

A subset $K \subset F$ is called a **Köthe space** if $K = K^{**}$. For a Köthe space K, the space K^* is also a Köthe space and is called the **associate Köthe space** of K. If K^* is the associate of K, then, by proposition 2, K is the associate of K^*.

In particular, F itself is a Köthe space.

PROPOSITION 3. F^* is the vector lattice of bounded measurable functions on S each of which vanishes outside of some S_n.

Proof. Let $f \in F$ and let g be bounded, measurable, and vanishing outside of one of the S_n. There is an M such that $|g(t)| < M$, $t \in S$. Then

$$\int_S |f(t)g(t)|\,dt = \int_{S_n} |f(t)g(t)|\,dt \leq M \int_{S_n} |f(t)|\,dt < \infty.$$

Hence, $g \in F^*$.

Suppose g is unbounded. Then g is unbounded on some S_n (since we are dealing with equivalence classes, this means that every function equivalent to g is also unbounded on S_n). It is not hard to construct a summable function f on S_n such that $\int_S |g(t)f(t)|\,dt = \infty$. Then $g \notin F^*$.

Suppose the support of g is not in any S_n. Then, there is a sequence $\{S_{n_k}\}$, $a_k > 0$, $k = 1, 2, \ldots$, $T_k \subset S_{n_k} \sim S_{n_k - 1}$, $\mu(T_k) > 0$, and $|g(t)| > a_k$ on T_k. Let

$$f_k = \frac{1}{a_k \mu(T_k)} \chi_{T_k}.$$

Then $f = \sum_{k=1}^{\infty} f_k \in F$ and $\int_S |f(t)g(t)|\,dt = \infty$. Thus $g \notin F^*$.

If K and L are Köthe spaces and $K \supset L$, then $K^* \subset L^*$. Thus, F is the largest Köthe space and F^* is the smallest Köthe space.

If $p > 1$, then L_p and L_q, for $1/p + 1/q = 1$, are associated Köthe spaces. This holds since $\int_S |f(t)g(t)|\,dt < \infty$ for every $g \in L_p$ if and only if $f \in L_q$, and these particular spaces do not depend on the choice of $\{S_n\}$.

For every Köthe space K, locally convex topologies, which are compatible with the order relation in K, may be introduced in K in terms of the associate K^* of K. In this connection, we say that a set $A \subset K^*$ is admissible if, for every $f \in K$,

$$\sup \left[\int_S |f(t)g(t)|\,dt : g \in A \right] < \infty.$$

For every admissible $A \subset K^*$ and $f \in K$, let

$$p_A(f) = \sup \left[\int_S |f(t)g(t)|\,dt : g \in A \right].$$

PROPOSITION 4. For every admissible $A \subset K^*$, p_A is a semi-norm on K, compatible with the order relation in K.

The proof is a direct and simple computation.

Now, let $[A]$ be a collection of admissible sets in K^* which covers K^*, i.e., every $g \in K^*$ belongs to at least one $A \in [A]$. The set of semi-norms p_A, $A \in [A]$, then defines a locally convex topology in K.

In order to show this we must see that, for every $f \in K, f \neq 0$, there is an $A \in [A]$ such that $p_A(f) > 0$. Clearly, it suffices to show that for every $f \in K$ there is $g \in K^*$ such that $\int_S |f(t)g(t)|\, dt > 0$. Indeed, there is a $g \in F^*$ with this property. For, there is an S_n and $T \subset S_n$ such that $\mu(T) > 0$ and either $f > 0$ or $f < 0$ on T. Let $g = \chi_T$.

We thus have

Proposition 5. For every collection $[A]$ of admissible sets in K^*, which covers K^*, the corresponding set of semi-norms p_A, $A \in [A]$, converts K into a locally convex topological vector lattice.

It is clear that the hypothesis of proposition 5 can be weakened and the conclusion still hold. For, in the proof, we only need that $[A]$ should cover F^*. Moreover, it should be apparent that it is enough that the scalar multiples of the $A \in [A]$ cover F^*.

We note that there is a finest topology in K obtained in this way from K^*. This is the one obtained by letting $[A]$ be the set of all admissible sets in K^*.

There is a special case of particular interest. This is the one where the finest topology is given by a single admissible set $A \subset K^*$. In this case, K is a normed space.

Proposition 6. If K is a normed space, with respect to the finest topology defined in K by means of K^*, then K is a Banach space.

Proof. There is an $A \subset K^*$ such that

$$\|f\| = \sup \left[\int_S |f(t)g(t)|\, dt : g \in A\right].$$

Suppose $\{f_n\}$ is a Cauchy sequence in K. Since this is the finest Köthe topology in K, it follows that for every $g \in K^*$,

$$\lim_{n,m\to\infty} \int_S |f_n(t) - f_m(t)|\, |g(t)|\, dt = 0.$$

But $K^* \supset F^*$. So, by letting g be in turn the characteristic function of each S_m, it follows that $\{f_n\}$ is a Cauchy sequence in $L_1(S_m)$, for every m. By a diagonal process, $\{f_n\}$ has a subsequence, which we also designate by $\{f_n\}$, which converges almost everywhere to a function f. Now,

$$\int_S |f(t)g(t)|\, dt \leq \liminf_{n\to\infty} \int_S |f_n(t)g(t)|\, dt < \infty,$$

since $|fg|$ is the almost everywhere limit of $\{|f_n g|\}$.

Let $\epsilon > 0$. Let $g \in A$, and let n be such that

$$\int_S |f_m(t) - f_n(t)|\,|g(t)|\,dt < \epsilon$$

for every $m > n$. Then,

$$\int_S |f(t) - f_n(t)|\,|g(t)|\,dt \leq \liminf_{m\to\infty} \int_S |f_m(t) - f_n(t)|\,|g(t)|\,dt \leq \epsilon.$$

Since there is an N such that $n, m > N$ implies

$$\int_S |f_n(t) - f_m(t)|\,|g(t)|\,dt < \epsilon$$

for every $g \in A$, it follows that, for $n > N$,

$$\int_S |f(t) - f_n(t)|\,|g(t)|\,dt \leq \epsilon$$

for every $g \in A$. This shows that $\{f_n\}$ converges to f in our space.

In particular, if $K = L_p$, $p > 1$, then the unit ball $A \subset L_q = K^*$ is admissible and defines the L_p norm in K.

Let K be a Köthe space with the finest topology determined by K^*. With this topology, K has a topological dual K'. For every $g \in K^*$, the linear functional,

$$\varphi(f) = \int_S f(t)g(t)\,dt$$

is defined on K and is evidently continuous. Thus K^* has a natural imbedding in K'. In many cases, $K^* = K'$. In the particular case, $K = F^*$, K^* is generally a proper subset of K'.

We close this section with brief mention of two special cases.

(a) Let S be the interval $[0, 1]$ and let μ be Lebesgue measure. Then $F = L_1[0, 1]$ and F^* is the set of bounded measurable functions. In this case, the Köthe spaces, which are Banach spaces with the finest topologies as given by their associated spaces, may be defined as follows:

Let $A \subset L_1[0, 1]$ be a bounded set, in the L_1 norm, such that $1 \in A$ and, if $f \in A$ and $|g| \leq |f|$ then $g \in A$. Let

$$K = \left\{f : \sup\left[\int_0^1 |f(t)g(t)| : g \in A\right] < \infty\right\}.$$

It is not hard to see that K is a Köthe space,

$$K^* = \bigcup[cA : c \in R],$$

and that K, with the finest topology defined by K^*, is a Banach space with norm

$$\|f\| = \sup\left[\int_0^1 |f(t)g(t)|\,dt : g \in A\right].$$

We leave the details to the reader.

(b) Let S be the set of natural numbers, and let μ be the measure which is

1 for each number. The set F of locally summable functions consists of all sequences of real numbers, and F^* consists of those sequences which vanish except for a finite number of terms.

EXERCISES

1.1 Prove that a collection $\mathcal{B}$ of open sets is a base for a topological space $(X, \mathcal{G})$ if and only if for every $x \in X$ and $G \in \mathcal{G}$, such that $x \in G$, there is an $H \in \mathcal{B}$ such that $x \in H$ and $H \subset G$.

1.2 Let X be the set of pairs of real numbers, ordered by means of $(x, y) > (x', y')$ if either $x > x'$ or $x = x'$ and $y > y'$. Then X is a totally ordered set. Let the open intervals in X be a base for the topology in X. Show that the space obtained is metrizable.

1.3 Let X be the set of all real functions on R which vanish except at a well-ordered subset of R. For $f, g \in X$, let $f > g$ if $f(x) > g(x)$ at the first real number x where they are not equal. Then X is a totally ordered set. Show that X is not metrizable.

1.4 Let $X = R$. Let G be open in X if it is an open set in the usual topology, minus a countable set. Let $\mathcal{G} = [G]$. Show that $(X, \mathcal{G})$ is a Hausdorff topological space which is not metrizable.

1.5 If $S \subset R$ is measurable, then x is said to be a point of density of S if, for every $\epsilon > 0$, there is a $\delta > 0$ such that if I is an interval, $x \in I$, and $m(I) < \delta$, then

$$\frac{m(S \cap I)}{m(I)} > 1 - \epsilon.$$

Let G be open if G is measurable and every point of G is a point of density of G. Let $\mathcal{G} = [G]$. Show that $(S, \mathcal{G})$ is a Hausdorff topological space which is not metrizable.

1.6 Show that if $(X, \mathcal{G})$ has a countable base then every base has a countable subset which is also a base.

2.1 If X is a compact space and $\{f_n\}$ is a sequence of decreasing functions which converges to zero on X, show that the convergence is uniform.

2.2 A topological space is said to be Lindelöf if every covering of the space by a set of open sets has a countable subcover. Show that the space of exercise 1.5 is not a Lindelöf space.

2.3 For every $\alpha \in A$, let X_α be a 2 point space all of whose subsets are open. For what cardinal numbers for A is

$$\prod [X_\alpha : \alpha \in A]$$

metrizable? Prove.

2.4 Show that if X is a Hausdorff space, and $S \subset X$ is compact with the induced topology, then S is a closed subset of X. Conversely, if S is closed in a compact X, then it is compact with the induced topology.

2.5 If $S \subset X$, where X is a topological space, show that $x \in \bar{S}$ if and only if for every open set G such that $x \in G$, the set $G \cap S$ is non-empty.

2.6 Show that the closed unit ball B in $L_2[0, 1]$ is weakly compact in the sense that if $\{f_n\} \subset B$ is such that $\left\{\int_0^1 f_n g\right\}$ is Cauchy for every $g \in L_2$, then there is an $f \in B$ with $\int_0^1 fg = \lim_{n\to\infty} \int_0^1 f_n g$, for every $g \in L_2$.

3.1 Show that a topological vector space, satisfying (d), is a Hausdorff space.

3.2 State necessary and sufficient conditions for a collection of sets in a vector space X to be a base at 0 for a topology in X for which X is a topological vector space.

3.3 Show that if X is a topological vector space, for every $a \in R$, $a \neq 0$, the mapping

$$f_a : X \to X$$

defined by $f_a(x) = f(ax)$, $x \in X$, is a homeomorphism.

3.4 Define the product of a set of topological vector spaces and prove that it is a topological vector space.

3.5 For what cardinalities are products of metrizable topological vector spaces also metrizable?

4.1 If X is a vector space and X^* is its algebraic dual, show that $\dim X^* \geq \dim X$, equality holding if and only if $\dim X < \infty$.

4.2 If X is a finite dimensional vector space, show that the topology on X for which X is a topological vector space is unique.

5.1 Give details of the proof that the equivalence classes of measurable functions on [0, 1] are a metric space with metric

$$d(f, g) = \int_0^1 \frac{|f(t) - g(t)|}{1 + |f(t) - g(t)|}\, dt.$$

5.2 Give details of the proof that the above metric d and the metric δ defined in the text are equivalent.

5.3 Show that the space $L_p[0, 1]$ has a minimal total set for every $p \geq 1$. Hint: Try the Haar functions.

5.4 If $\{f_1, f_2, \ldots\}$ is a complete orthonormal set for $L_2[a, b]$, show that for every n there is a bounded g such that $\{gf_{n+1}, gf_{n+2}, \ldots\}$ is also total.

6.1 Show that the product of locally convex topological vector spaces is locally convex and define the semi-norms in the product in terms of those in the factors.

6.2 If X is a vector space and t_1 and t_2 are topologies, for each of which X is a locally convex topological vector space with the same topological dual, show that the closed convex sets in X are the same for the two topologies.

6.3 Let X be an infinite dimensional locally convex topological vector space whose topological dual is the entire algebraic dual of X. Show that X is not a Banach space.

6.4 Describe the dual of the product of topological vector spaces.

6.5 Let $\{X_n\}$ be an increasing sequence of Banach spaces such that, for every n, the identity mapping

$$i_n : X_n \to X_{n+1}$$

is continuous. Show that there is a finest topology in $X = \bigcup_{n=1}^{\infty} X_n$ such that the identity mappings

$$j_n : X_n \to X$$

are all continuous.

6.6 Define a system of semi-norms for the topology of the space in exercise 6.5.

6.7 Prove that the space defined in exercise 6.5 is not metrizable.

6.8 In a vector space X a **manifold** is a set $M = x + Y$, where Y is a subspace of X. M is a **supporting manifold** of a convex $S \subset X$ if $S \cap M \neq 0$, and for every $x \in S \cap M$, every open segment through x which is in S is also in M. A supporting manifold consisting of one point is called an **extreme point.** A supporting manifold is called a **supporting hyperplane** if, together with a point in X, it spans X. Show that a compact convex S in a locally convex topological vector space has a supporting hyperplane.

6.9 If X is a locally convex topological vector space, and $S \subset X$ is compact and convex, show that every supporting hyperplane of S contains at least one extreme point of S.

6.10 If X is a locally convex topological vector space, and $S \subset X$ is compact and convex, show that S is the smallest closed convex set containing its extreme points.

6.11 Give an example of a closed bounded convex set, in a locally convex topological vector space, which has no extreme points.

6.12 Let X be a locally convex topological vector space. A closed convex set $A \subset X$ is called a **barrel** if for every $x \in X$, $ax \in A$ for some $a \neq 0$ and if $x \in A$, $|a| \leq 1$ implies $ax \in A$. X is called a **barrel space** if every barrel in X contains an open set containing 0. Show that a vector space X admits at most one barreled topology for which a given subspace $Y \subset X^*$ is the dual of X.

6.13 Show that a locally convex topological vector space which is locally compact is finite dimensional.

7.1 Show that every Fréchet space is barreled.

7.2 Let X be a Fréchet space which is not a Banach space. Let X' be the dual of X. For every bounded set $A \subset X$, we define a semi-norm

$$p_A(x') = \sup\,[|x'(x)| : x \in A].$$

Show that, with this topology, X' is not a Fréchet space.

7.3 Prove that the space defined in exercise 6.5 is barreled.

7.4 Generalize the result of exercise 7.3.

7.5 A barreled space X is called a Montel space if every closed bounded set in X is compact. Show that the only Banach spaces which are Montel spaces are finite dimensional.

7.6 Show that the space of entire functions is a Montel space which is a Fréchet space.

7.7 Show that if X is a Montel space, then if semi-norms are defined in X' as in exercise 7.2, X' is also a Montel space.

7.8 Show that the results of exercises 7.6 and 7.7 assure the existence of Montel spaces which are not Fréchet spaces.

7.9 Let D be the vector space of real functions of a real variable each of which has compact support and is infinitely differentiable. Define a locally convex topology in D so that a sequence $\{f_n\}$ converges to zero in the topology if and only if $\{f_n\}$ has a common compact support, converges uniformly to zero and, for every $k = 1, 2, \ldots$, the sequence $\{f_n^{(k)}\}$ of kth derivatives converges uniformly to zero.

7.10 Show that the space D of exercise 7.9 is not metrizable but is barreled.

7.11 A continuous linear functional on D is called a distribution. Show that if f is locally summable (i.e., for every compact $K \subset R$, $f\chi_K$ is summable), then the functional $\varphi(g)$ is a distribution, where

$$\varphi(g) = \int fg.$$

7.12 For every distribution φ, the linear functional φ' defined by $\varphi'(f) = -\varphi(f')$ is called the derivative of φ. Justify the name derivative and show that φ' is a distribution.

7.13 A distribution φ is said to have compact support if there is an n such that for every $f \in D$, which vanishes on $[-n, n]$, $\varphi(f) = 0$. If φ has compact support, show there is an integer k and a distribution ψ, determined by a summable function as in exercise 7.11, such that φ is the kth derivative of ψ.

7.14 Let $\{\varphi_n\}$ be a sequence of distributions such that, for every $f \in D$, $\{\varphi_n(f)\}$ converges. Let $\varphi(f)$ be the limit functional. Show that φ is a distribition.

7.15 If μ is a regular measure on R, finite on compact sets (and such that for every bounded measurable E and $\epsilon > 0$ there are compact K and open G such that $\mu(G) - \epsilon < \mu(E) < \mu(K) + \epsilon$), show that

$$\varphi(f) = \int f\,d\mu$$

is a distribution. Characterize the functions whose derivatives are measures of this sort.

8.1 Give details of the proof that the space of all sequences is an FK space, with semi-norms $p_n(x) = |a_n(x)|$, $n = 1, 2, \ldots$, where $x = (a_1(x), a_2(x), \ldots)$.

8.2 Give details of the proof that if X and Y are Fréchet spaces and f is a continuous linear mapping of X into Y, then $f(X)$ is either all of Y or is of the first category in Y.

8.3 Prove that if X_n, $n = 1, 2, \ldots$, is a sequence of FK spaces, then $X = \bigcap_{n=1}^{\infty} X_n$ is an FK space.

9.1 Show that the convergence field of a regular matrix does not contain all bounded sequences.

9.2 Show that every sequence is in the convergence field of some regular matrix.

9.3 A matrix A is said to be row finite if every row contains only finitely many non-zero terms. If A is row finite, describe the semi-norms for $C(A)$.

9.4 Show that, for every $\alpha > 0$, the (C, α) method is regular.

9.5 Show that if $\alpha > \beta$, then (C, α) is strictly stronger than (C, β).

10.1 An ordered group G is a group and an ordered set such that $x \geq y$ implies $x + z \geq y + z$ for every $z \in G$. $x \in G$ is called **positive** if $x \geq 0$, the group identity. G is called **directed** if, for every $x, y \in G$, there is $z \in G$ such that $z \geq x, z \geq y$. Show that G is directed if and only if every $x \in G$ is the difference between positive elements.

10.2 An ordered group G is called **lattice ordered** if $x, y \in G$ implies $\sup(x, y)$ exists. Show how every directed ordered group may be imbedded in a lattice ordered group.

10.3 Show that in a lattice ordered group G, $x, y, z \in G$ implies

$$\sup[x, \inf(y, z)] = \inf[\sup(x, y), \sup(x, z)].$$

10.4 A lattice ordered group G is archimedean if $x > 0$ and $ny \leq x$, for all n, implies $y \leq 0$. Show that every archimedean lattice ordered group is abelian.

10.5 A lattice ordered group is said to be complete if every set with an upper bound has a least upper bound. Show that a lattice ordered group can be imbedded in a complete lattice ordered group if and only if it is archimedean.

10.6 In a lattice ordered group G, show that $x, y, z \in G$ implies

$$\sup(x + y, x + z) = x + \sup(y, z).$$

10.7 Show that the ordered group of differentiable real functions is not a lattice ordered group.

10.8 Show that the lattice ordered group of continuous functions on $[0, 1]$ is not complete. Describe its completion.

11.1 Describe a locally convex topology, on the continuous functions with compact support on a locally compact space, so that the dual is the set of Radon measures.

11.2 Show that this dual is the same as the order dual.

12.1 For the real line R, with Lebesgue measure, show that the set of locally summable functions depends on the choice of $\{S_n\}$.

12.2 If g is unbounded (not equivalent to any bounded function) and vanishes outside a set of finite measure, show that there is a summable f such that $\int fg\, d\mu = \infty$.

12.3 Show that the spaces $L_p, p \geq 1$, are independent of the decomposition $\{S_n\}$.

12.4 For every admissible $A \subset K^*$, show that the functional p_A, defined in the text, is a semi-norm compatible with the order relation in K.

12.5 Show that the spaces K of example (a) are Banach spaces.

12.6 If a space K of exercise 12.5 is such that $f \in K$ and $\lim_{n \to \infty} \mu(T_n) = 0$ implies $\{f\chi_{T_n}\}$ converges to 0 in K, show that K^* is the topological dual of K.

12.7 If a space K of example (*b*) is a Banach space, with the finest topology determined in K by K^*, and if $\{a_n\} \in K$ implies $\{a_1, \ldots, a_m, 0, \ldots\}$, $m = 1, 2, \ldots,$ converges in K to $\{a_n\}$, show that K^* is the topological dual of K.

12.8 Let φ be right continuous for $t \geq 0$, positive, non-decreasing, with $\varphi(0) = 0$ and $\lim_{t \to \infty} \varphi(t) = \infty$, and let $\Phi(t) = \int_0^t \varphi(u)\, du$. Let ψ be defined by

$$\psi(t) = \sup\,[u : \varphi(u) \leq t],$$

and $\Psi(t) = \int_0^t \psi(u)\, du$. These are called **complementary functions.** Show that, for every $u, v \geq 0$,

$$uv \leq \Phi(u) + \Psi(v).$$

12.9 If there is an $M > 0$ and a t_0 such that $t \geq t_0$ implies $\Phi(2t) \leq M\Phi(t)$, show that the set of functions for which $\int \Phi(|f(t)|)\, dt < \infty$ is a Köthe space whose associate is the set of functions for which $\int \Psi(|f(t)|)\, dt < \infty$.

12.10 Show that in a space of exercise 12.9 a set is compact if and only if it is closed, bounded, and the integral means converge uniformly on the set (in the space).

CHAPTER 6

BANACH ALGEBRAS

6.1 Definition and Examples

Let X be a Banach space in which the standard vector space operations $(x, y) \to x + y$ and $(a, x) \to ax$ are defined and also a multiplication operation $(x, y) \to xy$.

The set X, together with the operations $(x, y) \to x + y$ and $(x, y) \to xy$, is assumed to be a ring and the norm is assumed to satisfy the Banach space conditions and

$$\|xy\| \leq \|x\| \, \|y\|.$$

The ring X need not have a multiplicative identity, but if it does have an identity e, then $\|e\| \geq 1$, since $\|x\| = \|ex\| \leq \|e\| \, \|x\|$.

It is easy to show that there is then an equivalent norm for which $\|e\| = 1$. (This means that the identity mapping of X with one norm onto X with the other norm is a homeomorphism.)

Such a system, with or without an identity, is called a **Banach algebra.**

We give some examples of Banach algebras.

(a) Let X be a compact Hausdorff space, and let $C(X)$ be the set of continuous, complex valued, functions on X. Then $C(X)$ is closed with respect to point-wise multiplication of functions, and multiplication of functions by scalars. With the usual norm

$$\|x\| = \max\,[|x(t)| : t \in X],$$

$C(X)$ is a Banach space. Moreover, a very easy computation shows that $\|xy\| \leq \|x\| \, \|y\|$ so that $C(X)$ is a Banach algebra. It is a commutative ring, and has an identity given by the function which is identically 1.

(b) Now, let X be a locally compact Hausdorff space, and let $C(X)$ be the set of complex valued continuous functions on X which vanish at infinity. This means that, for every $\epsilon > 0$, there is a compact set $K \subset X$ such that $|x(t)| < \epsilon$ for every $t \notin K$. With $\|x\| = \max\,[|x(t)| : t \in X]$, $C(X)$ is again a Banach algebra. It is commutative, but does not have an identity if X is not compact.

(c) Let X be the set of equivalence classes of summable complex valued functions on the real line R, i.e., $x \in X$ if x is measurable and $\int_{-\infty}^{\infty} |x(t)|\, dt < \infty$.

Then X is a vector space with the usual point-wise operations. However, the point-wise product of summable functions need not be summable. A natural definition of product is the convolution of functions. The convolution $x * y$ of summable functions x and y is summable, where the convolution is defined by

$$(x * y)(t) = \int_{-\infty}^{\infty} x(t-u)y(u)\, du.$$

Indeed,

$$\int_{-\infty}^{\infty} \left| \int_{-\infty}^{\infty} x(t-u)y(u)\, du \right| dt \leq \int_{-\infty}^{\infty}\int_{-\infty}^{\infty} |x(t-u)y(u)|\, du\, dt$$
$$= \int_{-\infty}^{\infty} |x(u)|\, du \int_{-\infty}^{\infty} |y(u)|\, du.$$

Hence, not only is $x * y \in X$, but $\|x * y\| \leq \|x\|\,\|y\|$, so that we have a Banach algebra. It is designated as $L_1(R)$.

$L_1(R)$ is commutative, but has no identity. However, there are sequences of functions in $L_1(R)$ which act as a substitute for the identity for certain purposes. As an example, let

$$e_n(t) = \begin{cases} n & \text{if } |t| < \dfrac{1}{2n} \\ 0 & \text{if } |t| \geq \dfrac{1}{2n}, \end{cases}$$

$n = 1, 2, \ldots.$

Then, for any $x \in L_1(R)$,

$$(x * e_n)(t) = n \int_{-1/2n}^{1/2n} x(t+u)\, du.$$

Then

$$\|x - x * e_n\| = \int_{-\infty}^{\infty} \left| x(t) - n \int_{-1/2n}^{1/2n} x(t+u)\, du \right| dt.$$

But we have seen in Chapter 3 that the limit of this integral is zero as n approaches infinity. It follows that for every $x \in L_1(R)$,

$$\lim_{n\to\infty} \|x - x * e_n\| = 0.$$

In general, an **approximate identity** for $L_1(R)$ is a sequence $\{e_n\}$ of non-negative functions which converges uniformly to zero on any set which does not have 0 as a limit point and $\lim_{n\to\infty} \int_A e_n = 1$, for every open set A containing 0.

(d) Let H be a complex Hilbert space, and let X be the set of bounded linear operators

$$T : H \to H.$$

We define the operations

$$T_1 + T_2 \text{ by } (T_1 + T_2)(x) = T_1(x) + T_2(x),\ aT \text{ by } (aT)(x) = aT(x),$$

and

$$T_1T_2 \text{ by } (T_1T_2)(x) = T_1(T_2(x)),$$

for every $x \in H$.

With $\|T\|$ defined in the usual way for bounded operators, X is easily seen to be a Banach algebra. X has an identity, but is not commutative.

(e) The subset Y, which consists of the completely continuous operators of H into H is easily seen to be a subalgebra of X.

(f) Example (d) holds for any Banach space.

6.2 Adjunction of Identity

If X is a Banach algebra without identity, it is an easy matter to extend X so that the extended Banach algebra has an identity. Let C be the set of complex numbers, and let $\tilde{X}$ be the set of all pairs (x, a), $x \in A$, $a \in C$. Define operations in $\tilde{X}$ as follows:

$$(x, a) + (y, b) = (x + y, a + b),$$
$$c(x, a) = (cx, ca),$$
$$(x, a)(y, b) = (xy + ay + bx, ab).$$

Then it is easy to check that $\tilde{X}$ is an algebra. Define a norm in $\tilde{X}$ by

$$\|(x, a)\| = \|x\| + |a|.$$

It is easy to check that this has the properties of a norm and that

$$\|(x, a)(y, b)\| \le \|(x, a)\|\ \|(y, b)\|.$$

It is also easy to verify that a sequence $\{(x_n, a_n)\}$ in X is Cauchy if and only if $\{x_n\}$ is Cauchy in X and $\{a_n\}$ is Cauchy in C. If $x = \lim_{n\to\infty} x_n$ in X and $a = \lim_{n\to\infty} a_n$ in C, then $(x, a) = \lim_{n\to\infty} (x_n, a_n)$ in $\tilde{X}$. We thus know that $\tilde{X}$ is a Banach algebra. The mapping

$$\varphi : X \to \tilde{X},$$

for which $\varphi(x) = (x, 0)$, preserves the algebraic operations and the norm.

Since $(x, a)(0, 1) = (x, a)$, the element $(0, 1)$ is the identity in $\tilde{X}$.

Although this imbedding can always be made, it can usually be circumvented by other devices, as will be seen in the sequel.

6.3 Haar Measure

An analogue to $L_1(R)$ may be defined for every locally compact topological group G. For this purpose, we have to know what is meant by the Haar measure on G.

A **topological group** is a set G which is

(a) a group,
(b) a Hausdorff topological space, and
(c) the mappings $(x, y) \to xy$ of $G \times G$ onto G and $x \to x^{-1}$ of G onto G are continuous.

In particular, every topological vector space is a topological group. Moreover, just as in the special case of a topological vector space, a base for the open sets may be given as the left and right translations of a base for the open sets containing the identity e.

Recall that a topological space X is said to be compact if for every collection $U = [U_\alpha]$ of open sets such that $X = \bigcup U_\alpha$, there is a finite subcollection such that $X = \bigcup_{k=1}^{n} U_{\alpha_k}$. X is said to be **locally compact** if every $x \in X$ is contained in an open set whose closure is compact.

By a **left invariant measure** μ on a locally compact topological group G, we mean a measure on the σ algebra $\mathcal{S}$ generated by the compact sets, such that

(a) if E is compact, then $\mu(E) < \infty$; if E is open, then $\mu(E) > 0$,
(b) if E is measurable and $x \in G$, then xE is measurable and $\mu(xE) = \mu(E)$.

A right invariant measure is defined similarly. A left invariant measure exists and is unique, except for a constant factor. We shall indicate a proof of existence. The method is to compare the sets in $\mathcal{S}$ with a given compact set F with non-empty interior.

Let E be a compact set. For every open set U, containing e, we shall compare the "U size" of E with the "U size" of F. The "U size" of a set $A \subset G$ will be the smallest number of left translations of U whose union contains A. We shall designate the "U size" of A by

$$n(A, U).$$

We then let

$$\mu_U(E) = \frac{n(E, U)}{n(F, U)}.$$

Clearly, $\mu_U(E)$ is a finite positive number. Indeed, if we let $n(E, F)$ be the smallest number of left translations of F such that E is in their union, it is easy to see that $n(E, F)$ is finite. Moreover,

$$\text{(a)} \qquad 0 \leq \mu_U(E) \leq n(E, F)$$

follows from the easy to prove relation

$$n(E, F)n(F, U) \geq n(E, U).$$

The set function $\mu_U(E)$ has the further properties:

(b) $$\mu_U(xE) = \mu_U(E),$$

(c) $$\mu_U(E_1 \cup E_2) \leq \mu_U(E_1) + \mu_U(E_2),$$

and

$$\mu_U(E_1) \geq \mu_U(E_2) \quad \text{if} \quad E_1 \supset E_2.$$

Finally, suppose that $E_1U^{-1} \cap E_2U^{-1} = 0$. Then E_1 may be covered by left translations $x_1U, \ldots, x_nU$ of U and E_2 may be covered by left translations $y_1U, \ldots, y_mU$ of U such that

$$\left(\bigcup_{i=1}^{n} x_iU\right) \cap \left(\bigcup_{j=1}^{m} y_jU\right) = 0,$$

and we have

(d) $$\mu_U(E_1 \cup E_2) = \mu_U(E_1) + \mu_U(E_2).$$

The desired measure μ will be a "generalized limit of μ_U as U tends to zero." We proceed to indicate how this is defined.

Let X be the topological product of the closed intervals $[0, n(E, F)]$ as E varies over all compact sets. Then X is a compact space. For every open set U, containing e, the point ξ_U, whose coordinate at place E is $\mu_U(E)$, is in X. This is so because $0 \leq \mu_U(E) \leq n(E, F)$.

For every U, consider the set

$$S(U) = [\xi_V : V \text{ open}, e \in V, V \subset U].$$

The sets $\overline{S(U)}$ are closed, and it follows from the fact that the intersection of every finite set of open neighborhoods of e is an open neighborhood of e that the sets $\overline{S(U)}$ have the finite intersection property. Since X is compact, we have

$$\bigcup[\overline{S(U)} : U] \neq 0.$$

Let μ be any element of X contained in this intersection. Then μ is a set function defined on the compact subsets of G. It is a relatively easy matter to show that μ may be extended to $\mathcal{S}$ so that it is a left invariant measure, and we leave the details to the reader.

A discussion of uniqueness is not vital to our needs and will be omitted.

For the special case where G is abelian, every left invariant measure is also right invariant. We shall consider only abelian groups, and shall speak of invariant measure as **Haar measure**. Since the groups are abelian, we use the additive notation for the group operation.

Now, let $L_1(G)$ be the set of summable functions, on a locally compact abelian topological group G, with respect to a Haar measure on G. Then, just as for $L_1(R)$, $L_1(G)$ is a Banach algebra with multiplication given by

$$(f * g)(x) = \int f(x - y)g(y)\, dy$$

Also, just as for $L_1(R)$, it follows that

$$\|f * g\| \leq \|f\| \, \|g\|.$$

Moreover, it follows from the fact that G is abelian that $f * g = g * f$. We omit the proof, but give the proof of

PROPOSITION 1. $L_1(G)$ has an identity if and only if G is discrete (i.e., every point is an open set).

Proof. Suppose G is discrete. Then a Haar measure in G is one for which the identity e has measure 1. The function E, which is 1 at e and 0 everywhere else, is in $L_1(G)$. For every $f \in L_1(G)$, and every $x \in G$,

$$\begin{aligned}(E * f)(x) &= \int_G f(x - y)E(y)\, dy \\ &= \sum_{y \in G} f(x - y)E(y) = f(x).\end{aligned}$$

Hence E is the identity for $L_1(G)$.

Suppose, conversely, that $L_1(G)$ has an identity E. Let μ be a Haar measure for G. We show that there is a $k > 0$ such that, for every neighborhood U of e,

$$\mu(U) \geq k.$$

Suppose otherwise. Then, by absolute continuity of the integral, there is a neighborhood U of e such that

$$\int_U |E(x)|\, dx < \frac{1}{2}.$$

Let V be a neighborhood of e such that $V = -V$ and $V + V \subset U$. Then, for every $x \in G$,

$$|\chi_V(x)| = |(E * \chi_V)(x)| = \left| \int_G \chi_V(x - y)E(y)\, dy \right| \leq \int_U |E(x)|\, dx < \frac{1}{2},$$

where χ_V is the characteristic function of V. But this contradicts the fact that $\chi_V(x) = 1$ for every $x \in V$. This shows that there is a $k > 0$ such that every open set has measure greater than k.

Suppose there is an open set U in G which has finite measure but contains infinitely many points. Let n be a positive integer and let $x_1, x_2, \ldots, x_n$ be n distinct points in U. It can be shown that there are disjoint open sets $U_1, \ldots, U_n$, with $x_i \in U_i \subset U$, $i = 1, \ldots, n$. Now,

$$\mu(U) \geq \sum_{i=1}^{n} \mu(U_i) \geq nk.$$

Since $\mu(U) < \infty$, this is impossible. Hence every open set in G, of finite measure, must be finite. In other words, G is discrete.

6.4 Commutative Banach Algebras, Maximal Ideals

We shall now consider arbitrary commutative Banach algebras. We first suppose that the Banach algebra has an identity e.

PROPOSITION 1. If X is a commutative Banach algebra, with an identity e, then $\|e - x\| < 1$ implies x has an inverse.

Proof. Observe that, for every n,

$$\|e - x\|^n \geq \|(e - x)^n\|.$$

Then, the series

$$e + (e - x) + (e - x)^2 + \dots$$

is such that, for every n and p,

$$\|(e - x)^{n+1} + \dots + (e - x)^{n+p}\| \leq \|e - x\|^{n+1} + \dots + \|e - x\|^{n+p}.$$

This implies that the series converges to a point $y \in X$. But

$$xy = [e - (e - x)][e + (e - x) + (e - x)^2 + \dots]$$

and it is easy to see that the product on the right converges to e. Thus, y is the inverse of x.

COROLLARY. The set of points in X for which the inverse exists is open.

Proof. Suppose x has an inverse x^{-1}. Since the norm is continuous on X and the algebraic operations are continuous, there is a neighborhood U of e such that, for every $z \in xU$,

$$\|e - zx^{-1}\| < 1.$$

It follows, by proposition 1, that zx^{-1} has an inverse. But then z has an inverse.

It can be shown easily that the mapping $x \to x^{-1}$ on the open set for which the inverse exists is continuous, but we leave the proof to the reader.

We now consider X merely as an algebra. Certain subsets of X, called ideals, are of special importance. A subset $I \subset X$ is called an **ideal** if

(a) $I \neq X$,

(b) $x, y \in I$ and $a, b \in C$ implies $ax + by \in I$,

(c) $x \in I, y \in X$ implies $xy \in I$.

We consider the following examples of ideals.

(i) Let $C(S)$ be the algebra of continuous functions on a compact Hausdorff space S. Let $A \subset S$ be any non-empty subset of S. Let I be the set of $f \in C(S)$ which vanish on A. Then it is trivial to verify that I satisfies (a), (b), and (c) so that I is an ideal.

(ii) We consider the algebra $L_1(R)$. We shall assume some properties of the Fourier transform of a function $f \in L_1(R)$. The Fourier transform of a function $f \in L_1(R)$ is the function Tf defined by

$$Tf(t) = \frac{1}{2\pi} \int_{-\infty}^{\infty} f(x)e^{-itx}\,dx.$$

The properties we need are that for every $f, g \in L_1(R)$ and $a, b \in C$,

$$T(af + bg) = aTf + bTg$$

and

$$T(f * g) = Tf \cdot Tg,$$

where the product on the right is the point-wise product. We should note that this last fact is the reason for the naturalness of convolution as the multiplication operation in $L_1(G)$.

Let $A \subset R$ be any non-empty set. The set $I \subset L_1(R)$ of functions f for which Tf vanishes on A is then easily seen to be an ideal in $L_1(R)$.

(iii) Every algebra X has a trivial ideal consisting of the one element 0. This is called the null ideal. Suppose X has an identity e. Then, if X has no ideals besides the null ideal, it follows that X is a field. In order to prove this, let $x \in X$, $x \neq 0$. Consider the set

$$I = [xy : y \in X].$$

This set clearly has properties (b) and (c) of an ideal and contains elements different from 0; in particular, x itself. Since X contains no proper ideals (i.e., ideals different from the null ideal), it follows that $I = X$. Hence, there must be $y \in X$ with $xy = e$, so that x has an inverse and X is a field.

In an algebra with identity, e cannot be in any ideal. If I were an ideal and $e \in I$, then $x = ex \in I$ for every $x \in X$ so that $X = I$. But this is impossible.

A **maximal ideal** I is an ideal which is not a proper subset of any ideal in X.

Proposition 2. If X is a commutative Banach algebra with identity, every ideal I in X is contained in a maximal ideal M in X.

Proof. Consider the ideals in X containing I to be ordered by inclusion. Let $\{I_\alpha\}$ be a maximal chain in this ordered set. We need only show that

$$M = \bigcup I_\alpha$$

is an ideal. For this, we first observe that since, for every α, $e \notin I_\alpha$, we have $e \notin M$. Hence, $M \neq X$.

Let $x, y \in M$ and $a, b \in C$. There are α, β such that $x \in I_\alpha$, $y \in I_\beta$. If $I_\beta \supset I_\alpha$, then $ax + by \in I_\beta \subset M$. Finally, let $x \in M$, $y \in X$. There is an α such that $x \in I_\alpha$. Then $xy \in I_\alpha \subset M$. Hence M is an ideal. If M were not a maximal ideal, then $\{I_\alpha\}$ would not be a maximal chain of ideals.

PROPOSITION 3. If X is a commutative Banach algebra with identity, then for every ideal $I \subset X$, the closure $\bar{I}$ of I is also an ideal.

Proof. We first note that I contains no element which has an inverse. For, if $x \in I$ and x^{-1} exists, then $xx^{-1} = e \in I$. Since the set of elements of X which have inverses contains e as an interior point, $e \notin \bar{I}$. Hence $\bar{I} \neq X$.

Let x, $y \in \bar{I}$ and a, $b \in C$. It follows readily from the continuity of the algebraic operations that $ax + by \in \bar{I}$. Moreover, it follows in similar fashion that if $x \in \bar{I}$ and $y \in X$, then $xy \in \bar{I}$. Hence $\bar{I}$ is an ideal.

PROPOSITION 4. x^{-1} exists if and only if x is in no ideal.

Proof. We have already observed that if x^{-1} exists, then x is in no ideal. For the converse, suppose x^{-1} does not exist. Let

$$I = [xy : y \in X].$$

Then $e \notin I$ so that $I \neq X$. It is easily verified that I has the other properties of an ideal.

As always in this section, let X be a commutative Banach algebra with identity. Let I be a closed ideal in X. We consider the quotient algebra X/I. We shall define a norm in X/I for which it turns out to be a Banach algebra.

The elements $\xi \in X/I$ are the subsets of X of the form $x + I$, $x \in X$. Then

$$\xi + \eta = [x + y : x \in \xi, y \in \eta],$$
$$a\xi = [ax : x \in \xi],$$
$$\xi\eta = [xy : x \in \xi, y \in \eta].$$

It is easy to see that these operations are clearly defined, and that X/I is an algebra with additive identity I and multiplicative identity E, where E is the element of X/I to which e belongs. We define a norm in X/I by

$$\|\xi\| = \inf [\|x\| : x \in \xi].$$

By the continuity of the group operation, every ξ is a closed subset of X. Suppose $\|\xi\| = 0$. Then there is a sequence $\{x_n\} \subset \xi$ with $\lim_{n \to \infty} \|x_n\| = 0$. Since ξ is closed, $0 \in \xi$, so that $\xi = I$. Thus $\|\xi\| = 0$ if and only if $\xi = I$.

For every $a \in C$ and $\xi \in X/I$,

$$\|a\xi\| = \inf [\|ax\| : x \in \xi]$$
$$= |a| \inf [\|x\| : x \in \xi] = |a| \cdot \|\xi\|.$$

For every $\xi, \eta \in X/I$,

$$\begin{aligned}\|\xi + \eta\| &= \inf [\|x + y\| : x \in \xi, y \in \eta] \\ &\leq \inf [\|x\| + \|y\| : x \in \xi, y \in \eta] \\ &= \inf [\|x\| : x \in \xi] + \inf [\|y\| : y \in \eta] \\ &= \|\xi\| + \|\eta\|.\end{aligned}$$

For every $\xi, \eta \in X/I$,

$$\begin{aligned}\|\xi\eta\| &= \inf [\|xy\| : x \in \xi, y \in \eta] \\ &\leq \inf [\|x\| \, \|y\| : x \in \xi, y \in \eta] \\ &= \inf [\|x\| : x \in \xi] \cdot \inf [\|y\| : y \in \eta] \\ &= \|\xi\| \, \|\eta\|.\end{aligned}$$

In order to show that X/I is a Banach algebra, it remains only to prove completeness.

Let $\{\xi_n\}$ be a Cauchy sequence in X/I. Let $x_1 \in \xi_1$; there is $x_2 \in \xi_2$ such that $\|x_2 - x_1\| < 2\,\|\xi_2 - \xi_1\|$. There is $x_3 \in \xi_3$ such that $\|x_3 - x_2\| < 2\,\|\xi_3 - \xi_2\|$. In this way, for every n there is $x_n \in \xi_n$ such that $\|x_n - x_{n-1}\| < 2\,\|\xi_n - \xi_{n-1}\|$. The sequence $\{x_n\}$ is evidently a Cauchy sequence. Let $x = \lim_{n\to\infty} x_n$ and let ξ be the element of X/I to which x belongs. Since the mapping of X onto X/I which takes each x into the ξ to which it belongs is continuous, it follows that $\xi = \lim_{n\to\infty} \xi_n$. We have thus proved

PROPOSITION 5. If X is a commutative Banach algebra, and I is a closed ideal in X, then X/I is a Banach algebra with norm

$$\|\xi\| = \min [\|x\| : x \in \xi].$$

We need the fact from algebra that if X is a commutative ring with identity, and M is a maximal ideal in X, then X/M is a field. This is true because if there were $\xi \in X/M$, $\xi \neq M$, which had no inverse, then the multiples of ξ would be an ideal I in X/M. The set $\bigcup[\xi : \xi \in I]$ is then easily seen to be an ideal in X which has M as a proper subideal. This contradicts the assumption that M is a maximal ideal.

We are now ready to prove a theorem which is vital for the subject.

THEOREM 1. The only normed field X is the complex number field (within an isomorphism).

Proof. Let e be the multiplicative identity in X. We shall show that every $x \in X$ is of the form ae, $a \in C$. Suppose then that there were an $x \in X$ such that $x \neq ae$ for every $a \in C$. Since X is a field, it then follows that

$$(x - ae)^{-1}$$

exists for every $a \in C$.

By continuity of the inverse, it follows that

$$\frac{[x - (a + h)e]^{-1} - (x - ae)^{-1}}{h} = [x - (a + h)e]^{-1}(x - ae)^{-1}$$

has a limit, as h converges to 0 in C, and this limit is given by $(x - ae)^{-2}$. Thus the function $(x - ae)^{-1}$ of the complex variable a, with values in X, has a derivative everywhere. Moreover, as a tends to infinity,

$$\|(x - ae)^{-1}\| = |a^{-1}| \left\| \left(\frac{x}{a} - e \right)^{-1} \right\|$$

tends to zero.

Now, let f be any continuous linear functional on the Banach space X. By a direct computation, the complex function

$$f((x - ae)^{-1})$$

of the complex variable a has a derivative everywhere. Moreover, since as a tends to infinity, the norm of $(x - ae)^{-1}$ tends to zero, we have

$$\lim_{a \to \infty} f((x - ae)^{-1}) = 0.$$

Hence, $f((x - ae)^{-1})$ is a bounded entire function, therefore a constant, and the constant is obviously zero. But this holds for every $f \in X'$ so that, by the Hahn-Banach theorem, $(x - ae)^{-1} = 0$. But this is impossible. Hence $x = ae$ for some $a \in C$, and X is isomorphic with C.

COROLLARY. If X is a commutative Banach algebra, with an identity, and M is a maximal ideal in X, then X/M is isomorphic with the complex numbers.

6.5 The Set $C[\mathscr{M}]$

Given a commutative Banach algebra X with identity, the last corollary allows us to associate, with every $x \in X$, a function on the set $\mathscr{M}$ of maximal ideals in X.

Let $x \in X$. For every $M \in \mathscr{M}$, let $\hat{x}(M)$ be the element of X/M to which x belongs. Then $\hat{x}(M)$ is a complex number. We thus have a mapping of X into the set of complex functions on $\mathscr{M}$. In particular, the image of 0 is the zero function, since $0 \in M$ for every $M \in \mathscr{M}$, and the image of e is the function identically 1, since e is in the multiplicative identity of X/M for every $M \in \mathscr{M}$.

Let $x, y \in X$. Then, for every $M \in \mathscr{M}$,

$$\widehat{x + y}(M) = \hat{x}(M) + \hat{y}(M),$$

and

$$\widehat{xy}(M) = \hat{x}(M)\hat{y}(M),$$

and for $x \in X$, $a \in C$, and every $M \in \mathcal{M}$,

$$\widehat{ax}(M) = a\hat{x}(M).$$

This follows since the mapping of X onto X/M is a homomorphism for every $M \in \mathcal{M}$.

Hence, the mapping we have defined is a homomorphism of the algebra X into the function algebra of complex functions on $\mathcal{M}$ with the usual point-wise operations.

Now, for every $M \in \mathcal{M}$, and $x \in X$, let $x \in \xi \in X/M$. Then

$$|\hat{x}(M)| = \|\xi\| = \inf [\|y\| : y \in \xi] \leq \|x\|.$$

Thus $\hat{x}$ is bounded, and with the sup norm,

$$\|\hat{x}\| \leq \|x\|.$$

Thus the mapping which takes x into $\hat{x}$ is a norm decreasing homomorphism of the algebra X into the function algebra.

We shall show that there is a natural topology in $\mathcal{M}$ for which $\mathcal{M}$ is compact and the functions $\hat{x}$ are continuous.

However, we first give a simple and interesting application which does not use this fact.

Let X be the set of complex functions of a real variable of the type

$$x(t) = \sum_{n=-\infty}^{\infty} a_n e^{int}$$

where

$$\sum_{n=-\infty}^{\infty} |a_n| < \infty.$$

Then X is an algebra with respect to the usual point-wise operations for functions. If we define the norm by

$$\|x\| = \sum_{n=-\infty}^{\infty} |a_n|$$

then X is easily seen to be a commutative Banach algebra with identity.

We prove

THEOREM 1. If $x \in X$ is never zero, then its inverse exists.

Proof. Let M be a maximal ideal in X. For $x = e^{it}$, let $\hat{x}(M) = a$. Then

$$|a| \leq \|e^{it}\| = 1.$$

For $x = e^{-it}$, then $\hat{x}(M) = a^{-1}$. So,

$$|a^{-1}| \leq \|e^{-it}\| = 1.$$

It follows that $|a| = 1$. Let $a = e^{it_0}$. Consider next any finite series

$$x(t) = \sum_{n=-N}^{N} a_n e^{int}.$$

It is clear that

$$\hat{x}(M) = \sum_{n=-N}^{N} a_n e^{int_0}.$$

It follows readily, and we leave the easy details to the reader, that for every $x \in X$,

$$\hat{x}(M) = x(t_0).$$

Thus, M is the set of functions in X which vanish at t_0.

This means that if x does not vanish anywhere, then it is in no maximal ideal. But this implies that x^{-1} exists.

6.6 Gelfand Representation for Algebras with Identity

Again, let X be a commutative Banach algebra with identity, and let $\mathcal{M}$ be the set of maximal ideals in X. For every $x \in X$ there is a corresponding $\hat{x}$ which is a bounded function on $\mathcal{M}$. We now define a topology in $\mathcal{M}$. It is the coarsest topology for which the functions $\hat{x}$ are continuous. A subbase for the topology is given by the sets

$$x^{-1}(\sigma) \subset \mathcal{M}$$

for all open spheres σ in C and all $x \in X$.

We show that, with this topology, $\mathcal{M}$ is a compact Hausdorff space. Our method is to show that $\mathcal{M}$ may be imbedded as a weakly closed set in the unit sphere in X' with the weak topology. Since the latter space is a compact Hausdorff space, this will prove that $\mathcal{M}$ is compact.

Now, to every $M \in \mathcal{M}$ there corresponds an x'_M defined by

$$x'_M(x) = \hat{x}(M).$$

Then x'_M is a complex valued function on X. We show that $x'_M \in X'$.

x'_M is linear since

$$x'_M(ax + by) = \widehat{ax + by}(M) = a\hat{x}(M) + b\hat{y}(M) = ax'_M(x) + bx'_M(y).$$

x'_M is bounded since

$$|x'_M(x)| = |\hat{x}(M)| \leq \|x\|.$$

This shows that $x'_M \in X'$.

Moreover, the last inequality implies that $\|x'_M\| \leq 1$ for every $M \in \mathcal{M}$.

We next show that

$$[x'_M : M \in \mathcal{M}]$$

is closed in X' with its weak topology. Accordingly, let x' be in the weak closure of this set. Since $x'_M(e) = 1$, for every $M \in \mathcal{M}$, $x'(e) = 1$. Hence

$x' \neq 0$. For every non-zero $x, y \in X$ and $\epsilon > 0$ there is an $M \in \mathcal{M}$ such that

$$|x'(x) - x'_M(x)| < \frac{\epsilon}{\|y\|}, \; |x'(y) - x'_M(y)| < \frac{\epsilon}{\|x\|}$$

and $|x'(xy) - x'_M(xy)| < \epsilon$.

Since $x'_M(xy) = x'_M(x)x'_M(y)$, we then have

$$\|x'(xy) - x'(x)x'(y)\| \leq \|x'(xy) - x'_M(xy)\|$$
$$+ \|x'_M(xy) - x'_M(x)x'_M(y)\| + \|x'_M(x)\| \, \|x'_M(y) - x'(y)\|$$
$$+ \|x'(y)\| \, \|x'_M(x) - x'(x)\| \leq \epsilon + \|x\| \frac{\epsilon}{\|x\|} + \|y\| \frac{\epsilon}{\|y\|} = 3\epsilon.$$

Since this holds for every $\epsilon > 0$, we have $x'(xy) = x'(x)x'(y)$. Thus x' is a bounded non-trivial homomorphism of the algebra X into the complex numbers. As such, its null space is a maximal ideal K in X. But then $x' = x'_K$. Thus

$$[x'_M : M \in \mathcal{M}]$$

is compact in the weak topology. But the open sets in $\mathcal{M}$ are precisely those induced by the weak topology in the unit sphere in X'. We thus have

THEOREM 1. If X is a commutative Banach algebra with identity, there is a norm decreasing homomorphism of X into the algebra $C(\mathcal{M})$ of continuous functions on the compact Hausdorff space of maximal ideals in X, topologized with the coarsest topology for which the images $\hat{x}$ of $x \in X$ are continuous.

6.7 Analytic Functions

In order to study further properties of $C(\mathcal{M})$, it is necessary to discuss analytic functions of a complex variable with values in a Banach algebra.

Let G be an open set in the complex plane. Let x be a mapping from G into a Banach algebra X. We say that x is analytic in G if, for every $c \in G$, there is a $\varphi \in X$ such that

$$\lim_{h \to 0} \left\| \varphi - \frac{x(c + h) - x(c)}{h} \right\| = 0.$$

We write $x'(c)$ for φ. It is called the **derivative** of x at c. x' is also a mapping from G into X.

PROPOSITION 1. If x is analytic on G and f is a continuous linear functional on X, then the function

$$c \to f(x(c))$$

is a complex valued analytic function on G.

Proof. Since

$$f\left(\frac{x(c + h) - x(c)}{h}\right) = \frac{f(x(c + h)) - f(x(c))}{h},$$

and f is continuous, the convergence in X of

$$\frac{x(c+h)-x(c)}{h} \quad \text{to} \quad \varphi = x'(c)$$

implies that

$$\lim_{h\to 0} \frac{f(x(c+h)) - f(x(c))}{h} = f(x'(c)).$$

It is to proposition 1 and the Hahn-Banach theorem that much of the theory of an analytic function of a complex variable, with values in a Banach algebra, is due.

Let Γ be a curve of class C' in the complex plane, and let x be a continuous function on Γ with values in X. We define the integral of x on Γ.

Let Γ be given by a pair f, g of continuously differentiable functions on $[0, 1]$. Let

$$\pi = [0 = t_0 < t_1 < \ldots < t_n = 1]$$

be a partition of $[0, 1]$ and let $p_i = (f(\tau_i), g(\tau_i))$, $\tau_i \in [t_{i-1}, t_i]$, $i = 1, \ldots, n$, and $p = (p_1, \ldots, p_n)$. Let

$$\sigma(\pi, p) = \sum_{i=1}^{n} x(p_i)\sqrt{\{f'(\tau_i)\}^2 + \{g'(\tau_i)\}^2}(t_i - t_{i-1}).$$

We state without proof, the proof being just as in the standard case well known to the reader, that for every $\epsilon > 0$ there is a $\delta > 0$ such that if $\|\pi\| < \delta$, $\|\pi'\| < \delta$, then

$$\|\sigma(\pi, p) - \sigma(\pi', p')\| < \epsilon$$

for every choice of p and p'. It follows that for every sequence $\{\pi_n\}$, whose norms converge to zero, and every $\{p^{(n)}\}$, the sequence

$$\{\sigma(\pi_n, p^{(n)})\}$$

converges in X, and always to the same value. This value is

$$\int_\Gamma x(z)\, dz.$$

Proposition 2. If x is analytic on an open set G, if Γ is a simple closed curve of class C' such that Γ and its interior are in G, then

$$\int_\Gamma x(z)\, dz = 0.$$

Proof. Let

$$y = \int_\Gamma x(z)\, dz.$$

Then for every continuous linear functional f on X, it follows from the definition of the integral as a limit of Riemann sums that

$$f(y) = \int_\Gamma f(x(z))\, dz.$$

Since $f \circ x$ is analytic, we have

$$\int_\Gamma f(x(z))\,dz = 0.$$

Hence $f(y) = 0$ for every $f \in X'$ so that, by the Hahn-Banach theorem, $y = 0$.

PROPOSITION 3. If x and Γ are as in proposition 2, then for every z in the interior of Γ, we have

$$x(z) = \frac{1}{2\pi i}\int_\Gamma \frac{x(\zeta)}{\zeta - z}\,d\zeta.$$

We omit the proof of this proposition and of the fact that, just as in the classical case, if x is analytic on an open set, then all its derivatives exist and the Cauchy formula

$$x^{(n)}(z) = \frac{n!}{2\pi i}\int_\Gamma \frac{x(\zeta)}{(\zeta - z)^{n+1}}\,d\zeta$$

is valid.

From this, we obtain

PROPOSITION 4. If x is analytic in the open disk $|z - z_0| < r$, then there is a Taylor series

$$x(z_0) + x'(z_0)(z - z_0) + \dots + x^{(n)}(z_0)\frac{(z - z_0)^n}{n!} + \dots$$

which converges absolutely to x in the disk.

Proof. Let $|z - z_0| < r' < r$. Then $\|x(\zeta)\|$ is continuous, hence bounded, on the circle $|\zeta - z_0| = r'$. Now,

$$\frac{x(\zeta)}{\zeta - z} = \frac{x(\zeta)}{\zeta - z_0}\cdot\frac{1}{1 - \dfrac{z - z_0}{\zeta - z_0}} = \sum_{n=0}^{\infty}\frac{x(\zeta)}{(\zeta - z_0)^{n+1}}(z - z_0)^n,$$

where the series converges uniformly on $|\zeta - z_0| = r'$. It follows that term by term integration is valid and, by the Cauchy integral formula, the proposition is proved.

6.8 Isomorphism Theorem for Algebras with Identity

Let $x \in X$. By the **spectrum** of x we mean the set of complex numbers a for which $(x - ae)^{-1}$ does not exist.

PROPOSITION 1. For every $x \in X$, the spectrum of x is equal to the set of values assumed by $\hat{x}(M)$, $M \in \mathcal{M}$.

Proof. Suppose $\hat{x}(M) = a$, $M \in \mathcal{M}$. Then $\hat{x}(M) = a\hat{e}(M)$, or

$$\widehat{(x - ae)}(M) = 0.$$

Thus $x - ae \in M$. This means that $(x - ae)^{-1}$ does not exist, so that a is in the spectrum of x.

Conversely, suppose $(x - ae)^{-1}$ does not exist. Then $x - ae \in M$ for some $M \in \mathcal{M}$, so that $\hat{x}(M) = a$.

PROPOSITION 2. For every $x \in X$,

$$\sup\,[\,|x(M)| : M \in \mathcal{M}] = \lim_{n\to\infty} \sqrt[n]{\|x^n\|}.$$

Proof. Let $\sup |\hat{x}(M)| = a$. Then, by proposition 1, $x - ze$ has an inverse whenever $|z| > a$. Thus

$$z(e - zx)^{-1} = \left(\frac{1}{z}e - x\right)^{-1}$$

exists whenever $|z| < 1/a$. It is analytic in this disk, as is seen by a direct computation of the derivative. Hence, it is given by the Taylor series

$$z(e - zx)^{-1} = z + z^2x + \dots + z^{n+1}x^n + \dots,$$

which converges absolutely for $|z| < 1/a$. Fix $0 < |z| < 1/a$. Then

$$\lim_{n\to\infty} \|z^nx^n\| = 0.$$

It follows that, for all n sufficiently large,

$$\|x^n\| \le \frac{1}{|z|^n}.$$

Hence,

$$\limsup_{n\to\infty} \sqrt[n]{\|x^n\|} \le \frac{1}{|z|}$$

whenever $|z| < 1/a$, so that

$$\limsup_{n\to\infty} \sqrt[n]{\|x^n\|} \le a.$$

On the other hand, we know that

$$\|x\| \ge \sup\,[\hat{x}(M) : M \in \mathcal{M}],$$

for every $x \in X$. In particular,

$$\|x^n\| \ge \sup\,[\hat{x}^n(M) : M \in \mathcal{M}] = a^n.$$

Hence,

$$\sqrt[n]{\|x^n\|} \ge a,$$

and

$$\liminf_{n\to\infty} \sqrt[n]{\|x^n\|} \ge a.$$

We say that x is in the **radical** of X if

$$\lim_{n\to\infty} \sqrt[n]{\|x^n\|} = 0.$$

We then have

COROLLARY 1. x is in the radical of X if and only if x is contained in every maximal ideal.

Thus the radical of X is also the intersection of the maximal ideals in X.

An algebra is called **semi-simple** if the intersection of its maximal ideals consists of 0 alone.

COROLLARY 2. The canonical mapping of X into $C(\mathcal{M})$ is one-one if and only if X is semi-simple.

Suppose now that, for every $x \in X$, $\|x^2\| = \|x\|^2$. Since

$$\max [|\hat{x}(M)| : M \in \mathcal{M}] = \lim_{n\to\infty} \sqrt[n]{\|x^n\|} = \lim_{n\to\infty} \sqrt[2^n]{\|x^{2^n}\|} = \lim_{n\to\infty} \|x\| = \|x\|,$$

it follows that the canonical mapping of X into $C(\mathcal{M})$ is a norm preserving isomorphism. In particular, this condition implies semi-simplicity.

Suppose next that a mapping of X into X which takes each x into an x^* exists such that

$$(ax + by)^* = \bar{a}x^* + \bar{b}y^*,$$
$$(x^*)^* = x$$
$$(xy)^* = y^*x^*.$$

Such a mapping is called an **involution.**

For example, in $C(X)$, the mapping which takes each function into its complex conjugate is an involution. A similar remark holds for $L_1(G)$. In the Banach algebra of bounded operators on a Hilbert space, the mapping which takes each operator into its adjoint operator is an involution.

We prove

THEOREM 1. If X is a commutative Banach algebra, with an identity and an involution, such that for every $x \in X$,

$$\widehat{(x^*)} = (\bar{\hat{x}})$$

and

$$\|x^2\| = \|x\|^2,$$

then $\hat{X} = C(\mathcal{M})$, and the canonical mapping is an isometry.

Proof. We first note that if $M_1 \neq M_2$, there is an $x \in X$ such that $\hat{x}(M_1) \neq \hat{x}(M_2)$. For, let $x \in M_1$, $x \notin M_2$. Then $\hat{x}(M_1) = 0$, $\hat{x}(M_2) \neq 0$.

Let $x \in X$. Define

$$x_1 = \frac{1}{2}(x + x^*), \quad x_2 = \frac{1}{2i}(x - x^*).$$

Then,

$$x_1{}^* = \frac{1}{2}(x^* + x) = x_1$$

and

$$x_2{}^* = -\frac{1}{2i}(x^* - x) = x_2.$$

It follows that $\hat{x}_1$ and $\hat{x}_2$ are real, and

$$x = x_1 + ix_2.$$

Now, $\hat{x}(M_1) \neq \hat{x}(M_2)$ implies either

$$\hat{x}_1(M_1) \neq \hat{x}_1(M_2) \text{ or } \hat{x}_2(M_1) \neq \hat{x}_2(M_2).$$

Let R be the subset of $\hat{X}$ of real valued functions. Then R is an algebra over the reals which, as has been shown above, satisfies the Stone-Weierstrass condition. Hence, R is dense in the set of continuous real functions on $\mathcal{M}$. It follows that $\hat{X}$ is dense in $C(\mathcal{M})$.

But $\|x^2\| = \|x\|^2$ implies that the mapping $X \to \hat{X}$ is an isometry. Since X is complete, so is $\hat{X}$. Hence, $\hat{X} = C(\mathcal{M})$.

6.9 Algebras without Identity

We now remove the hypothesis that the commutative Banach algebra X has an identity.

First, let $\tilde{X}$ be the Banach algebra obtained by adjoining an identity to X. Let $\tilde{I}$ be any ideal in $\tilde{X}$ which is not a subset of X. Consider the set

$$I = X \cap \tilde{I}.$$

Then I is a proper subset of X. For, otherwise, $\tilde{I} \supset X$ and, since $\tilde{I} \neq \tilde{X}$, this implies $\tilde{I} = X$. But this contradicts the assumption that $\tilde{I}$ is not a subset of X. Next, $x, y \in I$ and $a, b \in C$ implies $ax + by \in I$ and $x \in I$, $y \in X$ implies $xy \in I$. Hence, I is an ideal in X.

Since $\tilde{I}$ is not a subset of X, it contains an element of the form

$$y = x - e, x \in X.$$

For every $z \in X$,

$$-z + xz = (x - e)z \in I,$$

since $(x - e)z \in \tilde{I}$ and $-z + xz \in X$. There is thus an $x \in X$ such that $xz - z \in I$, for every $z \in X$. Such an element is called an **identity modulo *I*.** If an ideal I is such that there is an identity modulo I in X, then I is called a **regular** ideal.

We have shown above that for every ideal $\tilde{I}$ in $\tilde{X}$, which is not a subset of X, $I = \tilde{I} \cap X$ is a regular ideal in X.

Conversely, let I be a regular ideal in X, and let x be an identity modulo I. Let

$$\tilde{I} = [z : z \in \tilde{X},\ xz \in I].$$

Now, $\tilde{I}$ is not a subset of X. For $x - e \notin X$. But

$$x(x - e) = x^2 - x \in I,$$

so that $x - e \in \tilde{I}$.

Next, $I = \tilde{I} \cap X$. For, $z \in \tilde{I} \cap X$ implies $z \in X$ and $xz \in I$. But

$$xz - z \in I,$$

so that $z \in I$. Conversely, $z \in I$ implies $z \in X$ and $xz \in I$ so that $z \in \tilde{I}$.

That $\tilde{I}$ is an ideal is an easy verification which we omit.

We show that if $\tilde{I}$ and $\tilde{J}$ are ideals in $\tilde{X}$, neither a subset of X, then $I = \tilde{I} \cap X$ equals $J = \tilde{J} \cap X$ implies $\tilde{I} = \tilde{J}$.

There are $x, y \in X$ such that $x - e \in \tilde{I}$, $y - e \in \tilde{J}$. Then

$$yx - y = y(x - e) \in I$$
$$yx - x = x(y - e) \in J = I,$$

so that $y - x \in I$.

Suppose $ae + z \in \tilde{I}$. Then $ax + xz \in I$. But $-z + xz = z(-e + x) \in I$. Then $ax + z = ax + xz - z(-e + x) \in I$. Accordingly,

$$ae + z = a(e - y) + a(y - x) + ax + z \in \tilde{J}.$$

Hence $\tilde{I} \subset \tilde{J}$. In the same fashion, $\tilde{J} \subset \tilde{I}$, and we have proved

PROPOSITION 1. The ideals in $\tilde{X}$ which are not subsets of X are in one-one correspondence with the regular ideals in X by the mapping

$$\tilde{I} \to I = \tilde{I} \cap X.$$

COROLLARY. The maximal ideals in $\tilde{X}$, different from X, are in one-one correspondence, by the above mapping, with the maximal regular ideals in X.

We note, moreover, that if X is a commutative Banach algebra without identity, then if M is a regular maximal ideal in X, the quotient algebra X/M is isomorphic to the complex field.

Indeed, suppose $\tilde{X}$ is the extension of X obtained by adjoining the identity, and let $\tilde{I}$ be any ideal in $\tilde{X}$ which is not a subset of X. Then every coset $\tilde{I} + (x + ae)$ of $\tilde{I}$ has non-empty intersection with X. For, if $a = 0$, then $x \in \tilde{I} + (x + ae)$. Suppose $a \neq 0$. Let $y + be \in \tilde{I}$, $b \neq 0$. Then,

$$-\frac{a}{b}y - ae \in \tilde{I} \text{ and } -\frac{a}{b}y + x \in X \cap [\tilde{I} + (x + ae)].$$

We next show that for every $x \in X$,

$$I + x = (\tilde{I} + x) \cap X.$$

For, $y \in I + x$ implies $y \in \tilde{I} + x$ and $y \in X$. Conversely, $y \in (\tilde{I} + x) \cap X$ implies $y = z + ae + x$ and $y = t \in X$. Then $a = 0$ and $y = z + x$. Then, since $z \in \tilde{I}$ and $z \in X$, we have $z \in I$ and $y \in I + x$.

This shows that $\tilde{X}/\tilde{I}$ is isomorphic with X/I. In particular, if M is a maximal regular ideal in X, then X/M is isomorphic with the complex field.

For every $x \in X$, and every maximal regular ideal M in X, let $\hat{x}(M)$ be the element of X/M to which x belongs. This defines a mapping from X into the set of complex functions on the set $\mathcal{M}$ of maximal regular ideals in X. But, from the isomorphism of X/M with $\tilde{X}/\tilde{M}$, the function $\hat{x}$ is also a function on the set $\tilde{\mathcal{M}} \sim \{X\}$, of maximal ideals in $\tilde{X}$. Since $x \in X$, and X is a maximal ideal in $\tilde{X}$, these are precisely the functions in $(\hat{\tilde{X}})$ which vanish at the maximal ideal X.

Thus $\hat{X}$ is an algebra of continuous functions on $\tilde{\mathcal{M}}$ which vanish at the point X. Identifying each maximal regular ideal M with the maximal ideal $\tilde{M}$ in $\tilde{X}$ which contains it, the space $\mathcal{M} = \tilde{\mathcal{M}} \sim \{X\}$, with the topology induced by the topology in $\tilde{\mathcal{M}}$, is locally compact. For every open set $G \subset \tilde{\mathcal{M}}$, with $X \in G$, the set $\tilde{\mathcal{M}} \sim G$ is a compact subset of $\tilde{\mathcal{M}}$. There is a G of this sort such that, for every $\tilde{M} \in G$, $|\hat{x}(\tilde{M})| < \epsilon$, given $\epsilon > 0$ and $\hat{x} \in \hat{X}$.

We say that a function f on a locally compact space vanishes at infinity if, for every $\epsilon > 0$, there is a compact set such that $|f(t)| < \epsilon$ on the complement of the set. By the above, the functions $\hat{x}$ on $\mathcal{M}$ are continuous and vanish at infinity.

The topology in $\mathcal{M}$ may be defined directly as the coarsest topology for which the functions $\hat{x}$ on $\mathcal{M}$ are continuous, but we do not discuss this approach here.

We have proved

THEOREM 1. If X is a commutative Banach algebra without identity, there is a norm decreasing homomorphism of X into the algebra $C(\mathcal{M})$ of continuous functions, which vanish at infinity, on the locally compact Hausdorff space of maximal regular ideals in X, topologized by the coarsest topology for which the images $\hat{x}$ of $x \in X$ are continuous.

(The proof that the mapping is norm decreasing is the same as for the case of an algebra with identity.)

PROPOSITION 2. For every $x \in X$,

$$\sup |\hat{x}(M)| = \lim_{n \to \infty} \sqrt[n]{\|x^n\|}.$$

Proof.

$$\sup |\hat{x}(\tilde{M})| = \lim_{n\to\infty} \sqrt[n]{\|x^n\|}\,.$$

But $\hat{x}(M) = \hat{x}(\tilde{M})$ and $\hat{x}(X) = 0$.

COROLLARY 1. If X is a Banach algebra without identity, then the radical of X is the intersection of its maximal regular ideals.

COROLLARY 2. The canonical mapping of X into the continuous functions on $\mathcal{M}$, which vanish at infinity, is one-one if and only if X is semi-simple.

We finally have

THEOREM 2. If X is a commutative Banach algebra with involution, but without identity, such that $\widehat{(x^*)} = \overline{(\hat{x})}$ and $\|x^2\| = \|x\|^2$, for every $x \in X$, then $\hat{X} = C(\mathcal{M})$, the algebra of continuous functions on $\mathcal{M}$, which vanish at infinity, and the canonical mapping is an isometry.

Proof. Just as for theorem 1, Sec. 6.8, except that the form of the Stone-Weierstrass theorem which is used says that, if the function 1 is not in the given algebra A, then A consists of all continuous functions on the compact space X which vanish at a given point.

6.10 Application to $L_1(G)$

We apply some of the above results to the case of the group algebra, $L_1(G)$, where G is a locally compact abelian group.

We first discuss approximate identities in $L_1(G)$. Let $\{U_\alpha\}$ be a directed set of neighborhoods of 0 in G which forms a base for the topology at 0. For each α, let F_α be a continuous function on G, such that

(a) $$F_\alpha(t) \geq 0 \text{ for all } t \in G,$$

(b) $$F_\alpha(t) = 0 \text{ for all } t \notin U_\alpha,$$

and

(c)

$$\int_G F_\alpha(t)\, dt = 1.$$

Such a system of functions is called an **approximate identity** in $L_1(G)$. (For the case $L_1(R)$ we defined approximate identity somewhat more generally.) $L_1(G)$ has an identity only if G is discrete. The approximate identity assumes many of the roles of an identity.

PROPOSITION 1. For every $f \in L_1(G)$,

$$\lim_\alpha \|F_\alpha * f - f\| = 0.$$

Proof. We note that $(F_\alpha * f)(t) = \int_G f(t-u)F_\alpha(u)\,du$, and that $f(t) = \int_G f(t)F_\alpha(u)\,du$. Then

$$\begin{aligned}\|F_\alpha * f - f\| &= \int_G dt\left|\int_G [f(t+u) - f(t)]F_\alpha(u)\,du\right|\\ &\le \int_G dt\int_G |f(t+u) - f(t)|F_\alpha(u)\,du\\ &= \int_G \left\{\int_G |f(t+u) - f(t)|\,dt\right\}F_\alpha(u)\,du\\ &= \int_{U_\alpha} \left\{\int_G |f(t+u) - f(t)|\,dt\right\}F_\alpha(u)\,du.\end{aligned}$$

But, for every $\epsilon > 0$, there is an α_0 such that $\alpha > \alpha_0$ implies $\int_G |f(t+u) - f(t)|\,dt < \epsilon$ for every $u \in U_\alpha$. The result then follows.

For every $u \in G$, let f_u be the function given by $f_u(t) = f(t+u)$. We now state

Corollary. If $u \in G$ and $f \in L_1(G)$, then

$$\lim_\alpha \|F_{\alpha,u} * f - f_u\| = 0.$$

We shall need the characters of the group G. By a **character** χ of G we understand a continuous complex-valued function on G such that, for every $t \in G$, $|\chi(t)| = 1$, and for every t, $u \in G$, $\chi(t+u) = \chi(t)\chi(u)$. It is easily seen that the point-wise product of characters is a character and that the characters form a group.

It is an important fact that the characters in G are in one-one correspondence with the maximal ideals in $L_1(G)$, and we now discuss this relationship.

Proposition 2. For every maximal regular ideal M in $L_1(G)$,

$$\lim_\alpha \hat{f}_{\alpha,t}(M)$$

exists, is a character in G, and is independent of the choice of approximate identity $\{f_\alpha\}$.

Proof. Let $f \in L_1(G) \sim M$. Then $\hat{f}(M) \neq 0$. Now,

$$\lim_\alpha \|f_t - f * f_{\alpha,t}\| = 0,$$

and

$$\lim_\alpha |\hat{f}_t(M) - \hat{f}(M)\hat{f}_{\alpha,t}(M)| = 0.$$

Hence,

$$\lim_\alpha \hat{f}_{\alpha,t}(M) = \frac{\hat{f}_t(M)}{\hat{f}(M)}.$$

The details of the proof that $\lim\limits_{\alpha} \hat{f}_{\alpha,t}(M)$ is a character are left to the reader. It is clearly independent of the choice of $\{f_\alpha\}$. We designate the character associated in this way with M by χ_M.

We next present an important formula relating f to χ_M.

PROPOSITION 3. For every $f \in L_1(G)$, and every M, we have

$$f(M) = \int_G f(t)\chi_M(t)\,dt.$$

Proof. A set in a locally compact space is said to be σ compact if it is contained in the union of countably many compact sets. It is not very hard to show, and we leave the proof to the reader, that, if $E \subset G$ and $\mu(E) < \infty$, then E is σ compact. It follows that for every neighborhood U of e, E may be covered by a countable set of translations of U. This also holds for the support of f since it is easily seen to be the union of countably many sets of finite measure.

Suppose f is non-negative. Since $\chi_M(t) = \lim\limits_{\alpha} \hat{f}_{\alpha,t}(M)$, for every $\epsilon > 0$ there is an α such that

$$|\hat{f}_{\alpha,t}(M) - \chi_M(t)| < \epsilon.$$

Let U be such that $UU^{-1} \subset U_\alpha$, and let $E_1, E_2, \ldots, E_n, \ldots$ be such that they are disjoint, the support of f is contained in their union, and each is contained in a translation of U. Let

$$f_n(t) = f(t)C_{E_n}(t)$$

where C_{E_n} is the characteristic function of E_n. Then, for $t \in E_n$,

$$\begin{aligned}
&\left| \hat{f}_n(M) - \int_G f_n(t)\chi_M(t)\,dt \right| \\
&\qquad = \left| \frac{\hat{f}_n(M)}{\int f_n(t)\,dt} - \int_G \frac{f_n(t)}{\int f_n(t)\,dt}\chi_M(t)\,dt \right| \int_G f_n(t)\,dt \\
&\qquad = \left| \int_{E_n} [\hat{f}_{\alpha,t}(M) - \chi_M(t)] \frac{f_n(t)}{\int f_n(t)\,dt} \right| \int_G f_n(t)\,dt \\
&\qquad \leq \epsilon \int_G f_n(t)\,dt = \epsilon \int_{E_n} f(t)\,dt.
\end{aligned}$$

But, then, by summing over n,

$$\left| \hat{f}(M) - \int_G f(t)\chi_M(t)\,dt \right| \leq \epsilon \int_G f(t)\,dt.$$

As a corollary, we obtain the fact that $M_1 \neq M_2$ implies $\chi_{M_1} \neq \chi_{M_2}$.

Let χ be a character in G. For each $f \in L_1(G)$, we consider the complex number $\int_G f(t)\chi(t)\,dt$. It can be shown that this mapping of $L_1(G)$ into the complex numbers is an algebraic homomorphism. The only difficulty is with multiplication. Not all of $L_1(G)$ is mapped into 0. For suppose $f \in L_1(G)$ and $\int_G f(t)\, dt \neq 0$. Then

$$\int_G f(t)\overline{\chi(t)}\chi(t)\, dt \neq 0.$$

It follows that

$$M_\chi = \left[f : \int_G f(t)\chi(t)\, dt = 0\right]$$

is a maximal regular ideal in $L_1(G)$. Moreover, it is not hard to prove that for every character χ, we have $\chi = \chi_{M_\chi}$. It follows from the above that the characters in G are in one-one correspondence with the maximal ideals in $L_1(G)$.

As an example, let G be the circle of real numbers modulo 1. The characters on G are easily seen to be the functions $e^{in\pi t}$, $n = 0, \pm 1, \pm 2, \ldots$. The maximal regular ideals are thus in one-one correspondence with the integers. Thus, for $f \in L_1(G)$ and any maximal regular ideal n, we have

$$\hat{f}(n) = \int_G f(t)e^{int}\, dt.$$

These are simply the Fourier coefficients of f.

The theory we are discussing is accordingly seen to be simply that of Fourier analysis on an arbitrary locally compact abelian group. A surprisingly large portion of the theory holds in this setting, which gives a deeper insight into the nature of things. The interested reader will have no trouble finding books and papers where this subject is developed. In particular, the books by Naimark [1] and Loomis [1] and articles by Gelfand [1], Raikov [1], and Naimark [2], can be recommended.

EXERCISES

1.1 In a Banach algebra, with identity e, show that there is an equivalent norm for which $\|e\| = 1$.

1.2 If X is a Banach space, show that the set of bounded operators of X into itself, with the operator norm, is a Banach algebra.

1.3 Find a sequence $\{p_n\}$ of algebraic polynomials which forms an approximate identity for $L_1(I)$, where I is the interval $[-1, 1]$.

1.4 Find a sequence $\{t_n\}$ of trigonometric polynomials which forms an approximate identity for $L_1(J)$, where J is the interval $[-\pi, \pi]$.

1.5 Give a sequence $\{\varphi_n\}$ of functions of class C^∞ which forms an approximate identity for $L_1(R)$.

1.6 Show that every Banach algebra A is isomorphic to a subalgebra of the algebra of bounded operators of a Banach space into itself.

1.7 If A is a semi-simple Banach algebra and it admits another norm for which it is also a Banach algebra, show that the two Banach algebras are equivalent.

2.1 Verify that the system defined in Sec. 6.2 is indeed a Banach algebra with identity.

3.1 In a topological group, show that the left translations of a base for the open sets containing the identity form a base for all the open sets.

3.2 Define topological group by axioms on a neighborhood system of e.

3.3 In a topological group, show that the component of the identity is an open and closed subgroup.

3.4 Show that if $x_1, \ldots, x_n$ is a finite subset of an open set U in a locally compact group, there are pair-wise disjoint open $U_i \subset U$, $x_i \in U_i$, $i = 1, \ldots, n$.

3.5 Prove the easy-to-prove relation

$$n(E, F)n(F, U) \geq n(E, U).$$

3.6 Show that the set function μ, defined for compact sets in G, may be extended to a left invariant measure on $\mathcal{S}$.

3.7 Give an example of a locally compact topological group whose Haar measure is not totally σ finite.

3.8 If G is a locally compact group with Haar measure μ, then if $\mu(E) < \infty$, show that E may be covered by a countable set of compact sets in G.

3.9 Define a "natural" topology for the multiplicative group $R - \{0\}$ and show that this yields a topological group.

3.10 Determine Haar measure explicitly for this group.

3.11 Do the same as in exercise 3.10 for the multiplicative group of complex numbers.

3.12 Define a topology for the group of rotations of the 2 sphere and show that this is a topological group.

3.13 Define a left invariant measure explicitly for the group of exercise 3.12.

3.14 If G is an abelian locally compact group, give the details of the proof that $L_1(G)$ is an abelian Banach algebra.

3.15 Show that if G is a locally compact abelian group and $f \in L_1(G)$ and U is any neighborhood of e, then the support of f may be covered by a countable set of translations of U.

4.1 Show that if X is a commutative Banach algebra with identity and H is the open set on which the inverse exists, the mapping $\varphi : x \to x^{-1}$ is continuous on H.

4.2 If $f, g \in L_1(R)$ and T is the Fourier transform, show that

$$T(f * g) = Tf \cdot Tg.$$

4.3 Define the Fourier transform for the n dimensional case, and prove the result of exercise 4.2 for this case.

4.4 Given an $A \subset R$, show that the set I of functions $f \in L_1(R)$ for which $T(f)$ vanishes on A is an ideal in $L_1(R)$.

4.5 Are there ideals in $L_1(R)$ which are not of the type described in exercise 4.4?

4.6 Give details of the proofs that if $x, y \in \bar{I}$ and $a, b \in C$, then $ax + by \in \bar{I}$; and that if $x \in \bar{I}$ and $y \in X$, then $xy \in \bar{I}$.

4.7 Give details of the proof that for every continuous linear functional f on the Banach space X, $f((x - ae)^{-1})$ is an entire function.

5.1 If X is the set of complex functions of a real variable of the type

$$x(t) = \sum_{n=-\infty}^{\infty} a_n e^{int},$$

where

$$\sum_{n=-\infty}^{\infty} |a_n| < \infty \quad \text{and} \quad \|x\| = \sum_{n=-\infty}^{\infty} |a_n|,$$

show that X is a Banach algebra with identity.

6.1 If x' is a bounded non-trivial homomorphism of a commutative Banach algebra X, with identity, into the complex numbers, show that its null space is a maximal ideal in X.

7.1 With $\sigma(\pi, p)$ defined as in Sec. 6.7, show that for every $\epsilon > 0$ there is a $\delta > 0$ such that $\|\pi\| < \delta$, $\|\pi'\| < \delta$ implies

$$\|\sigma(\pi, p) - \sigma(\pi', p')\| < \epsilon.$$

7.2 If x is analytic in an open set G, and Γ is a simple closed curve of type C', such that Γ and its interior are in G, show that

$$x(z) = \frac{1}{2\pi i} \int_\Gamma \frac{x(\zeta)}{\zeta - z}\, d\zeta$$

for z in the interior of Γ.

7.4 Show that if $y = \int_\Gamma x(z)\, dz$, Γ of class C', then for every continuous linear functional f on X,

$$f(y) = \int_\Gamma f(x(z))\, dz.$$

9.1 Show that if X is compact, the maximal ideals in $C(X)$ correspond to points.

9.2 Find all the maximal regular ideals in the Banach algebra of continuous functions on R which vanish at infinity.

9.3 Let A be a commutative Banach algebra with maximal regular ideal space $\mathcal{M}$. For every $S \subset \mathcal{M}$, the kernel of S is defined as $k(S) = \bigcap [M : M \in S]$. Then $k(S)$ is a closed ideal. If I is an ideal, its hull is defined as $h(I) = [M : I \subset M]$. Show that for every $S \subset \mathcal{M}$, $\bar{S} = h(k(S))$.

10.1 Give the details of the proof that $\lim_{\alpha} \hat{f}_{\alpha,t}(M)$ in proposition 2 is a character.

10.2 In the character group $\hat{G}$ of a group G, a topology is introduced by taking as a base for the topology at the group identity those sets of characters determined by open sets A containing 1 and compact sets $K \subset G$, as those characters which take K into A. Show that $\hat{G}$ is then a topological group.

10.3 Show that $\hat{R}$ is isomorphic with R.

10.4 Show that $\hat{G}$ is discrete if and only if G is compact.

10.5 Show that $\hat{G}$ is compact if and only if G is discrete.

10.6 Show that $\widehat{G \times H} = \hat{G} \times \hat{H}$ both algebraically and topologically.

10.7 For every character χ in G show that the mapping $f \to \int_G f(t)\chi(t)\,dt$ is a homomorphism of $L_1(G)$ into the complex numbers.

10.8 Show that, for every character χ, we have $\chi = \chi_{M_\chi}$.

10.9 Show that the characters for the circle of real numbers modulo 1 are the functions $e^{in\pi t}$, $n = 0, \pm 1, \pm 2, \ldots$.

10.10 Let G be the group of integers modulo 2 and $H = G \times G \times \ldots$, a denumerable product. Discuss the character group of H.

10.11 Identifying sequences of 0's and 1's with real numbers, discuss the characters of the group H in exercise 10.10 as functions on $[0, 1]$. Show that they form a complete orthonormal set for $L_2[0, 1]$.

REFERENCES

Aronszajn, N., and K. T. Smith, *Functional Spaces and Functional Completion*, Annales de l'Institut Fourier, t. VI, 1956, p. 125–85.

Bari, N., *Trigonometrical Series* (in Russian). Moscow, 1961.

Gelfand, I., *Normierte Ringe*, Matematiceskii Sbornik, N.S. 9, 1941, p. 3–23.

Goffman, C., *Real Functions*. New York: Holt, Rinehart & Winston, Inc., 1953.

Hardy, G. H., *Divergent Series*. Oxford: Clarendon Press, 1956.

Hardy, G. H., and W. W. Rogosinski, *Fourier Series*. New York: Cambridge University Press, 1950.

Hausdorff, F., *Mengenlehre*. New York: Dover Publications, Inc., 1944.

Kelley, J. L., *General Topology*. Princeton, N. J.: D. Van Nostrand Co., Inc., 1955.

Kuratowski, C., *Topologie I*. Warsaw-Lwow: Monografie Matematyczne, 1933.

Loomis, L. H., *An Introduction to Abstract Harmonic Analysis*. Princeton, N. J.: D. Van Nostrand Co., Inc., 1953.

Lorch, E. R., *Spectral Theory*. New York: Oxford University Press, 1962.

Naimark, M. A., (1) *Normed Rings*, (translated from Russian). Groningen: P. Noordhoff, 1960; (2) *Rings with Involution*, Translation, American Math. Soc., No. 25, 1950.

Natanson, I. P., *Konstruktive Funktionentheorie*, (translated from Russian). Berlin: Akademie Verlag, 1955.

Nehari, Z., *Conformal Mapping*, New York: McGraw-Hill Book Company, 1952.

Raikov, D. A., "Die harmonische Analyse auf kommutativen Gruppen mit Haarschem Mass und die Theorie der Charaktere" (translated from Russian), *Sowietische Arbeiten zur Funktionalanalysis*. Berlin, 1954.

Widder, D. V., *The Laplace Transform*. Princeton; Princeton Press, 1941.

Zeller, K., *Theorie der Limitierungsverfahrung*. Berlin: Springer, 1958.

Zygmund, A., *Trigonometrical Series*, Vol. I. New York: Cambridge University Press, 1959.

GENERAL REFERENCES

Akhiezer, N., and I. M. Glazman, *Theory of Linear Operators in Hilbert Space*, (translated from Russian). New York: Ungar, 1961.

Banach, S., *Théorie des opérations linéaires*. Warsaw: Monografie Matematyczne, 1932.

Bourbaki, N., *Espaces Vectoriels Topologiques, Éléments de mathématique, livre V*. Paris: Hermann, 1953 and 1955.

Bourbaki, N., *Intégration, Éléments de mathématique, livre VI*. Paris: Hermann, 1952.

Day, M. M., *Normed Linear Spaces*. Berlin: Springer, 1958.

Dieudonné, J., and L. Schwartz, *La dualité dans les espaces (F) et (LF)*, Annales de l'Institut Fourier, t I, 1950, p. 61–101.

Dunford, N., and J. T. Schwartz, *Linear Operators I*. New York: Interscience, 1958.

Halmos, P. R., *Measure Theory*. Princeton, N. J.: D. Van Nostrand Co., Inc., 1950.

Lyusternik, L. A., and W. I. Sobolew, *Elemente der Funktionalanalysis* (German translation). Berlin: Akademie Verlag, 1955.

Riesz, F., and B. St.-Nagy, *Leçons d'analyse fonctionelle*, 3rd ed. Budapest: Akademiai Kiado, 1955.

Saks, S., *Theory of the Integral*. Warsaw-Lwow: Monografie Matematyczne, 1937.

Taylor, A. E., *Introduction to Functional Analysis*. New York: John Wiley & Sons, Inc., 1958.

Vulikh, B. Z., *Introduction to Functional Analysis* (translated from Russian). London: Pergamon, 1963.

Zaanen, A. C., Linear Analysis. Amsterdam: North-Holland Publishing Co., 1953.

INDEX

Absolutely continuous measure, 132
Adjoint of a transformation, 84
Algebra, 33
  Banach, 248
Algebraic dual, 52
Almost everywhere, 113
Approximate identity, 249, 269
Arc length, 40
Arzelà-Ascoli theorem, 28

Banach algebra, 248
Banach lattice, 236
Banach limits, 64
Banach space, 71
Base for a topology, 206
Basis:
  Hamel, 55
  orthogonal, 177
  Schauder, 101
Bergman kernel, 188
Bessel's inequality, 176
Bounded:
  functional, 72, 233
  set, 211
  totally, 25
  transformation, 72
  uniformly, 28

Category, 21
Cauchy-Schwarz inequality, 4, 6, 165
Cauchy sequence, 11
Chain, 53
Character, 270
Characteristic number, 85
Closed set, 9, 208
Closed transformation, 97
Closed graph theorem, 98
Closure of a set, 9, 208
Coarser topology, 206
Compact, 24, 208
  locally, 251
Compact transformation, 83
Complete metric space, 11
Complete set, 173, 191
Completion, 20
  functional, 185
Connected, 28
Continuity, 27, 207
  absolute, 132
  equi-, 28
  semi-, 38
  uniform, 27
Contraction, 17
Convergence:
  field, 231
  in measure, 118
  weak, 86, 202 (exercise 2.8)
Convergent sequence, 8
Convex, 7, 58, 211
  locally, 217
Curve, 39

Deficiency, 57
Dense, 9
  everywhere, 9
  nowhere, 21
Dimension, 56, 183
Directed set, 246 (exercise 10.1)
Directed sum, 51, 100
Dominated convergence theorem, 127
Dual:
  algebraic, 52
  of $C[a, b]$, 94
  of l_p, 93
  of L_p, $p > 1$, 142
  of L_1, 146
  space, 73

Egoroff's theorem, 118
Entire functions, 220
Equicontinuity, 28
Ergodic theorem:
  individual, 148
  mean, 172
Everywhere dense, 9

Fatou theorem, 126
Field:
  convergence, 231
  normed, 257
Finer topology, 206
First category, 21
FK space, 224
Fourier expansion, 175–77
Fréchet space, 224
Fubini's theorem, 161 (exercise 6.4)
Functional, 52
  bounded (*see* Bounded transformation)
  linear, 52
  positive, 233
Functional completion, 185

Graph of a transformation, 98
Group:
  locally compact, 251
  ordered, 59
  topological, 251

Haar functions, 194
Haar measure, 252
Hahn-Banach theorem, 60, 62, 73
Hamel basis, 55
Hilbert space, 166
Holder inequality, 2, 6, 136
Hyperplane, 57

Ideal, 254
  maximal, 255
Identity, approximate, 249
Independent, linearly, 55
Individual ergodic theorem, 148
Inner product, 165
Inner product space, 166
Integrable function, 124
Integral, 120–24, 128
  Lebesgue, 120–24
  Riemann-Stieltjes, 95
Interior point, 9
Involution, 265

Isometry, 20

Kernel:
  Bergman, 188
  reproducing, 186
Köthe space, 239

$L_1(G)$, 252, 269
Lattice:
  Banach, 236
  vector, 233
Lebesgue integral, 120–24
Lebesgue measure, 115
Limit point, 9
Linear:
  functional, 52
  independence, 55
  space (*see* Vector space)
  transformation, 52
Lipschitz condition, 17
Locally compact group, 251
Locally convex space, 217

Mapping (*see* Transformation)
Maximal:
  element, 53
  ideal, 255
Mean ergodic theorem, 172
Measurable function, 115, 212
Measurable set, 110–14
Measure, 109–15
  absolutely continuous, 132
  convergence in, 118
  Haar, 252
  Lebesgue, 115
  Radon, 237
  signed, 129
  singular, 134
  totally finite, 114
  totally σ finite, 115
Metric, 1
  uniform, 8
Metric space, 1
Metrizable, 207, 219
Minkowski inequality, 3, 5
Müntz' theorem, 181

Neighborhood, 9
Norm, 71
  semi-, 71, 217
  of a transformation, 72
Normable space, 211

Normal family, 35
Normed field, 257
Nowhere dense set, 21
Null space, 57

Open mapping theorem, 98
Open set, 9, 206
Operator (*see* Transformation):
  positive, 102
Ordered set, 232
  partially, 53
Orthogonal, 167
  basis, 177
  set, 173
Orthonormal set, 173

Parseval's formula, 177
Partially ordered set, 53
Product:
  inner, 165
  topology, 208
Projection, 100, 170
Projection theorem, 170
Positive functional, 233
Positive operator, 102

Rademacher system, 197
Radical, 265
Radon measure, 237
Radon-Nikodym theorem, 132
Reflexive space, 91
Regular ideal, 266
Regular method, 87, 228
Reproducing kernel, 186
Riesz-Fischer theorem, 184
Riesz representation theorem, 96

Schauder basis, 101
Schwarz inequality, 4, 6, 165
Second category, 21
Semi-continuity, 38
Seminorm, 71, 217
Semi-simple, 265
Separable space, 9, 183
Sgn z, 93
Signed measure, 129
Singular measure, 134
Space:
  Banach, 71
  $BV[a, b]$, 6
  $C[a, b]$, 6
Space (*cont.*)
  compact, 208
  complete metric, 11
  of entire functions, 220
  FK, 224
  Fréchet, 224
  Hilbert, 166
  Köthe, 239
  l_p, 5
  L_p, 135–48
  linear (*see* Vector space)
  locally convex, 217
  m, 75 (*see also* l_p, $p = \infty$)
  $M[a, b]$, 6
  of measurable functions, 212
  metric, 1
  normable, 211
  reflexive, 91
  separable, 9, 183
  vector, 50
  topological, 206
  topological vector, 210
Spectrum, 263
Sphere, 8
Stone-Weierstrass theorem, 34
Subbase for topology, 206
Subspace, 2, 52
Summable function, 123
Summand, direct, 51, 100

Topological group, 251
Topological space, 206
Topological vector space, 210
Topology, 206
  base for, 206
  coarser, 206
  finer, 206
  product, 208
  subbase for, 206
  weak, 209
Totally bounded, 25
Totally finite measure, 114
Totally σ finite measure, 115
Total set, 57, 86, 214
Total variation, 131
Transformation:
  adjoint, 84
  bounded, 72
  closed, 97
  compact, 83
  graph of a, 98

Transformation (*cont.*)
  linear, 152
  positive, 102
Tychonoff theorem, 208

Uniform boundedness, 28
  principle of, 76
Uniform continuity, 27
Uniform metric, 8

Variation, total, 131
Vector lattice, 233
Vector space, 50
  topological, 210

Walsh system, 200
Weak convergence, 86, 202 (exercise 2.8)
Weak topology, 209
Weierstrass approximation theorem, 32